LET'S BREAK BREAD TOGETHER II

BRUNCHES & LUNCHES
AND
SUPPERS ON THE GO

Minister's Message

Reflecting on the number of church suppers and bake sales in the United Church, a friend of mine is fond of saying that the church depends on eating, and being fed.

I don't know how true that is, but I do know my reaction from "Let's Break Bread Together": foods, recipes, and eating are extremely popular throughout the dominion. We heard from old friends and new friends; from Nanaimo to Corner Brook. We even had letters from folks in Jamaica and Kenya. In these letters, the cookbook was merely an entree into conversations about who we are and what we are about. The mail we received was a wonderful by-product of the project.

For those of us fortunate enough to read these letters, they demonstrated a vitality and vibrance among church folk from all over this nation, and even from the far-flung parts of the world. It appears from the mail received, Volume I was a hit. It is the hope of our congregation that "Brunches, Lunches and Suppers on the Go" will bring similar delight.

Yours in Christ,
Terry Hidichuk

We proudly present our new cookbook "Let's Break Bread Together II Brunches, Lunches and Suppers on the Go". This fine collection of favorite recipes would not have been possible without the overwhelming number of submissions from churches throughout Canada, and we sincerely thank you. Our hope is that you will enjoy preparing these wonderful dishes for family and friends for years to come.

Cookbook Committee
United Church in Meadowood
Winnipeg, Manitoba

Thanks to Derksen Printers for their help with the publication of this cookbook.

ISBN:1-55099-019-5

Compiled and Published by the United Church in Meadowood, Winnipeg, Manitoba

Printed by Derksen Printers Ltd., Steinbach, Manitoba, R0A 2A0

Table of Contents

MEASUREMENTS AND WEIGHTS

Equipment

3 teaspoons	15 ml	= 1 tablespoon	15 ml
4 tablespoons	60 ml	= ¼ cup	60 ml
5-⅓ tablespoons	79 ml	= ⅓ cup	79 ml
8 tablespoons	118 ml	= ½ cup	118 ml
16 tablespoons	237 ml	= 1 cup	237 ml
1 fluid ounce	30 ml	= 2 tablespoons	30 ml
8 fluid ounces	237 ml	= 1 cup	237 ml
16 fluid ounces	473 ml	= 2 cups or 1 pint	473 ml
32 fluid ounces	946 ml	= 4 cups or 1 quart	946 ml

Food

1 cup butter margarine	237 ml	= ½ pound	227 g
1 cup Cheddar cheese grated	237 ml	= ¼ pound	114 g
1 cup eggs	237 ml	= 4-5 whole eggs or 8 egg whites or 12 egg yolks	
1 cup all-porpose flour	237 ml	= ¼ pound	114 g
1 envelope of gelatine (unflavored)		= ¼ ounce or 1 tablespoon	7 g 15 ml
1 cup lard or solid vegetable fat	237 ml	= ½ pound	227 g
1 medium lemon (juice)		= 1½ fluid ounces (3 tablespoons)	45 ml
1 cup chopped nut meats	237 ml	= ¼ pound	114 g

Dry Measure

0.035 ounces	1 gram	g
1 ounce	28.35 grams	g
1 pound	453.59 grams or 0.45 kilograms	kg
2.21 pounds	1 kilogram	kg

Liquid Measure

1 teaspoon	4.9 milliliters	ml
1 tablespoon	14.8 milliliters	ml
½ cup	118.3 milliliters	ml
1 cup	237 milliliters	ml
1.06 quarts	1000 milliliters or 1 liter	l

Brunches and Lunches

Easter Brunch

Easter Sunday Brunch

(12-20 people)

Hors d'oeuvres
Crab Mousse Ring
Crudités and Dip

Appetizer
Apple Shrimp Cocktail

Entrées
Freshly Squeezed Orange Juice
Savoury Stuffed Crêpes
Bacon & Eggs Supreme
Wild Rice Casserole
Easter Nest
Hot Cross Buns
Selections of Jams & Honey

Dessert
Fresh Fruit Platter and Dip
Strawberry Rhubarb Chiffon Pie
Sweet Nest
Tea
Coffee

This menu was prepared by Karen Bate, the winner of our congregations ''Brunch Contest''.

Hors d'oeuvres

Crab Mousse Ring

1 - 10 oz. can cream of mushroom soup
1 - 6 oz. pkg. (168 g) cream cheese
1 envelope unflavoured gelatin
¼ cup cold water
½ cup finely chopped celery
½ cup finely chopped green onions
1 cup mayonnaise
1 - 5 oz. can crab meat
¼ tsp. curry powder

Heat mushroom soup and cream cheese, stirring until smooth. Add gelatin to cold water and soften 5 minutes. Add gelatin mixture to soup mixture. Add celery, onions, mayonaise, crab meat, and mayonnaise, mixing well. Pour into 4 cup mould. Chill overnight.

Place purple and/or green grapes in the center of the ring. Surround the ring with crackers and a few sprigs of parsley.

Crudités Dip

Wash and cut a variety of fresh vegetables (carrots, broccoli, cauliflower, celery, cherry tomatoes, mushrooms, cucumber, etc.) Arrange on a platter with a dressing of your choice (Ranch, Caesar, etc.) or the following dip.

1 cup sour cream
¾ tsp. sugar
½ tsp. salt
¼ tsp. fresh ground pepper
¾ tsp. celery seeds
1 tbsp. chopped fresh chives
1 tbsp. chopped fresh parsley

Mix all ingredients well and chill before serving.

Place dip in a hollowed out small red cabbage or green pepper. Take a small slice of the bottom of the cabbage so it will be more stable. If using a round tray, fan out the vegetables. If using a rectangular tray, arrange them in alternating rows.

Appetizer

Apple and Shrimp Cocktail

1½ cups cooked wild rice (white rice as
  alternative)
2 small tomatoes
2 small red eating apples
½ green pepper
1 stalk celery
Salt and pepper to taste
1 cup peeled shrimp or prawn
Thousand Island salad dressing

Mix together cold rice, skinned, chopped
tomatoes and diced apple. Dice pepper, remove
core and seeds, dice celery, add to rice. Add
shrimp and seasoning, then enough Thousand
Island dressing to moisten.

Line individual dishes with leaf lettuce (use
shrimp cocktail dishes, wide mouthed cham-
pagne glasses, cream soup bowls, scallop shells
or small fancy bowl/cup of your choice). Add
a scoop of salad and sprinkle lightly with
paprika for colour. Garnish with a lemon wedge
on edge of dish, and a whole shrimp and sprig
of parsley on top of the salad.
Makes 4 servings.

Entrées

Freshly Squeezed Orange Juice

Juice appropriate number of oranges for
number of guests. Amount of juice obtained
from one orange varies according to variety and
freshness. Chill, pour into small glasses before
serving. Garnish side of glass with maraschino
cherry if desired.

Whatever you are - be that.
Whatever you say - be true.
Straightforwardly act.
Be loved in fact.
Be nobody else but you.

Savoury Stuffed Crêpes

Crêpes:
  1½ cups flour
  ½ tsp. baking powder
  ½ tsp. salt
  2 cups milk
  2 eggs
  2 tbsp. oil
  ½ tsp. vanilla

Mix flour, baking powder and salt. Stir in remaining ingredients and beat with a hand mixer until smooth. Lightly butter the skillet and
preheat over medium heat until butter is bubbly. Pour a scant ¼ cup of batter into the skillet
and cook crepe on both sides until light brown.
Stack crêpes, separated by waxed paper.

Cheese Sauce:
  1 cup milk
  1 tbsp. cornstarch
  1 tsp. butter
  ½-1 cup cheese

Combine milk, butter and cornstarch. Cook
in microwave or saucepan until thick, then add
cheese and stir until smooth.

Filling:
  1 small onion, finely chopped
  ½ lb. mushrooms, finely chopped
  1 or 2 tomatoes, skinned and chopped
  4-6 oz. diced cooked ham
  ½ tsp. marjoram
  Pinch cayenne
  Salt and pepper to taste
  Parmesan cheese
  Butter for frying

Melt butter in frying pan. Add onion and
cook until golden. Add mushrooms and cook
1-2 minutes. Stir in ham and tomatoes. Season
with marjoram, cayenne, salt, and pepper and
simmer for 5 minutes. Fill crêpes with filling,
roll, and place in a 9x13'' ovenproof dish. Pour
the cheese sauce over the crêpes. Sprinkle with
Parmesan cheese. Bake at 350°F for 12-15
minutes until warmed through, then broil until
golden brown.

Use an oven-to-table casserole, if possible.
Garnish with a few finely chopped fresh chives
or a few sprigs of parsley.
Makes 12 crêpes.

Bacon and Eggs Supreme

¼ cup butter
¼ cup flour
1 cup table cream (or milk)
1 cup milk
¼ tsp. each thyme, basil, marjoram
¼ cup chopped parsley
1 lb. sharp cheddar cheese, grated
18 eggs, hardboiled and sliced in half
   lengthwise
1 lb. bacon, cooked and crumbled
2 cups bread crumbs
¼ cup melted butter

Melt first ¼ cup butter in medium saucepan or microwave. Add flour, milk, and cream, stirring to make a smooth, thick, cream sauce. Stir in herbs and cheese, stirring until the cheese melts. Arrange eggs in a large greased flat baking dish (about 9x13" or 3 litres). Layer the crumbled bacon on top of the eggs. Pour the sauce over the top. Mix the bread crumbs and melted butter and sprinkle over the top. Refrigerate until needed (may be made 1 or 2 days in advance). When ready to serve, bake for 30 minutes at 350°F (180°C).

Use an oven-to-table casserole, if possible. Garnish with a few finely chopped fresh chives or a few sprigs of parsley.

Wild Rice Casserole

2 cups uncooked wild rice
1 medium onion
2 stalks celery, sliced
1½ cups sliced fresh mushrooms
Butter for frying
½ cup toasted slivered almonds
2-3 tbsp. white cooking wine (optional) or
   apple juice
1 tbsp. butter

Cook wild rice until kernels burst and rice is tender. Do not overcook. (See "notes" for instructions on cooking wild rice.) Fry onions in butter until golden. Add celery and mushrooms and cook until excess moisture has evaporated. Place cooked rice in large buttered casserole. Mix in vegetable mixture and toasted slivered almonds. Sprinkle with wine, and dot the top with butter. Cook, covered, in 350°F (180°C) oven for twenty minutes or until warmed through, stirring once.

Serve in casserole dish. Garnish with an "almond flower": Use parsley as a background, place whole almonds in a circle as flower petals, with a small mushroom cap for the center of the flower.
Yield: 10-12 ½ cup servings.

Easter Nest

4 cups all-purpose flour
1 - 8 g envelope instant yeast
¼ cup granulated sugar
1 tsp. salt
2 tbsp. margarine
½ cup milk
½ cup water
2 eggs, slightly beaten
½ cup mixed candied fruit
¼ cup chopped almonds
¼ cup melted margarine
5 coloured raw eggs

Set aside 1 cup of the flour. Combine the remaining flour, instant yeast, sugar and salt. Combine margarine, milk and water and heat until hot to the touch (125-130°F or 50-55°C). Stir hot liquids into dry mixture. Mix in eggs. Stir in enough flour to make a soft dough that does not stick to the bowl. Turn out onto a floured board and knead until smooth and elastic (about 15 minutes). Knead fruit and nuts into the dough until they are evenly distributed. Cover the dough and let rest for 10 minutes. Divide in half, rolling each piece into a 24-inch (60 cm) rope. Twist ropes together loosely and form into a ring on a greased baking sheet. Place coloured raw eggs into the spaces in the twist. Cover and let rise until doubled in bulk (about 40-50 minutes). Brush with melted margarine and bake at 350°F (180°C) for 30-35 minutes. Cool on wire racks and frost.

Frosting:
   1 cup icing sugar
   1 tsp. milk
   ¼ tsp. vanilla or almond flavoring

Combine icing sugar, milk and vanilla or almond flavouring and stir until smooth. Drizzle icing onto the cooled nest.

Center of ring may be filled with small silk spring flowers. Serve with butter.
Yield: 1 ring

Hot Cross Buns

4 cups all-purpose flour
1 - 8 g pkg. instant yeast
¼ cup granulated sugar
½ tsp. salt
1 tsp. ground cinnamon
¼ tsp. ground cloves or allspice
¼ tsp. ground nutmeg or mace
½ cup raisins or currants
¼ cup chopped candied lemon peel
¼ cup water
1 cup milk
¼ cup margarine
1 egg
1 egg yolk
1 tbsp. water
1 cup icing sugar
1-2 tbsp. lemon juice or milk

Set aside 1 cup of the flour. Combine remaining flour, instant yeast, sugar, salt, cinnamon, cloves, nutmeg, raisins, and lemon peel in a large bowl. Combine margarine, milk and water and heat until hot to the touch (125-130°F or 50-55°C). Stir hot liquids into dry ingredients. Mix in egg. Stir in enough flour to make a soft dough that does not stick to the bowl. Turn out onto a floured board and knead 5 minutes until smooth and elastic. Divide into 12 equal pieces. Shape each piece into a smooth ball, pinching at the bottom to seal. Place seam side down on a greased baking sheet about 2" (5 cm) apart. Place baking sheet over a shallow pan half filled with boiling water, cover, and let rise for 40 minutes. Remove baking sheet from pan of water. Mix egg yolk with 1 tablespoon water and brush over the surface of the buns. Bake at 375°F (190°C) for 10-12 minutes. Cool on wire rack. Mix icing sugar and lemon juice to desired consistency and drizzle in the form of a cross on each bun.

Place in cloth-lined wicker basket. Serve with butter, jams and honey.
Yield: 12 buns.

Dessert

Fresh Fruit Platter and Dip

Choose a selection of fresh fruit (strawberries, bananas, grapes, apple slices, orange slices, melon, etc.) and serve with the following dip. Bananas and apple slices may be sprinkled with lemon juice to prevent browning.

1 - 500 mL tub Cool Whip
1 - 113 g pkg. vanilla instant pudding
1½ cups milk
½ cup sour cream
1 tbsp. Grand Marnier (or other favourite) liquor (optional) or orange juice

Make up pudding using either 2 cups of milk as specified on the box or the combination of milk and sour cream given above. Mix equal parts of Cool Whip and pudding. Add liquor. Blend well and chill.

Arrange fruit and dip on a platter alternating contrasting colours of fruit.

Sweet Nests

1 tub of your favourite flavour of frosting
4 cups chow mein noodles
Assorted small chocolate Easter eggs,
    jelly beans, etc.

Place a sheet of waxed paper over a cookie sheet. Heat the frosting in a saucepan over low heat until it is liquid, stirring occasionally. Remove from heat. Stir in the chow mein noodles until they are coated. Drop the mixture by ½ cupfuls onto the waxed paper. Leave 1" space between nests. Make a crater in each scoop using the back of a spoon. Place eggs or jelly beans into each nest.

Place each nest on a doily-lined dessert plate. Top with small pom-pom bunnies or chicks if desired.

Strawberry Rhubarb Chiffon Pie

Graham wafer pie crust:
2 cups graham wafers
⅓ cup melted margarine

2 cups rhubarb, cut into chunks (fresh or frozen)
2 tbsp. sugar
¼ cup water
1 - 3 oz. pkg. strawberry flavoured jelly powder
1 - 10 oz. pkg. frozen strawberries, sweetened
½ cup whipping cream

Line a 9" (23 cm) pie plate with graham wafer crust and bake until lightly browned. Cool. Combine rhubarb, sugar, and water in a saucepan. Simmer uncovered 5-10 minutes or until rhubarb can be broken with a fork, and is tender. Remove from heat and add the jelly powder, stirring until completely dissolved. Add frozen block of strawberries and stir until berries are separated. Chill until slightly thickened. When the fruit mixture begins to thicken, whip the cream until stiff. Fold into the fruit mixture. Pour into the cooled pie shell and chill about 3 hours.

The last part of this recipe reads "Garnish with additional whipped cream if you are up to it!"

NOTES

1. All recipes are given in their original form. Amounts may be increased or decreased appropriately, according to the number of guests. Savory Stuffed Crêpes and Wild Rice Casserole freeze very well so the full recipes can be made if desired, with the excess frozen for future use.
2. Although this brunch has been designated for 12-20 people, it can be scaled down for a smaller number of guests (e.g. 8). If serving a smaller number, plan on seating all of the guests, if a larger number is expected, the table may be set up as for a smorgsbord.
3. **General Presentation:** Use the Easter Nest (bread) as a the centerpiece. Put small vases of fresh spring flowers at either end of the table. For a larger group, place plates, cutlery, and napkins at one end of the table and arrange the menu items around the table, with the desserts at the opposite end. (Serve the hors d'oeuvres in advance.) The sweet nests may be placed in a semi-circle around the other desserts, or given to parting guests as a gift. If a smaller number of guests is expected, place the sweet nests at each place setting backed by a fan-folded napkin. Place a name card in each nest to help seat your guests.
4. Many of these dishes may be made in advance. The crêpes and wild rice casserole freeze well and may be made well in advance if desired. The Bacon and Eggs Supreme may be made 1 or 2 days in advance. The wild rice for the Apple Shrimp Cocktail may be precooked and frozen as well. Both the Crab Mousse Ring and the Strawberry Rhubarb Chiffon Pie are chilled dishes which should be made the day before. In other words, the preparation may be spread out over a week. Very little is necessary on the actual day, giving you a chance to relax and enjoy your party.
5. Tips on cooking wild rice: For both the casserole and the cocktail, 100% wild rice is recommended and *not* a mixture such a Uncle Ben's. The latter has a variety of rice grades in it and does not cook evenly enough for these dishes. To cook wild rice, place the measured amount in a strainer and rinse thoroughly under very hot water for 2 minutes or so. Place in a large pot with three times the amount of water as rice. Cover and bring to a full boil, then reduce the heat but maintain a steady boil. Stir it lightly with a fork occasionally (you can "peek", unlike with ordinary rice). Cook for approximately 40 minutes, or until the kernels split, showing the white interior on most of the grains. Depending on the quality of the rice, an additional 5-15 minutes may be needed (the higher the quality, the longer the cooking time). It should still be chewy when done, not soft or mushy. Turn off the heat, drain any excess water, and return the pot to the cooling element. Fluff the rice gently and leave uncovered on the element for 10-15 minutes, fluffing every 5 minutes or so with a fork. During this extra (and optional) time, the rice gets loftier. The decreasing heat eliminates any extra moisture and helps to prevent mushiness. At this stage, the rice can be used in recipes, or packaged and frozen for future use.

Beverages

Fruit Smoothie

250 mL berries*
250 mL milk
250 mL plain yogurt
2 mL vanilla
25 mL honey
Dash of nutmeg

Put berries in blender. Blend until smooth. Add milk, yogurt, vanilla, honey and nutmeg and blend until smooth. Serve immediately.
*Use fresh or partially thawed berries or canned fruit of any kind.

St. Paul's United Church
Harrowsmith, Ont.

Rhubarb Drink

4 cups rhubarb, cut up
6 cups water
1 cup sugar
¼ cup lemon juice
½ cup frozen, undiluted orange juice
2 litres ginger ale

Cook rhubarb and water and put through sieve. Add sugar and allow to cool. Add lemon juice and orange juice. Just before serving add ginger ale.

Taymouth United Church
Taymouth, N.B.

Cranberry Cooler Punch

1 - 1.14 L bottle cranberry juice
1 - 177 mL can frozen orange juice
  concentrate
1 L bottle ginger ale
1 orange, thinly sliced

Mix all together. Yield 20 - 125 mL servings.
United Church in Meadowood
Winnipeg, Manitoba

Ariel's Punch

1 - 48 oz. unsweetened pineapple juice
1 - 12 oz. pink lemonade, undiluted
1 - 12 oz. orange juice, undiluted
1 - 26 oz. ginger ale
1 pkg. frozen strawberries

Mix the juices together and add ginger ale and strawberries just before serving. Serves approximately 20-25 (4 oz. servings).

First United Church
Cambridge, Ont.

Hot Apple Drink

2 - 48 oz. cans apple juice
⅓-½ cup brown sugar
1 tsp. whole cloves
1 tsp. whole allspice
3 cinnamon sticks
¼ tsp. salt (optional)

Tie cloves and allspice in bag. Put all ingredients in large pan. Simmer ½ hour and serve hot.

Stone United Church
Rockwood, Ont.
United Church in Meadowood
Winnipeg, Man.

Cranberry Orange Punch

2 - 32 oz. cranberry cocktail
1½ cups Realemon concentrate
⅔ cup sugar
2 - 12 oz. cans orange soda pop
½ cup orange liqueur, optional

Combine cranberry cocktail, Realemon concentrate and sugar in large bowl and stir until sugar is dissolved. Add pop and liqueur before serving, also ice and perhaps cherries or orange sections.

Port Stanley United Church
Port Stanley, Ont.

Mulled Fruit Nectar

2 - 12 oz. tins apple juice
1 - 12 oz. frozen orange juice concentrate, thawed
1 cup cranberry juice cocktail
3 sticks cinnamon (approx. 2½" ea.)
1 tsp. whole cloves
Orange slices or additional cinnamon sticks (optional)

At least 20 minutes or up to 2 days before serving: in a 3-quart saucepan place apple juice, orange juice concentrate, cranberry juice cocktail, broken cinnamon sticks and cloves. Over medium high heat bring to boil. Reduce heat to low, cover and simmer 10 minutes. Remove and discard spices if making ahead, cool, cover and refrigerate up to 2 days. I transfer to slow cooker on low to keep warm if using right away.

To serve: If made ahead, reheat, pour hot mixture into mugs. Garnish with orange slices or cinnamon sticks.
Yield: 7 - 6 oz. servings.

Fenwick United Church
Fenwick, Ont.

A Nice Punch

1 - 48 oz. can pineapple juice
1 - 48 oz. can fruit punch
2 lge. bottles ginger ale
1 can frozen orange juice
1 can frozen lemonade

Do not dilute frozen juice and lemonade before adding to other liquids. Slice oranges and float on top. Add maraschino cherries and ice cubes.

Victoria Street United Church
Goderich, Ont.

Iced Tea

Place 2 tea bags in an electric 12 cup coffee perk. Fill coffee pot with water and switch on. When your tea has brewed, pour contents into a container, e.g. ice cream pail. Repeat this procedure once more. Add ½ to ¾ cup of sugar and 1 tin of frozen lemonade. Stir mixture well and refrigerate for several hours. Simply delicious.

Zion Calvin United Church
Darlingford, Man.

Punch

1 can orange juice, frozen
1 can pink lemonade, frozen
1 large can pineapple juice
1 pkg. cherry Kool-Aid
1 cup white sugar
2 quarts water (ice cubes)

Dissolve white sugar and Kool-Aid in small amount of hot water. Add to juices. At serving time place above in punch bowl and add:
2 bottles ginger ale
1 bottle 7-Up

Add ice cubes. Serves 25.

Ruthilda United Church
Ruthilda, Sask.

Grape Sparkle

1 cup sugar
1 cup water
3 cups (24 oz. bottle) grape juice
1½ cups orange juice, fresh or diluted frozen concentrate
2 cups cold water
2 - 25 oz. bottles ginger ale

Boil together sugar and 1 cup water for three minutes to make a simple sugar syrup. Chill. Combine sugar, syrup with chilled fruit juices and water. Just before serving add ginger ale. Makes about 12 servings.

Beachville United Church
Beachville, Ont.

Fruit Punch

1½ cups sugar
1 qt. strong hot tea
1 qt. orange juice
1 cup lemon juice
1 qt. ginger ale
Fresh mint leaves

Dissolve the sugar in hot tea. Mix with juices. Pour over a block of ice (may use ice cubes). Just before serving add ginger ale. Sprinkle fresh mint leaves on the top.
Yield: 3½ quarts.

Zion Evangelical United Church
Pembroke, Ont.

Punch for 50 People

6 lge. bottles ginger ale (may use 7 if more ginger ale is liked)
48 oz. can grapefruit juice
48 oz. can orange juice (may use unsweetened juices)
1 frozen can orange juice
1 can frozen lemon juice (or bottled lemon)
Oranges and lemons (approx. 4 of each), thinly sliced to use as garnish
Cherries, optional
Approx. 8 cups plain black tea, cold
48 oz. can pineapple juice, optional

Cherries may be used for color as well as for taste. Black tea is the main base for punch. Pineapple juice makes it quite sweet. Serve with ice cubes floating on top to cool the punch. Three or four 26 ounce bottles alcohol may be used with this recipe if so desired. I like this as a cooling punch without alcohol.

Zion Evangelical United Church
Pembroke, Ont.

Hot Cider Punch

2 quarts cider
½ cup orange juice
2 tbsp. lemon juice
1 tsp. orange rind
5" cinnamon stick
½ tsp. cloves
½ cup sugar
Nutmeg
Whole cloves

Mix all together. Bring to a boil. Simmer. Then keep hot to serve. Makes a beautiful hot punch for fall and winter gatherings. We used it for a fall outdoor wedding, made pots of it. The aroma is just as inviting as the taste. A great "come-all-ye"! Recipe may be doubled, tripled, till the pot is full. Spices may be changed to suit taste.

St. John's United Church
Kemptville, Ont.

Punch

2 litres lime sherbet
3 - 750 mL bottles of 7-Up

Excellent for Christmas.

Orono United Church
Orono, Ont.

Frosty Golden Punch

1 - 6 oz. can frozen lemonade concentrate
1 - 6 oz. can frozen orange juice
1 - 6 oz. can frozen pineapple juice
1 - 12 oz. can or 1½ cups apricot nectar
½ cup lemon juice
2 pts. lemon sherbet
2 L bottle ginger ale

Add water to frozen concentrates as per can directions. Add apricot nectar and lemon juice. Refrigerate to blend flavours. Just before serving spoon in slightly softened sherbet and carefully pour ginger ale down side of punch bowl. Makes 20-25 ½ cup servings.

Wilmot United Church
Fredericton, N.B.

Advent Supper Cocktail
(or Ellanor's Hot Cinnamon Punch)

4 large (355 mL) cans frozen orange juice, thawed and strained to remove all pulp (use clean nylon stocking)
4 cans water
4 - 48 oz. cans cranberry cocktail
4 litres apple juice (in carton)
8 sticks cinnamon, broken
2 tsp. each whole cloves and allspice

Put spices in basket of 55 cups (or larger) percolator and the remaining ingredients in bottom. Perk as for coffee.
Note: If not sweet enough, add 1-2 cups sugar to taste.

Foothills United Church
Calgary, Alta.

Pauline's Party Punch

1 - 48 oz. can (1.3 L) pineapple juice
1 - 12½ oz. can (355 mL) frozen orange concentrate
1 - 12½ oz. can (355 mL) frozen lemonade
1 - 12½ oz. can (355 mL) frozen limeade
2 litres Canada Dry ginger ale
1 litre soda water
1 pkg. frozen strawberries

Mix all together and serve, adding pop last. This may be mixed beforehand, except for ginger ale, soda water and strawberries. Serves 50.

St. James United Church
Antigonish, N.S.

Tropical Slush

2 ripe bananas
4 tsp. honey (liquid)
Juice of 1 lime
3 cups pineapple juice
1 cup finely crushed ice

Place all ingredients in blender. Blend until smooth.
Serves 4.

Asbury West United Church
Toronto, Ont.

Soy Milk

½ cup soybeans
2½ cups boiling water

Wash and soak beans overnight. Blend beans with boiling water. Purée in blender for one minute. Strain mixture to collect soy milk and then cook over low heat for 20 minutes. Stir often as soy milk has a tendency to burn. Cool the milk and pour into a clean container, cover and refrigerate. Dilute and sweeten to taste.

Chinese United Church
Vancouver, B.C.

HELPFUL HINTS:
A fruit juice ice block is the ideal way to keep your punch cool without diluting the flavour. Simply pour some complimentary fruit juice into a plastic bowl. Add some fruit slices and freeze until ready to use.

Helpful Hints

Drain Cleaner: Place 2 tablespoons of baking soda in the drain. Pour 2 tablespoons vinegar into the drain. Place stopper in the drain to contain bubbles. Pour a full kettle of boiling water down the drain. Repeat if necessary.
Window/Glass Cleaner: 1 part vinegar, 1 part water.
All-Purpose Cleaner: 4 tablespoons soda, 1 quart water. Use on all surfaces as a no scratch scouring powder, all-purpose cleanser. Rinse surface.

United Church in Meadowood
Winnipeg, Man.

A Thanksgiving Prayer

Thanks to Thee, O Lord for these;
Harvest moon through maple trees;
Autumn colours, red and gold;
Nights so clear and crispy cold;
Kettles full of simmering fruit;
Sacks of beans, and parsnip root;
Geese in V-shaped southward flight;
Indigo of early night;
Vines with pumpkins bright and bold;
Indian summer, days of gold;
Now for blessings everywhere;
God accept our humble prayer.

Trinity United Church
Coronation, Alta.

Soups

"Hearty Bean Soup"

1 onion, chopped
3 or 4 carrots, sliced
1 tbsp. flour

Sprinkle onion and carrots with flour and fry lightly in margarine.

Add:
1 - 19 oz. can Italian tomatoes or
stewed tomatoes
1 - 14 oz. can red kidney beans
3 cups water
Any or all of the following:
Slices of celery, zucchini, grean beans
lima beans, broccoli, cauliflower, or
whatever vegetable is available

Simmer until vegetables are cooked. Let stand overnight to mellow! Delicious. Freezes well.

Advocate United Church
Advocate Harbour, Nova Scotia

Bean Soup with Parsley & Garlic

1 tsp. chopped garlic
½ cup olive oil
2 tbsp. chopped parsley
2 cups dried white beans

Soak beans overnight covered in 2 inches of cold water. The next day simmer the beans for about 2 hours in chicken or beef broth (4-6 cups).

Put olive oil and garlic in frying pan and cook until lightly coloured. Add parsley, stir 2 or 3 times then add to the beans and broth. Add salt and pepper to taste. Cover and simmer for 6-8 minutes. Put ½ cup beans in food processor, purée; put back into pot. Cover and simmer for another 6-8 minutes. Nice with toasted Italian bread.

Wesley United Church
Regina, Sask.

Borscht

(Russian Beet Soup)

¼ green cabbage
3 or 4 carrots
2 medium beets
1 onion
Salt and pepper

Shred all above ingredients.

Add:
2 cups cooked tomatoes
1½ lbs. lean stewing beef or hamburger

Simmer for 2-3 hours. Pour into soup bowls and top with 1 tablespoon sour cream, if desired (can be added at table).

This soup can be frozen. Excellent soup to make in fall when all vegetables are fresh from garden. Excellent for weight loss diets.

Zion United Church U.C.W.
Ostrander, Ont.

Russian Borscht

4 cups raw potatoes, diced
2 cups cooked navy beans
1 cup pickled beets, with juice
Salt to taste
½ cup sour cream

Cook potatoes in salted water until tender. Add beans and beets. Bring to a boil. Add sour cream and serve.

Robert McClure United Church
Calgary, Alta.

Place your recipe book inside a see-through plastic bag to prevent "spoiling" while cooking. Can be easily wiped and kept clean.

Use the crust piece (end) of a loaf of bread to keep stuffing in the turkey instead of skewers or lacing the bird shut.

United Church in Meadowood
Winnipeg, Man.

Hamburger Vegetable Soup

We had a large number of submissions for the basic soup with some variations. They are listed below and give you the opportunity to create a made-to-order soup.

Sauté:
1 lb. ground beef
1 medium onion, diced
1 cup chopped celery

Add liquids to make a total of 8-12 cups depending on how chunky you like your soup.

1 qt. canned tomatoed
1 - 28 oz. can tomato juice
1 - 10 oz. can tomato soup
1 - 10 oz. can beef consomme
Water

Spices as desired:
Salt (approx. 1½ tsp.)
⅛ to ¼ tsp. pepper
1 tbsp. ground cumin
1 bay leaf
½ tsp. thyme
1 tsp. Worcestershire sauce
½ to 1 tsp. parsley
1 tbsp. basil
1 tsp. garlic powder
1 tsp. oregano
2-3 beef Oxo cubes
1 envelope onion soup mix
1 envelope tomato-vegetable soup mix

Vegetables: to make 4-8 cups
Cauliflower
Carrots
Potatoes
Cabbage
Mushrooms
Corn
Zucchini
Green beans
Green pepper

Other Additions:
1 can kidney beans
1 can pork & beans
½ to ¾ cup pasta, uncooked
¼ to ½ cup rice, uncooked
¼ cup pearl barley, uncooked

Simmer 1 to 2 hours till vegetables and pasta are tender and soup is full of flavor.

Westcott United Church, Conn, Ont.
Moorefield United Church, Moorefield, Ont.
Mount Forest United Church, Mount Forest, Ont.
Goshen United Church, Varna, Ont.
Dundas St. United Church, Woodstock, Ont.
Carlyle United Church, Carlyle, Sask.
Bethel United Church, Forestburg, Alta.
Buchin United Church, Buchin, Ont.
Greenbank United Church, Uxbridge, Ont.
Berwick United Church, Berwick, N.S.
Foothills United Church, Calgary, Alta.
Old Barns United Church, Old Barns, N.S.
Rosenort United Church, Regina, Sask.
Humbervale United Church, Etobicoke, Ont.
Grace United Church, Caledonia, Ont.
Trinity - St. Andrews United Church, Renfrew, Ont.
St. Andrews United Church, Atwater, Sask.

Winter Beef Vegetable Soup

7-8 lbs. beef bones
1 lb. minced beef steak
2 tbsp. salt
1 tsp. pepper
1 pkg. soup mix
10 medium potatoes
1 small turnip
12 carrots
6 medium onions
2 cups celery, sliced
1 cup chopped cabbage
2 qts. canned tomatoes
2 cups elbow macaroni
2 tbsp. parsley

Boil beef bones for 2 hours in 8 litres water and 2 tablespoons salt. Set in cold place overnight. (I set it in the garage)

Next day: Remove all fat from top and discard. Remove bones and take all meat pieces off and chop. (Throw bones out). Heat stock and meat, salt and pepper. Prepare soup mix by covering with water and bring to boil. Set aside for 1 hour (off heat).

Scrub and pare potatoes, turnip, carrots and onions. Put vegetables in processor and add to soup broth. Cook for 1 hour. Add soup mix, celery, cabbage, and tomatoes. Let cook for another hour. Add macaroni and parsley. Cook for another 20 minutes till macaroni is cooked. Add salt and pepper to taste.

Makes 4-5 ice cream pails or fill jars ⅔ full and freeze. Enough for all winter.

Rivers United Church
Rivers, Man.

Cream of Broccoli Soup

2 cups (packed) cut up broccoli, including
   trimmed stalks
2 cups hot water
¼ bay leaf
2 tbsp. chopped onion
2 chicken bouillon cubes
4 tbsp. margarine
5 tbsp. flour
½ cup 10% cream
½ cup milk

Combine the prepared broccoli in a pot with
hot water, bay leaf, onion and bouillon cubes.
Bring to a boil and simmer covered for about
15 minutes. In a large pot melt margarine, stir
in flour until blended then add cream and milk.
(If concerned about fat content - use all skim
milk, still quite good). When broccoli and onion are done drain and reserve ½ cup of liquid.
Stir this into the white sauce. Cool vegetables
and liquid a bit and place in blender. Blend until
reduced to a purée (a bit at a time, so it doesn't
overflow). Add purée to white sauce and stir to
blend. Stir until it reaches a boil. Serve with
croutons, made by toasting ⅓'' cubes of bread
in the oven at 325°F until golden. Freezes well.
Serves 4.

Rapid City United Church
Rapid City, Man.

Cream of Broccoli Soup

2 cups chopped celery
1 cup finely chopped onion
10 oz. pkg. chopped broccoli
1 cup cottage cheese
2 cups whole milk
1 - 10 oz. can cream of chicken soup,
   undiluted
½ tsp. salt (if desired)
Pinch of white pepper

Cook celery, onions and broccoli in 2½ quart
covered casserole in microwave on HIGH for
6 minutes, stirring after 3 minutes. Set aside.
Blend cottage cheese in blender until very
smooth; add milk and blend again. Add chick-
en soup, blend again. Add blended mixture to
cooked, undrained vegetables. Microwave on
HIGH until heated through (without boiling).
Add salt and pepper.
Yield: 6 servings.

Knox United Church
Didsbury, Alta.

Cauliflower & Cream Cheese Soup

2 litres chicken broth
1 medium head cauliflower
2 bay leaves
4 peppercorns
1 tbsp. parsley flakes
1 small tub light cream cheese

Chop cauliflower into small pieces. Add with
seasonings to chicken broth and boil until
tender. Add water to make 2 litres. Pour into
blender, add cream cheese and blend until
smooth. Garnish with fresh parsley.

Winnipeg Presbytery
Winnipeg, Man.

Cream of Carrot and Cheddar Soup

Sauté in large kettle:
   2 tbsp. butter or margarine
   ½ cup finely chopped onion

Add and simmer until vegetables are tender:
   1 lb. carrots (8-10), shredded
   1 lb. potatoes (3-5), shredded
   6 cups chicken broth
   ½ tsp. thyme
   1 bay leaf
   ⅛ tsp. Tabasco sauce (or more to taste)
   ½ tsp. Worcestershire sauce
   ½ tsp. sugar
   Salt and pepper to taste

When vegetables are tender purée in blender.
Return to kettle.

Add:
   1½ cups milk
   1-2 cups cheddar cheese, shredded

Stir and heat until cheese is melted. Discard
bay leaf. Sprinkle with parsley to serve. This
soup freezes well.

Shanly United Church
Spencerville, Ont.

Golden Carrot Soup

¼ cup butter
1 sliced medium onion
1 small garlic clove (optional)
5 cups water
2½ cups sliced carrots
¼ cup long grain rice
2 tbsp. chicken bouillon mix
Salt
Chopped parsley

Melt butter in medium saucepan. Sauté onion and garlic until tender. Add water, carrots, rice and bouillon mix. Bring to a boil. Cover and simmer 25 minutes. Spoon vegetable mixture, part at a time into blender continer. Cover and blend until smooth. Add salt and parsley to taste.
Makes 4 generous servings.
(190 calories per serving)

Trinity United Church
Schumacher, Ont.
Zion Evangelical United Church
Pembrooke, Ont.

Curried Carrot and Leek Soup

4 medium leeks
2 lbs. carrots (about 14 medium)
½ cup butter
4 tsp. curry powder
1 tsp. cumin
½ tsp. nutmeg
5 cups chicken stock
¼ cup frozen orange juice concentrate
2 cups whipping cream
2 tsp. salt
Freshly ground pepper

Slice leeks (white part and about 1 inch of green). Peel carrots, then slice into rounds. In large saucepan, melt butter; add leeks and carrots and cook over medium heat, stirring, for about 15 minutes.
Stir in curry powder, cumin, nutmeg, chicken stock and orange juice concentrate. Bring to boil, reduce heat and simmer, covered for 20 minutes or until vegetables are tender.
Purée soup in food processor or blender or pass through food mill. Just before serving, return soup to saucepan; add cream, salt and pepper to taste. Bring to boil. Add more chicken stock if desired.
Makes 10-12 servings.

Brooklin United Church
Brooklin, Ont.

Cheddar Cheese Soup

¼ cup butter or margarine
1 clove garlic, cut in half
¼ cup chopped onion
2 medium carrots, grated
½ cup chopped celery
¼ cup flour
1 tsp. salt
¼ tsp. pepper
2 cups milk
2 cups grated cheddar cheese

Melt butter; add garlic and cook gently for 3 minutes. Remove and discard garlic. Turn heat to low and add onion, carrots and celery. Cover tightly and cook gently until tender. Add flour, salt and pepper and stir to blend. Remove from heat and add all the milk. Return to heat and cook, stirring, until mixture is thick and smooth. Add cheese and continue to cook, stirring, over low heat until cheese is melted and blended in. Serve immediately.
Yield: 4 servings

Ashton United Church
Ashton, Ont.

Chicken Gumbo Soup

1 - 3-4 lb. chicken
2 onions, coarsely chopped
4 or 5 carrots, cubed
2 stalks celery, chopped
1 tbsp. parsley
Pinch of garlic powder, optional
2 chicken bouillon cubes
2 or 3 fresh tomatoes or
    1 medium tin of tomatoes
½ tsp. savory

Cook chicken pieces in seasoned water to cover until cooked but still firm. Cool and remove chicken and cut in bite-size pieces. Chill broth and remove excess fat. Add water to make 6 cups liquid and add bouillon cubes, vegetables and seasonings. Cook until carrots are crisp tender. Add chicken, tomatoes and macaroni shells or noodles. Simmer for 15-20 minutes covered. Add water or broth if soup is too thick.

Wyevale United Church
Wyevale, Ont.

Chicken Noodle Soup

2½ lb. broiler chicken, cut up
4 carrots, sliced
1 large onion, sliced
1 tsp. sugar
2 cups uncooked thin egg noodles
1 qt. water (more may be required to thin soup)
4 medium stalks of celery, sliced
1 tbsp. salt
3 chicken bouillon cubes

Heat all ingredients, except noodles, to boiling point in 4-quart Dutch oven. Reduce heat. Cover and simmer until chicken is cooked (approximately 45-60 minutes). Skim off fat if necessary. Remove chicken from broth. Debone chicken, cut into pieces and return to pot. Add noodles and continue cooking until noodles are tender. This soup freezes well. For a variation rice can be substituted for the noodles.

Humphrey Memorial United Church
Moncton, N.B.

Turkey Gumbo Soup

2 cups (500 mL) cooked turkey, coarsely chopped
2 cups (500 mL) turkey broth
1 clove garlic, minced
1 small onion, chopped
1 can (398 mL) stewed tomatoes
1 bay leaf
1 tbsp. (15 mL) dried parsley
½ tsp. (2 mL) basil
Dash of pepper
¼ cup (62 mL) uncooked rice

Combine all ingredients in a large saucepan. Bring to a boil and simmer covered until rice is cooked. Remove bay leaf and serve.

St. Paul's United Church
Fairview, Alta.

Quick Clam Chowder Soup

1 can creamed corn
1 can cream of potato soup
1 can clam chowder soup
1 can Carnation milk (evaporated)
Dash of Worcestershire sauce

Oil Springs United Church
Oil Springs, Ont.

Seafood Chowder

4 medium potatoes, cubed
1 cup finely chopped onion
1 cup finely chopped celery

Cook with water to cover for 20 minutes.

Add:
1 can evaporated milk
1 can mushroom soup
1 soup can 2% milk

Add:
½ lb. cubed fish (sole, Boston blue fish, etc.)
1 - 12 oz. pkg. crab flavoured seafood flakes

Cook 10 minutes.

Add:
1 cup frozen peas
½ cup grated carrots
Sprinkle with paprika

Serves 6-8.

Pioneer Memorial Church
Hamilton, Ont.

Hawk Lake Fish Chowder

1 large onion, chopped
½ red pepper, chopped
½ green pepper, chopped
⅔ cup sliced celery
1 cup coarsely grated carrot
2 cups cubed potatoes
Salt and pepper and garlic to taste
1 medium sized lake trout
¼ cup chopped parsley
1 cup corn kernels
1 tin 2% evaporated milk
Skim milk, as needed

Sauté onions, peppers and celery in butter, oil or bacon drippings for 5 minutes. Add carrots and potatoes and water or stock to cover. Lay whole trout on top and simmer until vegetables and fish are cooked. Take skin and bones from fish and break in chunks. Add seasonings, parsley and corn. Just before serving add milk and heat through.

Melville United Church
Stouffville, Ont.

Clam Chowder Soup

Approx. 15-20 small clams in the shell or
  2 - 7½ oz. cans minced clam
Water
5 medium sized potatoes, diced
1 large onion, diced
2 slices bacon, diced
Clam liquid
¼ cup (⅛ lb.) butter or margarine
¼ cup flour
1½ cups milk
Salt and pepper to taste

If fresh clams are used, scrub them well and place in a pan with about 1 cup water in the bottom. Cover and bring to a simmer. Steam about 5 minutes, or until shells open and clams are just tender. Pull clams from shells; strain liquid through a fine mesh wire strainer lined with cloth and reserve. Measure, you should have about 2 cups.

If canned clams are used, drain them, reserving the liquid. Place potatoes, onion, and bacon in a saucepan and nearly cover them with clam liquid and water, cover and simmer until potatoes are just tender. Meanwhile, make a thick white sauce by melting the butter over low heat in a pan large enough to hold the chowder. Add flour and stir until bubbly and blended. Add milk and cook stirring constantly until thick. Add clams and potato mixture with its liquid to the sauce. Thin to consistency you like with water; season with salt and pepper. Heat, stirring, just to the boiling point before serving. Makes 6 to 8 servings.

Smoky Lake United Church
Smoky Lake, Alta.

Easy Lobster Bisque

In saucepan blend the following:
  1 can undiluted condensed cream of
    mushroom soup
  1 can undiluted condensed cream of tomato
    soup
  1 soup can milk
  1 cup light cream

Heat, but do not boil. Pick over and flake 1 pound can lobster. Add to soup. Heat well, sprinkle with snipped parsley.
Makes 4 servings.

Salisbury United Church
Salisbury, N.B.

Pacific Chowder

2 potatoes
1 onion
½ cup green pepper
½ cup celery
2 cups milk
1 tbsp. flour
1 can cream style corn
1 can Red Pacific sockeye salmon
Salt and pepper to taste

Chop vegetables in bite-sized pieces. Cover with water and cook for 8 minutes. Add 2 cups milk and flour. Continue cooking until thickened. Add 1 can cream style corn and 1 can flaked salmon. Heat and simmer 5 minutes. Add salt and pepper to taste. Serve with thick slices of French bread.

Trinity United Church
Ingersole, Ont.

Cheesy Fish Soup

1 lb. fish fillets, fresh or frozen
2 tbsp. butter
½ cup finely chopped onion
1 cup finely chopped carrot
½ cup finely chopped celery
¼ cup flour
½ tsp. salt
Dash paprika
2 cups chicken stock
3 cups milk
½ cup processed cubed cheese

Thaw frozen fillets enough to cut into 1-inch cubes. Melt butter and sauté onion, carrot and celery until onion is transparent. Blend in flour, salt and paprika. Gradually add stock and milk. Cook, stirring constantly until thickened. Add fish and simmer about 5 minutes for fresh fish - 10 minutes for frozen. Add cheese and stir until melted.
Makes 6 cups.

Northlea United Church
Toronto, Ont.

It's not enough to save
And a little too much to dump
And there's nothing to do but eat it
That makes the housewife plump.

Old Fashioned Bacon and Corn Chowder

6 slices bacon, cut into cross-wise strips
1 medium onion, thinly sliced
4 cups cooked potatoes, cut into ¼-inch slices
2 cups boiling water
1 lb. can cream style corn
1 qt. milk
Salt and pepper to taste
Dash of Worcestershire sauce (if desired)
1 - 10 oz. can condensed clam chowder (can be omitted)

Cook bacon until crisp and golden. Add onions. Cook five minutes stirring frequently. Add potatoes, boiling water, corn and milk. Bring to boiling point, but do not boil. Season with salt and pepper and Worcestershire sauce. Combine clam chowder (if using) with approximately 1 cup water. Return to boil and simmer about 5 minutes. Serves 6.

Hudson Bay United Church
Hudson Bay, Sask.

Meatball Sauerkraut Soup

1 lb. ground beef
1 medium onion, chopped
3 large carrots, diced
3 large potatoes, diced
1 - 28 oz. tin tomatoes
1 - 14 oz. tin sauerkraut
Salt
Pepper
Garlic powder
1 egg
⅓ cup bread crumbs

Meatballs: Combine ground beef with salt, pepper and garlic powder to taste. Mix with egg and bread crumbs. Shape into bite-sized meatballs. Brown in heavy skillet in 1 tablespoon oil.
Soup: Transfer meatballs to soup pot, drain fat from skillet and rinse with water for soup stock. Add vegetables and tomatoes. Simmer until just tender. Add sauerkraut (including juice) 15 minutes before serving.

Trinity United Church
Capreol, Ont.

Summer Soup

4 cups V-8 juice
1 small can broken shrimp
⅓ cup green pepper, finely chopped
⅓ cup celery, finely chopped
2-3 green onions, finely chopped
2-3 tsp. Worcestershire sauce
2-3 drops Tabasco sauce

Combine all the ingredients and chill. You may wish to add more of the shrimp, celery and green pepper. Serve cold.

United Church in Meadowood
Winnipeg, Man.

Chili Soup

Salt
8 oz. lean ground beef
1 onion, chopped
1 clove garlic, chopped
½ tsp. or more chili powder
¼ tsp. cumin
¼ tsp. oregano
Black pepper to taste
1 - 14 oz. can plum tomatoes
1 cup beef stock or water
1 - 14 oz. can kidney beans, undrained
1 cup shredded low fat cheese (optional)

Heat heavy saucepan over medium high heat and sprinkle bottom lightly with salt. Add beef, stirring with wooden spoon to break up pieces, cook until browned for about 5 to 7 minutes. Add onion, garlic, chili powder, cumin and oregano. Cook stirring occasionally until onion is soft.

Add tomatoes and stock; bring to boil, reduce heat and simmer covered for 1 hour. Add beans and salt and pepper to taste and simmer covered for 15 minutes more. If soup becomes too thick add a little more stock. Serve in heated bowls and garnish with cheese, if using. Makes 4 servings, 240 calories each with cheese garnish and 160 calories without cheese. This soup freezes well.

Britannia United Church
Ottawa, Ont.

Bolton United Church Thanksgiving Stone Soup

A favourite recipe within our church. Each year we ask the children to bring a vegetable on Thanksgiving Sunday. During the children's story the vegetables are collected, the story of stone soup is recalled, then the Sunday school chops and dices the vegetables into the waiting hot broth. If the children are fast and the minister's sermon a bit long, the soup will be ready for serving after the service.

1 medium sized grade A stone (preferably granite)
1 lb. ground beef
2 medium sized onions
3 medium sized carrots
2 stalks celery
½ cup barley
¼ cup powdered beef soup base
Assorted other vegetables
Salt and pepper
Worcestershire sauce

Brown ground beef. Remove fat. Add onions and fry until clear. Season with salt, pepper and Worcestershire sauce. Place stone in large pot with 6-8 cups of boiling water. Add beef mixture, carrots, celery, barley and any other vegetables desired. Mix in powdered beef soup base to taste. Cook until vegetables and barley are tender. Serves 10 to 12 people.

When serving a large church group, it is best to prepare the stock and add the barley the night before and have already boiling so that the children's vegetables can be cooked quickly on Sunday morning.

The Story of Stone Soup

Once upon a time there was a traveller who went from town to town visiting. One day he entered a tiny village and discovered that everyone was unhappy. The children were hungry and fighting with each other. The parents were arguing. Neighbours were feuding. He asked some of the children if they would like to join him in a delicious pot of stone soup. Since they had never heard of stone soup and thought that the idea was ridiculous, the traveller soon had a large group of children looking on. The traveller went on to explain, that he had the necessary stone for the soup, but since he had forgotten a pot, he wondered if one of the children might be good enough to bring one from home. Since he was travelling, he didn't have water either, so another child ran to fetch a pail full. The traveller went on to explain that carrots go well with stone soup, so another child ran home and brought back a carrot. Soon all the children were running home for various vegetables and seasonings. Each child's offering was added to the pot. Before too long a huge pot of stone soup was ready, and everyone within the village sat down to enjoy it. The fighting stopped. Neighbours who hadn't spoken in years began to visit. And it truly was a wonderful Thanksgiving meal.

Bolton United Church
Bolton, Ont.

Chunky Pizza Soup

1 tbsp. oil
1 small onion, chopped
½ cup sliced mushrooms
¼ cup slivered green pepper
1 - 28 oz. can tomatoes, undrained
1 cup beef stock
1 cup thinly sliced pepperoni
½ tsp. dried basil
1 cup shredded mozzarella cheese

In saucepan heat oil on medium heat and stir-fry onions, mushrooms and green pepper until softened. Add the rest of the ingredients except for cheese. Ladle soup into oven-ready bowls. Sprinkle cheese on top of soup. Broil until cheese is bubbly or microwave 1-1½ minutes. A quick lunch for hungry teens on the go.

Brucefield United Church
Brucefield, Ont.

Corn Chowder

4 slices bacon, finely cut
1 medium sized onion, diced

Sauté bacon and onion in pan until slightly brown.

Add:
1 medium sized potato, diced
1 cup cooked corn
Water, enough to simmer until potatoes are tender
Salt and pepper to taste
3 cups milk

Bring to boiling point and slightly thicken with mixed flour and water as for gravy. Boil for 2 minutes.
Serves 4 or 5.

Chilliwack United Church
Chilliwack, B.C.

Chippier Soup

1 lb. hamburger, browned
1 cup chopped onion
1 cup chopped celery
1 cup green pepper or zucchini
1 cup cabbage
1 cup diced potatoes
1 cup sliced carrots
1 - 28 oz. can tomatoes
6 cups water or
    4 cups water and 2 cups tomato juice
2 tsp. salt
1 tsp. Worcestershire sauce
1 tsp. pepper
2 bay leaves

Simmer above ingredients for 1 hour. Then add 1 can kidney beans or pork and beans, ½ cup macaroni. Cook 30 minutes longer. Makes large amount. Freezes well.

Springvale United Church
Hagersville, Ont.

Chunky Leek and Cabbage Soup

3 cups chicken stock
1 onion, chopped
2 cups chopped leeks (white part only)
1½ cups peeled, diced potatoes
2 cups chopped green cabbage
1 cup milk
Salt and pepper
Chopped fresh dill, pepper or green
    onions

In large pan bring stock, onion, leeks and potatoes to boil. Cover and reduce heat; simmer 20 minutes or until vegetables are tender. Add cabbage, cook covered 5 to 8 minutes or until tender. Stir in milk. Season with salt and pepper to taste. Sprinkle dill, parsley or green onions on each serving. Makes about 6 servings, each with 97 calories and 2 grams of fat.

Grace United Church
Trenton, Ont.

Mushroom & Leek Soup

½ cup (125 mL) butter
2 bunches leeks
½ lb. (250 g) mushrooms, chopped
3 cups (750 mL) milk
Dash cayenne pepper
¼ cup (50 mL) flour
1 tsp. (5 mL) salt
1 cup (250 mL) chicken broth
1 tbsp. (15 mL) sherry or lemon juice

Wash leeks, slice, use white part only. In ¼ cup of butter, sauté until tender but not brown. Remove and set aside. In remaining butter, sauté mushrooms until soft, about 10 minutes. Blend in flour, salt and cayenne pepper. Gradually stir in broth and milk. Cook, stirring constantly until mixture thickens and comes to a boil. Add leeks, sherry or lemon juice, salt and pepper to taste. Simmer for 10 minutes. Serve with thin slices of lemon and sprinkling of parsley if desired.

Caistorville United Church, Canfield, Ont.
Cooksville United Church, Mississauga, Ont.
Beaconsfield United Church, Beaconsfield, Que.
Wesley United Church, Vandorf, Ont.

Leek Soup

3 tbsp. butter or margarine
2 cups sliced leeks
1 small onion
2 cups sliced raw potatoes
2 cups water
2 chicken bouillon cubes
1½ tsp. salt
2 cups hot milk
2 tbsp. minced fresh parsley

Melt butter in medium sized saucepan. Add leeks and pared sliced onions. Sauté 5 minutes or until tender. Add potatoes, water, cubes and salt. Cover. Simmer 15 minutes or until vegetables are tender. Pour into blender container. Cover. Blend at high speed one minute or until smooth. Add to hot milk. Reheat to serving temperature. Garnish with parsley.
Makes 5-6 servings.

North Kildonan United Church
Winnipeg, Man.

Meatless Minestrone Soup

½ cup salad oil
1 clove garlic, minced
2 cups chopped onion
1 cup chopped celery
4 tbsp. chopped parsley
1 - 14 oz. can tomato paste
2 Oxo cubes in 2 cups of water
9 cups water
1 cup chopped cabbage
2 carrots, sliced
2 tsp. salt
¼ tsp. pepper
⅛ tsp. oregano
1 can chick peas
1 cup cooked spaghetti

Brown onion, garlic and celery in oil. Add the next ingredients with the exception of the chick peas and spaghetti. Bring to a boil and simmer for 1 hour. Add chick peas and spaghetti. Cook for 10 minutes.

St. Giles United Church
Hamilton, Ont.

Microwave French Onion Soup

6 tbsp. butter
3 - 10½ oz. cans condensed beef consomme
1 tbsp. Worcestershire sauce
3 large onions, halved & thinly sliced
1½ cups water
¼ cup dry wine or sherry (optional)
1 tsp. salt
½ tsp. pepper (to taste)

In large glasss bowl or casserole cook butter on MED.-HIGH for 1½ minutes or until melted. Add onions. Cover; cook on HIGH for 20 minutes or until onions are completely soft, stirring twice during cooking. Add consomme, water and wine. Cover; cook on HIGH for 10 minutes or until boiling. Pour into individual serving bowls. Top each with a slice of French bread and sprinkle with Parmesan cheese. Cook on MED.-HIGH for 6 minutes or until cheese is melted.

Buchanan-Eastwood United Church U.C.W.
Edmonton, Alta.

Onion Chowder

Fry until brown:
¼ cup bacon, chopped

Add:
2 cups onions, chopped

Continue cooking until onions are yellowed colored.

Add:
2 cups water
3 cups raw potatoes, diced

Cook 30 minutes or until potatoes are tender.

Add:
2 cups milk
2½ tsp. salt
½ cup cream
¼ tsp. pepper

Mix together until smooth:
1 tbsp. flour
1 tbsp. water

Stir flour and water until a smooth paste. Add to soup. Boil 2 minutes stirring frequently.
Note: I use more bacon and add either carrots and celery. If I don't have cream I use a little extra flour.
Good on a cold day.

Plunkett United Church
Plunkett, Sask.

Potato Chowder

2 cups hot water
2 chicken bouillon cubes
3 medium potatoes, peeled & halved
1 medium onion, thinly sliced
1 large carrot, thinly sliced
2 large stalks celery, sliced
3 cups milk
¼ cup margarine
¼ tsp. pepper
1 tsp. salt

Dissolve cubes in water. Bring to a boil. Add potatoes. Cook until soft. Remove potatoes from pot. Add other vegetables. Cook until tender. Mash potatoes. Return to pot and add milk, margarine, salt and pepper. Heat through, but do not boil. Serve with a sprinkling of parsley, green onion tops or chives.

Garden City United Church
Victoria, B.C.

Dutch Green Pea Soup

1 lb. split green peas
8 pts. water
1 pork hock or ham bone
Small piece of salt bacon (optional)
Smoked pork sausage
2 leeks (or onions)
2 or 3 celery stalks with greens
Celery root

Soak peas overnight, then rinse in cold water and add to 8 pints of water. Add pork hock and salt bacon. Simmer about 3 hours, stirring now and then. Add cut up vegetables. Simmer until done, season with salt and pepper and ½ teaspoon thyme. Half an hour before serving add smoked sausage. One grated potato thickens the soup and 1 grated carrot gives it color. This soup will be thick the second day.

Robinson Memorial United Church
London, Ont.

Special Potato Soup

2-3 tbsp. butter or margarine
1 large onion, sliced
½ cup thinly sliced carrot (optional)
½ cup diced celery (optional)
1 garlic clove, minced
4 cups diced potatoes
2-3 cups chicken stock
1½ tsp. salt
¼ tsp. pepper
1 tsp. parsley flakes
1½-2 cups milk
½ cup grated cheddar cheese for garnish
or 1½ cups diced cheddar cheese

Put first 5 ingredients into large saucepan. Sauté vegetables until onion is soft and clear. Add potatoes, chicken stock, salt, pepper and parsley. Bring to a boil. Cover and simmer slowly until vegetables are cooked. Stir occasionally. Stir in milk. Heat without boiling. Garnish with grated cheese or stir in diced cheese for a cheesy potato soup.

Mount Royal United Church, Saskatoon, Sask.
First United Church, Cambridge, Ont.
Sandwich United Church, Windsor, Ont.
St. Paul's United Church, Harrowsmith, Ont.
Consul United Church, Consul, Sask.
Ochre River United Church, Ochre River, Man.
Hickson United Church, Hickson, Ont.

High Protein Pea Soup

½ cup split green peas
¼ cup barley
¼ cup lima beans
1 carrot
1 celery stalk
1 medium size potato
1 medium size onion (or less)
1½ qts. water
2 tbsp. chicken base
Bay leaf (optional)
Green pepper (optional)
Salt and pepper to taste

Soak beans and barley overnight. Bring all to a boil and cover and simmer gently.

Zion Evangelical United Church
Pembroke, Ont.

Savory Potato-Cheese Soup

2 cups diced peeled raw potatoes
1 cup chopped onion
½ cup diced celery
2½ cups boiling water
2½ tsp. salt
¼ cup butter or margarine
¼ cup all-purpose flour
¼ tsp. pepper
½ tsp. dry mustard
1½ tsp. steak sauce
2 cups milk
3 cups well packed sharp cheddar cheese, grated
1 tsp. minced parsley
1 - 28 oz. can stewed tomatoes

Put first 4 ingredients and 1 teaspoon salt in Dutch oven or heavy kettle. Bring to boil, cover and simmer about 15 minutes. Add tomatoes. In a saucepan, melt butter and blend in flour. Slowly add milk, to prevent lumps. Add cheese and stir until melted. Add remaining salt, pepper, mustard and steak sauce. Cook, stirring constantly, until smooth and thickened. Add cheese and simmer on low till smooth. Then add it to potato/tomato mixture. Simmer for a few minutes.
Makes about 1½ quarts.
Note: Do not boil, for this will cause the cheese to curdle.

Zion Evangelical United Church
Pembroke, Ont.

Bacon and Potato Chowder

6 slices bacon, diced
1 cup chopped onion
3 cups diced, raw potatoes
3 cups water
3 chicken bouillon cubes
½ tsp. salt
3 tbsp. flour
1 large can undiluted
Carnation evaporated milk

Fry bacon in a large saucepan until crisp. Drain well; set aside. Reserve 2 tablespoons drippings. Sauté onion in the drippings 5 minutes. Add potatoes, water, bouillon cubes and salt. Heat to boiling. Cover and simmer until potatoes are tender. Mix flour with a small amount of milk to make a paste; gradually stir in remaining milk. Add to potato mixture. Cook over medium heat, stirring constantly until mixture comes to a boil. Garnish with reserved bacon. Makes about 6 cups.

Brooklin United Church
Brooklin, Ont.

Tomato Chowder

2 cups potatoes, cubed
¾ cup onion, minced
1 cup celery, chopped
3 cups chopped ripe tomatoes
2 tsp. salt
¼ tsp. pepper
¼ tsp. oregano (optional)

Combine in large saucepan. Cover with 2½ cups water and bring to a boil. Reduce heat and simmer until vegetables are tender.

3 tbsp. butter or margarine, melted
¼ cup flour
½ tsp. dry mustard
2 cups milk
1½ tsp. salt
¼ tsp. pepper
½ to ¾ cup grated cheese

Combine the above. Heat and stir in a heavy saucepan until thick and smooth. Add to vegetable mixture. Add parsley and Worcestershire sauce to taste (optional). Stir and heat. Cool if to be put in cartons for freezing. Add more milk when reheating if desired.

Killarney United Church
Killarney, Man.

Trinity United Church
Coronation, Alta.

Tomato Juice Soup

1 envelope onion soup mix
1 large can tomatoes or tomato juice
1 large green pepper
1 large bunch celery
3-6 onions
1 head cabbage

Cut up vegetables. Cover with water in large pot. Bring to a boil, then simmer 2 hours.
Optional: add 1 tablespoon basil, 1 can mushrooms and 1 can string beans.

Kings Kirk United Church
Belleisle Creek, N.B.

Rice and Tomato Soup

4½ cups water
¼ cup uncooked rice
¼ cup chopped celery leaves
½ cup chopped onions
1¼ tsp. salt
¼ tsp. pepper
2 cups canned tomatoes

Add all ingredients except tomatoes and bring to a boil. Simmer 14 minutes. Add canned tomatoes. Make a thickening of cornstarch and water. Add some hot liquid to it. Blend. Add to soup and stir well. Simmer for 10 minutes. Serves 5.

Lake Cowichan United Church
Lake Cowichan, B.C.

Cream of Tomato Soup

Sauté:
2 tbsp. margarine
2 tbsp. chopped onion

Blend in:
3 tbsp. flour
2 tsp. sugar
1 tsp. salt
⅛ tsp. pepper
Dash of garlic salt, basil, oregano, thyme

Remove from heat.

2 cups tomato juice
2 cups cold milk

Gradually stir in tomato juice. Bring to a boil, stirring constantly. Boil 1 minute. Stir hot tomato mixture into cold milk. Heat almost to boiling and serve.

Wyoming United Church
Wyoming, Ont.

Tomato Soup

2½ cups milk
2 tbsp. soft butter
3 tbsp. all-purpose flour
1½ tsp. salt
¼ tsp. pepper
1 - 28 oz. can tomatoes
1 thinly sliced onion (optional)
2 tbsp. sugar
Sprinkle of cinnamon (optional)
Pinch of soda

Scald milk in a large double boiler and stir in a mixture of butter, flour, salt and pepper. Cook until thickened. Chop tomatoes into small pieces and place in another saucepan. Add onion, sugar, cinnamon and soda. Bring to a boil and simmer 10 minutes. Stir slowly into cream sauce mixture. Season to taste.
Note: Make ahead and refrigerate. Reheat anytime.

Westway United Church, Etobicoke, Ont.
Rutherglen United Church, McAuley, Man.

"All Occasion" Tomato Vegetable Soup

4-5 chicken bouillon cubes
4 qts. water

Dissolve chicken bouillon cubes in water.

Add:
Chopped cabbage
Carrot
Turnip
Celery
1½ cups frozen peas
Corn

Add:
1 can whole tomatoes, mashed
1 - 7¼ oz. can tomato paste
½ cup macaroni
Sprinkle some parsley; a few crushed chilies and pepper for flavor. Lastly, add macaroni to thicken. You may also use rice or noodles if desired. A bit of fried hamburger is good also for variety. Simmer for 2-3 hours. This is convenient to have on hand for large crowds. Delicious and nourishing!

Cape North United Church
Cape North, Vict. Co., N.S.

Mushroom Soup

½ lb. fresh mushrooms, thinly sliced
½ cup finely chopped onion
2 chicken cubes
2 cups boiling water
¼ cup butter
3 tbsp. flour
1½ tsp. salt
⅛ tsp. poultry seasoning
3 cups milk

In a medium saucepan, combine first four ingredients, and let simmer. In a large pan melt butter, add flour, salt and seasoning. Gradually stir in milk. Stir over medium heat constantly until smooth and thickened. Stir in mushroom mix undrained. Serve hot. Make and serve immediately. May be reheated next day.

St. John's United Church
Alliston, Ont.

Hearty-Vegetable Chowder

2 slices bacon, diced
½ cup chopped onion
1 - 10 oz. (284 mL) can beef broth
1 - 14 oz. (398 mL) can spaghetti sauce
1 cup water
¼ tsp. dried basil leaves, crushed
2 cups frozen or fresh mixed vegetables
½ cup spiral-shaped pasta
2 cups milk
2 tbsp. flour
Salt and pepper
Grated Parmesan cheese (optional)

Cook bacon until crisp in large saucepan. Drain, reserve drippings. Set bacon aside. Cook onion in bacon drippings until tender. Stir in beef broth, spaghetti sauce, water and basil. Add vegetables and pasta. Bring to a boil. Reduce heat, cover and simmer 10 minutes or until vegetables are tender.

Combine milk and flour until smooth. Stir into chowder. Cook and stir until mixture comes to a boil and thickens. Add salt and pepper to taste. Sprinkle reserved bacon and Parmesan cheese over each serving if desired.
Preparation Time: 10 minutes.
Cooking Time: 20 minutes.
Yield: about 7 cups.

St. Andrew's United Church
Glenavon, Sask.

Zucchini Cream Soup

3 medium zucchini, unpeeled and sliced thin
¼ lb. butter
1 medium onion, finely chopped
3½ cups chicken broth or
   3 chicken bouillon packets, dissolved
   in 3½ cups hot water
½ cup coffee cream or milk
Pepper and salt to taste
¼ tsp. each of dried dill weed, basil
   and savory
Sour cream (optional)

Sauté zucchini and onion in butter until limp. Add chicken broth. Cover and simmer 15 minutes. Add salt and spices. Purée in blender. Refrigerate at least 6 hours. Reheat and add cream and serve, with sour cream swirled on top. Purée can be frozen during zucchini season when they're plentiful - prior to the addition of cream or milk.
220 calories per serving.
Makes 6 servings.

Britannia United Church
Ottawa, Ont.

Good Soup!

1 cup chopped onions
1 cup shredded cabbage
½ cup sliced leeks
1 cup chopped celery
1 lb. sweet or hot Italian sausage
8 cups beef broth
1 tsp. basil leaves
½ tsp. thyme
½ tsp. oregano
1 tsp. dried parsley
1 cup pasta, spirals or shells
1 - 28 oz. can Italian plum tomatoes, cut up
1 can chick peas
1 cup chopped or sliced carrots
2 cups sliced zucchini

Cook sliced sausage and onions until onions are tender. Add everything except zucchini and pasta. Bring to a boil; then simmer about 50 minutes. Add pasta; cook another 10 minutes. Add zucchini; cook another 15-20 minutes. Make ahead - refrigerate - reheat - improves!
Makes about 12 servings.

Central United Church
Port Colborne, Ont.

Ham and Cabbage Soup

¼ cup butter or margarine
1 cup chopped celery
1 cup chopped onion
½ cup chopped green pepper
1 garlic clove, crushed
2 tbsp. all-purpose flour
1 tsp. dried oregano leaves
¼ tsp. crushed bay leaf
¼ tsp. pepper
2 - 10¾ oz. cans undiluted chicken broth
1½ cups water
1½ cups ham, cut into ¼" wide
   julienne strips
3 cups shredded green cabbage
Sour cream (optional)

In a 5-quart Dutch oven, put 2 tablespoons butter, over medium heat, sauté celery, onion, green pepper and garlic, stirring until onion is soft - about 5 minutes. Add flour, oregano, bay leaf and pepper. Stir until well blended - 2 minutes. Combine chicken broth with water to make 4 cups. Gradually add chicken broth and ham to vegetable mixture, blend well. Bring to a boil; reduce heat, simmer, covered - 20 minutes.

Meanwhile, in remaining 2 tablespoons butter in a medium skillet, sauté shredded cabbage, stir about 3 minutes. Add 1 tablespoon water, cook covered, just until cabbage is crisp, not soft. Add cabbage to soup. Serve if desired, with sour cream.
Makes 6 servings - 1½ quarts.

St. Andrews United Church
Bow Island, Alta.

Crock Pot Vegetable Soup

3 tbsp. margarine
3 carrots, sliced
1 cup chopped cabbage
1 small onion
3 tomatoes, chopped
1 - 14 oz. can green beans
7 cups boiling water
2 cubes chicken bouillon
2 cubes beef bouillon
1 - 14 oz. can red kidney beans, well drained
Pinch of dried sage
Salt and pepper to taste
½ cup macaroni

Cook slowly, about 8 hours until vegetables are tender. Add macaroni ¾ hour before using.

College Hill United Church
Belleville, Ont.

Salads

Meal in a Salad

Chicken Salad

½ cup mayonnaise
Dash of white vinegar
½ cup whipping cream (1 cup whipped)
3 cups white meat diced (cooked chicken
  or turkey)
Salt and pepper to taste
½ cup toasted almonds
½ cup diced celery

Combine mayonnaise and vinegar. Fold in whipped cream, salt and pepper. Add diced chicken, almonds and celery. Serve with Orange Soufflé on broken lettuce leaves.
Como Lake United Church
Coquitlam, B.C.

Orange Soufflé

1 envelope unflavored gelatin (1 tbsp.)
½ cup white sugar
2 egg yolks
1 tsp. grated orange peel
1 tsp. grated lemon peel
½-1 cup whipping cream (whipped)
Dash salt
1¼ cups orange juice
4 tsp. lemon juice
1 cup orange sections

Mix gelatin, sugar and salt in pan. Beat together egg yolks and ¾ cup of orange juice. Stir into gelatin mixture. Cook over medium heat, stirring constantly until mixture comes to a boil. Remove from heat and stir in orange and lemon peel and remaining juices. Chill, stirring occasionally until the mixture mounds when dropped from spoon. Stir in orange sections. Fold in whipped cream. Pour into ring mold. Chill until set.

To serve, unmold soufflé onto a glass plate and mound chicken in centre. Garnish with almonds.
Serves 8.
Como Lake United Church
Coquitlam, B.C.

Salad Crab Louis

Louis Dressing:
1 cup Miracle Whip
¼ cup whipping cream, whipped
¼ cup chili sauce
¼ cup chopped green pepper
¼ cup chopped green onion
1 tsp. lemon juice
Salt to taste

1 head lettuce or mixed greens
3 cups cooked crabmeat or more
2 large tomatoes, cut in wedges
2 hard-cooked eggs, cut into wedges

Combine ingredients for dressing and chill. Line bowl with lettuce. Arrange crab on top, reserving claws for finish. Circle with tomato and egg wedges. Dash with salt. Pour ¼ cup dressing over salad. Sprinkle with paprika. Top with claw meat. Pass remaining dressing.
Forest Hills United Church
Dartmouth, N.S.

Taco Salad

1 lb. ground beef, fried, drained
1 pkg. taco seasoning
1 - 250 mL bottle Thousand Island dressing
1 - 200 g bag of taco chips, slightly crushed
3-4 tomatoes, chopped
1-2 green peppers, diced
1 onion, chopped
1 head lettuce

Mix altogether, adding taco chips and dressing just before serving. Makes a large bowl. Variation: Substitute the Thousand Island dressing with French or Russian dressing.
Thedford United Church, Thedford, Ont.
McClure United Church, Winnipeg, Man.
St. Rose United Church, St. Rose du Lac, Man.
Essex United Church, Essex, Ont.

Macaroni Salad

2 cups macaroni, cooked
2 cups cubed ham
2 cups cubed cheddar cheese
2 cups sliced mushrooms
1 large tomato, diced
1 cup diced sweet pickles
⅓ cup chopped green onions
½ cup diced celery
½ cup Italian dressing
½ cup sour cream
½ tsp. seasoned salt

Mix well and serve chilled.

Zion Evangelical United Church
Pembroke, Ont.

Ham Rolls in Jelly Salad

2 pkgs. lemon flavored gelatin
3 cups hot water
½ cup white vinegar
¼ cup lemon juice
1 tsp. Worcestershire sauce
4 dashes Tabasco
8 oz. pkg. cream cheese (room temperature)
1 tbsp. prepared horseradish
1 tbsp. minced parsley
1 tsp. cream
1 tbsp. drained sweet pickle relish
1 tsp. cream
8 slices cooked ham
Lettuce
Sliced hard-cooked eggs

Dissolve gelatin in hot water. Add vinegar, lemon juice, Worcestershire sauce and Tabasco and chill until syrupy. Divide cream cheese into equal parts. Blend horseradish, parsley and 1 teaspoon cream into one part. Blend pickle relish and 1 teaspoon cream into other part. Lay ham slices out on table and divide cream cheese mixtures up evenly among them, spreading the cream cheese across one end of the ham slices. Roll the slices up around the cheese. Pour a thin layer of the gelatin mixture into a glass baking pan about 12x7x2''. Lay ham rolls in the gelatin. Add remaining gelatin. Chill until set. Cut around each roll at serving time and lift out with a spatula onto lettuce. Serve 1 or 2 for each serving. Garnish with sliced hard-cooked eggs. Serves 4 or 8.

Bethesda of Forest Glen United Church
Mississauga, Ont.

Jellied Salads

Strawberry Salad Mold

2 - 6 oz. pkgs. strawberry Jell-O
2 cups boiling water
2 - 16 oz. pkgs. frozen strawberries in juice, sliced
1 - 20 oz. can crushed pineapple in juice
1 - 16 oz. container sour cream at room temperature

Dissolve Jell-O in boiling water. Add frozen strawberries including juice. Add pineapple and juice . Work quickly, before mixture begins to set. Pour half of mixture into a 13x2'' flat container. Spread sour cream over top. Add remainder of gelatin as third layer. Refrigerate until set.

Greenwood United Church
Greenwood, Ont.

Apricot-Orange Jellied Salad

1 - 14 oz. can apricots, drained (reserve juice)
1 - 3 oz. pkg. orange Jell-O
1 - 4 oz. pkg. cream cheese
1 can mandarin oranges, drained

Heat 1 cup apricot juice to a boil. Add gelatin, stir, let cool. Combine gelatin, cheese and apricots and blend. Let partially set in a bowl, approximately 1 hour. Add oranges. Turn into a mold.

Greenwood United Church
Greenwood, Ont.

Orange Sherbet Salad

1 - 3 oz. pkg. strawberry Jell-O
1 - 3 oz. pkg. orange Jell-O
1⅓ cups boiling water
½ pint orange sherbet
1 - 14 oz. tin crushed pineapple, drained
1 - 10 oz. tin mandarin oranges, drained and cut up

Dissolve Jell-O in boiling water. Add sherbet, stirring until melted. Add fruits and chill.

Grace United Church
Dunnville, Ont.

Orange Perfection Salad

3 oz. pkg. orange Jell-O
1 cup boiling water
2 tbsp. sugar
Dash salt
½ cup cold water
½ cup juice
1 tbsp. vinegar
1 orange, peeled and diced
1 cup shredded cabbage
½ cup diced celery

Dissolve jello in boiling water. Add sugar and salt. Add cold water, juice and vinegar. Chill until partially set and fold in orange, cabbage and celery. Chill until set.

Zion Evangelical United Church
Pembroke, Ont.

Bing Cherry Jellied Salad

1 - 3 oz. pkg. cherry Jell-O
1 cup boiling water
1 - 15 oz. can pitted bing cherries (or equal
    amount of home canned bing cherries)
½ cup sliced, chopped celery
½ cup toasted, slivered almonds

Dissolve Jell-O in boiling water. Drain cherries. Place juice in measuring cup, add water or cooking wine to make one cup. Add to the boiling water/Jell-O mixture. Chill until egg white consistency. Fold in remaining ingredients. Spoon into desired mold and let set.

Kirkfield Park United Church
Winnipeg, Man.

Beet Salad

1 - 3 oz. (85 g) pkg. cherry Jell-O
1 cup hot water
1½ cups cooked grated beets
1 grated apple
½ cup chopped celery
½ small chopped onion
2 tbsp. white sugar
½ cup vinegar, add cold water to make 1 cup

Dissolve Jell-O in hot water, let cool. Add beets, apple, celery, onion, sugar and vinegar water. Mix well and leave set.

Zion Evangelical United Church
Pembroke, Ont.

Cran-Raspberry Mold

1 - 6 oz. pkg. raspberry Jell-O
1¾ cups boiling water
1 - 14 oz. can cranberry sauce
1 - 19 oz. can crushed pineapple
1 cup sour cream

Dissolve Jell-O in boiling water. Add cranberry sauce, stirring until melted. Add undrained pineapple. Chill until partially set. Pour half of mixture into a 6½ cup ring mold. Chill until almost firm. Leave remaining Jell-O at room temperature. Spread sour cream evenly over firm Jell-O. Gently spoon remaining Jell-O mixture on top of sour cream layer. Chill until firm.
Makes 12 servings.

Hickson United Church
Hickson, Ont.

Christmas Jell-O

2 cups applesauce
1 large pkg. cherry Jell-O
1½ cups ginger ale

Heat applesauce to boiling. Remove from heat and add Jell-O and ginger ale. Pour into a bowl or jelly mold. If using 1 small pkg. Jell-O, decrease ginger ale to 1 cup.

Port Stanley United Church
Port Stanley, Ont.

Molded Salmon

1 tsp. salt
1 tsp. dry mustard
1 tbsp. sugar
¾ cup sweet milk or cream
¼ cup vinegar
2 eggs or 3 egg yolks
¼ cup cold water
1½ tbsp. gelatin
1 large can salmon

Make salad dressing of first six ingredients. Soften gelatin in cold water. Dissolve in hot dressing, stirring constantly. Add salmon, turn into moistened mold. Chill. Unmold on lettuce and garnish with parsley and hard boiled eggs or olives.
Additions: Peas, diced celery or gherkins.

North St. United Church
Goderich, Ont.

Cranberry-Orange Salad

1 - 11 oz. can mandarin orange sections,
  drained
1 - 3 oz. pkg. orange Jell-O
1 cup boiling water
1 - 8 oz. can (1 cup) jellied cranberry sauce
1 tbsp. lemon juice
⅓ cup chopped pecans

Dissolve gelatin in boiling water. Add cranberry sauce; beat with rotary beater till smooth. Stir in lemon juice. Chill till partially set. Fold in oranges and pecans.

Grace United Church
Dunnville, Ont.

Cottage Cheese Salad

1 lemon or pineapple Jell-O dissolved in
  ½ cup hot water
½ lb. cottage cheese
⅓ cup salad dressing
½ cup chopped celery
½ cup chopped walnuts, optional
1 - 14 oz. can crushed pineapple, partially
  drained

Mix last five ingredients, then fold into Jell-O. Pour into mold and set overnight. Garnish with green or red cherries.

Gibsons United Church
Gibsons, B.C.

Molded Corn Beef Salad

2 beef bouillon cubes
1 cup boiling water
1 - 3 oz. pkg. lemon Jell-O
8 oz. pkg. cream cheese
2 cups diced celery
¼ cup diced onion
4 hard cooked eggs, diced
1 - 12 oz. can corned beef, cut in small pieces
1 cup salad dressing

Dissolve cubes in boiling water. Add Jell-O. Stir. Blend dressing and cheese. Then add celery, onion, eggs and corned beef. Mix and turn into loaf pan and chill.

Ontario St. United church
Clinton, Ont.

Jellied Ham and Celery Salad

1 pkg. lime Jell-O
1¾ cups boiling water
¼ cup vinegar
½ tsp. salt
1 cup chopped ham
1½ cups chopped celery
1 tbsp. chopped onion
2 tbsp. sweet pickles, chopped fine

Dissolve Jell-O in water. Add vinegar and salt. Chill. When thickening fold in ham, celery, onion and pickles. Pour in bowl or individual dishes. Chill. Serve on lettuce and garnish with sliced tomatoes. I also add a little grated cheese and ½ cup salad dressing.

King's Kirk United Church
Belleisle Creek, N.B.

Rainbow Salad

3 oz. pkgs. Jell-O, 1 raspberry, 1 lemon,
  1 lime, 1 orange
1 cup sour cream

Mix raspberry Jell-O using 1 cup hot water and ⅔ cup cold water. Pour half into an 8x8'' glass pan. Chill until set. In remainder put 1½ tablespoons sour cream and beat with beater on low. Pour over first mixture and chill until set. Repeat using lemon Jell-O, then lime and then orange.

Trinity United Church
Vankleek Hill, Ont.

Horseradish Salad

1 - 3 oz. lemon Jell-O powder
1½ cups boiling water
¼ cup horseradish
½ cup Miracle Whip
¼ cup milk
½ pkg. Dream Whip

Dissolve Jell-O in boiling water, put in fridge to partially set. Stir horseradish into Miracle Whip, beat milk and Dream Whip together. Fold or beat the mixture altogether in the Jell-O and chill.

Victoria Street United Church
Goderick, Ont.

Easy Tomato Aspic

5¼ cups V-8 juice
3 bay leaves
3 - 3 oz. pkgs. lemon Jell-O
6 tbsp. lemon juice

Heat juice and bay leaves to boiling point. Remove from heat and take out bay leaves. Stir in Jell-O until dissolved. Add lemon juice. Cool. Refrigerate. When starting to thicken, pour into oiled mold.

Wesley United Church
Vandorf, Ont.

Pink Party Salad

1 - 3 oz. pkg. lemon Jell-O
1 can condensed tomato soup
1 cup Miracle Whip salad dressing
1 tbsp. finely chopped onion
¼ cup chopped almonds
1 cup finely chopped celery
2 tbsp. green pepper
½ cup boiling water
6 oz. white cream cheese

Dissolve Jell-O in boiling water. Add cream cheese and beat vigorously. Add other ingredients. Put in oiled mold and chill.

Belmont United Church
Belmont, Ont.

Summer Salad

1 small can crushed pineapple, do not drain
1 - 8 oz. carton cottage cheese
1 pt. carton Cool Whip
1 - 3 oz. pkg. strawberry Jell-O
¾ cup water
½ cup sugar

Bring pineapple, juice, water and sugar to a boil for 1 minute. Add Jell-O and let cool to soft set. Fold in cottage cheese and Cool Whip. Refrigerate until firm.

Caledonia United Church
Caledonia, Queen's County, N.S.

Tomato and Cheese Salad

20 oz. can tomato juice
1 celery stalk
¼ cup chopped onion
1 small lemon Jell-O
½ cup white sugar
½ tsp. salt
1 tbsp. vinegar
Pepper
1 tbsp. butter
1 - 8 oz. pkg. cream cheese
7 tbsp. Miracle Whip
¾ cup finely chopped celery
¼ cup chopped nuts
2 tsp. finely chopped onion

Simmer tomato juice with celery stalk and ¼ cup chopped onion for 15 minutes; strain. Add lemon Jell-O, sugar, salt, vinegar and pepper. Bring to a boil, add butter. Pour into mold and let set. Mix cream cheese, Miracle Whip, chopped celery, nuts and onion. Spread on set tomato Jell-O. Refrigerate overnight. This Jell-O may be inverted onto a plate if desired.

Highgate United Church
Highgate, Ont.

Sunny Marshmallow Salad

1 - 3 oz. pkg. orange Jell-O
1 cup boiling water
½ cup cold water
1 tbsp. lemon juice
1 - 8 oz. pkg. Philadelphia cream cheese
1½ cups mini marshmallows
Lettuce
Mandarin orange sections

Dissolve orange Jell-O in boiling water, add cold water and lemon juice. Gradually add to softened cream cheese, mixing until well blended. Chill until almost firm. Fold in marshmallows. Pour into one quart mold. Chill until firm. Unmold on lettuce, surround with orange sections.

River Hebert Pastoral Charge
River Hebert, N.S.

Salad
Caesar Salad

1 head Romaine lettuce
1 clove garlic
½ cup Parmesan cheese
Bacon bits
Sliced mushrooms
Croutons

Oil Dressing:
  ¼ to ½ cup olive oil
  2 tbsp. red wine vinegar

Egg Dressing:
  1 raw egg, slightly beaten
  ½ tsp dry mustard
  2 crushed cloves garlic
  ½ tsp. pepper
  1 tbsp. lemon juice

Rub edge of glass bowl with clove of garlic, break up Romaine lettuce and place in bowl. Shake together olive oil and red wine vinegar. Mix together egg, mustard, garlic, pepper and lemon juice, and let sit a few hours in fridge. Pour oil mixture over lettuce. Toss, then pour egg mixture over lettuce. Toss and add Parmesan cheese, bacon bits, mushrooms and croutons.

United Church in Meadowood
Winnipeg, Man.

Armenian Spinach Salad

2 bunches fresh spinach
1 red onion, thinly sliced
1 cucumber, thinly sliced
½ cup black olives
1 cup Feta cheese
Pepper

Dressing:
  ⅔ cup olive oil
  ⅓ cup lemon juice

Wash, dry and tear spinach. Combine all ingredients in salad bowl. Combine oil and lemon juice in jar and shake well. Pour over salad and toss.
Serves 4-6.

Nisbet Memorial United Church
Prince Albert, Sask.

Orange and Watercress Salad

1 med. head lettuce
2 bunches watercress
6 oranges
2 tbsp. chopped mint
1 tbsp. grated orange peel
Lemon dressing

Wash and drain lettuce and watercress. Peel and slice oranges into rounds. Combine watercress, oranges, mint and orange peel. Mix well. Place lettuce in bowl and cover with the watercress and orange mixture. Pour lemon dressing over and serve immediately.

Lemon Dressing:
  4 tbsp. lemon juice
  ½ tsp. sugar
  ¼ tsp. salt
  Pinch of white pepper
  4 tbsp. salad oil

Dissolve sugar in lemon juice. Combine with remaining ingredients and mix thoroughly. Serves 6.

Lakeshore Drive United Church
Morrisburg, Ont.

Family Favourite Romaine Salad

1 large head Romaine lettuce
1 cup bean sprouts
2 hard boiled eggs, chopped fine
5 slices bacon, cooked and crumbled

Tear lettuce into bowl, sprinkle sprouts, bacon and eggs over top. Pour dressing over top. Toss together and serve at once.

Dressing:
  ¼ cup salad oil
  ¼ cup granulated sugar
  2 tbsp. ketchup
  1 tbsp. vinegar
  1 tbsp. grated onion
  1 tbsp. Worcestershire sauce

Blend all ingredients together. Best when made a few hours early and allowed to let sit.

Columbus United Church
Columbus, Ont.

Artichoke Zucchini Salad

3 small zucchini
1 - 14 oz. can artichoke hearts, quartered
½ cup olive oil
¼ cup red wine vinegar
1 tbsp. fresh lemon juice
2 tbsp. grated Parmesan cheese
2 tbsp. grated onion
¾ tsp. Worcestershire sauce
1 tsp. salt
¾ tsp. fresh ground pepper
¾ tsp. sugar
¾ tsp. basil
¾ tsp. oregano
¾ tsp. dry mustard
1 head Romaine lettuce
2-3 tbsp. parsley, chopped
1 cup fresh mushrooms, sliced

Slice zucchini, with skin on, thinly and place in bowl. Add artichoke hearts, drained. Combine all other ingredients except lettuce, parsley, mushrooms, in a blender and blend 30 seconds. Pour over artichokes and zucchini. Marinate at least 2 hours. Tear lettuce into bite size pieces and put into salad bowl. Add parsley and sliced mushrooms. Just before serving add artichokes and zucchini with marinade. Toss.

United Church in Meadowood
Winnipeg, Man.

Oriental Spinach Salad

⅓ cup roasted peanuts
½ lb. fresh spinach
10 cherry tomatoes
4 thin slices red onion
2 tbsp. rice-wine vinegar
Salt
1 tbsp. soy sauce
⅛ tsp. cayenne pepper
6 tbsp. peanut oil

Chop peanuts and de-stem spinach. Wash the leaves and tear into pieces. Cut tomatoes into halves and add to onions and spinach. In a small jar, shake together vinegar, salt, soy sauce and cayenne until salt dissolves. Add oil and shake again to combine ingredients. Pour this dressing over salad and toss well.

Knox United Church
Gainsborough, Sask.

Shrimp Salad

1 tsp. salt
½ tsp. sugar
2 tbsp. vinegar
1 tbsp. curry powder
2 tbsp. soya sauce
½ tsp. Accent
½ cup oil
1 cup rice, cooked
10 oz. peas, cooked
1 can shrimp
2½ cups chopped celery
1 can chow mein noodles

Boil together salt, sugar, vinegar, curry powder, soya sauce, Accent and oil. Cook rice and cool. Cook peas and cool. Drain and rinse shrimp. Combine rice, peas, shrimp, celery and chow mein noodles. Pour the hot sauce over the salad ingredients. Cool and serve.
Variation: Reduce white rice to ½ cup and add ½ cup wild rice, cooked. It adds a nutty flavour.

Westminster United Church
The Pas, Man.

Golden Salmon Potato Salad

1 - 15½ oz. can salmon
4 cups diced cooked potatoes
1 small onion, chopped
2 tbsp. finely chopped parsley
1 cup diced celery
1 tsp. salt
2 tbsp. light cream
4 tbsp. prepared mustard
2 tbsp. white sugar
2 tbsp. vinegar
¼ tsp. salt
Few grains pepper
Lettuce

Drain salmon and break into bite size chunks. Toss lightly with potatoes, onions, parsley, celery and salt. Combine cream with mustard, sugar, vinegar, salt and pepper. Beat until light and fluffy and pour over salmon mixture. Toss gently until well mixed. Cover and let stand about 1 hour in refrigerator. Serve on lettuce.

Vaughan's United Church
Lr. Vaughan's, Hants County, N.S.

Tomato and Pasta Salad

2 cups bowtie or spiral pasta, cooked and
    cooled
2 ripe tomatoes, chopped
2 green onions, chopped
½ green pepper, chopped
½ cup chopped cucumber

Mix vegetables and pasta together in casserole
dish or salad bowl. Pour sauce over top. Stir
through. Refrigerate overnight or at least 2-3
hours.

Sauce:
    ⅔ cup white sugar
    ½ cup salad oil
    ⅓ cup ketchup
    ¼ cup vinegar
    1 tsp. salt
    ¼ tsp. pepper
    1 tsp. paprika

Park Avenue United Church
Saint John, N.B.

Tomato Salad

3 lge. tomatoes, cut in thin wedges, then
    halved
2 green onions, chopped
½ med. green pepper, cut in julienne strips

Dressing:
    ⅓ cup salad oil
    3 tsp. vinegar
    1 tsp. salt
    1 tsp. sugar
    1 tsp. celery seed
    ½ tsp. paprika
    ¼ tsp. dry mustard
    ⅛ tsp. pepper

Combine vegetables. Combine dressing ingre-
dients in a jar with a tight fitting lid. Shake.
Pour dressing over vegetables and toss lightly.
Marinate at room temperature for 2 hours. Chill
for ½ hour before serving.
Makes 4 servings.

First United Church
Cambridge, Ont.

One Pot Pasta Salad

2 cups corkscrew noodles
½ bag mixed frozen vegetables (cauliflower/
    broccoli mixture)
½ cup Miracle Whip
½ cup Zesty Italian dressing
¼ cup grated Parmesan cheese

Cook noodles according to package directions. Two minutes before noodles are done,
throw frozen vegetables in pot, finish cooking.
Mix last three ingredients together. When noodles are cooked run cold water over noodles and
vegetables until cool. Drain. Mix dressing mixture into noodles and vegetables.

Thedford United Church
Thedford, Ont.

Carrot Salad

3½ cups shredded carrots
1 cup small marshmallows
¼ cup pineapple tidbits, drained
1 cup white seedless raisins
½ cup coconut
1 cup mayonnaise or Miracle Whip
2 cups Cool Whip

Combine salad dressing and Cool Whip. Mix
together all other ingredients and fold into salad
dressing mixture.

Grace United Church
Port Dover, Ont.

Onion Salad

2 lge. Spanish onions, sliced and separated

Marinade:
    1 cup vinegar
    1 cup sugar
    ¼ cup boiling water

Dressing:
    ½ cup salad dressing or sour cream
    Celery seed, optional

Mix marinade well and pour over onions.
Marinate overnight. Drain onions well. Add
salad dressing and celery seed and stir well. Any
mild onions can be used.

Emmanuel United Church
Saskatoon, Sask.

Marinated Vegetable Salad

2 cups thinly sliced cucumber
1 med. onion, sliced and separated into rings
½ cup chopped celery
¾ cup sugar
1 tsp. celery seed
¼ tsp. pepper
2 cups thinly sliced carrots
1 cup vinegar
¼ cup salad oil
1 tsp. salt
Lettuce

In a large bowl, combine cucumber, carrots, onion and celery. To make dressing, in a bowl combine vinegar, sugar, salad oil, celery seed, salt and pepper. Mix well. Pour over vegetables. Stir gently. Cover and refrigerate several hours or overnight, stirring occasionally. To serve, drain the vegetables reserving marinade. Mound vegetables in lettuce-lined bowl. Store leftovers in marinade in the refrigerator. Serves 6-8.

Humphrey Memorial United Church
Moncton, N.B.

Spinach Salad

3 hard boiled eggs
1 bag fresh spinach torn up in pieces
Grated mozzarella cheese
Bacon bits

Dressing:
¼ cup vinegar
Less than ¾ cup white sugar
½ to ⅔ cup oil
½ med. onion, chopped
Salt and pepper to taste
A few drops Worcestershire sauce

Place spinach in large bowl. Chop up eggs over it. Mix dressing ingredients altogether, and pour over spinach and egg. Top with cheese and bacon bits. Serves 6-8.

Port Mouton United Church
Port Mouton, N.S.

Carrot and Raisin Salad

½ cup raisins
1½ cups grated raw carrots
1 tbsp. lemon juice
⅓ cup orange sections
¼ cup mayonnaise
¼ tsp. salt

Plump raisins in boiling water for 5 minutes. Drain and combine with chopped orange sections and carrots. Mix remaining ingredients together, then toss all together.

Foam Lake United Church
Foam Lake, Sask.

Olive Nut Salad

1 - 3 oz. pkg. lime Jell-O
1 cup boiling water
¾ cup chilled, unsweetened apple juice
½ cup grated carrots
¼ cup sliced olives
¼ cup chopped green pepper
½ cup chopped pecans

Dissolve Jell-O in boiling water. Stir in apple juice. Chill until egg white consistency. Fold in carrots, olives, green pepper and nuts. Place in a greased mold. Chill.

Kirkfield Park United Church
Winnipeg, Man.

Fusilli Chicken Salad

8 oz. fusilli pasta, cooked and drained
2 cups diced cooked chicken
2 cups seeded diced tomatoes
1 cup sliced celery
1 green pepper, julienne strips
½ cup chopped onion
1½ cups sour cream, regular or light
¼ cup grated Parmesan cheese
2 tbsp. lemon juice
1 tsp. basil leaves
Salt and pepper to taste

Combine first 6 ingredients in a large bowl. Wisk remaining ingredients together, toss salad. Cover and chill at least 2 hours to blend flavours.
Makes about 6 servings.

Zion United Church
Thessalon, Ont.

Summer Chicken Salad

2 cups diced cooked chicken
1 pint halved strawberries
1 sliced banana
1 can pineapple chunks
1 tbsp. lemon juice
½ cup salad dressing
Toasted slivered almonds
Lettuce

Sprinkle lemon juice over the banana. Add chicken, strawberries and pineapple. Toss with slivered almonds and serve on a generous bed of crisp lettuce.

Middle River United Church
Middle River, N.S.

Chicken Cabbage Salad

2 cups cubed, cooked chicken
2 cups shredded cabbage
¼ cup coarsely chopped sweet pickles
½ cup diced celery
½ cup coarsely chopped nuts
¼ cup mayonnaise
Salt and pepper to taste

Combine chicken, cabbage, chopped pickles, nuts and celery. Add mayonnaise and toss together thoroughly. Serve on lettuce and garnish with sliced or quartered tomatoes or hard cooked eggs.
Yield: 6 servings.

Hammond United Church
Maple Ridge, B.C.

Chicken Rice Waldorf Salad

1½ cups Minute instant brown rice
1 cup reduced calorie mayonnaise
1 lge. red apple
1 tbsp. lemon juice
2 cups diced cooked chicken
1 cup diced celery
1 cup seedless green grapes

Prepare rice as directed on package. Mix apple with lemon juice (to keep apple from turning dark), stir into rice mixture with remaining ingredients. Chill.

St. Luke's United Church
Islington, Ont.

Crunchy Chicken Salad

5 cups diced cooked chicken
1 cup chopped celery
8 oz. can water chestnuts, drained & sliced
1 cup pineapple tidbits, drained
1 cup seedless grapes (red or green)

Dressing:
1 cup Miracle Whip salad dressing
1 cup sour cream
2 tbsp. sugar
1 tsp. seasoning salt

Serve on lettuce leaf. Top with sliced olive. Other ingredients you may want to add are:
½ cup toasted almonds
½ cup chopped green and ripe olives
Hard cooked eggs
¼ cup pickle relish
Serves 8 to 10.

Olds United Church, Olds, Alta.
George St. United Church, St. John's, Nfld.
Two Hills United Church, Two Hills, Alta.

Super Supper Salad

1 pkg. vanilla pudding powder (4¾ oz.)
3 cups milk
1 pkg. dessert topping mix (4 oz.)
1 cup milk
1 tsp. vanilla
1 tin mandarin oranges, drained
1 tin pineapple chunks, drained
1 red apple, diced
2-3 dozen seedless green grapes or pint basket of fresh strawberries
2 bananas

Cook vanilla pudding powder in 3 cups milk. Cool. Whip dessert topping mix with 1 cup milk and vanilla. Combine with cooled pudding. Add prepared oranges, pineapple, apple, and grapes or strawberries. Add bananas just before serving. Store covered in fridge. Serve with angel cake.

Hamiota United Church
Hamiota, Man.

Lemon Fruit Salad

1 can chunk pineapple
1 can mandarin oranges
1 can fruit cocktail
1 can lemon pie filling
8 oz. Dream Whip
1 tsp. lemon juice

Drain pineapple, mandarin oranges and fruit cocktail overnight. Any other fruit of your choice may be added. (Bananas only if salad being used in day one.) Add fruit to lemon pie filling, prepared Dream Whip and lemon juice. Chill.

Cambridge St. United Church
Lindsay, Ont.

Cabbage Salad

6 cups shredded cabbage
½ cup peanuts
½ cup mayonnaise
¼ cup sour cream
2 tbsp. sugar
2 tbsp. vinegar

Combine the cabbage and the peanuts. Mix the rest of the ingredients and mix with the cabbage. This is very good.

Harrow United Church
Harrow, Ont.

Pink Cloud Salad

1 can cherry pie filling
1 can crushed pineapple, drained
1 can Eagle Brand milk
1 lge. tub Cool Whip
1 - 3 oz. pkg. cherry Jell-O (dry)

Mix altogether in a bowl. Stir and serve. A very good traveller and keeper.

St. Andrews United Church
Outlook, Sask.

Fresh Fruit Salad

1 egg, well beaten
¼ cup honey
1 tbsp. fresh lime juice
½ cup whipping cream, whipped
8 cups fresh fruit - cantaloupe, strawberries, grapes, bananas, apples, oranges, etc.
¼ cup peanuts, chopped
Crisp salad greens

Combine egg, honey, lime juice in pan. Cook over medium heat, stirring until thick. Remove from heat. Cool 30 minutes. Fold in whipped cream. Chill until ready to use. Just before serving blend fruits and nuts. Arrange on crisp greens. Garnish with dressing.

Greenwood United Church
Greenwood, Ont.

Cranberry Salad

2 cups fresh cranberries coarsely chopped
3 cups mini marshmallows
¾ cup sugar
2 cups chopped apple
2 cups seedless green grapes
¼ cup chopped pecans or walnuts
1 cup Cool Whip

In a large bowl combine cranberries, marshmallows and sugar. Cover and refrigerate for 8 hours or overnight. Before serving add apples, grapes and nuts. Fold in Cool Whip. Refrigerate until serving. Garnish as desired.

Cliffcrest United Church
Scarborough, Ont.

Fruit Dip

1 - 250 mL container whipping cream
1 tbsp. white sugar
¾ cup orange juice
1 pkg. instant pudding, any variety

Whip the whipping cream. Add sugar. Beat again. Stir in orange juice and the instant pudding. Serve with your favorite fruits.

Orono United Church
Orono, Ont.

Coconut Fruit Dip

2 cups sour cream
10-12 coconut cookies, crushed
¼ cup brown sugar

Mix well. Chill. Serve in a gutted pineapple surrounded with cut up pieces of your favourite fruit.

Elimville United Church
Exeter, Ont.

Fruit Salad

2 eggs
2 tbsp. vinegar
2 tbsp. water
4 tbsp. sugar
2 tbsp. butter

Cook in double boiler. Cool. Add butter and **1 package of prepared Dream Whip** or **Cool Whip (500 mL).**

Add to 1st mixture:
2 oranges
1 can pineapple tidbits (drained)
2 cups miniature marshmallows
1 apple cut fine
1 banana

Cool until ready to serve.

Coal Dale United Church
Coal Dale, Ont.

Pistachio Salad

1 - 106 g pkg. pistachio instant pudding
1 - 19 oz. tin crushed pineapple, juice and all
1 cup mini marshmallows
½ cup chopped walnuts
500 mL container Cool Whip or prepared
    Dream Whip

Mix pineapple and pudding until it begins to thicken. Add marshmallows and walnuts. Fold in whipped topping gently. Chill

Innerkip United Church, Innerkip, Ont.
Wilkie United Church, Wilkie, Sask.
Crescent Ft. Rouge United Church, Winnipeg, Man.
Stockholm United Church, Stockholm, Sask.
South Cayuga Pastoral Charge, Dunnsville, Ont.

Spiced Cranberries

1 qt. cranberries (16 oz.)
2 cups white sugar
1 cup cold water
¾ cup raisins, washed
½ tsp. cloves, ground (can use whole ones if
    desired)
1 tsp. cinnamon
1 tsp. vinegar

Combine all ingredients. Cook over medium heat until slightly thick and cranberries have popped. Stir often. Cool and refrigerate. Would not have Christmas or Thanksgiving without these.

Royal York Rd. United Church
Etobicoke, Ont.

How come opportunity rarely knocks but temptation pounds away every day.

Zucchini Pickles

3 cups zucchini
1 med. head cabbage
½ cup salt
3 lbs. onions
5 apples

Cut into small pieces and soak overnight in 2 quarts hot water and salt. In the morning drain.
Add:
1½ pts. vinegar
2 tsp. allspice
4 tsp. turmeric
½ cup prepared mustard
8 cups sugar

Boil until soft.

Add:
1 lge. tin corn
1 lge. tin tomatoes
1 cup flour
Plus enough water to thicken

(More spices may be added.)

First United Church
Hopeall Trinity Bay, Nfld.

Salad Dressings

Mayonnaise

2 eggs
1 cup white sugar
2 cups milk
1 cup vinegar
4 tsp. dry mustard
4 tbsp. flour

Mix together. Bring to a boil and remove from heat. Add **2 tablespoons butter**. Made in the microwave, it's easy.

River Hebert Pastoral Charge
River Hebert, N.S.

Coleslaw Dressing

1 cup mayonnaise
½ cup sugar
¼ cup oil
¼ cup vinegar
Salt and pepper to taste

Place ingredients in a bottle. Shake until mixed. Keep refrigerated.

Harrow United Church
Harrow, Ont.

Russian Salad Dressing

1 cup tomatoes
½ cup olive oil
½ cup lemon juice
1 small green onion
1 tbsp. honey
2 tsp. salt
1 tsp. paprika
1 tsp. horseradish (optional)
1 clove garlic (optional)

Place all ingredients in food processor. Blend until smooth. Makes about 16 fluid ounces.

Robert McClure United Church
Calgary, Alta.

Fruit Salad Dressing

1 - 500 g container light yogurt, plain
1 - 500 mL Cool Whip
2 tbsp. sugar
2 tsp. almond extract

Whip together.

Wesley United Church
St. Andrews, N.B.

Tasty Tomato Dressing

1 tsp. salt
1 tsp. paprika
⅓ cup sugar
2 tbsp. lemon juice
¼ cup vinegar
⅓ cup ketchup
½ cup Mazola oil

Serve over freshly sliced raw tomatoes.

Orono United Church
Orono, Ont.

Blender Caesar Salad Dressing

¼ cup salad oil
2 tbsp. lemon juice
1 egg
6"-8" anchovy paste from tube
1 clove garlic or garlic powder to taste
¼ tsp. salt
¼ tsp. dry mustard
Dash pepper

Put all ingredients in blender. Blend at high speed for 1 minute. Pour over:
1 head Romaine lettuce, broken
⅓ cup freshly grated Parmesan cheese
Croutons

Toss just before serving. This dressing can be kept refrigerated up to 3 weeks.

United Church in Meadowood
Winnipeg, Man.

Honey-Celery Seed Dressing

⅔ cup sugar
1 tsp. dry mustard
1 tsp. paprika
1 tsp. celery seed
¼ tsp. salt
⅓ cup honey
⅓ cup vinegar
1 tbsp. lemon juice
1 tbsp. grated onion
1 cup salad oil

Mix dry ingredients. Blend in honey, vinegar, lemon juice and onion. In a slow stream, add 1 cup salad oil, beating with electric mixer until thick. Keeps well in refrigerator. Recipe can be doubled. Beware! It's addictive!

First United Church
St. Thomas, Ont.

Salad Dressing

⅓ cup ketchup
¼ cup white sugar
½ tsp. garlic salt
2 tsp. Worcestershire sauce
½ tsp. salt
¾ cup salad oil
½ cup vinegar

Mix together and pour over salad greens.

Orono United Church
Orono, Ont.

Church Supper Coleslaw Dressing

1 jar (1 L) of salad dressing
3 cups white sugar
⅓ cup vegetable oil
½ cup white vinegar

Combine all ingredients, mixing well. Store in refrigerator.

Fallowfield United Church
Nepean, Ont.

Cheater's Caesar Salad Dressing

½ cup Hellmann's light mayonnaise
½ cup low fat Danone 1% yogurt
1 tbsp. lemon juice
1 clove garlic, crushed and minced
1 tsp. Worcestershire sauce
¼ cup Parmesan cheese

Mix all together and enjoy!! Fabulous and keeps well in the refrigerator.

Bolton United Church
Bolton, Ont.

French Dressing

¾ cup white sugar
¾ cup salad oil
½ cup vinegar
1 - 10 oz. can tomato soup
2 tsp. celery seed
¼ tsp. garlic powder

Place all ingredients in jar and shake well. Refrigerate. Shake well before serving.

First United Church
St. Thomas, Ont.

Cabbage Coleslaw

(Feeds approx. 400-450)

20 medium cabbages, chopped
3 qts. onions (1 qt. of red onion can be substituted for colour)
3 qts. grated carrots
2 qts. salad dressing
1 large bottle diet Italian dressing
2 tbsp. Mrs. Dash extra spicy
1 tbsp. pepper

Mix the above 3 ingredients in large plastic container. Add the next two ingredients or until moist enough. Then add extra spicy Mrs. Dash and pepper to the above ingredients. This recipe is much easier if prepared ½ at a time.

Stone United Church
Rockwood, Ont.

Muffins

Applesauce Bran Muffins

1 cup All-Bran
¼ cup milk
⅓ cup oil
1 egg
½ cup maple syrup or ⅓ cup brown sugar
1 cup applesauce
1½ cups flour
3 tsp. baking powder
½ tsp. soda
½ tsp. salt
½ tsp. cinnamon
½ cup raisins

Stir first 6 ingredients together. Add dry ingredients and stir just to moisten. Bake at 375°F for 15-20 minutes.

Danville -Asbestos Trinity United Church
Danville, Que.
Ontario Street United Church
Clinton, Ont.

Applesauce-Oatmeal Muffins

1 cup margarine
1½ cups brown sugar
2 eggs
2 cups flour
½ tsp. cinnamon
2 tsp. baking powder
½ tsp. baking soda
½ tsp. salt
1½ cups applesauce
1 cup raisins
2 cups oatmeal
1 cup chopped nuts

Cream margarine and sugar. Beat in eggs. Add dry ingredients (mixed together) alternately with applesauce. Stir in raisins, oats and nuts. Fill muffin pans ¾ full. Bake at 350°F (180°C) for about 25 minutes. Allow baked muffins to 'set' for 10 minutes or more before removing from pans.

St. Paul's United Church
Fairview, Alta.

Apple Lemon Streusel Muffins

2 cups flour
½ cup sugar
3 tsp. baking powder
1 tsp. salt
½ cup margarine
1 apple, peeled and diced
2 tsp. grated lemon rind
1 egg
⅔ cup milk
¼ cup chopped nuts
2 tbsp. sugar

Mix flour, ½ cup sugar, baking powder and salt. Cut in margarine to make a crumbly mixture. Reserve ½ cup crumbly mixture for topping. Stir apple and 1 teaspoon rind into crumbly mixture. Beat egg and milk together and add to apple crumbly mixture. Fill greased or lined muffin tins ¾ full. Blend reserved crumbs with 1 teaspoon rind, nuts, and 2 tablespoons sugar. Sprinkle over muffins. Bake at 375°F for 25-30 minutes.

Marsden United Church
Marsden, Sask.

Bran Muffins

1½ cups flour
1 cup bran
1 tsp. baking powder
Salt
1 cup brown sugar
2 tbsp. butter
1 egg

Mix batter with enough milk to make a stiff batter and pop in the oven. Bake at 375°F for 15-20 minutes.

Lavenham United Church
Lavenham, Man.

Apple 'n Cheddar Muffins

2 cups all-purpose flour
⅓ cup granulated sugar
1 tsp. baking powder
½ tsp. baking soda
¼ tsp. salt
¼ tsp. cinnamon
1 cup grated sharp cheddar cheese
⅓ cup grated Parmesan cheese
1 egg
1 cup buttermilk or sour milk
¼ cup oil
1 med. size tart apple, finely chopped
¼ cup grated cheddar cheese, optional

Combine flour, sugar, baking powder, baking soda, salt, cinnamon and cheeses in large mixing bowl. Beat egg, buttermilk, oil and apple together thoroughly. Add liquid ingredients all at once to dry ingredients. Stir until just moistened. Fill greased muffin cups ¾ full. Sprinkle tops with ¼ cup cheddar cheese if desired. Bake at 400°F (200°C) for 18-22 minutes.
Makes 12 muffins.

Carrville United Church
Richmond Hill, Ont.

Marc's Butterscotch Apple Muffins

1 cup (250 mL) all-purpose flour
1 cup (250 mL) natural bran
½ cup (125 mL) brown sugar
1½ tsp. (7 mL) baking powder
¼ tsp. (1 mL) baking soda
¾ cup (175 mL) butterscotch chips
¼ cup (50 mL) raisins
1 egg, slightly beaten
¼ cup (50 mL) vegetable oil
1 Granny Smith apple, peeled, cored and
   finely chopped
2 tsp. (10 mL) cinnamon sugar

Preheat oven to 400°F (200°C). Combine dry ingredients in a large bowl. In another bowl combine liquid ingredients. Pour liquid ingredients over the dry ingredients and stir just to combine. Gently fold chopped apple into batter. Divide batter evenly among paper-lined muffin cups and sprinkle with cinnamon sugar topping. Bake until muffins test done, about 20 minutes. Remove and cool on rack.

Centralia United Church
Centralia, Ont.

Refrigerator Bran Muffins
(Large Recipe)

2 cups natural bran
2 cups boiling water

Put together and let stand to cool.

1 cup oil
2 cups white sugar
4 eggs
1 L buttermilk
2½ cups whole wheat flour
2½ cups all-purpose flour
3 tbsp. baking soda
1 tbsp. salt
4 cups bran flakes
2½ cups raisins or dates

Note: 1 cup of oat bran can be used to replace 1 cup of the flour.
Mix everything in bowl with electric mixer. Bake at 300°F for 20-25 minutes. Will store 6 weeks in fridge (ice cream pail).
Hint: Put ¼ cup vinegar with 3¾ cups milk = 1 quart buttermilk.

Wilmar Heights United Church, Scarborough, Ont.
Orono United Church, Orono Ont.
Crescent Fort Rouge United, Winnipeg, Man.
Berwick United Church, Berwick, N.S.
Melville United Church, Stouffville, Ont.
Trinity United Church, Hopewell Hill, N.B.

Banana Muffins

1 cup sugar
1 cup Miracle Whip
2½ or 3 bananas, mashed
1 egg
1 tsp. vanilla

Mix together in bowl. Add gradually:
2 cups all-purpose flour
1 tsp. baking powder
1 tsp. soda
½ tsp. salt
Chopped nuts, if desired

Bake at 375°F for 15-20 minutes.

Elimville United Church
Exeter, Ont.

Orange Bran Muffins

1 cup oil
4 eggs
1 tsp. baking powder
2 cups oat bran
1½ cups sour milk
1 cup raisins
1 cup brown sugar
2 cups flour
2 tsp. soda
2 cups bran
1 orange, juice and chopped rind and pulp

Beat oil and brown sugar. Beat in eggs, one at a time. Stir in the chopped orange. Mix in the flour which is sifted with the baking powder and soda alternately with the milk. Add the oat and wheat brans and raisins. Place in muffin tins lined with paper cups. Bake in a 400°F oven for 15 minutes or until toothpick comes out clean.
Yield: 24 large muffins.

St. Paul's United Church
Souris, Man.

Chocolate Chip Bran Muffins

¼ cup shortening
⅓ cup brown sugar
¼ cup molasses
2 eggs
1 cup milk
1½ cups natural wheat bran
1 cup flour
1½ tsp. baking powder
½ tsp. baking soda
½ tsp. salt
½ cup chocolate chips

Cream shortening and sugar. Add molasses and well beaten eggs. Add milk and bran. Combine remaining ingredients and add to mixture and stir to blend. Fill muffin tins ⅔ full and bake at 350°F for 15-18 minutes. Raisins may be used instead of chocolate chips if you increase the sugar to ½ cup.

Port Royal United Church
Charlottetown, P.E.I.

Carrot Bran Muffins

¾ cup oil (Mazola or Crisco)
1 cup brown sugar
1 tsp. salt
1 egg
⅓ cup milk
2 cups grated carrot

Mix together.

1⅓ cups flour
1⅓ cups natural bran
2 tsp. cinnamon
1 tsp. baking soda
1 tsp. baking powder
½ cup currants or raisins

Mix together and add to top mixture. Stir only enough to mix flour in. Bake at 350°F 20-25 minutes. Use muffin papers, fill ⅔ full. Sprinkle tops with sesame seeds before baking.

St. Stephen's United Church
Red Bank, N.B.

Oat Bran Banana Raisin Muffins

1 egg, lightly beaten
½ cup milk
¼ cup vegetable oil
½ cup granulated sugar
1 cup mashed bananas
1 tsp. vanilla
1 cup whole wheat flour
1 tsp. baking soda
1 tsp. baking powder
1 cup oat bran
½ cup raisins

Combine egg, milk, oil, sugar, vanilla and bananas. Mix well. In another bowl, mix the rest of the ingredients. Stir into the egg mixture and mix until the ingredients are just combined. Spoon into 12 muffin tins and bake at 400°F for 20-25 minutes or until firm to the touch. For cholesterol free muffins use skim milk and replace the egg with 2 egg whites, slightly beaten.

Central United Church, Port Colburne, Ont.
Trinity United Church, Verona, Ont.
Onanole United Church, Onanole, Man.

Chocolate Chip Party Muffins

1½ cups all-purpose flour
½ cup sugar
2 tsp. baking powder
½ tsp. salt
1 egg, slightly beaten
½ cup milk
¼ cup vegetable oil
½ cup semisweet chocolate chips
¾ cup crushed pineapple, well drained
½ cup chopped nuts
¼ cups chopped maraschino cherries, well
    drained

Combine flour, sugar, baking powder and salt. Add egg, milk and oil. Stir just until blended. Stir in chocolate chips, pineapple, nuts and cherries. Fill greased muffin pan ⅔ full. Bake at 400°F for 25-30 minutes. Makes 12 muffins.

Grace United Church
Port Dover, Ont.

Chocolate Cheesecake Muffins

1 - 3 oz. pkg. cream cheese
2 tbsp. sugar
1 cup flour
½ cup sugar
3 tbsp. unsweetened cocoa
2 tsp. baking powder
½ tsp. salt
1 beaten egg
¾ cup milk
⅓ cup cooking oil

In small bowl, beat cream cheese and 2 tablespoons sugar until light and fluffy. Set aside. In a large bowl, stir together flour, ½ cup sugar, cocoa, baking powder and salt. Make a well in centre of dry ingredients. Combine egg, milk and oil. Add all at once to dry ingredients, stirring just until moistened. Batter will be lumpy. Spoon about 2 tablespoons of chocolate batter into each greased small muffin cup or paper cup. Drop 1 teaspoon of cream cheese on top and then more chocolate batter. Bake at 375°F for 20 minutes.
Yield: 12 muffins.

St. Andrew's United Church
Truro, N.S.

Chocolate Chip Banana Muffins

1¾ cups flour
½ cup sugar
3 tsp. baking powder
½ tsp. salt
½ cup chocolate chips
1 egg
¼ cup oil
¼ cup milk
1 cup mashed bananas (3 medium)

Mix first 5 ingredients in large bowl. Mix thoroughly and make a well in the centre. Beat egg till frothy. Mix in oil, milk and bananas. Pour into well. Stir until moistened. Batter will be lumpy. Fill greased muffin tins ¾ full. Bake at 400°F for 20-25 minutes.
Yield: 12-14 muffins.

Camrose United Church
Camrose, Alta.

Chocolate Chip Banana Bran Muffins

1 cup (250 mL) whole wheat or all-purpose
    flour
1 cup (250 mL) natural bran
1 tsp. (5 mL) baking powder
1 tsp. (5 mL) baking soda
Jumbo chocolate chips, enough to put 4
    in each muffin
¼ cup (50 mL) margarine or oil
½ cup (125 mL) granulated sugar
2 eggs
¼-⅓ cup (50-75 mL) buttermilk
1 cup (250 mL) mashed bananas (3 medium)

Measure dry ingredients into a bowl. Stir to combine. Make a well in centre. Cream margarine, sugar, one egg until well blended. Beat in second egg. Mix bananas and sour milk. Add to egg mixture. Pour all at once into well. Mix until moistened (ignore lumps). Fill muffin tins ½ full. Put 4 jumbo chips on each muffin. Fill another ¼ full. Bake at 400°F (200°C) for 10 minutes. Turn heat to 375°F for another 10 minutes or until done.
Note: The chocolate chips must be jumbo size. The smaller ones will melt.

Rivers United Church
Rivers, Man.

Banana Cranberry Muffins

⅓ cup sugar
⅓ cup oil
1 egg, beaten
1 med. banana, mashed
1 tsp. vanilla
½ cup All-Bran
½ cup whole cranberries
1½ tsp. vinegar
1 tsp. soda
1 cup plus 2 tbsp. milk
1 tsp. baking powder
½ tsp. salt
1½ cups flour

Cut cranberries in half or coarsely chop if you prefer. Mix soda, vinegar, milk and beat well. Add the egg, banana, oil, vanilla and sugar and mix together. In a bowl, stir together flour, salt and baking powder. Add the liquid ingredients all at once to the flour mixture, stirring to moisten. Fold in the cranberries and All-Bran. Fill greased muffin cups and bake at 375°F for 14 minutes.

Kirk-McCall United Church
St. Stephen, N.B.

Cranberry Pumpkin Muffins

2 eggs
2 cups sugar
1 cup solid pumpkin
½ cup oil

Beat eggs. Add sugar, pumpkin and oil. Mix well. Sift together:
2¼ cups flour
1 tbsp. pumpkin pie or other spice
1 tsp. baking soda
½ tsp. salt

Add to first ingredients and mix only until moistened. Stir in:
1 cup finely chopped cranberries

Bake in greased muffin tins for ½ hour at 350°F. Test for doneness.
Makes 3 dozen.

Adolphustown Centennial U.E.L. United Church
Napanee, Ont.

Blueberry Pumpkin Muffins

1⅔ cups flour
1 tsp. baking soda
½ tsp. baking powder
½ tsp. salt
1 tsp. cinnamon
½ tsp. allspice
1 cup canned pumpkin
¼ cup evaporated milk
⅓ cup shortening
1 cup firmly packed brown sugar
1 egg
1 cup blueberries
1 tbsp. flour
Streusel

Combine first six ingredients. Combine pumpkin and evaporated milk until blended. Cream shortening and sugar in large mixing bowl. Add egg; beat until mixture is fluffy. Add flour mixture alternately with pumpkin mixture, beating well after each addition. Combine blueberries and flour. Gently stir into batter. Makes 12 large muffins, 18 medium. Sprinkle streusel over top of muffins. Bake in 350°F oven for 40 minutes or until toothpick comes out clean.

Streusel: Combine **2 tablespoons flour, 2 tablespoons sugar** and **¼ teaspoon cinnamon.** Cut in **1 tablespoon butter** until mixture is crumbly.

Knox United Church
Gainsborough, Sask.

Pumpkin Muffins

3 cups canned pumpkin
1 cup canola oil
1 cup honey
3 eggs

Beat above well. Add:
3 cups flour
1 tsp. baking powder
1 tsp. baking soda

Fold into mixture and add:
1 cup raisins
1 cup sunflower seeds, walnuts or chocolate chips

Bake at 400°F or 375°F (depends on your oven) for 20 minutes.

Crescent Fort Rouge United Church
Winnipeg, Man.

Blueberry Orange Muffins

2½ cups (625 mL) flour
¾ cup (175 mL) sugar
2 tsp. (10 mL) baking powder
1 tsp. (5 mL) baking soda
½ tsp. (2 mL) salt
½ cup (125 mL) butter
1 cup (250 mL) orange yogurt
2 eggs, lightly beaten
2 tsp. (10 mL) grated orange rind
1¼ cups (300 mL) fresh or thawed, drained
    blueberries

In large bowl, mix together flour, sugar, baking powder, baking soda and salt. Cut in butter until mixture resembles fine crumbs. In small bowl, combine yogurt, eggs and orange rind. Add all at once to flour mixture. Stir just until combined. Gently fold in blueberries. Divide batter evenly among 12 large greased muffin cups. Bake in 400°F (200°C) oven for 20-25 minutes or until done. Serve warm with butter. Makes 1 dozen.

Pine River United Church
Pine River, Man.

Pineapple Muffins

1⅔ cup sifted flour
2 tbsp. sugar
3 tsp. baking powder
½ tsp. salt

Sift together in bowl.

Combine:
1 beaten egg
⅔ cup well drained, crushed pineapple
½ cup pineapple syrup
⅓ cup milk
¼ cup cooking oil
¼ tsp. vanilla

Add to dry ingredients. Sprinkle top of muffins with **2 tablespoons sugar** mixed with ½ **teaspoon cinnamon**. Bake at 375°F for 15-20 minutes.

Mirror United Church
Mirror, Alta.

Blueberry Muffins

1¾ cups flour
3 tsp. baking powder
½ tsp. baking soda
2 eggs
1 cup milk
½ tsp. vanilla
¼ cup oil or margarine
¾ cup sugar
¾ cup-1 cup blueberries
½ tsp. salt

Sift dry ingredients together. Add beaten eggs, vanilla and oil. Add sugar and mix. Add milk, mix small amount of sugar with berries and add. Bake at 375°F for about 30 minutes. Frozen berries may be used. Substitute saskatoon berries for blueberries for a change.

Stanley United Church, Stanley, N.B.
Two Hills United Church, Two Hills, Alta.
Oak Ridge United Church, St. Stephen, N.B.

Rhubarb Muffins

1¼ cups firmly packed brown sugar
½ cup salad oil
1 egg
2 tsp. vanilla
1 cup buttermilk
1½ cups diced rhubarb
½ cup chopped walnuts
2½ cups all-purpose flour
1 tsp. soda
1 tsp. baking powder
½ tsp. salt

Cinnamon topping:
  1 tbsp. melted butter
  ⅓ cup brown sugar
  1 tsp. cinnamon

In a large bowl, combine sugar, oil, egg, vanilla and buttermilk. Beat well. Stir in rhubarb and walnuts. In a separate bowl, stir together flour, soda, baking powder and salt until thoroughly blended. Stir dry ingredients into rhubarb mixture just until blended. Spoon batter into greased muffin cups, filling them about ⅔ full. Top with cinnamon topping. Bake at 400°F for 20-25 minutes. Yield: 20 muffins.

St. Stephen's United Church
Red Bank, N.B.

Rhubarb Pecan Muffins

2 cups all-purpose flour
¼-½ cup sugar
1½ tsp. baking powder
½ tsp. baking soda
1 tsp. salt
¾ cup chopped pecans
1 large egg
¼ cup vegetable oil
2 tsp. grated orange peel
¾ cup orange juice
1¼ cups finely chopped fresh rhubarb

In large bowl combine flour, sugar, baking powder, baking soda, salt and nuts. In medium bowl beat egg. Add oil, orange peel and juice. Add to flour mixture all at once, and stir just until batter is moist. Stir in rhubarb. Lightly grease 12 large muffin cups and fill ¾ full. Bake at 350°F for 25-30 minutes.
Makes 12 muffins.

St. Paul's United Church, Ormstown, Que.
Binbrook United Church, Binbrook, Ont.
Asbury and West United Church, Toronto, Ont.

Orange Oatmeal Muffins

1 cup quick oats
½ cup orange juice
Grated rind of 1 orange
½ cup boiling water
½ cup butter, melted
½ cup brown sugar
½ cup white sugar
2 eggs
½ cup chopped dates
½ cup pecans, chopped
1¼ cups all-purpose flour
1 tsp. baking powder
1 tsp. baking soda
1 tsp. salt
1 tsp. vanilla

Heat oven to 350°F. Line 14-18 muffin cups with paper baking cups. Soak oats in orange juice and boiling water for 15 minutes. Add orange rind. Beat eggs into oat mixture. Stir in dates and pecans. In a separate bowl stir together melted butter and sugars. Combine oats with butter mixture. Add dry ingredients to batter. Stir thoroughly. Add vanilla and stir. Bake 20-22 minutes or until golden.

Central Avenue United Church, Fort Erie, Ont.
Westminster United Church, Medicine Hat, Alta.

Cranberry Oat Muffins

2 cups quick cooking rolled oats
2 cups sour milk (¼ cup lemon juice & 1¾ cups milk)
2 cups flour
2 tsp. baking powder
1 tsp. baking soda
1 tsp. salt
1½ cups brown sugar
2 eggs, beaten
½ cup melted margarine or butter
2 cups fresh or frozen cranberries, halved or 2 cups fresh or frozen blueberries

Mix oats and sour milk. Let stand. Combine flour, baking powder, baking soda, salt and brown sugar. Mix together. Add eggs and butter to oat mixture and mix well. Add flour mixture all at once to oat mixture. Stir just to moisten. Stir in berries. Fill cups ¾ full. Bake at 400°F 15-20 minutes.
Makes 2 dozen muffins.

Bolton United Church
Bolton, Ont.
North Kildonan United Church
Winnipeg, Man.

Cranberry Muffins

Dry mixture:
2 cups all-purpose flour
3 tsp. baking powder
½ tsp. salt
¾ cup fresh cranberries
½ cup powdered sugar

Moist mixture:
1 lge. egg
4 tbsp. vegetable oil
¼ cup granulated sugar
1 cup milk

Preheat oven to 350°F and prepare 12 muffin cups. Combine first 3 ingredients of dry mixture in a large bowl. Chop cranberries and combine with powdered sugar in a small bowl. In a medium bowl beat egg lightly and combine all ingredients of moist mixture. Add moist mixture to dry mixture all at once and stir briefly. Carefully fold in the cranberry-sugar mixture. Fill prepared cups ⅔ full. Bake for 20 minutes.

Cole Harbour United Church
Dartmouth, N.S.

Sour Cream Pineapple Muffins

¼ cup white sugar
1 egg
¼ cup soft butter
1 cup sour cream
1½ cups flour
1 tsp. baking powder
½ tsp. baking soda
1 cup very well drained, crushed pineapple

Beat together first 4 ingredients. Sift together dry ingredients. Add moist ingredients to dry ingredients. Stir only until blended. Stir in pineapple. Bake at 375°F for 20 minutes.

Asbury & West United Church
Toronto, Ont.

Deluxe Health Muffins

1½ cups very hot water
¼ cup molasses
½ cup natural bran
½ cup rolled oats
3 tbsp. granulated sugar
3 tbsp. brown sugar
½ cup whole wheat flour
½ cup all-purpose flour
¼ cup graham flour
½ cup skim milk powder
3 tbsp. wheat germ
1 tbsp. baking powder
½ tsp. baking soda
Salt to taste
⅓ cup cooking oil
2 lge. eggs
2 tsp. vanilla
½ cup coconut
½ cup walnuts
½ cup sunflower seeds
1 cup raisins
½ cup chopped dried apricots
½ cup chopped dates

In large beater bowl combine water and molasses. Add the bran and oats and let soak 15 minutes. Meantime, combine sugars, flours, skim milk powder, wheat germ, baking powder, baking soda, and salt. Add to and beat into soaked bran and oats mixture, the oil, eggs and vanilla. Stir in the nuts and fruits. Add dry ingredients and combine. Spoon batter into large muffin tins ⅞ full. Bake at 350°F for 20 minutes.
Yield: 1 dozen muffins.

Grace United Church
Thornbury, Ont.

Muffins That Taste Like Donuts

1¾ cups flour
1½ tsp. baking powder
½ tsp. salt
½ tsp. nutmeg
¼ tsp. cinnamon
⅓ cup oil
¾ cup sugar
1 egg
¾ cup milk

Combine flour, baking powder, salt, nutmeg and cinnamon. Combine oil, sugar, egg and milk. Add dry ingredients to this, stir only to combine. Bake at 350°F for 15-20 minutes. Shake muffins out and while hot, dip in melted margarine, then in sugar and cinnamon: **¼ cup melted margarine, ⅓ cup sugar, 1 teaspoon cinnamon** mixed together.

Sawyerville United Church, Sawyerville, Que.
Crescent Fort Rouge United Church, Winnipeg, Man.

It is bad to have an empty purse. But an empty head is a whole lot worse.

Raspberry-Cheese Muffins

3 cups all-purpose flour
1 cup granulated white sugar
1 tbsp. baking powder
1 tsp. salt
4 oz. cream cheese
3 eggs
½ cup vegetable oil
½ cup melted butter or margarine
1 cup milk
1 cup fresh or frozen unsweetened raspberries

Mix cream cheese, eggs, oil, butter and milk. Stir in raspberries. If frozen, thaw enough to separate and put into egg mixture. Quickly mix in dry ingredients and fill tins ⅔ full. For lightly glazed tops, sprinkle with a little sugar on each muffin before baking. Bake 15-20 minutes at 400°F.

Kirkfield Park United Church
Winnipeg, Man.

Carrot Muffins

1 cup sugar
¾ cup oil minus 1 tbsp.
2 eggs
1¼ cups flour
¼ tsp. salt
1 tsp. baking powder
1 tsp. soda
½ cup raisins
¼ cup walnuts
1 cup grated carrots

Mix sugar and oil. Add eggs, stir in flour, baking powder, soda and salt. Add carrots and nuts. Fill muffin cups ⅔ full. Bake at 350°F for 20 minutes.

Sawyerville United Church
Sawyerville, Que.

Rosemary Parmesan Muffins

1½ cups buttermilk or sour milk
2 lge. eggs
3 tbsp. olive oil
2½ cups cake flour
2 heaping tsp. baking powder
1 tsp. baking soda
1 cup freshly grated Parmesan cheese
1 tsp. dried rosemary, crumbled

Beat eggs and oil and buttermilk. Stir flour, baking powder and soda. Add ½ cup Parmesan cheese, stir in rosemary. Make a well in the dry ingredients. Mix in wet mixture, stir. Sprinkle ½ cup Parmesan cheese over muffins. Bake at 350°F for 20-25 minutes. (May add a pinch of salt, or no salt as the cheese is salty.)

Trinity United Church
Coronation, Alta.

Buttercup Muffins

¾ cup brown sugar
¾ cup oil or 1 cup butter
1 egg, well beaten
1 tbsp. molasses
1 cup sour milk
1 tsp. vanilla
1 cup flour
1 tsp. baking powder
¼ tsp. salt
1 tsp. soda
½ tsp. nutmeg
1½ cups graham flour or 1½ cups graham wafer crumbs

Bake at 400°F till rises, then lower temperature to 350°F and bake 25 minutes. Makes 16-18 muffins.

St. Andrew's United Church
Wakefield, Que.

Porridge Muffins

Combine:
1½ cups flour
¼ cup sugar
1 tbsp. baking powder
½ tsp. salt
½ cup raisins

In a separate bowl stir:
½ cup milk
1 beaten egg
2 tbsp. oil
1 cup cooked oatmeal

Combine two mixtures. Mix well. Spoon into muffin tins. Bake at 400°F 15-20 minutes.

Cambray Pastoral Charge
Cambray, Ont.

Blueberry-Lemon Muffins

1¾ cups all-purpose flour
½ cup white sugar
3 tsp. baking powder
1 cup milk
½ cup melted butter
1 egg
½ tsp. salt
1 cup frozen blueberries
Grated rind of 1 lemon

Stir together dry ingredients and add frozen blueberries. Combine egg, milk, melted butter and rind and stir into flour mixture and blueberries, stirring just to moisten. Do not beat. Bake in 350°F oven for 20 minutes. While hot, dip in melted butter and then dip in white sugar.

Bloomingdale United Church
Bloomingdale, Ont.
Middle River United Church
Baddeck, N.S.

Cherry Muffins

1½ cups flour
½ cup oat bran
1 tbsp. baking powder
Salt
1 cup chocolate chips
1 cup walnuts or pecans
2 eggs
⅓ cup oil
½ cup milk
⅔ cup brown sugar
1 can cherries, pitted, cut (save ½'s for top of each muffin

Mix first six ingredients. Add the rest. Stir gently until well mixed. Makes 12 large muffins. Bake 20 minutes at 375°F.

Trinity United Church
Portage la Prairie, Man.

Snow Muffins

3 tbsp. butter
1 cup brown sugar
2 cups flour
3 tsp. baking powder
1 tsp. salt
1 cup milk or water
1½ cups clean white snow
¾ cup raisins or currants

Mix together butter and sugar. Sift flour, bak-ing powder and salt together. Add to creamed mixture alternately with milk or water. Fold in snow and raisins or currants. Put in greased muffin tins. Bake for 10 minutes at 400°F and 15 minutes at 325°F or until lightly browned.

St. Paul's United Church
Mildmay, Ont.

Wheat Germ Muffins

1 tbsp. butter
¾ cup white sugar
1 cup wheat germ
1 egg
1 cup buttermilk or sour milk
1 cup whole wheat flour or 1 cup all-purpose flour
1 tsp. baking soda
1 tsp. vanilla

Cream butter and sugar; add wheat germ, flour, and soda, then egg, milk and vanilla. Stir just enough to moisten. Bake 15 minutes at 400°F.
Makes 12 medium muffins.

Grace United Church
Hanover, Ont.

Chocolate Chip Muffins

1 cup sugar
½ cup butter
2 eggs
1 tsp. vanilla
½ tsp. salt
1 cup cream or yogurt
1 tsp. soda
2 cups flour
½ tsp. baking powder
¾ cup chocolate chips

Topping:
¼ cup chocolate chips
2 tbsp. brown sugar
1 tsp. cinnamon
2 tbsp. nuts (optional)

Combine sugar, butter, eggs, vanilla, salt, and cream. In a separate bowl, combine dry ingredients, then add to sugar mixture, stirring only to moisten. Put batter into muffin tins, sprinkle with topping. Bake at 350°F for 20-25 minutes.

Stanley United Church
Stanley, N.B.

Coffee Cakes & Quick Breads

Cherry Streusel Coffee Cake

2¼ cups flour
¾ cup granulated sugar
⅔ cup butter or margarine
½ tsp. baking soda
½ tsp. baking powder
¾ cup undiluted Carnation evaporated milk
1 tbsp. lemon juice
1 egg
1 tsp. almond extract
1 can cherry pie filling
⅓ cup sliced almonds

Combine flour and sugar in large bowl. Cut in butter until mixture is crumbly. Set aside ½ cup of mixture. Combine evaporated milk and lemon juice. Stir well and leave stand 5 minutes. Add egg and extract; beat well. Add to dry ingredients. Stir until moistened. Spread ⅔ of batter over bottom and about 1 inch up the side of 9" springform pan. Spread pie filling over batter. Drop small spoonsful of remaining batter over pie filling. Stir almonds into reserved crumb mixture. Sprinkle evenly over cake. Bake at 350°F for 50-55 minutes.

North Kildonan United Church
Winnipeg, Man.

Pinch Cake

5 cups tea biscuit mix
1 cup white sugar
1 tbsp. cinnamon
1 cup chopped pecans or walnuts

Topping:
1 cup brown sugar
½ cup melted butter
½ cup melted butter

Mix tea biscuit mix according to directions. Blend sugar, cinnamon and nuts. Butter a bundt cake pan and sprinkle an extra ½ cup of nuts around the bottom. Drop and roll half of the dough by tablespoon into the sugar/cinnamon/nut mixture. Arrange on bottom of pan. Pour half of the topping over the dough. Sprinkle some of the sugar/cinnamon/nut mixture over this. Repeat layer with remaining dough, topping and sugar/cinnamon/nut mixture in the same way. Pour second ½ cup melted butter over all. Bake at 350°F for 30 minutes or until done.

Lakeshore Drive United Church
Morrisburg, Ont.

Overnight Blueberry Coffeecake

1 egg
½ cup sugar
1¼ cups sifted flour
2 tsp. baking powder
¾ tsp. salt
⅓ cup milk
3 tbsp. butter or margarine, melted
1 cup fresh blueberries
2 tbsp. sugar

Night before: Lightly grease an 8x8x2" baking pan. In medium-size bowl, with wooden spoon, beat egg. Gradually add ½ cup sugar, beating until well combined. Sift together flour, baking powder and salt. Add to sugar mixture alternately with milk; beat well after each addition. Add the melted butter and beat thoroughly. Gently fold in blueberries. Pour batter into prepared pan. Sprinkle top with 2 tablespoons sugar. Refrigerate overnight. To serve next day preheat oven to 350°F. Bake 35 minutes, or until top springs back when lightly touched with fingertip. Brush top with 1 tablespoon butter. Cut into squares; serve warm with butter.
Serves 9.

Mount Bruno United Church
St. Bruno, Que.

Cheddar Streusel Coffee Cake

1¾ cups all-purpose flour
⅓ cup sugar
3½ tsp. baking powder
¾ tsp. salt
⅓ cup chilled butter
1 cup shredded cheddar cheese
1 egg
¾ cup milk
½ tsp. vanilla

In a large bowl stir together flour, sugar, baking powder and salt. Beat eggs well, stir in milk and vanilla. Add all at once to dry ingredients. Stir just to moisten. Spread half of batter in greased 8 inch square pan, top with half of streusel topping. Repeat layering. Bake at 375°F for 25-30 minutes. Serve warm with butter.

Topping:
½ cup brown sugar
⅓ cup chopped nuts
1 tsp. cinnamon

St. Paul's United Church
Sarnia, Ont.

Coffee Cake

2 cups (500 mL) sifted flour
1 tbsp. (15 mL) baking powder
¼ tsp. (1 mL) salt
4 tbsp. (50 mL) shortening
½ cup (125 mL) white sugar
1 egg, well beaten
¾ cup (175 mL) milk

Grease a 9x9x2'' pan. Sift together flour, baking powder and salt. Cream shortening and white sugar. Beat in egg. Add dry ingredients alternately with milk.

Topping:
½ cup (125 mL) brown sugar
1 tsp. (5 mL) cinnamon
½ cup (125 mL) chopped walnuts

Pour half the batter into prepared pan. Sprinkle half of mixture of brown sugar, cinnamon and nuts over the batter. Add remaining batter and sprinkle remaining brown sugar on top. Bake for 30-35 minutes at 350°F (180°C).

St. Paul's United Church
Boissevain, Man.

Cream Cheese Coffee Cake

2 - 3 oz. pkgs. Philadelphia cream cheese, softened
4 tbsp. confectioners sugar
2 tbsp. lemon juice
2 cups all-purpose flour
1 tsp. baking powder
1 tsp. baking soda
¼ tsp. salt
1 cup white sugar
½ cup butter or margarine, softened
3 eggs
1 tsp. vanilla
1 - 8 oz. container sour cream

Topping:
¼ cup sugar
1 tsp. cinnamon
¼ cup finely chopped walnuts
¼ cup red cherries, quartered

Grease and flour 10'' tube pan. Beat cream cheese, confectioners sugar and lemon juice until fluffy. Set aside. In medium bowl, stir together flour and the next three ingredients. In large bowl, with electric mixer on medium, beat sugar and butter until fluffy. Add eggs and vanilla. Beat well. Beat in dry ingredients alternately with sour cream to egg mixture until well blended. Pour half of batter in prepared pan. Spoon cream cheese mix on top to within ½'' from edges. Spread remaining batter over cheese mix. Sprinkle topping over top. Bake 40-45 minutes in 350°F oven. Test at center with toothpick. Cool for 10 minutes on wire rack. Remove from pan and cool on wire rack 10 minutes longer and serve warm, or cool completely.

Wilmot United Church
Fredericton, N.B.

Married Woman's Cake

1 lb. of true love
1 lb. of perfect trust and confidence
1 lb. of cheerfulness
A pinch of unselfishness
A sprinkle of interest in all your husband does

Mix well with a gill of the oil of sympathy. Put into a tin of contentment. Flavor with a bright fireside and a loving kiss. Bake well all your life.

Westlock United Church
Westlock, Alta.

Golden Syrup Coffee Cake

1 egg
1 cup milk
⅓ cup salad oil
½ tsp. ground ginger
2 cups biscuit mix (2 cups flour, ½ whole
  wheat and ½ white) (3 tsp. baking powder,
  1 tsp. salt)
2 tbsp. golden syrup

Topping:
¾ cup dry cereal flakes
½ cup golden syrup
2 tsp. milk

Preheat oven to 425°F. Beat egg and milk together. Add golden syrup and ginger and beat. Add 2 cups biscuit mix and beat until smooth. Pour into 8x8'' pan. Sprinkle cereal flakes on top. Dribble syrup and milk on top. Cook for ½ hour or until cooked through on middle rack of oven.

Trinity United: Ecumenical Centre
Nanaimo, B.C.

Rhubarb-Strawberry Coffee Cake

Rhubarb-strawberry filling
3 cups all-purpose flour
1 cup sugar
1 tsp. salt
1 tsp. baking soda
1 tsp. baking powder
1 cup butter or margarine
1 cup buttermilk or sour milk
2 slightly beaten eggs
1 tsp. vanilla
¾ cup sugar
½ cup all-purpose flour
¼ cup butter or margarine

Prepare rhubarb-strawberry filling; set aside to cool. In large mixing bowl stir together the 3 cups flour, 1 cup sugar, salt, baking soda, and baking powder. Cut in the 1 cup butter or margarine till mixture resembles fine crumbs. Beat together buttermilk, eggs, and vanilla; add to flour-butter mixture. Stir just till moistened. Spread half the batter in a greased 13x9x2'' baking pan.

Spread cooled rhubarb-strawberry filling over batter in baking pan. Spoon remaining batter in small mounds atop fruit filling. Combine ¾ cup sugar and ½ cup flour; cut in the ¼ cup butter or margarine till mixture resembles fine crumbs. Sprinkle crumb mixture over batter. Bake in 350°F oven for 40 to 45 minutes. Makes 1 coffee cake.

Rhubarb-Strawberry Filling: In saucepan combine 3 cups fresh or frozen cut-up rhubarb and one 16-ounce package frozen sliced strawberries. Cover and cook rhubarb and strawberries about 5 minutes. Stir in 2 tablespoons lemon juice. Combine 1 cup sugar and ⅓ cup cornstarch; add to rhubarb mixture. Cook and stir 4 to 5 minutes more or till thickened and bubbly.

Central United Church
Lunenburg, N.S.

Raspberry Coffee Cake

⅔ cup sugar
¼ cup cornstarch
¾ cup water or raspberry juice
2 cups raspberries
1 tbsp. lemon juice

Cook and then set aside to cool.

Cake:
3 cups flour
1 cup sugar
1 tbsp. baking powder
1 tsp. salt
1 tsp. cinnamon
1 cup butter
2 eggs
1 cup milk
1 tsp. vanilla

Combine dry ingredients and cut in butter. Add eggs, milk and vanilla. Spread ½ the batter in two buttered round 8'' pans or one 9x13''. Drizzle filling and spread evenly over batter. Drop other half of batter over filling in small teaspoonsful.

Topping:
¼ cup butter
½ cup flour
½ cup sugar
¼ cup chopped almonds

Mix together and sprinkle over cake. Bake in 350°F oven for 40 minutes.

Knox United Church
Gainsborough, Sask.

Crumb Top Coffee Cake

1 - 8 oz. pkg. cream cheese
1 cup sugar
½ cup margarine
2 eggs
1¾ cups flour
1 tsp. baking powder
½ tsp. baking soda
¼ tsp. salt
¼ cup milk
1 tsp. vanilla
1 - 12 oz. jar raspberry jam
½-¾ cups chopped walnuts or pecans

Combine softened cream cheese, sugar and softened margarine, mixing until well blended. Add eggs and beat well. Add flour, sifted with the baking powder, baking soda and salt. Add the flour mixture alternately with the ¼ cup milk, mixing well after each addition. Add vanilla and mix well. Pour half the batter into a well greased and floured 9x13x2'' baking pan. Cover batter with the raspberry jam, spreading evenly over entire surface. Cover jam with other half of batter. Spread crumb topping over batter.

Topping:
¼ cup sugar
¼ cup flour
2 tbsp. softened margarine
½ tsp. ground cinnamon
1 tsp. ground nutmeg
½ cup chopped walnuts or pecans

Mix sugar, flour, margarine, cinnamon and nutmeg. Blend with pastry blender or fork, adding nuts, mixing until mixture resembles coarse crumbs (mixing with hand if necessary). Spread this mixture completely to cover over top of batter. Bake in preheated 350°F oven for 1 hour or until toothpick comes out clean.

First United Church
Truro, N.S.

The love in your heart wasn't put to stay.
Love isn't love until you give it away.

Quick Breads

Pink & White Loaf Cake

1¾ cups cake flour
½ tsp. baking powder
½ tsp. salt
¼ cup milk
1 tsp. food coloring
¼ cup shortening
3 eggs
½ tsp. vanilla
½ tsp. almond extract

Mix well. Divide dough in half and add coloring to one. Spoon into greased loaf pan (alternately) and bake at 325°F for one hour. Cool in pan for 10 minutes and remove.
Note: Any food coloring may be used according to preference or season.

Rivers United Church
Rivers, Man.

Christmas Brazil Nut Loaf

Grease and line with greased brown paper a 9x5'' loaf pan. Set oven at 300°F (150°C).
Combine:
1¼ cups all-purpose flour
¾ tsp. baking powder
¼ tsp. salt

Add:
3 cups Brazil nuts, whole
2 cups dates, whole, pitted
1 cup glace cherries, whole

Cream together:
½ cup margarine, softened
¾ cup sugar

Add:
3 eggs
1 tsp. vanilla
1 tsp. almond extract

Beat in eggs one at a time. Stir in vanilla and almond extract. Fold together, press into loaf pan. Bake 1½ to 1¾ hours. Store (in airtight container) a few weeks before slicing.

Grace United Church
Trenton, Ont.

Apple Bread

2 cups finely diced apple, peeled and seeded
1 cup sugar
¼ cup salad oil
1 egg, beaten
1 cup all-purpose flour
1 tsp. salt
1 tsp. baking soda
1 tsp. cinnamon
½ cup coarsely chopped walnuts
½ cup raisins or currants

Toss apples with sugar, let stand 30 minutes. Add oil and egg, blending well. Sift flour, salt, soda and cinnamon into apple mix. Stir thoroughly. Mix in nuts and raisins. Pour into 9x5x3" bread pan. Bake at 350°F for 50-60 minutes or until bread tests done (be sure it is cooked right to the bottom). Cool in pan for 10 minutes and turn out on rack. When cool, wrap the foil and refrigerate or freeze up to 2 months.

Salem United Church
Colborne, Ont.

Date and Pineapple Quick Bread

1 cup chopped dates
1 cup boiling water
1 - 14 oz. can crushed pineapple and juice

Simmer until of jamlike consistency. Add 2 tablespoons soda to warm fruit mixture. Add to the cooled fruit mixture:
1 cup white sugar
4 tbsp. butter or oil
2 unbeaten eggs
4 cups all-purpose flour
1 tsp. salt
2 tsp. vanilla
1 cup chopped walnuts

Bake in greased and floured loaf pans at 350°F for approximately 25 minutes. This may also be baked in 14 ounce tins (6). Makes 2 loaves.

Grace United Church
Port Dover, Ont.

Spicy Squash Bread

2 cups flour
1 tsp. baking powder
1 tsp. baking soda
½ tsp. salt
½ tsp. cinnamon
½ tsp. nutmeg
¼ tsp. ginger
¼ tsp. allspice
2 eggs
1 cup granulated sugar
½ cup brown sugar, lightly packed
½ cup oil or melted shortening
1 cup cooked squash, mashed
¼ cup orange juice or water
1 cup raisins
½ cup chopped nuts

Mix flour, baking powder, soda, salt and spices in bowl. Beat eggs. Add sugars, oil, squash and orange juice. Combine with flour mix. Stir only until blended. Stir in raisins and nuts. Pour into 9x5" loaf pan. Bake in 350°F oven approximately 1 hour. (Test with toothpick before removing.) Cool in pan 15 minutes, then turn out on wire rack. When cold wrap well and let ripen in fridge.
Note: Pumpkin can be used in place of squash. Home cooked vegetables are often moist and you may not require the orange juice or water in this recipe.

Emmanuel United Church
Saskatoon, Sask.

Annapolis Valley Applesauce Bread

1 cup hot unsweetened applesauce
3 tbsp. shortening
1 egg
½ cup sour milk
½ cup molasses
1 tsp. salt
1½ cups flour
1 tsp. soda
1 cup rolled oats
1 cup raisins

Cream shortening. Add molasses, egg and milk. Beat well. Add the flour, sifted with the salt and soda. Add oats and raisins. Blend well. Mix in the applesauce, combining well. Pour into greased and floured 9x5x2" loaf pan. Bake at 375°F for 45 minutes.

Berwick United Church
Berwick, N.S.

Best Pumpkin Bread

1⅔ cup all-purpose flour
½ tsp. baking powder
1 tsp. baking soda
¾ tsp. salt
1 tsp. cinnamon
¼ tsp. cloves
¼ tsp. nutmeg
½ tsp. ginger
1½ cups brown sugar
⅓ cup milk
⅓ cup cooking oil
1 tbsp. molasses
2 lge. eggs
1 cup pumpkin
½ cup raisins or walnuts

Mix dry ingredients. Mix liquids. Add to dry ingredients. Thoroughly blend. Add raisins or nuts. Bake in well greased 9½x5" loaf pan at 350°F for 1 hour or until done or in a 9x12" cake pan for 35 minutes at 375°F.

Emmanuel United Church
Waterloo, Ont.
Trinity United Church
Coronation, Alta.

Chocolate Zucchini Loaf

2½ cups all-purpose flour, unsifted
½ cup cocoa
2½ tsp. baking powder
1½ tsp. baking soda
1 tsp. salt
1 tsp. cinnamon
¾ cup soft butter or margarine
2 cups sugar
3 eggs
2 tsp. vanilla
2 tsp. grated orange peel
2 cups coarsely shredded zucchini, unpeeled
1 cup milk
1 cup pecans or walnuts, chopped

Combine all dry ingredients and set aside. Beat together butter and sugar until well blended. Add eggs, one at a time, beating well after each addition. With spoon stir in vanilla, orange peel and zucchini. Alternately stir in dry ingredients and milk into zucchini mixture, adding nuts with last addition. Pour batter into a greased and floured 10" tube pan or bundt pan or 2 loaf pans. Bake at 350°F for about 1 hour or until a toothpick inserted in center of cake comes out clean. Cool in pan for 15 minutes. Turn out on cake rack to cool thoroughly. Glaze if you wish.

Glaze:
2 cups icing sugar
2 tbsp. milk
1 tsp. vanilla

Mix together and beat until smooth. Drizzle glaze over cake. Slice thin. Freezes well.

Wilberforce United Church
Wilberforce, Ont.
Foam Lake United Church
Foam Lake, Sask.

Strawberry Bread

2 - 10 oz. pkgs. frozen strawberries, thawed
4 eggs, beaten
1¼ cups salad oil
3 cups flour
2 cups white sugar
3 tsp. cinnamon
1 tsp. baking soda
1 tsp. salt
1 cup chopped nuts

Heat oven to 350°F. Grease and flour two 9x5" pans. In medium size bowl, stir berries, eggs and oil. Set aside. In large bowl combine flour, sugar, cinnamon, baking soda, salt and nuts. Add berry mixture and stir or mix until blended. Pour into pans and bake 1 hour. Makes 2 loaves.

Kirkfield Park United Church
Winnipeg, Man.

Date Pumpkin Loaf

Sift together:
1¾ cups all-purpose flour
1 tsp. soda
1 tsp. cinnamon
Pinch salt

Cream:
¾ cup pumpkin
½ cup salad oil
1 scant cup white sugar
2 eggs
Vanilla

Add dry ingredients, then stir in 1¼ cups dates, finely chopped and ½ cup chopped nuts. Bake at 350°F for approximately 1 hour.

Hickson United Church
Hickson, Ont.

Cheese and Date Ribbon Loaf

Batter:
2 cups all-purpose flour
4 tsp. baking powder
½ tsp. salt
½ cup white sugar
1 cup grated strong cheese (old cheddar)
⅓ cup shortening
1 cup milk
1 egg, slightly beaten

Filling:
½ cup brown sugar
1 tsp. cinnamon
1 tbsp. flour
1 cup chopped dates
¼ cup soft butter
⅓ cup chopped nuts (for top)

Combine filling ingredients. Grease a loaf pan. Preheat oven to 350°F. Sift flour with baking powder, salt and sugar. Stir in cheese. Cut in shortening. Add slightly beaten egg and milk all at once. Stir just until moistened. Spoon one-third batter in pan. Sprinkle with one-half filling mixture. Spoon another third of batter and then sprinkle remaining filling and batter over the top. Sprinkle with nuts. Bake 1 hour and cool thoroughly before slicing.

Grace United Church
Trenton, Ont.

Cranberry Raisin Bread

2 cups flour
1 cup sugar
1½ tsp. baking powder
1 tsp. salt
½ tsp. baking soda
¼ cup butter
1 egg, beaten
1 tsp. grated orange peel
¾ cup orange juice
1½ cups light raisins
1½ cups cranberries, cut in half

Sift flour, sugar, baking powder, salt and soda into a large bowl. Cut in butter until mixture is crumbly. Add egg, orange peel and juice, all at once. Stir just until mixture is moist. Fold in raisins and cranberries. Spoon into a greased loaf pan. Bake at 350°F for 1 hour and 20 minutes.

First United Church
Corner Brook, Nfld.

Blueberry Nut Bread

3 cups flour
4 tsp. baking powder
¾ tsp. salt
3 tbsp. butter or margarine
1 cup milk
¾ cup sugar
1¼ cups fresh blueberries
½ cup chopped walnuts
2 eggs, well beaten

Prepare dry ingredients: flour, baking powder and salt. Beat eggs well. Gradually add white sugar and mix thoroughly. Add milk and melted fat. Add dry ingredients to wet ingredients and stir only enough to blend. Carefully fold in blueberries and nuts. Pour into greased large loaf pan (13x4½''). Bake in 325°F oven for about 45-50 minutes, longer if frozen blueberries are used. This loaf is better when fresh!

First United Church
Trenton, N.S.

Orange Pecan Loaf

⅔ cup sugar
¼ cup butter
2 lge. eggs
2 cups flour
½ tsp. salt
1 tbsp. baking powder
Dash nutmeg
1 cup pineapple-orange juice
½ tsp. vanilla
⅔ cup chopped pecans

Beat sugar, butter and eggs. Combine dry ingredients. Mix juice and vanilla. Alternately add wet and dry. Stir in nuts. Put in greased 9x5x3'' pan. Bake at 350°F for 1 hour. Test with toothpick. Remove from pan. Cool.

Glaze:
1 cup icing sugar
1-2 tbsp. orange juice

Use pastry bag to decorate. Put about **8 pecan halves** on top.

St. David's United Church
Upsalquitch, N.B.

Yukon Orange Bread

2 medium oranges
⅓ cup water
1 cup sugar
1 egg
¾ cup sugar
2 cups flour
2 tsp. baking powder
1 tsp. salt
¾ cup milk

Finely shred peel of the oranges and simmer in water for about 6 minutes until peel softens. Add 1 cup white sugar and simmer for another 15 minutes or until slightly thickened. Cool. Meanwhile, in mixing bowl, beat egg and ¾ cup sugar. Alternately add sifted dry ingredients with milk, beginning and ending with dry ingredients. Add cooled orange mixture and fold in well. Pour into small to medium greased loaf pan. Bake at 350°F for 1 hour. This loaf is a sweet tea bread with a tasty crunch crust.

Rexdale United Church
Rexdale, Ont.

Apricot Cream Cheese Loaf

½ cup chopped raisins
½ cup chopped dried apricots
2 cups water

Simmer in a covered saucepan for 20 minutes. Cool and drain.

1½ cups sugar
1 cup butter
8 oz. cream cheese
4 eggs
2¼ cups flour
1½ tsp. vanilla
1½ tsp. baking powder
½ cup chopped pecans

Cream sugar, butter, cheese and vanilla. Add eggs, one at a time, beating after each addition. Add flour and baking powder. Fold in fruit and nuts. Bake in two loaf pans at 350°F for approximately 45 minutes or in a tube pan for at least 1 hour. (Use Philadelphia Lite cream cheese.)

Kirkfield Park United Church
Winnipeg, Man.

Apricot Loaf

1 cup chopped apricots
4 tbsp. melted margarine
1½ cups granulated sugar
4 cups flour
2 tsp. baking powder
¾ tsp. salt
1 tsp. baking soda
3 eggs, beaten
1½ cups orange juice
½ tsp. grated orange rind

Measure and combine dry ingredients - flour, baking powder, baking soda and salt. Mix margarine and sugar well; add eggs and blend well. Add orange rind. Add apricots to flour mixture and combine alternately with orange juice to creamed mixture. Mix well and pour into two loaf pans (4x11'') and bake in 325°F oven for about 40-45 minutes. This loaf freezes well.

First United Church
Trenton, N.S.

Tropical Prune Bread

2 cups flour
1 cup white sugar
2 tsp. baking powder
2 tsp. cinnamon
½ tsp. nutmeg
½ tsp. salt
1 cup coarsely chopped prunes
½ cup shredded coconut
½ cup chopped walnuts
2 cups shredded carrots
¾ cup vegetable oil
¼ cup milk
3 eggs, beaten
2 tsp. vanilla

In a large bowl combine flour, sugar, baking powder, cinnamon, nutmeg and salt. Add coconut, prunes and nuts. Toss to blend thoroughly. Add carrots, oil, eggs and vanilla. Mix just to blend. Turn into greased and floured 9x5x3'' loaf pan. Smooth top. Bake at 350°F for 1 hour and 15 minutes until bread is springy to the touch and begins to push away from sides of pan. Cool 15 minutes. Turn out onto rack. Wrap in plastic or foil while slightly warm. Store 24 hours before slicing. Makes 1 large loaf.

Nashwaaksis United Church
Fredericton, N.B.

Yeast Breads, Biscuits & Buns

Pretzels

1¼ cups lukewarm water
1 pkg. yeast
½ tsp. sugar
4½ cups flour
1 egg yolk
1 tbsp. milk
Coarse salt (pickling type)

Place water, sugar and yeast in a bowl and let stand for 1 hour. Mix with flour and knead for about 10 minutes. Let dough rise in a greased, covered bowl until double in bulk. Punch dough down and form into pretzels. Place on a greased baking sheet and apply egg wash made by mixing egg yolk and milk. Sprinkle with salt. Cover and let rise until not quite double in bulk. Bake at 475°F for about 10 minutes or until nicely browned. Cool on rack.

St. Paul's United Church
Mildmay, Ont.

Jiffy Cinnamon Rolls

4-5 cups all-purpose flour, divided
1 box (9 oz.) one-layer white cake mix
2 pkgs. (¼ oz. each) quick rise yeast
1 tsp. salt
2 cups warm water (120°-130°F)
2 tbsp. butter or margarine
½ cup sugar
1 tbsp. cinnamon

In a large mixing bowl, combine 3 cups flour, cake mix, yeast, salt and warm water. Mix until smooth. Add enough remaining flour to form a soft dough. Turn out onto a lightly floured surface; knead until smooth, about 6-8 minutes. Roll dough into a 9x18'' rectangle. Spread with butter and sprinkle with sugar and cinnamon. Roll dough jelly roll style, starting with the long end. Slice the roll into 1'' circles; place on greased cookie sheets. Cover and let rise in a warm place until doubled, about 15 minutes. Bake at 350°F for 15-18 minutes. Frost.

St. Andrew's Glenavon Church
Glenavon, Sask.

Pita Bread

3½-4 cups all-purpose flour
1 tsp. salt
1 tbsp. instant yeast
2 tbsp. vegetable oil
¼ tsp. sugar
1¼ cups warm water (110°F)

Combine flour and salt in processor. Pulse to mix. Mix together water, sugar and yeast and set aside to soften. Stir occasionally until foaming starts (10-15 minutes). Add oil and mix. Add slowly to running processor until a loose ball forms. Process for 1-2 minutes to form gluten. Place in a greased bowl and turn to coat both sides, cover and place in a warm place for 45-60 minutes until about double in bulk. Try a cold oven with the light on and door closed. Punch down and divide with a sharp knife into 12 sections. Roll each into a ball and let rest for 10 minutes. On a lightly floured surface, start at the center of a ball and roll to the outside until a 5-6 inch circle is formed. Do not go back and forth. Place each round on an ungreasd cookie sheet, cover with a towel and let rest for 30 minutes. Bake at 400°F for 10-12 minutes or until the surface is lightly browned and puffed up. Remove from the pan and wrap immediately in foil to keep the crust soft. Cool and store in closed container or bread wrapper. Cut in half and fill pocket with your favourite fillings. Makes 12 pitas

Grace United Church
Port Dover, Ont.
Nashwaaksis United Church
Fredericton, N.B.

Dirty Dishes

Thank God for dirty dishes,
They have a tale to tell
While other folks go hungry
We're eating very well.
With home and health and happiness,
We shouldn't ought to fuss
For by this stack of evidence,
God's very good to us.

Gilford United Church
Gilford, Ont.

Pineapple Criss Cross Coffee Cake

Basic Sweet Dough
  2 or 3 tbsp. yeast
  2 tsp. sugar
  ½ cup warm water

Mix yeast and sugar and dissolve in warm water. Let stand 10 minutes.

  1 cup milk
  ½ cup sugar
  2 tsp. salt
  ¾ cup cold water
  ¼ cup soft margarine
  2 eggs
  7-8 cups flour

Heat milk. Stir in sugar, salt, margarine and water. Beat eggs and add milk mixture and 2 cups of flour. Beat all until smooth. Add 5-6 cups of flour to make a soft dough. Knead 5-10 minutes till dough is smooth and elastic. Place in greased bowl, cover and let rise in a warm place until double in bulk. Punch down and cut in equal portions. Shape each portion as desired.

Coffee Cake Filling:
  ¼ of basic sweet dough recipe
  ¾ cup crushed, drained pineapple
  ¼ cup brown sugar
  ¼ cup coconut
  ⅛ tsp. cinnamon

Honey Glaze:
  3 tbsp. soft butter
  ½ cup icing sugar
  ½ cup liquid honey
  ½ tsp. vanilla

Roll dough into an 8x12" rectangle. Spread pineapple mixture on center of rectangle. Cut slashes 2" long 1" apart along each long side of dough. Fold these cut pieces across the filling alternately from side to side to make the top look criss-cross. Brush top with honey butter glaze. Sprinkle with slivered almonds. Cover lightly and let stand in a warm place until double in bulk (approximately 45 minutes). Bake at 350°F for 25-30 minutes. You may bake this in a rectangle pan or a round deep expansion pan, a 10" round is quite suitable. I prefer to put the glaze on after baking, right after I take it out of the oven.

St. Andrews United Church
Admiral, Sask.

Swedish Tea Ring

1 pkg. yeast
¼ cup warm water
¾ cup scalded milk
⅓ cup sugar
1 tsp. salt
⅓ cup shortening
4-4½ cups sifted all-purpose flour
2 eggs

Filling:
  2 tbsp. soft margarine
  ½ cup sugar
  2 tsp. cinnamon
  ½ cup seedless raisins

Soften yeast in warm water. Combine scalded milk, sugar, salt and shortening. Cool. Stir in 2 cups flour. Add eggs, beating well. Add yeast. Add only enough flour to make a soft dough. Knead until smooth. Place in a greased bowl and let rise in a warm place for 1½ hours. Punch down and let rise for 1 more hour. Divide dough, cover and let rest for 10 minutes. Roll into a 9x13" rectangle. Spread dough with margarine and sprinkle other ingredients on top. Roll and seal edges. Shape in ring, seam side down, on greased sheet. Snip with scissors at 1½" intervals and turn slightly. Cover and let rise 45 minutes. Bake at 375°F for 25-30 minutes. Drizzle with confectioners' icing.

Highgate United Church
Highgate, Ont.

Two Hour Buns

(No Knead)

  3 cups warm water
  6 tbsp. granulated sugar
  2 tsp. salt
  7 or 8 cups flour (to make a workable batter)
  2 tbsp. instant yeast (Fermipan)
  2 eggs
  6 tbsp. oil

Mix dry yeast and 4 cups flour, sugar and salt. Mix beaten eggs, oil, water and dry ingredients. Add remaining flour. Let rise 15 minutes. Punch down and let rise 15 minutes. Punch down. Form into rolls or bread. Let rise one hour. Bake at 350°F for 15 to 18 minutes or until brown and done. Brush tops with margarine.

Lakeshore Drive United Church
Morrisburg, Ont.
Stockholm United Church
Stockholm, Sask.

Pecan Cinnamon Buns

2½ cups milk
¾ cup butter
1 pkg. granular yeast
1 tsp. sugar (first amount)
½ cup lukewarm water
½ cup sugar (second amount)
2 eggs
7 cups unsifted flour
2½ tsp. salt
Cinnamon

Glaze:
1½ cups light brown sugar
⅓ cup soft butter
4 tbsp. light corn syrup
8 oz. whole pecans

Heat milk to scalding. In a large bowl measure ½ cup butter, ½ cup sugar and salt. Pour scalded milk over the above, and let cool to lukewarm. In cup or small bowl, add the 1 teaspoon sugar and ½ cup lukewarm water to the yeast and give it one stir; let stand 10 minutes. When milk mixture is cool, add yeast liquid. Beat the eggs slightly, add them and the flour. Mix with a large spoon, then turn out on a floured board and knead 100 times, adding flour to the board as needed. Shape into a ball and return to greased bowl. Turn dough in bowl until entire ball is greased. Let rise in a warm place until double in bulk. Punch down dough on floured board and knead 200 times. Cut dough into 3 equal pieces. With rolling pin roll dough into oblongs ¼'' thick. Spread with butter and sprinkle liberally with cinnamon. Roll up like a jellyroll, starting at the long side. Stretch to lengthen and tighten roll and slice into 1¼'' thick pinwheels. Place these close together in pans prepared with the glaze.

Glaze: Put over low heat, just enough to blend the sugar, butter and corn syrup. As soon as melted remove from heat. Cover bottom of pans with pecans (3 to a group where you'll place the pinwheels). Drizzle glaze over nuts, then place each piece of dough, cut side down, on the glaze. Cover, let rise in warm place about 1½ hours. Bake at 400°F placed on high rack in oven for 10 minutes, then reduce heat to 375°F for another 15 minutes.
Makes 3 square pans - approx. 27 buns.

McClure United Church
Edmonton, Alta.

Brown Buns

½ cup oatmeal
½ cup whole wheat flour
2 tsp. salt
¼ cup shortening
2 tbsp. molasses
2 tbsp. honey
1 cup boiling water
2 pkgs. yeast
½ cup warm water
1 tsp. honey
1 egg
2-4 cups white flour

Combine first 6 ingredients. Pour cup of boiling water over all. Mix and let stand till cool (not cold). While it cools dissolve yeast in warm water and honey. Add beaten egg to cooled mixture and mix in yeast. Add white flour till able to knead. Let rise till double in bulk. Put in pans and bake at 350°F for 40 minutes or less. Approximately 16 buns.

St. Andrew's United Church
Hemmingford, Que.

Sticky Buns

(Microwave Recipe)

¼ cup melted butter
⅓ cup brown sugar
2 tbsp. corn syrup
½ cup pecans
¼ cup maraschino cherries
1 - 10 oz. roll refrigerator biscuits

Add sugar and corn syrup to melted butter. Stir well and cook on HIGH 1-1½ minutes Sprinkle nuts and cherries on the bottom of a tube pan. Pour syrup on. Arrange refrigerator biscuits on top of syrup. Cook on MEDIUM for 4-6 minutes. Invert on serving tray and let stand a few minutes. Serve hot or cold. This recipe fills a small microwave tube pan. Double the amount for a larger pan.

Annesley United Church
Markdale, Ont.

White Bread

3-3½ cups unbleached all-purpose flour
2 lge. eggs
¼ cup sugar
1 cup milk, heated
1 tsp. salt
1 tsp. vanilla
½ cup oil
Pinch of nutmeg and mace
Grated peel of 1 lemon
1 scant tbsp. yeast
¼ cup warm water

Dissolve yeast in ¼ cup warm water and let rise for approximately 10 minutes. Add all ingredients (except flour) into blender and mix well. Add risen yeast and mix again. Add liquids to flour in bowl and mix gently. Hold some flour back. Dust dough with flour, cover bowl and let rise in fridge overnight or approximately 1½ hours. Knead in additional flour, till not sticky any longer.

For braided bread: Divide into 3 parts, roll and braid into loaf.

For round bread: Divide dough into 2 parts and form round loaf.

Brush with well beaten egg and sprinkle with sesame seeds. Let rise for approximately ½ hour. Bake 40-45 minutes in 375°F oven.

Kilbride United Church
Kilbride, Ont.

Multi-Grain Health Bread

½ cup shortening
½ cup honey
1 tbsp. and 1 tsp. salt
¼ cup light molasses
4 cups very hot water
2 eggs, beaten
2 cups large flake oatmeal
1 cup Red River cereal
1 tbsp. and 1 tsp. Fleishman's quick rise yeast
2 cups whole wheat flour
3 cups all-purpose flour
4 cups white flour

Combine shortening, honey, salt, molasses and hot water in a large bowl and stir until shortening is melted. Add enough cold water to eggs to make 2 cups and add to above. Add oatmeal and cereal. Combine yeast and whole wheat flour and add to above. Add 3 cups white flour to above and beat by hand or electric mixer until well mixed and smooth. Add 2 cups white flour and mix by hand. Add another 2 cups white flour and mix well. Add enough flour until dough comes away from bowl (1 cup). Turn out on well floured, large area and knead 5-8 minutes, adding small amounts of flour as needed. Grease top and rise in a warm, draft-free place for 1 hour or until doubled. Punch down and put into 4 or 5 well greased pans and let rise again until doubled in bulk (approximately ¾ hour). Preheat oven to 375°F. Bake loaves for 15-20 minutes. Turn loaves in oven and bake another 15-20 minutes (turn oven to 350°F if loaves are browning too fast or cover with foil). Loaves should be nicely browned and sound hollow when tapped. Remove from pans and cool on wire rack.

Dublin St. United Church
Guelph, Ont.

Braided Rueben Loaf

2½ cups flour
1 tbsp. sugar
1 tsp. salt
1 pkg. quick rise yeast
1 cup hot water
1 tbsp. margarine

Filling:
200 g shaved corned beef
¼ cup mayonnaise
2 tsp. prepared mustard
1 cup grated Swiss cheese
1 cup saurkraut, drained

Place half the flour, yeast, sugar and salt in bowl. Melt margarine in hot water. Add to flour and mix. Add balance of flour and mix well. Remove dough to board and rest for 10 minutes. Roll dough 14x10". Distribute corned beef down center of pastry. Spread mixture of mayonnaise and prepared mustard on top, then cheese and saurkraut last. Make 1" cutting slits along each side of filling to outer edge. Fold alternately to braid. Cover - leave in warm place to rise - ½ hour on greased cookie sheet. Brush top with mixture of **1 egg white**, beaten with **1 tablespoon water**. Bake at 400°F for 25 minutes. Serves 6-8.

Silver Heights United Church
Winnipeg, Man.

Pull Apart Bread

*(A delicious "Fergasa" type bread made with
frozen bread dough and a bundt pan.)*

2 loaves frozen bread dough
¼ cup melted butter
1 tsp. garlic powder
¼ cup grated Parmesan cheese
¼ cup chopped fresh parsley
2 or 3 green onions, chopped
½ (or more) grated cheddar cheese

Thaw bread dough, but do not let rise yet.
Cut dough into 20 pieces for each loaf. Mix all
remaining ingredients in small bowl. Dip each
piece of bread into butter mixture. Place in
greased bundt pan. Let rise 2 hours. Sprinkle
with more Parmesan cheese. Bake at 350°F for
30-35 minutes. Cover with foil after 15 minutes
so it doesn't get too brown. Remove from pan
soon after baking so it does not stick.

United Church in Meadowood
St. Vital, Man.

Variation: use 1 cup of grated Parmesan and
Romano cheese mixed instead of the Parmesan
and cheddar cheese.

Columbus United Church
Columbus, Ont.

Fermipan Bread

4½ cups water
½ cup white sugar or less
¾ cup powdered milk
3 eggs
¾ cup oil
4½ tsp. salt
**8 cups whole wheat flour, plus some white
flour**

Mix together first 6 ingredients. Add 2 cups
flour and 3 tablespoons Fermipan instant yeast.
Beat. Add enough flour white and whole wheat
to make a soft dough. Let rise 15 minutes and
punch down. Let rise 15 minutes and punch
down. Let rise 15 minutes and make into loaves.
Let rise 30-45 minutes. Bake at 350°F for about
40 minutes or until done. You must use Fermipan yeast and punch down even if it doesn't
look as if it has risen. Makes approx. 8 loaves.

Macoun United Church
Macoun, Sask.

Face God with the problem and then face the
problem with God.

Green Onion Cheese Bread

½ lb. soft butter
½ cup finely chopped green onion
3 tsp. dry mustard
Swiss cheese slices
2 tbsp. poppy seeds
1 lge. French bread

Cut crust off top, sides and end of bread.
Slice across loaf to bottom, but not through to
bottom. Mix soft butter, onions, dry mustard
and poppy seeds. Spread on both sides of each
slice. Add ½ Swiss cheese slice in each slit.
Cover whole loaf with remaining butter mixture
(iced like cake). Wrap all in foil, leaving top
open and bake in 400°F oven uncovered 15-20
minutes until crusty and light brown. Put on pan
that can go on table or bread board. The bottom of each slice, as served, needs to be cut
through for easy serving.

Sandford United Church
Sandford, Ont.

Lorianne's Coffee Bread

1 loaf frozen bread dough
Pecans, to taste
Glace cherries, to taste
⅓ cup butterscotch instant pudding powder
½ cup brown sugar
½ tsp. cinnamon
½ cup melted butter

Allow bread dough to thaw enough to cut into
eight pieces. Butter bundt pan well. Place cherries and pecans on bottom of greased pan. Place
bread dough on top of cherries and nuts. Sprinkle the pudding (dry), brown sugar and cinnamon over the bread dough. Drizzle melted
butter over above mixture. Cover with greased
paper. Put in warm place to rise and then bake
at 350°F for 30 minutes.

Trinity United Church
Schumacher, Ont.

Pringle Bread

Loaf of French bread, sliced
½ cup butter
1 tsp. thyme
1 tsp. parsley
¼ tsp. dry mustard
¼ tsp. sage
2 tbsp. onion, minced
Dash pepper

Mix ingredients together. Spread on slices. Put slices back in loaf form, wrap in foil, heat in oven and serve warm. (This amount of mixture is not quite enough for the whole loaf.)

Stanley United Church
Stanley, N.B.

Biscuits and Buns

Apple Rolls

¾ cup granulated sugar
⅓ cup water
Recipe of baking powder biscuits
4 apples
⅓ cup brown sugar
2 tbsp. butter
Cinnamon
Syrup

Boil sugar and water in covered saucepan for 3 minutes. Pour into an 8-inch square pan. Let cool while preparing a recipe of baking powder biscuits. Roll biscuit dough to ¼" thickness. Peel and chop apples and spread over surface of dough. Sprinkle with ⅓ cup brown sugar, cinnamon, and dot with butter. Roll up like a jelly roll, and cut into 1½" slices. Arrange rolls cut side up in syrup in pan. Bake in preheated oven at 450°F for 20-25 minutes. Serve warm topped with syrup from bottom of pan, and milk, whipped cream or ice cream. Serves 4.

Salisbury United Church
Salisbury, N.B.

The main difficulty with a liar is the necessity of a good memory.

Eva's Scones

¾ cup currants
3 cups flour
¾ cup white sugar
3 tsp. baking powder
1 cup margarine
¾ tsp. salt (optional)
1 egg, beaten and milk to fill 1 cup

Cover currants with boiling water and drain. Blend flour, sugar, baking powder, margarine and salt. Add egg and milk mixture. Add currants. Roll and cut in diamonds. Place on greased cookie sheet and bake at 425°F for 8-10 minutes.

Central United Church
Unionville, Ont.

Cheese Scones

¼ cup margarine
¼ cup milk
1 egg, beaten
2 cups all-purpose flour
¼ cup white sugar
1 tbsp. baking powder
1 cup grated cheese

Heat oven to 400°F. With pastry blender, blend margarine, sugar, flour and baking powder. Add milk and egg and blend well. Add cheese and stir only till blended. Knead out on floured board, pat with hands or roll to ½" thick. Cut with glass. Place on ungreased pan and bake until lightly browned.

Westminster United Church
Whitley, Ont.

Buttermilk Tea Biscuits

3 cups all-purpose flour
3 tsp. baking powder
½ tsp. soda
¼ tsp. salt
¼ cup white sugar
½ cup shortening

Combine dry ingredients and cut in shortening until crumbly. Add all at once 1½ cups buttermilk (or soured milk). Mix only until dough holds together. Knead a few times and flatten on floured board to 1" thickness. Cut out with biscuit cutter. Bake at 425°F for 12-15 minutes.

Thorndale United Church
Thorndale, Ont.

Cranberry Scones

¾ cup chopped fresh or frozen cranberries
¼ cup granulated sugar
2 cups all-purpose flour
4 tsp. baking powder
½ tsp. salt
2 tbsp. granulated sugar
½ cup shortening
⅔ cup milk

Combine cranberries with ¼ cup sugar, set aside. Combine flour, baking powder, salt and 2 tablespoons sugar; mix well. Cut in shortening. Stir in cranberries. Add milk all at once, stirring with a fork to make a soft dough. Knead lightly on a floured surface about 10 times. Roll out ½ inch thick. Cut in rounds or triangles. Place on ungreased baking sheet. Bake in 425°F oven for 10-12 minutes. Best served warm with butter.
Makes 12-18.

Salisbury United Church
Salisbury, N.B.

Butterscotch Biscuits

Basic biscuits
2 cups all-purpose flour
4 tsp. baking powder
½ tsp. salt
¼ cup shortening
¾ cup milk

Make up basic biscuit batter. Roll out 8x14'' and prepare the following:
½ cup softened margarine
⅔ cup brown sugar

Beat mixture till smooth. *Drop ½ teaspoon in 16 muffin tins that have been greased. Spread remaining mixture on 8x14'' batter. Roll up like jelly-roll and cut in ½'' slices. Place in muffin tins - cut side down. Cinnamon may be put on jelly roll. Bake at 375°F until done, 15-20 minutes.
*A little corn syrup can be put in muffin tins.

Salem United Church
Colborne, Ont.

Angel Biscuits

¼ oz. instant yeast
5 cups all-purpose flour
3 tsp. baking powder
1 tsp. salt
2 cups buttermilk
¼ cup warm water
3 tbsp. white sugar
1 tsp. baking soda
1 cup butter or margarine

Measure flour, sugar, baking powder, soda and salt into large bowl. Dissolve yeast in warm water and set aside. Cut butter into flour mixture until crumbly. Stir in yeast and buttermilk. Knead just enough to make dough hold together. Roll out on floured board until ¾'' thick and cut into biscuit shapes. Bake on greased cookie sheet at 400°F for 15 minutes. Great with casseroles or whatever.
Makes 2½ dozen.

Trinity United Church, Listowel, Ont.
Moorefield United Church, Moorefield, Ont.

Sweet Milk Biscuits

2 cups flour
¼ cup sugar
4 tsp. baking powder
½ tsp. salt
¼ cup lard or shortening
¼ cup butter
½ cup raisins, optional
1 egg
⅔ cup milk

Sift together first four ingredients. Cut in lard and butter until mixture is crumbly. Add raisins if using. Whisk egg and milk together. Stir into dry ingredients until a soft dough forms. Turn dough onto a lightly floured board. Knead 10 turns. Roll out to ¼'' thick. Cut with biscuit cutter. Put biscuits on a lightly floured baking sheet. Bake at 425°F for 18 minutes. Serve hot with butter and honey.

Ennismore United Church
Ennismore, Ont.

Coconut Tea Buns

4 cups flour
2 tbsp. baking powder
¾ cup sugar
1 cup coconut
1 cup butter or margarine
2 eggs, well beaten
¾ cup milk
1 cup raisins

Sift or blend together flour, baking powder, sugar and coconut. Blend in butter. Stir in eggs, milk and raisins. Stir with a fork to make a soft slightly sticky dough. Bake on ungreased baking sheet for 12-15 minutes in 400°F oven.

Garnish United Church
Garnish, Nfld.

Bread Stuffing

Enough bread stuffing for 5 turkeys, weighing between 20-25 pounds.

13 loaves of bread, crumbled
1 lb. butter
1 qt. chopped celery
1½ tsp. ginger
2 tbsp. poultry seasoning
1½ tsp. sage
2½ tbsp. salt
1 tsp. black pepper
2½ cups melted butter
5 cups water

Add seasonings to bread crumbs. Sauté butter, onion and celery. Add to the above 13 loaves. Divide into 5 plastic bags or containers. Add approximately **1 cup water** and **½ cup melted butter** to each container before stuffing. This is a moist stuffing. Bake turkey as usual.

This recipe can be doubled or even made into larger quantities. (Our church 4 times the recipe for 20 turkeys and has been served 40 years at our turkey supper every fall.)

Stone United Church
Rockwood, Ont.

Homemade "Grease Relief" Cakes

(Muffins or loaves will fall out of pans)

⅓ cup flour
⅓ cup oil
⅓ cup shortening

Mix in blender and pour into jar with lid. Keep in fridge. Put in microwave for 10 seconds on HIGH and brush on pan with pastry brush.

Oil Springs United Church
Oil Springs, Ont.

HELPFUL HINT:
For quick tea biscuits roll out the dough then just cut into squares.
If you roll out the tea biscuit dough to half the normal thickness and then fold it over in half before cutting your tea biscuits will be easier to split after baking.

Entrees

Pancakes

Pancakes

¾ cup all-purpose flour and
¾ cup whole wheat flour or
   1 cup all-purpose flour and ½ cup oat bran
3 tsp. baking powder
½ tsp. salt (optional)
3 tbsp. sugar
2 egg whites
3 tbsp. low fat margarine, melted
¼ tsp. vanilla
1¼ cups skim milk

Mix and sift dry ingredients. Add whole wheat flour or bran. Beat egg whites. Add milk. Make a well in center of dry ingredients, slowly add egg and milk mixture. Add melted margarine and flavoring. Mix only enough to make mixture smooth. Spray preheated griddle. Cook till bubbly then turn. Blueberries or other fruit may be added if desired.

Harrow United Church
Harrow, Ont.

Apple Pancakes

2 cups sifted all-purpose flour
2 tbsp. sugar
4 tsp. baking powder
1 tsp. salt
2 egg yolks, well beaten
2 cups milk
2 tbsp. butter or margarine, melted
1 cup finely grated apple
2 egg whites, stiffly beaten

Sift together dry ingredients. Combine egg yolks and milk. Pour into dry ingedients; stir well. Stir in butter and apple. Fold in egg whites. Let batter stand a few minutes. Cook on hot griddle. Makes seven 8-inch cakes. Serve with maple syrup.

Franklin Centre United Church
Franklin Centre, Que.

Pancake Mix

6 cups flour
1 tbsp. salt
6 tbsp. baking powder
6 tbsp. sugar
2 cups powdered milk

Mix well and store in airtight container on cupboard shelf.

To use:
Combine in a bowl:
1 egg, beaten
1 cup water
2 tbsp. oil
1½ cups pancake mix

Fry on hot ungreased griddle. Serves 3-4. Double recipe if a bigger batch is desired.

Wyoming United Church, Wyoming, Ont.
United Church in Meadowood, Winnipeg, Man.

Oatmeal Pancakes

1½ cups rolled oats
2 cups milk
½ cup whole wheat flour
½ cup all-purpose flour
1 tbsp. sugar
1 tbsp. baking powder
1 tsp. salt
½ tsp. cinnamon
2 eggs, beaten
¼ cup melted butter

In large bowl blend oats and milk and let stand 5 minutes. Stir together flour, sugar, baking powder, salt and cinnamon. Add dry ingredients, eggs and melted butter to oats, stirring until combined. Use ¼ cup measure and cook.
Makes 16-18 pancakes.

United Church in Meadowood
Winnipeg, Man.

Super Pancakes with Orange Sauce

1⅓ cups whole wheat flour
½ tsp. salt
2 tsp. baking powder
2 tsp. dry orange peel or
   1 tbsp. fresh peel
3 tbsp. oil
1 egg, beaten
3 tbsp. honey
¼ cup milk
¾ cup orange juice
1½ cups cottage cheese or ricotta

Stir dry ingredients together, then add egg, honey, milk, juice and oil. Don't stir too much. Make into four large pancakes. Stack them with cheese between each pancake. Serve warm orange sauce over the pancakes, cut in four wedges.

Orange Sauce:
   1 tbsp. cornstarch
   ¼ tsp. salt
   2 tbsp. grated orange peel or
      1 tbsp. dried rind
   ¼-½ cup honey
   1 tbsp. butter
   1 fresh orange sections
   1 cup orange juice

Mix cornstarch, salt, orange peel, and juice and honey in small pan. Bring to a boil, stir until thickened. Remove from heat, stir in butter to melt. Add orange sections and it's ready to serve.

Consul United Church
Consul, Sask.

Economy Pancake Syrup

Combine in saucepan:
   1 cup brown sugar
   3 cups water
   5 tsp. cornstarch

Cook until lightly thickened.

Add:
   1 tsp. maple flavoring

Store in refrigerator.

Bissell Memorial United Church
Andrew, Alta.

Zucchini Pancakes

2 cups grated zucchini
1 cup grated carrots
½ cup grated onion
2 eggs
1 tsp. salt
1 tsp. baking powder
1 tsp. chopped parsley
½ tsp. pepper
1 cup flour

In a mixing bowl combine all ingredients. For each pancake pour a large spoonful of batter onto a hot skillet. Brown on both sides for 2 to 3 minutes. Serve hot.

St. Andrew's United Church
Outlook, Sask.

Waffles

Banana Berry Waffles

(Featured on cover)

3½ cups sifted flour
2 tbsp. baking powder
2 tbsp. sugar
1½ tsp. salt
4 eggs, separated
3 cups milk
¾ cup cooking oil

Sift together flour, baking powder, sugar and salt. Beat egg whites until stiff but not dry. Set aside. Beat egg yolks until thick and lemon colored. Continue beating adding milk and oil. Add dry ingredients and beat until smooth. Fold in beaten egg whites. Pour 1 cup batter on preheated waffle grill.

Topping:
   1 cup strawberry ice cream, softened
   1 - 8 oz. carton strawberry yogurt
   1 - 10 oz. pkg. frozen strawberries, thawed
   1 cup banana chunks

Combine ice cream and yogurt. Combine strawberries and banana chunks. To serve, place a waffle on serving plate. Spoon ice cream yogurt mixture on top and top off with fruit.

United Church in Meadowood
Winnipeg, Man.

Peachy Waffles

3 eggs
1½ cups buttermilk
1¾ cups flour
2 tsp. baking powder
1 tsp. soda
½ tsp. salt
½ cup shortening
1 tsp. almond extract
1 cup sour cream
¼ cup packed brown sugar
4 cups sliced peaches

Beat eggs, beat in buttermilk, flour, baking powder, soda, salt and shortening with beater until smooth. Stir in extract. Pour batter from cup onto center of hot waffle iron. Bake until steaming stops. Lift off waffle carefully. Mix sour cream and sugar. Serve waffles topped with peaches and cream.

Shubenacadie United Church
Shubenacadie, N.S.

Company French Toast

½ cup margarine
1 cup brown sugar
1 tsp. cinnamon
Bread slices
6 eggs
1½ cups milk
Dash of salt

Melt margarine in 9x13 pan, add brown sugar and cinnamon. Mix well. Cover with 2 layers of bread slices. Beat 6 eggs and 1½ cups milk, dash of salt. Pour over bread slices. Cover and let stand in fridge overnight. uncover and bake at 300°F for 30 minutes or more. Cut in spears and invert on platter to serve.
Serves 4.

Consul United Church
Consul, Sask.

French Toast

Superduper French Toast

6 eggs
⅔ cup orange juice
⅓ cup Grand Marnier
⅓ cup milk
3 tbsp. sugar
¼ tsp. vanilla
¼ tsp. salt
Finely grated peel of 1 orange
8 - ¾-inch thick slices French bread
3-4 tbsp. butter

Beat eggs in large bowl. Add orange juice, Grand Marnier, milk, sugar, vanilla, salt and peel, mix well. Dip bread into egg mixture, turning to coat all sides. Transfer to 9x13 baking dish in single layer. Pour any remaining egg mixture over top. Cover and refrigerate overnight. (Liquid will absorb).

To cook melt butter in large skillet on medium heat. Add bread, cook both sides until brown, about 8 minutes. May be sprinkled with icing sugar. Serve with maple syrup.
Serves 4.

United Church in Meadowood, Winnipeg, Man.
Oil Springs United Church, Oil Springs, Ont.

Oven French Toast

1 (12 oz.) loaf French bread, cut in
   1-inch slices
8 large eggs
2 cups milk
2 cups half and half cream
2 tsp. vanilla
½ tsp. nutmeg
½ tsp. cinnamon
½ tsp. mace

Topping:
   ¾ cup softened butter
   3 tbsp. dark corn syrup
   1⅓ cups brown sugar
   1⅓ cups coarsely chopped pecans or
      walnuts

Heavily butter 9x13" pan. Fill pan with bread slices to within ½" of top. Set aside. In blender mix eggs, milk, half and half cream, vanilla and spices. Pour over bread slices. Refrigerate overnight. Make topping by combining all ingredients, set aside until time to bake toast. Spread topping over toast, bake at 350°F for 50 minutes until puffed and golden.
Serves 8-10.

Westlock United Church
Westlock, Alta.

Orange Upside-Down French Toast

¼ cup margarine
⅓ cup sugar or ½ cup maple syrup
¼ tsp. cinnamon
1 tsp. orange rind
6 eggs
1 cup orange juice
Thick sliced bread

Melt margarine and pour into a jelly roll pan. Mix sugar, cinnamon and orange rind and sprinkle over butter in pan. Combine eggs and orange juice. Dip slices of bread into egg mixture. Place in pan and bake at 350-375°F for 20-25 minutes. Watch closely as bottom burns easily. Eat with butter and syrup or delicious plain!

Battleford United Church
Battleford, Sask.

Christmas Brunch Stuffed French Toast

8 slices white bread
2 - 8 oz. pkgs. cream cheese
1 dozen eggs
2 cups milk
⅓ cup maple syrup

Remove crusts from bread and cube. Put ½ in the bottom of a 9x13" buttered baking dish. Cube cream cheese and put on top of the bread. Put remaining bread on top of cheese. Mix eggs and milk, then add maple syrup. Pour mixture over bread. Cover with plastic wrap and refrigerate overnight. Bake at 375°F for 45 minutes. Serve with more syrup and sausage or bacon. Decorate plate with fruit, e.g. orange slices, etc.

St. Paul's United Church
New Liskeard, Ont.

Too many committees waste hours and keep minutes.

The McNabb House B&B French Toast

3 eggs
1 cup milk
1 tbsp. sugar (rounded)
Pinch of salt
¼ tsp. nutmeg
½ tsp. vanilla

Beat together; Dip thick slices of French bread into egg mixture, coating well. Fry in hot 375°F pan until brown, turning bread once during cooking. Serve hot with syrup or preserves.

Wesley United Church
St. Andrews, New Brunswick

Egg Dishes

Western Style Oven Baked Omelette

4 tbsp. butter, divided
3 cups frozen hash brown potatoes
Salt and pepper
1½ cups chopped onion
½ cup coarsely chopped red or green pepper
1 tbsp. flour
1 cup coarsely chopped cooked ham
6 eggs
1 cup milk
½ tsp. seasoned salt

Melt 3 tablespoons butter in large frying pan. Add potatoes, cook turning occasionally until crusty and brown. Add salt and pepper to taste. Line the outside edge of shallow baking dish with potatoes. Melt remaining 1 tablespoon of butter in frying pan. Cook onions and green peppers until tender. Stir flour then ham into vegetable mixture. Beat together eggs milk and salt. Stir in vegetable ham mixture. Pour into center of prepared baking dish. Bake in preheated 325°F oven for 30 minutes or until set.

Keswick United Church
Keswick, Ont.

German Omelette

1 lb. (500 g) sausage meat
1 medium onion, chopped
2 tbsp. fresh parsley, chopped
1 tbsp. dry mustard
6 eggs
2 cups milk
3 slices crustless bread, cubed
1 cup grated cheddar cheese

Brown sausage, drain off excess fat. Add onion, parsley and mustard. Season with salt and pepper. Cook over medium heat until onion is tender (5 minutes). Mix together eggs, milk, bread and cheese then add to meat mixture and stir. Pour into greased 9'' baking dish. Place in fridge overnight, or may be cooked right away. Bake in preheated 350°F oven for 45 minutes. Serves 9.

Trinity United Church
Capreol, Ont.

Never Fail Omelette

2 tbsp. Minute tapioca
½ tsp. salt
¼ tsp. pepper
¾ cup milk
1 tbsp. butter
4 egg yolks, beaten
4 egg whites, stiffly beaten

Cook first four ingredients for 10 minutes. Add yolks stirring constantly. Fold in egg whites. In buttered 9'' frying pan cook slowly for 17 minutes. Dry in slow oven for 5 minutes. Cheese topping, onions and mushrooms can be added.

Glen Morris United Church
Glen Morris, Ont.

Oven Omelette

12 eggs
1 cup sour cream
1 cup milk
2 cups shredded cheddar cheese
1 can sliced mushrooms
3 green onions
2 cups diced, cooked ham, bacon, or
    crumbled sausage meat
Salt, pepper, parsley or basil for flavouring

Butter a 9x13'' glass pan. Beat eggs, sour cream, milk and seasonings until blended. Layer remaining ingredients. Pour the egg mixture over. Bake at 350°F for 45-60 minutes. Can be assembled the night before, covered, refrigerated and then baked for 60 minutes the next day.

Trinity United Church
Ingersoll, Ont.

Double Cheese Oven Omelet

1 tbsp. butter
1 cup fine curd cottage cheese
¾ cup shredded Swiss cheese
1 medium tomato, diced
1 tbsp. flour
1 tsp. dill weed
¾ tsp. salt
4 eggs

Combine cottage cheese, Swiss cheese, tomato, flour, dill weed and salt. Beat eggs to blend and combine with cheese mixture. Place butter in 9-inch pie plate and melt in pre-heated 350°F oven. Pour cheese mixture into hot pie plate and bake 30-35 minutes. Cut into wedges and serve immediately.

Lucan United Church, Lucan, Ont.
Fleetwood United Church, Surrey, B.C.

Sunday Eggs and Ham

2 dozen eggs
½ cup milk
½ cup margarine
2 lbs. canned ham
1 - 10 oz. can sliced mushrooms
2 - 10 oz. cans mushroom soup
½ cup cooking sherry
½ lb. sharp cheese

Beat eggs and milk. Melt margarine in pan and scramble eggs. Put into 9x13" pan. Chop ham, then sprinkle on eggs. Layer mushrooms on top of ham. Warm soup with sherry and spread over all. Grate cheese on top. Cover with foil and refrigerate until required. Bake at 300°F for 1 hour uncovered.

Central United Church, Lunenburg, N.S.
Fishburn - Marr U.C.W., Pincher Creek, Alta.

Mushrooms Benedict

1-2 large green peppers
3 tbsp. margarine
½ cup fresh, coarsely chopped mushrooms
⅛ tsp. salt
Dash freshly ground pepper
¾ cup sour cream
⅛ tsp. Worcestershire sauce
¼ tsp. Dijon mustard
¾ cup sharp shredded cheddar cheese
¼ cup dry sherry
3 English muffins, split, toasted and
   buttered
6 poached eggs

Sauce: Melt butter in saucepan, add chopped mushrooms and brown slightly. Stir in salt, pepper, sour cream, Worcestershire sauce, mustard and cheese. Stir over low heat until cheese melts. Add sherry.

Poached Eggs: Cut 6 rings (½" thick) from large green pepper(s) and put in frying pan. Break 1 egg into each ring, add 1 tablespoon sherry and 1 tablespoon water to pan. Cover and cook until eggs are set. Transfer to toasted muffin halves. Cover with hot Benedict sauce. Serve immediately.

Westfield United Church
Westfield, N.B.

Spanish Devilled Eggs

2 tbsp. chopped onion
1 tbsp. chopped green pepper
1 - 8 oz. can tomatoes

Use above 3 ingredients or you may use a can of stewed tomatoes.

1½ tsp. flour
½ tsp. sugar
1 tsp. butter
6-8 devilled eggs
¼ cup bread crumbs or
   crisp, crumbled bacon

Cook onion and green pepper in 1 tablespoon margarine. Add tomatoes and sugar, flour, salt and pepper. Pour into a 9x13" baking dish. Arrange egg halves which have been devilled in dish. Combine crumbs and butter (or bacon), sprinkle over top. Bake at 425°F for 10 minutes. To devil eggs: half the hardcooked eggs, remove yolk and mash. Blend in ½ teaspoon vinegar, ½ teaspoon prepared mustard and 2 tablespoons mayonnaise, salt and pepper. Refill the whites.

Westcott United Church
Conn, Ont.

Brunch Egg Casserole

2 cups seasoned croutons
1 cup shredded cheddar cheese
4 eggs, slightly beaten
2 cups milk
½ tsp. salt
½ tsp. prepared mustard
½ cup chopped green onion
Dash pepper
10 slices bacon, cooked crisp and crumbled
   (optional)

In bottom of greased 10x6x2" baking dish combine croutons and cheese. In a 4 cup measure (or bowl) combine eggs, milk, salt, pepper, mustard and onion, mix until blended. Pour over crouton mixture in casserole. Bake in 325°F oven uncovered for 55-60 minutes. Sprinkle crumbled bacon on top during last 10 minutes of baking.
Serves 6.

Streetsville United Church, Mississauga, Ont.
Westlock United Church, Westlock, Alta.
United Church in Meadowood, Winnipeg, Man.

Overnight Breakfast Casserole

6 slices bacon
¼ cup butter
4 cups milk
⅛ tsp. pepper
½ lb. cubed ham
½ cup flour
⅛ tsp. salt
16 eggs
1 cup evaporated milk
¼ cup butter
¼ tsp. salt

Sauté bacon, break into pieces and return to pan. Remove half the fat, add ham and ¼ butter and sauté. Sprinkle with flour and stir well. Add milk, stir and cook until thick. Add salt and pepper. Set aside while you prepare eggs. Beat eggs into evaporated milk; add salt. Melt ¼ cup butter in skillet, add egg and scramble until firm. In large 10" buttered casserole or pan put ½ egg mixture and cover with ½ sauce. Add other half of eggs and cover with remaining sauce. Put in fridge overnight. Bake at 275°F oven for 1 hour. Sprinkle with paprika or parsley.

Gibbons United Church
Gibbons, Alta.

Spinach Roll

1 cup flour
1 tsp. baking powder
½ tsp. salt
2 eggs, separated
2 cups milk
1 lb. spinach (cooked, drained and chopped)
¼ cup cooked ham, chopped
3 tbsp. butter
Pinch of grated nutmeg, pepper and salt

Sift flour with baking powder and salt. Beat egg yolks with milk and add to flour mixture. Blend quickly until smooth. Whisk egg whites stiff and fold into batter. Spread 1 tablespoon of butter, melted, evenly in a 10x14" (25x36 cm) jelly roll pan. Pour in batter and bake in a 350°F oven until set but not browned, about 20 minutes. Meanwhile, toss spinach and ham in 2 tablespoons butter with seasoning. Spread spinach mixture evenly over cooked pancake and roll jelly roll fashion. Serve sliced while hot, cover with your favorite cheese sauce.

St. Andrew's United Church
Tide Head, N.B.

Curried Eggs and Muffins

4 English muffins, split and toasted
8 hard-cooked eggs
¼ cup butter or margarine
¼ cup all-purpose flour
2 tsp. curry powder
½ tsp. salt
⅛ tsp. white pepper
2 cups milk

Toppings:
Crumbled cooked bacon
Sliced green onions
Shredded carrots
Chopped nuts
Shredded coconut
Chopped fully cooked ham
Chopped red and green pepper

Heat oven to 200°F. Arrange muffin halves on large ovenproof platter. Slice each egg lengthwise into 4 slices. Place 4 egg slices on each toasted muffin half. Cover platter with foil. Place in oven for 15-20 minutes.

In 4 cup measure, microwave butter on HIGH for 1¼ to 1½ minutes, or until melted. Stir in flour, curry powder, salt and pepper. Blend in milk. Microwave on HIGH for 7-9 minutes or until sauce thickens and bubbles, stirring twice.

Remove platter from oven. Remove foil. Spoon curry sauce over eggs and muffins. Sprinkle with desired toppings.

Advanced Preparation: Up to 1 day in advance, cook eggs, but do not peel. Refrigerate. To serve peel eggs and prepare recipe as directed above.

Shubenacadie United Church
Shubenacadie, N.S.

Spicy Scrambled Eggs

Bacon, ham or sausage
1 medium onion
3 stalks celery
Green pepper (to taste)
8 eggs
Curry, salt, pepper and garlic, to taste

Brown bacon, add onion, celery, peppers and spices. Cook vegetables until just crunchy, then add eggs. Cook and turn over, cook other side and serve. Serve with baking powder biscuits.

Trinity United Church
Hazlet, Sask.

Scrambled Egg Bake

2 tbsp. butter
½ tsp. salt
2 cups milk
1 cup diced bacon, cooked and drained
4 tsp. butter, melted
⅛ tsp. paprika
12-14 eggs, beaten
2 tbsp. flour
⅛ tsp. pepper
1 cup shredded cheddar cheese
3 tbsp. butter
¾ cup sliced mushrooms
½ cup soft bread crumbs
½ cup onions

In a saucepan, melt 2 tablespoons butter. Blend in flour with salt and pepper. Add milk slowly and cook and stir until bubbly. Add cheese gradually. Stir until cheese is melted. Set this mixture aside to cool. Cook onion until tender in the 3 tablespoons butter. Add eggs and cook and scramble until just set. Fold in mushrooms, along with bacon. Add to cheese sauce, making sure all eggs are folded in. Pour into buttered 9x13'' baking dish. Set in fridge overnight. Combine 4 teaspoons melted butter with bread crumbs. Sprinkle over egg mixture. Dust with paprika. Bake uncovered in 350°F oven 30 minutes.

Runnymede United Church, Toronto, Ont.
Trinity St. Andrew's United Church, Renfrew, Ont.

Mushroom & Swiss Baked Eggs

4 green onions, sliced
⅓ cup green pepper, diced
¾ lbs. mushrooms, sliced
3 tbsp. butter
2 tbsp. dry sherry (optional)
9 eggs
1 cup milk
¾ tsp. dry mustard
¾ tsp. tarragon
½ tsp. salt
¼ tsp. pepper
2½ cups Swiss cheese, shredded

In large skillet, cook onions, green peppers and mushrooms in butter until softened and most of moisture is evaporated. Add sherry and continue cooking for about 1 minute longer. In bowl beat together eggs, milk and seasoning. Stir in mushroom mixture and 2 cups cheese. Pour into greased 9-inch baking dish. Cover and refrigerate overnight. Next morning: bake, uncovered at 350°F for 40-45 minutes or until center is almost set. Sprinkle with remaining cheese and bake for 5 minutes or until cheese melts.
Makes 4-6 servings.

Temple Hill United Church
Markdale, Ont.

Festive Hash and Eggs

1 - 15 oz. can corned beef hash
4 eggs
½ cup milk
½ cup shredded Swiss cheese
Paprika

Spread hash in 4 individual casseroles. Make a hollow in each with the back of a spoon. Break one egg into each; do not season. Spoon 2 tablespoons milk over each, top with cheese. Bake, uncovered at 350°F for 18-20 minutes until almost set. Top with paprika, let stand 5 minutes.
Makes 4 servings.

Trinity United Church
Hazlet, Sask.

Bacon Frittata

1 tsp. vegetable oil
1 tsp. butter
8 eggs
10-12 slices bacon, cooked and crumbled
¼ tsp. basil
¼ tsp. oregano
Black pepper to taste
1 green onion
1 green or red pepper (optional)
1 cup cheddar cheese

Heat oil and butter in large frying pan. Beat eggs and seasoning and pour in pan. Sprinkle with bacon, onion and peppers and cheese. Cook over low heat until bottom is lightly done. Place pan in 350°F oven for a few minutes until top is set and cheese is melted. Serve at once.

St. Andrew's United Church
Sunderland, Ont.

Eggs Fooyung

4 eggs
1½ tsp. salt
Dash pepper
¾ cup chopped cooking onions
1 tbsp. soy sauce
1 cup chopped, cooked pork, chicken or
  shrimp
1 cup drained bean sprouts
4 tbsp. chopped green onions

Lightly beat eggs, salt and pepper. Stir in onion, soy sauce, meat, sprouts and green onion. Heat a small amount of oil in frying pan. Using ¼ cup measure, drop measured amount of mixture into hot oil, cooking only 4 mounds at a time, turning each when browned. Serve with sauce.

Sauce:
1 tbsp. soy sauce
1 tbsp. cornstarch
1½ cups chicken broth

Mix ingredients together and cook, stirring until thick.

Foam Lake United Church
Foam Lake, Sask.

Spinach-Chicken Souffle Roll

Spectacular and satisfying, this gourmet treat is worth the extra effort!

4 tbsp. butter or margarine
½ cup flour
2 cups milk
½ cup (2 oz.) grated Parmesan cheese
½ cup (2 oz.) shredded cheddar cheese
¼ tsp. salt
4 egg yolks, slightly beaten
4 egg whites, room temperature
Spinach-chicken filling, see below
4 slices cheddar cheese, cut in triangles

Spinach-Chicken Filling:
2 tbsp. butter or margarine
½ cup chopped onion
¼ lb. mushrooms, chopped
2 - 10 oz. pkgs. frozen chopped spinach,
  thawed and squeezed dry
1 cup diced cooked chicken
1 - 3 oz. pkg. cream cheese
⅓ cup dairy sour cream
2 tsp. Dijon mustard
Dash nutmeg
Salt and pepper to taste

In a medium saucepan over moderate heat, melt butter or margarine. Stir in flour. Cook and stir until blended, about 2 minutes. Slowly add milk, stirring constantly with a whisk. Stir over moderately high heat until batter comes to a boil and thickens. Stir in cheeses and salt. The batter will be very thick. Remove from heat. Add a small amount of batter to egg yolks. Mix well and add egg yolk mixture to saucepan. In a large bowl, beat egg whites until stiff but not dry. Fold a dollop of whites into batter, then gently fold remaining batter into egg whites. Preheat oven to 325°F (165°C). Grease a 15x10x1'' baking sheet or jelly roll pan. Line with waxed paper, leaving a little extra paper at each end; grease and flour waxed paper. Pour batter onto prepared waxed paper; spread evenly. Bake in lower third of oven 40 to 45 minutes until golden brown and surface springs back when lightly pressed.

Prepare Spinach-Chicken Filling; set aside. Remove souffle from oven; carefully loosen edges of waxed paper. Place another piece of waxed paper over souffle. Cover with a tray of another baking sheet and invert. Carefully remove baking sheet now on top and peel off waxed paper. Grease another baking sheet; set aside. Spread Spinach-Chicken Filling evenly over top of souffle. Roll up lengthwise, using the waxed paper to help roll. Souffle may crack. Slide roll seam-side down onto prepared baking sheet. Roll may be refrigerated overnight. It may also be flash frozen or frozen uncovered until solid, then wrapped in freezer foil and returned to freezer.

Before serving, bring souffle roll to room temperature. If frozen, unwrap and place on a baking sheet to bring to room temperature. Preheat oven to 375°F (190°C). Cover souffle roll with foil and reheat 20 minutes or until hot. Remove foil. Overlap triangles of cheese down center of roll. Place under broiler until cheese melts and is lightly browned. Slide a spatula under each end of roll and lift onto a platter. Makes 8 servings.

Spinach-Chicken Filling:
In a medium saucepan, melt butter or margarine. Saute onion and mushrooms until tender. Stir in spinach, chicken, cream cheese and sour cream. Cook and stir until cheese is melted. Add mustard, nutmeg, salt and pepper.

Variation: Substitute chicken with 8 ounces of cooked sausage meat.

United Church in Meadowood
Winnipeg, Man.

Mollie's Savory Eggs

1 cup grated cheese, mild or medium
2 tbsp. butter
½ cup cream (coffee or half and half)
1 tsp. dry mustard
Salt and pepper
6 eggs

Spray a 9" pan and spread the cheese and dot the butter on top. Mix cream, mustard, salt and pepper. Pour half of the cream mixture over cheese. Lightly beat the eggs and pour over mixture. Pour the remaining cream over eggs. Bake at 325°F for 30 minutes or until puffed up and brown around edge.

Beachville United Church
Beachville, Ont.

Quiche & Pies

Quiche

Easy crust - Butter a 9" pie plate. Sprinkle in bread crumbs and shake to coat. Chill 15 minutes.

Melt:
2 tbsp. butter

Add:
½ cup chopped onion
Cook until tender, set aside.

Sprinkle in chilled crust:
1 cup cubed ham
1½ cups grated cheddar cheese
Cooked onion

Combine:
2 eggs, beaten
1¼ cups milk
¼ cup flour
½ tsp. salt
½ tsp. pepper
Blend well. Pour over ingredients in pie shell. Bake at 375°F for 30-40 minutes or until a knife inserted comes out clean. Let stand 5 minutes. Serve hot or cold.

Note: This quiche may be made with tuna, salmon, broccoli, crisp bacon, cooked and broken up.

St. Mark's United Church
Whitby, Ont.

Crab Quiche

1½ cups shredded Swiss cheese
1 - 5 oz. can crab meat, drained and flaked or may substitute with 2 cups flavored seafood or sea legs
1 tbsp. finely chopped onion
1 tbsp. finely chopped celery
1 tbsp. chopped parsley
1 tbsp. flour
½ tsp. salt
3 eggs
1¼ cups light cream or evaporated milk

Toss together cheese, crab meat, onion, celery, parsley, flour and salt. Beat eggs lightly and stir into first mixture. Pour into greased quiche dish. Bake in 325°F for 40-45 minutes or until a knife inserted off center comes out clean. Cool 5 minutes. Cut and serve with tossed salad and hot tea biscuits.
Makes 6 servings.

Gordon Providence United Church
Bridgetown, Nova Scotia

Crustless Salmon Broccoli/Pea Quiche

1 tbsp. butter
1 medium onion, chopped
1 cup chopped broccoli or 1 cup peas
1 cup milk
4 large eggs
¾ cup Bisquick baking mix
¼ tsp. dried dill weed
½ tsp. salt
¼ tsp. pepper
1 - 213 g tin canned salmon, drained and flaked
1 cup grated Swiss cheese (or any grating cheese)

Melt butter and sauté onion for 4 minutes or until tender. Stir in broccoli and cook 1 minute. Beat together eggs, baking mix, dill, salt and pepper. Stir in salmon, cheese and broccoli mixture. Pour into greased 10-inch pie plate. Bake at 400°F for 30-35 minutes or until knife inserted close to center comes out clean. Let stand 5 minutes.
Makes 6 to 8 servings.

Fleetwood United Church, Surrey, B.C.
Crystal City United Church, Crystal City, Man.

Cheddar & Onion Quiche

1 unbaked 9-inch pie shell
1 cup finely chopped onion
2 tbsp. butter
2 cups shredded cheddar cheese
1 tbsp. flour
½ tsp. salt
3 eggs
1¼ cups light cream
Paprika

Prick pie shell well. Bake in preheated 425°F oven 5-7 minutes. Reduce oven temperature to 325°F. Sauté onion in butter until tender. Cool. Add cheese, flour and salt. Toss lightly to combine. Beat eggs slightly, stir in cream. Combine egg and cheese mixtures and pour into partially baked shell. Sprinkle lightly with paprika. Bake in preheated oven 40-45 minutes. Serve hot.

Hudson Bay United Church
Hudson Bay, Sask.

Ham Vegetable Quiche

⅓ cup (75 mL) margarine
1½ cups (375 mL) finely rolled crackers
¼ tsp (1 mL) dried basil leaves
1 cup (250 mL) grated Swiss cheese
½ cup (125 mL) julienne-strips cooked ham
1 - 10 oz. can cream of celery soup
3 eggs
½ cup (125 mL) milk
2 green onions, sliced
¼ cup (50 mL) diced green pepper
1 tbsp. (15 mL) flour

Preheat oven to 375°F. Place margarine in a 9'' pie plate. Heat in oven until melted. Remove and stir in cracker crumbs and basil. Press evenly over bottom and sides of plate. Sprinkle cheese and ham over bottom. Whisk together remaining ingredients and pour into plate. Bake at 375°F (190°C) for about 40 minutes or until set.
Makes 6 servings.

Central United UCW
Lunenburg, N.S.

Mushroom Crust Quiche

5 tbsp. butter
½ lb. mushrooms, coarsely chopped
½ cup (20) finely crushed soda crackers
¼ cup chopped green onions
2 cups shredded Swiss cheese
1 cup cottage cheese
3 eggs
¼ tsp. cayenne
¼ tsp. paprika

In frying pan melt 3 tablespoons butter, add mushrooms, cook until limp. Stir in crumbs. Turn into 9'' pie pan. Press mixture over bottom and up the sides. In same frying pan melt remaining 2 tablespoons butter. Add onion and cook until limp. Spread onions over mushroom crust. Sprinkle with shredded cheese. In a blender whirl cottage cheese, eggs and cayenne until smooth. Pour into crust and sprinkle with paprika. Bake in 350°F oven for 20-25 minutes or until knife inserted comes out clean. Let stand 10-15 minutes before cutting.

St. Andrew's United Church
Wakefield, Que.

Brunch Pie

3 tbsp. butter or margarine
2 cups frozen hash brown potatoes
½ tsp. celery salt & pinch of pepper
¾ cup sliced fresh mushrooms
½ cup chopped onion
½ cup chopped green pepper
5 eggs
½ cup milk
1 cup shredded cheddar cheese
6 slices bacon, cooked and crumbled

In frying pan, melt butter and sauté potatoes until browned and crusty, about 5 minutes. Sprinkle with celery salt and mix well. Spread evenly in 9-inch pie plate or quiche dish. Top with mushrooms, onion and green pepper. Whisk together eggs, milk and pepper. Pour into pan. Bake at 325°F for 30 minutes or until set. Remove from oven, sprinkle with cheese and bacon.
Makes 6 servings.

St. Andrew's United Church, Beaverton, Ont.
Rosemont United Church, Regina, Sask.

Strata-Various Pie

1 red pepper, cut in strips (optional)
¼ cup chopped onion
1 clove garlic, crushed
1 tbsp. butter
1 - 10 oz. pkg. frozen spinach, thawed
    and drained or
    approximately 4 cups coarsely chopped
    fresh spinach, washed and stems removed
3 eggs
1 - 6 oz. pkg. sliced ham
1 - 7 oz. pkg. Swiss or mozzarella cheese
    slices
Pastry for a double crust pie

Preheat oven to 400°F. In large frying pan, sauté onions and garlic in the butter. Add spinach; cover and cook until spinach wilts. Drain very well. Set aside. Whisk together the eggs. In an unbaked pie shell, layer half the ham, half the cheese and half the spinach mixture; cover with half of the egg mixture. Repeat the layers. Place a pie crust over the top. Crimp the edges. Bake pie on a cookie sheet for 30-35 minutes or until golden brown. Serve hot or cold.

Grenfell United Church, Grenfell, Sask.
Como Lake United Church, Coquitlam, B.C.

Italian Zucchini Crescent Pie

4 cups thinly sliced, unpeeled zucchini
1 cup coarsely chopped onion
½ cup butter or margarine
½ cup chopped parsley or 2 tbsp flakes
½ tsp. salt
½ tsp. pepper
¼ tsp. garlic powder
¼ tsp. basil
¼ tsp. oregano
2 eggs, well beaten
8 oz. mozzarella cheese, shredded
8 oz. can Pillsbury quick crescent dinner
    rolls
2 tsp. Dijon or prepared mustard

Melt butter and cook zucchini and onion until tender (about 10 minutes). Stir in parsley and seasonings. Blend eggs and cheese. Stir in vegetable mixture. Separate dough triangles and place in ungreased 10" pie plate. Press over bottom and up sides. Spread mustard over shell. Pour egg, vegetable mixture into pie shell. Bake at 375°F for 10 minutes, then at 350°F for 20 minutes (watch carefully).

Cooksville United Church
Mississauga, Ont.

Fran's Frugal Ham Flan

1 - 9" unbaked pie shell
2 tbsp. butter
½ cup chopped onion
½ cup sliced mushrooms
1 cup cubed ham
2 eggs, beaten
1½ cups milk
¼ cup flour
½ tsp. salt and pepper
1½ cups shredded cheddar cheese

Melt butter in frying pan. Sauté onions and mushrooms until tender. Sprinkle ham, cheese, onions and mushrooms in bottom of unbaked pie shell. Combine eggs and milk. Gradually blend in mixture of flour, salt and pepper. Pour into pie shell. Bake in preheated 375°F oven 30-40 minutes or until a knife inserted in center comes out clean. Let stand 5 minutes. Serve hot or cold.

Valley United Church
Truro, N.S.

Salmon Quiche

1 - 9" pie shell, unbaked or quiche pan
1 - 7¾ oz. tin red salmon
3 oz. shredded Gruyére or cheddar cheese
4 eggs
⅓ cup mayonnaise
2 tsp. lemon juice
¼ tsp. salt
Dash nutmeg, cayenne or paprika

Drain salmon juice into a measuring cup, add enough milk to make 1¾ cups. Discard dark skin from salmon and flake. Distribute salmon and shredded cheese in pie shell. Beat eggs, mayonnaise and lemon juice together and add salmon-milk juice mixture, salt and seasonings. Pour over salmon mixture. Sprinkle with paprika. Bake at 450°F for 15 minutes, then reduce heat to 325°F for 35 minutes or until set.

Wilmar Heights United Church
Scarborough, Ont.

Cheese Pie

Shell:
1 cup grated cheese
½ tsp. salt
¼ cup melted margarine
¾ cup flour
¼ tsp. dry mustard

Combine until smooth; knead 1 minute to soften and press into a 9'' pie plate.

Filling:
1½ cups egg noodles
2 cups thinly sliced onions
2 tbsp. margarine
2 eggs, slightly beaten
1 cup milk
Dash of salt and pepper
1 cup grated cheese

Cook and drain egg noodles. Sauté onions in margarine until tender. Remove from heat. Combine noodles and onions. Beat eggs slightly and slowly add milk, salt and pepper and grated cheese. Mix well. Place noodle mixture in pie shell, then add egg mixture. Bake at 350°F for 45 minutes or until knife inserted in center comes out clean.

Delta United Church
Hamilton, Ont.

Zucchini Pie

3 cup grated zucchini
1 cup biscuit mix (Tea Bisk)
4 eggs, beaten
½ cup vegetable oil
¾ cup grated cheese
¼ cup green onion, chopped
½ green pepper, chopped
2 cloves garlic, chopped
Seasoning salt
Pepper
1 cup bacon bits, ham or sausage, chopped

Fry meat. Beat eggs, then add remaining ingredients. Add meat and pour into a greased pie plate. Bake at 350°F for 35 minutes.

Bissell Memorial United Church, Andrew, Alta.
Westcott United Church, Conn., Ont.
Kipling United Church, Kipling, Sask.
Keswick United Church, Keswick, Ont.
Gilford United Church, Gilford, Ont.

Impossible Tuna Pie

1 - 6½ oz. can tuna or salmon
2 oz. chopped pimento
1 cup shredded cheddar cheese
1 small pkg. cream cheese, cut in cubes
¼ cup sliced green onions
2 cups milk
1 cup biscuit mix
4 eggs, beaten
¾ tsp. salt
Dash of nutmeg

Mix tuna, pimento, cheeses and onions in pie plate. Beat remaining ingredients until smooth, for 15 seconds in blender on high, or 1 minute with hand beater. Put in 10'' pie plate and bake 35-40 minutes at 400°F.

St. Andrew's United Church
Wakefield, Que.

Crustless Tuna Pie

1 - 7 oz. (200 g) can white tuna
4 eggs
1 cup sour cream
1 cup milk
½ cup flour
1 tsp. Worcestershire sauce
½ tsp. salt
½ tsp. dill weed
1½ cups grated cheddar cheese
½ cup finely chopped green pepper
⅓ cup grated Parmesan cheese
¼ cup finely chopped green onion

Drain tuna, flake and set aside. Combine eggs, sour cream, milk, flour, Worcestershire sauce, salt and dill weed in blender, food processor or electric mixer. Blend until smooth. Pour into greased 10'' or deep 9½'' pie plate. Sprinkle tuna, cheeses, green pepper and onion evenly over egg mixture. Stir lightly with a fork to dampen cheeses. Bake at 400°F for 25-30 minutes or just until set and golden. Let stand 5 minutes before slicing.
Makes 6 servings.
Variation: Replace tuna with salmon, shrimp, crab, cooked ham or chicken if desired.

Kingsview United Church
Oshawa, Ont.

Three Cheese Pie

1 cup shredded cheddar cheese
1 cup shredded mozzarella cheese
1 cup shredded Swiss cheese
1 medium onion, chopped
2 tbsp. all-purpose flour
4 eggs
1 cup milk
½ tsp. salt
½ tsp. Dijon mustard
½ tsp. Worcestershire sauce
2 medium tomatoes, sliced

Mix cheese, onion and flour. Spread in greased 10" pie plate. Beat eggs slightly, beat in milk, salt, mustard and Worcestershire sauce. Pour over cheese mixture. Cook uncovered in 350°F oven until set 35-40 minutes. Let stand 10 minutes, arrange tomato slices around edge of pie, overlapping slices slightly.

Port Perry United Church
Port Perry, Ont.

Garden Vegetable Pie

2 cups (500 mL) chopped broccoli or
    cauliflower or a mixture of both
½ cup (125 mL) cup chopped onion
½ cup (125 mL) chopped green pepper
¼ tsp. (2 mL) pepper
1 cup (250 mL) or 4 oz. grated cheese,
    cheddar is best
1½ cups (375 mL) milk
¾ cup (175 mL) Bisquick mix or your own
    biscuit mix before liquid is added
3 eggs
1 tsp. (5 mL) salt

Heat oven to 400°F (200°C) and grease a 10" (25 cm) pie plate. Add broccoli to 1 cup (250 mL) boiling, salted with ½ teaspoon (3 mL) water. Cover and cook until tender, drain. Place broccoli, onion, pepper, and cheese in plate. Beat remaining ingredients until smooth (1 minute) with hand mixer. Pour into pie plate. Bake until brown. Good hot or cold.

St. James United Church, Dartmouth, N.S.
Central Ave. United Church, Fort Erie, Ont.
St. Andrew's United Church, Scotstown, Que.

Chicken Aspic Pie

1 - 3 oz. pkg. lemon Jell-O
1 tbsp. plain gelatin
1 cup boiling water
1 - 7½ oz. can tomato sauce
1 tbsp. vinegar
½ tsp. salt
Dash of pepper
½ tbsp. grated onion
1½ cups chicken salad
1 baked, cooled 9" pie shell

Dissolve Jell-O and gelatin in boiling water. Add salt, pepper, onion, vinegar and tomato sauce. Chill until slightly thickened. Put ½ cup of gelatin mix in bottom of prepared shell. Chill until firm. Put chicken salad (prepared as desired with onion, celery, mayo) into shell. Pour remaining gelatin mix over and chill until firm.

Athens United Church
Athens, Ont.

Impossible Broccoli Pie

10 oz. thawed frozen broccoli
1 cup grated cheddar cheese
2 eggs
½ tsp. salt
¼ cup finely chopped onion
¾ cup milk
½ cup tea biscuit mix
⅛ tsp. pepper

Spray a 9" pie plate with Pam or grease lightly. Spread broccoli over the bottom of the pie plate. Sprinkle with onions and cheese. Blend eggs, milk, biscuit mix, salt and pepper well. Pour over cheese. Bake at 400°F for 25-35 minutes. Pie will be done when inserted knife comes out clean. Serve with a green salad and rolls.

Westminster United Church
The Pas, Man.

Broccoli Quiche

2 cups broccoli flowerets
1¼ cups half and half cream
4 eggs
½ tsp. pepper
Pinch of salt (optional)
4 oz. (125 g) cream cheese

Place small pieces of broccoli in 9''
microwave-safe pie plate. Microwave, covered
on HIGH for 3 minutes or until tender. Drain
well. Pat dry. In a bowl whisk cream with eggs
and seasonings. Whip cream cheese and add.
Lightly grease a 9'' pie plate and add mixture
including broccoli. Place on an inverted
microwave-safe cereal bowl. Microwave, uncovered on MEDIUM for 10-12 minutes until
almost set in center. Place on countertop for 5
minutes before cutting.
Serves 4.

Eastend Saskatchewan United Church
Eastend, Sask.

Impossible Shrimp Pie

1 or 2 cans drained shrimp
⅓ cup sliced green onions
½ tsp. dried basil
1 cup grated mozzarella cheese
1½ cups milk
3 eggs
¾ cup Bisquick
½ tsp. salt
¼ tsp. pepper

Heat oven to 400°F. Grease pie plate. Sprinkle shrimp, onions, basil and cheese in plate.
Beat remaining ingredients until smooth. Pour
into plate. Bake at 400°F until knife comes out
clean, about 30 minutes.
Serves 6-8

St. Paul's United Church
Halifax, Nova Scotia

Impossible Quiche Pie

2 - 6.5 oz. cans tuna, drained
2 cups shredded sharp cheese
6 oz. dry cottage cheese
½ cup chopped chives or green onion
3 oz. chopped pimento (optional)
4 cups milk
2 cups Bisquick baking mix
8 eggs
1 tsp. salt
Dash nutmeg

Mix tuna, cheeses, chives and pimento in
greased 9x13'' pan or 2 greased 9'' pie plates.
Beat remaining ingredients 15 seconds. Pour
into prepared pan or plates. Bake 40-45 minutes
at 400°F until knife inserted between center and
edge comes out clean. Substitute flakes of ham
plus ½ cup mushrooms instead of tuna for a
nice variation.

Grace United Church
Caledonia, Ont.

Spinach Rice Quiche
(no pastry)

3 eggs
1½ cups cooked long grain or wild rice
3 oz. grated sharp cheddar cheese
¾ tsp. salt
2½ cups spinach, cooked, drained and
    chopped
6 tbsp. milk
¾ cup drained sliced mushrooms
Pepper to taste

Preheat oven to 375°F. Beat 1 egg; add rice,
half of the grated cheese and salt. Mix well.
Press on bottom of quiche dish or 9-inch pan.
Beat remaining eggs. Stir in spinach, milk,
pepper, mushrooms and the rest of cheese.
Spoon over rice mixture. Bake 30 minutes. Cool
15-20 minutes before serving.

St. Andrew's United Church
Scotstown, Que.

Souffles

Zucchini Custard Souffle

1 medium onion, finely chopped
3 large eggs, well beaten
2 tbsp. flour
½ cup cream
Salt and pepper
1 cup cubed cheddar cheese
4 cups sliced zucchini

Steam zucchini briefly and drain. Combine with onions, eggs, flour, cream, salt and pepper and cheese. Pour into buttered souffle dish. Bake at 325°F for 75 minutes or until golden brown. Let stand before serving. Serve hot or cold.
Serves 6.

Westport United Church
Westport, Ont.

Ham and Cheese Souffle

9 slices bread, cubed (whole wheat/white mixture)
1½ cups chopped ham
1½ cups grated cheddar cheese
½ cup minced onion
¼ cup chopped green pepper (optional)
¼ cup minced parsley
Salt and pepper to taste
10 large eggs
2½ cups milk
¼ cup melted butter
2 tsp. dry mustard
½ cup grated Parmesan cheese
Paprika

Layer a third of the bread cubes in a buttered 2 quart (2 L) souffle dish. Top with half of the ham, cheese, onion, green pepper, parsley, salt and pepper. Repeat layers topping with the last third of the bread cubes. Beat eggs in bowl; add milk, cooled butter and dry mustard. Mix well. Pour over layers in dish. Sprinkle with Parmesan and paprika. Refrigerate overnight. Bake uncovered in a 350°F (180°C) oven for approximately 1 hour or until golden and puffed. Serve immediately.

Alsask United Church
Alsask, Sask.

Overnight Cheese Souffle

6 slices bacon
3 slices bread, spread with prepared mustard
2 cups grated cheese (strong)
2 cups milk
3 eggs
¼ tsp. salt

Grease a 9x13" casserole. Cut bread in 1" cubes. Place half the bread in casserole, cover with grated cheese, then repeat. Beat together the milk, eggs and salt. Cover bread with liquid and press down. Top with bacon, sprinkle with paprika. Refrigerate overnight or for at least 6 hours. Remove from fridge 1 hour before baking. Bake 1-1½ hours at 350°F.

Burgessville United Church
Burgessville, Ont.

Strata Souffle

3 cans flaked ham or chopped ham
2 pkgs. chopped broccoli, partially cooked and drained
6 eggs
12 slices bread, crusts removed
1½ cups grated Swiss cheese
3 cups milk
1 tsp. dry mustard
Salt and pepper
Parmesan cheese

Grease a 9x13" pan. Line with trimmed bread. Cover bread with ham and broccoli. Then a layer of Swiss cheese, followed by another layer of bread. Beat eggs with 3 cups milk, 1 teaspoon dry mustard, salt and pepper. Pour over layers and let stand in refrigerator overnight. Sprinkle with Parmesan cheese. Bake at 325°F for 15 minutes and reduce heat to 300°F for another 45 minutes. Cut into squares to serve.

Fraser Rd. United Church
Gander, Nfld.

Cheese Souffle

3 tbsp. Minute tapioca
½ tsp. salt
1 cup milk
¾ cup grated cheese
3 eggs, separated

In a saucepan combine tapioca, salt and milk. Bring to a boil over medium heat, stirring constantly. Remove from heat, add cheese and stir until melted. Beat egg yolks and add to above mixture. Fold in stiffly beaten egg whites. Turn into a greased baking dish. Place in a pan of hot water in a 350°F oven. Cook about 45-50 minutes or until done.
Serves 4 or 5.

Glen Morris United Church
Glen Morris, Ont.

Cheese

Cheese Fondue

This has the delightful flavour of a souffle and there is no worry of it falling if lunch is delayed.

1 cup scalded milk
1 cup stale bread crumbs
¼ lb. Velveeta cheese, cut into small
    pieces
1 tbsp. margarine
½ tsp. salt
3 egg yolks
3 egg whites

Mix first five ingredients. Add egg yolks which have been beaten until lemon coloured. Beat egg whites until stiff and cut and fold into rest of ingredients. Pour into buttered baking dish and bake at 350°F for 20 minutes until nicely brown.
Serves 4.

Vernon United Church
Vernon, Ont.

Egg and Cheese Rolls

1 - 125 g pkg. Philadelphia cream cheese
¼ lb. butter
4 boiled eggs

Mix cheese and butter. Grate eggs into mixture. Put on small rolls. Broil for a few minutes.

St. Giles United Church
Martinon, N.B.

Cheese Dreams

1 tbsp. butter
1 egg, beaten
½ tsp. salt
½ tsp. dry mustard
¼ tsp. paprika
1 tsp. Worcestershire sauce
2 cups Cheese Whiz
Bacon
Unsliced white bread

Cut bread in pieces 1½'' thick by 2'' long. Add butter, egg and seasonings to cheese. Mix to a paste and spread on top and sides of bread slices. Place small piece of bacon on top. (Fry bacon ahead of time.) Bake in 400°F oven for 5-10 minutes.
Note: Cheese dreams may be prepared in advance and frozen.

Zion Evangelical United Church
Pembroke, Ont.

Cheese Corn Puff

3 eggs, separated
¼ cup flour
2 tsp. sugar
½ tsp. salt
¼ tsp. dry mustard
¾ cup milk
3 tbsp. melted butter
8 oz. grated cheese
1 - 14 oz. can corn niblets, drained
2 tbsp. green pepper

Beat egg yolks. Mix flour, sugar, salt and mustard together. Add milk and melted butter. Mix until smooth, then add cheese, corn and pepper. Fold in beaten egg yolks. Lastly fold in well beaten egg whites. Put in greased baking dish. bake 350°F oven for 1 hour.

Heartz Memorial United Church
Weymouth, N.S.

Cheese Cracker Puff

32 soda crackers
6 slices processed cheese
3 tbsp. onion, finely chopped
2 cups milk
3 eggs, beaten
½ tsp. dry mustard
Dash salt
Dash pepper

Oil bottom of a 9x9'' square glass ovenproof dish. Cover bottom with a layer of crackers. Layer cheese slices, overlapping where necessary. Sprinkle onions over cheese. Cover with a layer of crackers. Combine milk, eggs and seasonings and pour over crackers. Let stand at least 1 hour. Bake at 325°F for 40-45 minutes. Sprinkle with paprika. Cut into squares to serve. Can be made ahead, covered and refrigerated until ready to bake. Serve with a salad. Serves 4.

St. Paul's United Church
Bancroft, Ont.

Recipe For a Happy Year

Take 12 fine, full grown months; see that these are free from all old memories of bitterness, rancour, hate and jealousy. Cleanse them completely from every clinging spite. Pick off all specks of pettiness and littleness, in short, see that these months are freed from all the past. Have them as fresh and clean as when they first came from the great storehouse of time. Cut these months into thirty or thirty-one equal parts. Do not attempt to make up the whole batch at one time (so many persons spoil the entire lot in this way), but prepare one day at a time, as follows:

Into each day, put equal parts of faith, patience, courage, work, (some people omit this ingredient and so spoil the flavour of the rest), hope, fidelity, liberality, kindness, rest (leaving this out is like leaving oil out of the salad - don't do it), prayer, meditation and one well selected resolution. Put in about a teaspoon of good spirits, a dash of fun, a sprinkling of play and a heaping cupful of good humour. Pour love into the whole mix with a vim. Cook thoroughly in fervent heat, garnish with a few smiles and a sprig of joy. Serve them with quietness, unselfishness and cheerfulness.

Westlock United Church
Westlock, Alta.

Buns and Sandwiches

Broccoli Cheese Roll

⅔ cup butter or margarine
¼ cup flour
½ tsp. salt
⅛ tsp. cayenne
1¼ cups milk
1 cup cheddar or Swiss cheese, shredded
2 cups broccoli, thawed and chopped
½ pkg. Phyllo dough
¼ cup dry bread crumbs

In a saucepan melt 4 tablespoons butter or margarine. Stir in flour, salt and cayenne until blended. Gradually add milk and stir until thickened and smooth. Stir in well drained broccoli and cheese. Cook until cheese is melted stirring constantly. Remove from heat.

In a small saucepan melt remaining butter. On waxed paper place 2 or 3 Phyllo sheets and brush with melted butter. Sprinkle with crumbs. Repeat until half the package of Phyllo is used. Preheat oven to 375°F. Beginning on the long side of the pastry, evenly spoon broccoli mixture to cover ½ the rectangle. Roll pastry, jelly roll fashion from broccoli side. Place roll seam down on 10x15 inch pan. Brush with more melted butter or margarine and cut with very sharp knife into 1-1½ inch slices. Bake 30 minutes. Serve warm. If not served immediately, can be wrapped in foil and refrigerated or frozen. Reheat at 375°F for 15 minutes. Fresh broccoli may also be used but be sure to steam first. Serve for lunch with salad and crusty rolls. Serves 8.

Eastend United Church
Eastend, Sask.

Christmas Appetizer

2 cups grated cheddar cheese
1 cup mayonnaise
1 cup finely chopped onion
1½ tbsp. summer savory

Mix well (even 24 hours ahead). Serve on halved tiny tea biscuits or quartered English muffins. Broil for 3-4 minutes.

St. Paul's United Church
Edmundston, N.B.

Mushroom Tarts

½ lb. mushrooms, finely chopped
¼ cup butter
3 tbsp. flour
¼ tsp. M.S.G. (Accent)
¼ tsp. salt
1 cup light cream
1 tsp. minced chives
1 tsp. lemon juice

Sauté mushrooms in butter for 5 minutes. Blend in flour, M.G.S. and salt. Stir in cream. Cook until thick. Add minced chives and lemon juice. Cool. Remove crusts from loaf of white bread. Roll slices thin. Cut circles to fit muffin tins. Butter one side of bread. Place buttered side against muffin tin. Fill with mushroom mixture. Freeze or bake at 400°F for approximately 10 minutes or until nicely browned.

Beverley Hills United Church
Downsview, Ont.

Ham and Horseradish Filling (Sandwiches)

1 can ham, approx. 1¼ cups
½ cup chili sauce
½ cup minced onion
2 tbsp. minced green pepper
1 tbsp. horseradish

Mix all together. Spread on bread. Very tasty filling.

St. Andrew's United Church
Tide Head, N.B.

Open Deviled Ham Sandwiches

4 English muffins, split
2¼ oz. tin deviled ham
1 cup grated cheddar cheese
⅓ cup finely chopped onions
⅔ cup finely chopped ripe olives
⅓ cup mayonnaise
½ tsp. curry powder

Set split muffins on cookie sheet, split side up. Combine all ingredients and spread on muffins, covering edges. Broil until bubbling and lightly brown. Serve with a tossed salad. Serves 4.

Hammond United Church
Maple Ridge, B.C.

English Muffins for Lunch

4 English muffins, split

Mix together:
1 cup grated cheddar
2 green onions, sliced
½ cup sliced black olives
Mayonnaise (to moisten)

Spread mixture on muffin halves and broil until bubbly and slightly brown.

Marshall Memorial United Church
Ancaster, Ont.

Vegetable Pizza

2 pkg. Pillsbury crescent dough

Lay dough out on rectangle (9x13) cookie sheet. Bake as directed. Cool.

Mix:
8 oz. cream cheese
¾ cup light Miracle Whip
¼ tsp. garlic powder
1 tsp. Italian seasoning
¼ cup Parmesan cheese

Spread on cool, cooked dough. Top with assorted vegetables, finely chopped (broccoli, cauliflower, celery, carrots, green onion, green and red pepper). Sprinkle with grated cheese.

Transcona Memorial United Church
Winnipeg, Man.

Ham and Cheese Sandwiches

1 cup sour cream
1 envelope onion soup mix (for 4 servings each)
12 slices ham, thinly sliced
12 slices cheese (Muenster)
Bread

Combine sour cream and soup mix. Trim crusts from bread. Spread all bread with soup mixture. Top each of 12 slices with ham, bread slice, cheese, bread slice with spread side down. Refrigerate covered. Cut each sandwich into 4ths, use toothpick to hold slices together.

St. Andrew's United Church
Tide Head, N.B.

Ham and Cheese Finger Rolls

Sliced ham
Cheese slices or Swiss cheese

Split rolls and put slice of cheese and ham in each. Line a pan with aluminum foil. Lay rolls on side and pack tightly.

Melt:
2 blocks (1 cup) margarine
1 tbsp. poppy seed
1 tsp. Worcestershire sauce
1 tsp. prepared mustard
1 tbsp. minced onion

Mix and pour over tightly-packed rolls. Cover with foil and refrigerate for 24 hours or overnight. Bake at 350°F for 30 minutes. Leave foil on while baking.

St. Stephen's United Church
Red Bank, N.B.

Breakfast Pizza

2¼ cups biscuit mix (Bisquick)
½ cup milk
2 tbsp. butter
10 eggs
¼ cup water or milk
½ tsp. salt
¼ tsp. pepper
½ cup pizza sauce
2 cups grated mozzarella cheese
1 cup bacon pieces, ham or sausage
1 can mushrooms, drained
1 tomato, sliced

Mix biscuit mix and milk to make a soft dough. Pat onto 12" greased pizza pan. Bake at 375°F for 15 minutes to partially cook. Melt butter in frying pan. Add eggs, milk, salt and pepper. Beat lightly to mix. Stir until cooked. Remove from heat.

Spread pizza sauce over crust. Cover with scrambled eggs. Sprinkle with cheese. Add any other toppings you prefer. Return to oven. Bake for about 15 minutes until topping is sizzling hot.

Warren United Church
Warren, Man.

Bacon Mushroom Roll-ups

8 slices bacon, diced
2½ cups fresh mushrooms, finely chopped
1 bunch green onions, chopped
1 large pkg. cream cheese
15 slices sandwich bread
¼ cup butter, melted

Cook bacon until crisp. Add onions and mushrooms. Cook 5-8 minutes until tender, set aside. Trim crusts from bread, flatten with rolling pin. Spread each slice with bacon and mushroom mixture. Roll up like jelly roll and secure with toothpick. Place each roll-up, seam side down on baking dish. Cover and chill for at least one hour. Or freeze in single layer, then package in air-tight container.

When using do the following: (If frozen, thaw at room temperature for 30 minutes.) Brush with melted butter. Bake at 375°F for 10-15 minutes or until lightly browned. Remove toothpicks, cut in half and serve warm.

Ruthilda United Church
Ruthilda, Sask.

Ham and Cheese Biscuits

2 cups all-purpose flour
1 tbsp. baking powder
1 tbsp. chopped fresh parsley
2 tsp. granulated sugar
½ tsp. baking soda
¼ tsp. salt
½ cup cold butter, cut in chunks
1 cup sour cream
2 tbsp. Dijon mustard
6 thin slices black forest ham
6 thin slices Swiss cheese

In bowl combine flour, baking powder, parsley, sugar, soda and salt. With pastry blender cut in butter until in tiny bits. With fork, stir in sour cream, mixing just until dough is formed. Turn onto lightly floured surface. Knead lightly about 8 times. Roll out dough to about ¼" thickness. Using a 4" round dough cutter cut dough into 12 rounds. With pastry brush spread each round with mustard. Cut ham and cheese into 4" rounds and divide among 6 of the rounds of dough. Top each with remaining dough mustard side down; press to seal. Place on baking sheet and bake at 425°F for 15-18 minutes. Serve warm with soup or salad.

Port Perry United Church, Port Perry, Ont.
United Church in Meadowood, Winnipeg, Man.

Stuffed Ham Loaf

1 loaf unsliced Italian bread
¼ cup mayonnaise or salad dressing
⅓ cup chopped parsley
1 - 8 oz. pkg. cream cheese
¾ cup celery, finely chopped
½ cup shredded cheddar cheese
2 tbsp. onion, finely chopped
¼ tsp. salt
2 - 4 oz. pkgs. ham (8 slices)
1 large dill pickle

Cut bread lengthwise, hollow out each half with fork leaving ½ inch thick shell (save insides for bread crumbs). Spread mayonnaise over hollows, sprinkle parsley over mayonnaise. Blend cream cheese, celery, cheddar cheese, onion and salt and spoon into bread halves, packing down well with back of spoon. Leave a small hollow down the center. Quarter pickle lengthwise. Roll each quarter inside a double thick slice of ham. Place rolls, end to end, in center of half of bread and top with other half. Wrap loaf tightly in transparent wrap. Chill several hours. To serve, cut into 16 slices.

Carberry United Church
Carberry, Man.

Egg and Tuna Turnover

4 hard cooked eggs, chopped
⅓ cup flaked tuna
1 tbsp. chopped onion
1 tsp. parsley (optional)
Pinch dill seed (optional)
1 - 10 oz. can undiluted cream of celery soup
1 - 8 oz. pkg. refrigerator crescent roll dough
1 tbsp. lemon

Preheat oven to 375°F. Thoroughly combine eggs, tuna, onions, parsley, dill seed and ⅓ of the soup. Separate dough into 4 rectangles only. Place ⅓ cup of the egg mixture and enclose it. Pinch edges to seal. Place turnovers on greased baking sheet. Bake 20 minutes. Meanwhile, make a sauce by combining remaining soup and lemon juice in saucepan. Heat and pour over baked turnovers to serve.
Serves 4.

Erie St. United Church, Ridgetown, Ont.
Cameron United Church, Cameron, Ont.
Lamont United Church, Lamont, Alta.

Tuna Melt

1 can white tuna
Mayonnaise
Cheese
Buns
Onion or celery (optional)

Mix tuna with mayonnaise. May add onion or celery if desired. Cut buns in half. Cover top of each half with tuna mixture. Place slice of cheese on top of each. Heat under broiler to melt cheese until bubbly. Serve with salad or soup for a quick meal.

Balzac United Church
Balzac, Alta.

Tuna on a Bun

1 can tuna
1 cup cubed Velveeta cheese
⅓ cup celery
12 dinner rolls
½ cup mayonnaise
3 hard cooked eggs
Small amount chopped onions
1 small pkg. potato chips

Mix tuna, cheese, mayonnaise, eggs, onion, celery and leave overnight. Split buns, spread with mixture. Place a dab of butter on top and sprinkle buns with crushed potato chips. Place in 350°F oven and heat thoroughly 10-15 minutes.

Zion Calvin United Church, Darlingford, Man.
Kincardine United Church, Kincardine, Ont.
Knox United Church, Redvers, Sask.
Wesley United Church, St. Andrews, N.B.
Hamiota United Church, Hamiota, Man.

Shrimp Boats

2 cans shrimp, small, broken
1 lb. cheddar cheese, grated
1 jar stuffed olives, chopped
½ cup oil
1 - 8 oz. can tomato sauce
¼ green pepper, chopped

Combine and spread on hotdog buns. Freeze on buns. Before broiling let thaw 20-30 minutes.

Trinity United Church
Portaga la Prairie, Man.

Sardines On Toast

For each person you need 2 slices of toast, buttered and put onto a plate. Cover with layer of sardines, layer of very thinly sliced raw onion, layer of sliced hard boiled egg. Lightly season with salt and pepper then cover with white sauce and second slice of toast and more white sauce.

White or Cream Sauce:
2 tbsp. flour
2 tbsp. butter
1 cup milk
¼ tsp. salt

Melt butter, slowly add flour and blend to paste. Gradually add milk, stirring constantly. Cook until thickened. Add salt. If a thinner sauce is desired use 1 tablespoon flour and 1 tablespoon butter.

Rapid City United Church
Rapid City, Man.

Magic Puff Tuna Sandwich

1 can tuna, drained
2 cups shredded cheddar cheese
¼ cup chopped onion
3 tbsp. lemon juice

Mix together:
1¼ cups Bisquick
¾ cup mayonnaise
1 egg

Combine above ingredients. Spread on six slices of bread. Bake at 450°F for 10 minutes or until puffy and brown.

St. Mark's United Church
Cannifton, Ont.

Pimento Cress Whirligig's

¼ cup chopped watercress leaves
1 jar pimento cheese
Red pepper seasoning
1 can salmon

Spread mixture on one slice of white bread. Also spread mixture on 1 slice dark bread. Place second on first slice. Roll up like jelly roll. Wrap tightly. Secure with toothpick. Put into refrigerator. Slice in 1-inch slices to serve.

St. Andrew's United Church
Tide Head, N.B.

Pizza Buns

6 slices bacon
1 small can tomato sauce
¾ cup oil
1 can cut mushrooms, drained
1 medium onion, grated
2 cups cheddar cheese, shredded
¼ tsp. garlic salt
1 tsp. seasoned salt
½ tsp. celery salt
½ tsp. onion salt
½ tsp. oregano

Mix well. Brown bacon and onions together. Weiners, sausage, hamburger or ham may be used instead of bacon. Spread on buns and broil until bubbly and browned. Mixture keeps well in the fridge or freezer in jars.

Alsask United Church, Alsask, Sask.
Hudson Bay United Church, Hudson Bay, Sask.
Division St. United Church, Owen Sound, Ont.
Wilkie United Church, Wilkie, Sask.

Chicken Rolls

4 double chicken breasts, cooked and chopped
1 tin crushed pineapple, drained
½ cup finely chopped celery

Mix with ¼ cup Miracle Whip salad dressing.

1 sandwich loaf, crusts off, cut horizontally
1 - 8 oz. pkg. Philadelphia cream cheese
Toasted pecans, crushed

Spread bread slices with chicken filling. Roll up and spread with cream cheese, then roll in crushed pecans and secure with toothpick and chill. Serve 2 rolls on lettuce leaf. Serve with cranberry Jell-O square.

Cranberry Jell-O Square
1 pkg. orange Jell-O
1 tin cranberry sauce
7 oz. ginger ale

Bring orange Jell-O and cranberry sauce to a boil. Add ginger ale. Chill until firm.

Pioneer Memorial United Church
Hamilton, Ont.

Brunch Sandwich Loaf

1 ½ cups cooked chicken, minced
½ cup finely chopped celery
¼ cup chopped toasted almonds
Salt and pepper to taste
¼ cup mayonnaise
1 cup cooked ham, minced
¼ cup sweet mustard pickles, finely chopped
2-3 tbsp. pickle sauce, to make a moist filling
8 oz. cream cheese, room temperature
2 tbsp. cranberry sauce
Sandwich loaf

Combine chicken, celery, almonds, salt and pepper and mayonnaise together. Chill. Combine ham, pickles and sauce. Chill. Beat the cream cheese until fluffy. Add cranberry sauce and beat until blended. Cut all crusts from sandwich loaf and slice loaf into 4 equal layers lengthwise. Spread the chicken filling on first and last slice. Spread ham filling on middle slice. Ice whole outside of loaf with cream cheese mixture. Chill several hours. Cut into thick slices and serve. Can be frozen. Serve with green salad.
Serves 10.

Maple Grove United Church
Bowamanville, Ont.

Phyllo Turkey Puffs

2 tbsp. butter or margarine
2 tbsp. flour
2 cups chicken broth
¾ cup milk
2 eggs, slightly beaten
1 tbsp. Parmesan cheese, grated
3 oz. cream cheese
¼ tsp. pepper
¼ tsp. nutmeg
2 cups turkey, cooked and cubed
½ cup butter, melted
12 sheets of frozen Phyllo dough, thawed

In saucepan melt butter, add flour gradually. Stir in broth and milk; cook over medium heat. Stir and thicken. Remove from heat; beat mixture into eggs, then return egg mixture to pan. Add cheese, pepper, nutmeg and turkey. Brush inside of muffin cups with melted butter, set aside. Stack 12 sheets of phyllo dough together, brush each with butter, cut into 6 pieces. Line muffin cups with phyllo, fill with turkey filling. Fold corners of pastry filling to cover, brush with melted butter. Bake at 375°F for 25-30 minutes or until puffed and golden. Let stand in pan 5 minutes before removing.

St. Paul's United Church
Bancroft, Ont.

Turkey French Toast Sandwiches

1 cup finely diced cooked turkey
2 tbsp. chopped green onion
¼ cup finely diced celery
¼ cup salad dressing
½ tsp. prepared mustard
½ tsp. salt
Dash of pepper
8 slices buttered bread
3 eggs
6 tbsp. milk
2 tbsp. butter

Filling: Mix first 6 ingredients. Spread filling on buttered bread making four sandwiches. Cut in half. Beat eggs and milk. Dip sandwiches in egg mixture and fry in butter until golden brown (2-3 minutes each side).
Makes 4 servings.

Wilkie United Church
Wilkie, Sask.

Cheesy Asparagus Sandwich

2 slices bread, toasted lightly
2 slices American cheese
10-12 cooked asparagus spears
1 egg, separated
1 tbsp. mayonnaise
Salt and pepper
Dash dry mustard
Paprika

Place toast on large microwave-proof plate. Top each piece with slice of cheese. Arrange asparagus spears on cheese. Beat egg whites stiff. Set aside. Beat yolk in small bowl; stir in mayonnaise, salt, pepper and dry mustard; fold in beaten egg white. Spoon mixture over asparagus, sprinkle with paprika. Microwave on HIGH for 2 minutes.
Makes 2 servings.

Eastend United Church Women
Eastend, Sask.

Curried Chicken and Almond Rolls

1 cup finely chopped cooked chicken
1 cup mayonnaise
¾ cup shredded cheddar cheese
⅓ cup finely chopped almonds
¼ cup chopped parsley, fresh
2 pkgs. shallots or 1 small onion, finely chopped
2 tsp. curry powder
2 tsp. lemon juice
½ tsp. each salt and pepper
18 slices of whole wheat sandwich bread
¼ cup melted butter

In large bowl combine: chicken, mayonnaise, cheese, almonds, parsley, shallots, curry powder, lemon juice, salt and pepper. Blend well. Cover and refrigerate for 30 minutes. Trim crust from bread. Roll slices, with rolling pin. Spread 2 tablespoons of chicken mixture on each slice and roll up. Cut each roll in 3 sections. Secure with toothpicks if needed. Place on baking sheet, seam side down. Brush with melted butter. Bake at 375°F for 15 minutes. Let cool. Then freeze uncovered in single layer on baking sheet. Package in air-tight containers and store in freezer. Do not thaw before reheating. To reheat, bake frozen rolls in single layer on baking sheet in 400°F oven for 10 minutes or until hot. Remove toothpicks before serving. Delicious and crispy!
Makes 54 rolls.

Nashwaaksis United Church
Fredericton, N.B.

Colby Bean Buns

½ lb. ground beef
1 can pork and beans
¼ cup barbecue sauce
Onion, to taste
4 hamburger buns
3 cups shredded Colby cheese

Brown meat and onion, drain fat. Add beans and barbecue sauce. Bring to a boil, reduce heat, simmer 5-10 minutes. Split buns, toast under broiler. Sprinkle some cheese on each bun half. Broil until melted. Spoon equal amounts of bean mixture onto each bun half. Top with remaining cheese. Place under broiler and cook until cheese is melted.
Serves 8.

Ruthilda United Church
Ruthilda, Sask.

Pizza Cups

(makes 40, recipe can be halved)

¼ lb. bacon
¾ to 1 lb. lean ground beef
1 - 5½ oz. can tomato paste
1 - 10 oz. can mushroom pieces and stems (use juice with enough water to fill and rinse out the tomato paste can)
½ cup water (see note above)
2 tbsp. dehydrated minced onion
1 tsp. Italian herb seasoning
1 tsp. oregano
4 - 7½ oz. cylinders or cans of refrigerated biscuits
1 - 19 oz. can pineapple dessert bits
½ lb. shredded or grated mozzarella cheese

Preheat oven to 400°F. Fry, drain and crumble the bacon; set aside. In the same pan, brown and drain the ground beef. In a small bowl, mix tomato paste, mushrooms, juice and water, minced onion and seasonings. Add to browned meat in pan; stir to mix, and simmer 5 minutes. Meanwhile, fill 40 well greased muffin tins or tart cups with refrigerated biscuits, pressing to cover bottoms and sides. Spoon a heaping spoonful of the meat mixture into each biscuit-lined cup. Top with crumbled bacon, pineapple bits, chopped green and/or red pepper, olives, or any other topping that you like. Sprinkle mozzarella cheese over each cup. Bake for 10 to 12 minutes or until golden brown.

If reducing the recipe by half or a quarter, you will have extra tomato sauce mixture to store in the refrigerator or freeze for another time. Baked pizza cups can be frozen and reheated.

Goshen United Church
Varna, Ont.

Cheese Rarebit

1 tbsp. butter
2 tbsp. flour
½ tsp. mustard
¼ tsp. salt, pepper to taste
1 cup milk
2 cups shredded cheese

Make sauce of first 6 ingredients, then blend in cheese. Serve on toast, wedges of hard cooked eggs, broccoli or asparagus may be added before spooning on the sauce.

Hudson Bay United Church
Hudson Bay, Sask.

Beef in Warmed Pita Pouches

1 tbsp. (15 mL) olive oil
1 lb. (500 g) lean ground beef
2 cloves garlic, minced
1 medium onion, finely chopped
2 tbsp. (30 mL) green pepper
1 tsp. (5 mL) finely chopped ginger
1 tsp. (5 mL) Tabasco sauce
2 medium tomatoes, chopped
2 tbsp. (30 mL) plain yogurt
6 pita pockets

Heat oil in large frying pan; add beef and cook over medium-high heat for 5 minutes. Drain off any fat. Stir in garlic, onion and green pepper. Cook 2-3 minutes. Add ginger, Tabasco sauce and tomatoes; mix well. Simmer over medium-low heat for 5-10 minutes; stir in yogurt. Warm pita pockets in oven or microwave. Divide beef mixture evenly among pockets. Serve immediately with coleslaw or a tossed green salad. Serves 6.

St. Andrew's United Church
Tide Head, N.B.

Ham & Asparagus Rolls

24 thin stalks asparagus, cooked or canned
12 thin slices cooked ham
2 tomatoes, peeled and chopped
1 cup table cream
1 cup grated Swiss cheese
1 tbsp. flour
2 tbsp. minced parsley
½ tsp. chervil
½ cup or less fine dry bread crumbs
2 tbsp. butter

Roll 2 stalks asparagus in each slice of ham. Lay rolls in buttered 9x13 baking dish. Sprinkle with tomatoes and grated cheese. Combine cream, flour, parsley and chervil, stirring until flour is smoothly blended with cream. Pour over all. Sprinkle with bread crumbs and dot with butter. Bake 20 minutes in a 400°F oven or until lightly browned and bubbling.

Bells Corners United Church
Nepean, Ont.

Dressing For Egg Sandwiches

½ cup vinegar
½ cup white sugar
¾ cup water
½ tsp. salt
1 egg
1 tsp. dry mustard
1 tbsp. cornstarch
Butter, the size of an egg

Cook until thick and use a small amount with mashed up hard boiled eggs for sandwiches.

St. Paul's United Church
Mildmay, Ont.

Dad's Denvers for Two

2 buttered bread slices
2 bacon slices
3 eggs
2 cheese slices

Semi-fry bacon. Set aside. Drain pan. Scramble eggs and salt and pepper to taste. Arrange buttered bread on broiler tray. Top with scrambled eggs, cheese and tomato slices, then bacon. Broil at 450°F until cheese is melted and bacon is crisp. If you don't have fresh tomatoes, use an undiluted can of tomato soup, heated and poured on at the table - like gravy.

Neidpath United Church Women
Swift Current, Sask.

Bacon Onion Treat

12 slices bacon
2 cups biscuit mix
1 egg
¾ cup milk
Herb seasoning
¼ cup shredded cheddar cheese
1 onion, thinly sliced

Fry 4 slices of bacon until crisp. Drain on towel and then crumble. In bowl combine biscuit mix, egg, milk, herb seasoning, and cheese. Shape batter into an 11-inch circle on a greased cookie sheet. Spread onions over top of circle and then lay remaining bacon on top, twisting each slice slightly. Bake 20-30 minutes in 400°F until golden brown and bacon is done. Serves 8.

Hillview United Church
New Liskeard, Ont.

"Crescent Roll" Lunch

1 pkg. Pillsbury crescent rolls

Arrange squares in 8 muffin tins, leaving a little of the corners of the dough to cover the roll.

Filling:
2 hard-boiled eggs, grated
5-6 slices cooked bacon, cut up
½-¾ cup grated cheddar cheese

Moisten with Miracle Whip or mayonnaise and fill into the dough in the muffin tins. Fold point over. Bake at 350°F. Serve with a salad.

Goshen United Church
Varna, Ont.

Casseroles

Tuna Vegetable Casserole

1 pie crust
1 cup shredded cheddar cheese
½ cup sliced celery
¼ cup chopped onion
½ cup mayonnaise or salad dressing
1 - 7 oz. can tuna
1 cup frozen peas and carrots
¼ cup bread crumbs
¼ cup chopped green pepper

Combine tuna, cheese, vegetables. Stir in salad dressing. Spoon into casserole. Cover with pie crust. Bake until slightly brown, about 40 minutes at 350°F.

Trinity United Church
Listowel, Ont.

Zucchini / Cheese Casserole

4 cups diced zucchini
1 cup grated cheese
1 medium onion
3 eggs
½ cup oil
1 tsp. salt
1 tsp. pepper
1 tsp. oregano
1 cup tea biscuit mix

Mix together. Put in oven for 45 minutes at 350°F.

Gilford United Church
Gilford, Ont.

Tuna Casserole

2 eggs
Milk
1 small pkg. potato chips, crushed
2 tins flaked tuna, drained
1 - 10 oz. (284 mL) can cream of mushroom or cream of chicken soup

Beat eggs and a little milk together. Add tuna, half the potato chips and the soup. Combine well. Put in a greased casserole and top with the rest of the chips. Bake ½ hour at 350°F (180°C).

St. James United Church
Dartmouth, N.S.

Pizza-in-a-dish

10 slices cubed French bread
2 cups salami, coarsely chopped
½ cup green pepper, diced
2 cups shredded mozzarella cheese
6 eggs
2½ cups milk
¾ cup spaghetti sauce

In an 8 cup deep baking dish, layer ⅓ each of the bread, salami, green pepper and cheese. Repeat to make 2 more layers. Beat together eggs and milk; pour over casserole. At this point, the casserole may be covered and refrigerated overnight if desired. Drizzle spaghetti sauce over casserole before baking. Bake uncovered in 350°F oven 1¼ hours or until puffed and golden.

Makes 6 to 8 servings.

Note: Mushrooms, onions or other pizza ingredients may be substituted for green peppers.

Crystal City United Church
Crystal City, Man.

Asparagus & Egg Casserole

3 cans asparagus, drained
6 hard-boiled eggs, sliced
1 can cheese soup

Thin soup with 1 or 2 tablespoons of milk. Layer asparagus, soup, eggs, soup and repeat. Cover with crumbs. Heat in 350°F oven until hot for 30-40 minutes. Fresh or frozen asparagus can be used and your favourite cheese sauce.

St. Paul's United Church
Perth, Ont.

3 Bean Pot

½ cup ketchup
1 cup brown sugar
3 shakes Worcestershire sauce
1 capful vinegar
Salt and pepper to taste
1 tin lima beans
1 tin pork 'n beans
1 tin kidney beans
1 large onion, chopped
2-3 stalks celery, chopped
1 lb. bacon
1 garlic clove, finely chopped

Cut bacon in small pieces and fry. Clean pan. Sauté onion, celery and garlic. Mix remainder of ingredients in large pot or crock pot. Add bacon, onion and celery. Bring to boil, then simmer several hours in a crock pot. Best made day before.

St. Paul's United Church
Kelowna, B.C.

Sausage Spinach Squares

3 tbsp. vegetable oil
1 onion, chopped
1 lb. sweet Italian sausage or breakfast
sausage, removed from casings and
crumbled
2 - 10 oz. pkgs. frozen spinach, squeezed
dry and chopped
1 cup (2 doz.) saltine cracker crumbs
4 eggs
½ cup milk or cream
1 tsp. salt (or less)
¼ tsp. black pepper
1 cup grated cheddar cheese

Heat oil in large skillet. Add onion and cook until lightly browned. Add sausage and break up well with spoon. Cook 10 minutes until sausage colours. Drain off excess fat. Stir in spinach and cook a few minutes combining ingredients well. Cool slightly. Stir in cracker crumbs. Beat eggs with milk or cream, salt, pepper and cheese. Stir in sausage mixture. Put in buttered 9x9'' pan. Bake at 350°F for 35 to 40 minutes until set. May be served cold or may be reheated at 350°F for 20 minutes.
Serves 8.

Emmanuel United Church
Sebringville, Ont.

Christmas Morning Wife Saver

16 slices white or egg bread, crusts removed
Canadian back bacon or ham slices
Slices of sharp cheddar cheese
6 eggs
½ tsp. pepper
¼ cup minced onions
½ tsp. salt
½ tsp. dry mustard
½ cup finely chopped green pepper
1 to 2 tsp. Worcestershire sauce
3 cups whole milk
¼ lb. butter
Dash of Tabasco sauce

In a 9x13'' buttered glass baking dish put 8 slices of bread in even layer. Cover bread with meat, sliced thinly. Lay slices of cheese on top of meat. Then cover with slice of bread (like sandwich). In a bowl beat eggs, salt and pepper, mustard, onion, peppers, sauce, milk and Tabasco. Pour over sandwich. Let stand overnight. In morning melt butter, pour over top. Cover with Special K or crushed corn flakes. Bake uncovered for 1 hour at 350°F. Let stand 10 minutes before serving. Serve with fresh fruit and hot cinnamon rolls.
Makes 8 servings.

Goshen United Church, Varna, Ont.
Hudson Bay United Church, Hudson Bay, Sask.
Highgate United Church, Highgate, Ont.
Keswick United Church, Keswick, Ont.
North Bedeque United Church, Summerside, P.E.I.
Thedford United Church, Thedford, Ont.
St. Mark's United Church, Whitby, Ont.
Fordwich United Church, Fordwich, Ont.
Kingston United Church, Kingston, N.S.
Woodrow United Church, Woodrow, Sask.
St. Andrew's United Church, Admiral, Sask.
St. Paul's United Church, Fairview, Alta.
First United Church, St. Thomas, Ont.
Harriston United Church, Harriston, Ont.
Kincardine United Church, Kincardine, Ont.
St. James United Church, Regina, Sask.
Renfrew United Church, Calgary, Alta.
Bethesda United Church, Lancaster, Ont.
Hawthorne United Church, Ottawa, Ont.
Westminister United Church, Mississauga, Ont.
Emmanuel United Church, Waterloo, Ont.
Central United Church, Bay Roberts, Nfld.
Zion Calvin United Church, Darlingford, Man.
Mount Carmel-Zion United Church, Morriston, Ont.
St. Andrew's United Church, Scotstown, Que.
Vernon United Church, Vernon, Ont.
Battle River United Church, Manning, Alta.
Wesley Memorial United Church, Moncton, N.B.
Minden United Church, Minden, Ont.
Grace United Church, Port Dover, Ont.
Springvale United Church, Hagersville, Ont.

Sausage and Spinach Casserole

2 eggs, slightly beaten
2 - 8 oz. pkgs. frozen spinach, cooked
  and drained
4 tbsp. butter, melted
8 oz. mozzarella cheese, cubed
1½ cups milk
1 cup flour
1 tsp. salt
1 tsp. baking powder
1 lb. pkg. mild pork sausage, cooked
  and broken

Combine all ingredients and bake in a greased
9x13'' pan at 350°F for 45 minutes.

Grantham United Church
St. Catharines, Ont.

Egg and Bacon Loaf

½ lb. bacon
2 cups flour
Sprinkle of salt
1 tbsp. sugar
1 tbsp. baking powder
1 egg, beaten
1 cup milk
1 cup grated cheese
¼ cup bacon fat

Fry chopped bacon until crisp. Drain on paper
towels. Cool. Combine dry ingredients and pour
in beaten egg, milk and fat. Stir just until
moistened. Pour into greased loaf pan and bake
for 30-40 minutes at 400°F.

Highgate United Church
Highgate, Ont.

Lasagna

1 - 9x13'' pan and 1 - 8'' square pan, greased
15 lasagna noodles, cooked just until
  tender

Sauce:
2 lbs. ground beef, browned
1 cup chopped onion
½ cup chopped celery
2 - 28 oz. cans spaghetti sauce, plain
1 - 10 oz. can mushroom pieces, drained

Assemble in three layers:
  5 lasagna noodles
  Ground beef sauce
  5 lasagna noodles
  2 eggs, beaten with 1 - 16 oz. container
    of 2% cottage cheese
  5 lasagna noodles
  Ground beef sauce
  Slices of mozzarella cheese, to cover
    sauce

Bake covered with foil at 350°F for
1 hour and uncovered for another ½ hour. Let
sit out of oven at least 15 minutes before cutting and serving. This freezes well for future use.
Serve with either tossed salad or Caeser salad
and garlic bread, warmed in foil or toasted.

Stoney Creek United Church
Stoney Creek, Ont.

Oktoberfest Beans

8 slices bacon
1 cup finely diced celery
1 cup finely diced onion
1 small can tomato paste
½ cup brown sugar
1 envelope spaghetti sauce mix
2 tbsp. prepared mustard
1 tsp. garlic salt
2 tsp. vinegar
2 cans lima beans, drained
1 can kidney beans, drained
1 - 28 oz. can pork and beans

Cook bacon until crisp, drain and crumble.
Add celery and onion to 2 tablespoons bacon fat
and sauté for 5 minutes. Add 1 cup of water
and all other ingredients, except beans. Bring
to a boil. In a 3 quart casserole, combine beans
and bacon. Stir in tomato mixture. Bake uncovered for 1 hour at 350°F.
Serves 10.

Donminister United Church
Don Mill, Ont.

Zucchini Casserole

¼ lb. melted butter
1 pkg. stuffing mix
1 cup sour cream
1 can cream of chicken soup
2 grated carrots
Salt and pepper
⅓ cup minced onion
2 lbs. zucchini, peeled and sliced
Bread crumbs or croutons

Boil zucchini for 10 minutes and drain. Mix together melted butter and stuffing mix. Add to this the sour cream, soup, carrots, salt and pepper and onion. Place ½ of mixture in casserole. Add ½ of zucchini. Repeat these 2 layers. Top with crumbs or croutons. Dot with butter. Bake at 350°F for 20-30 minutes.

Port Mouton United Church
Port Mouton, Queens Co., N.S.

Beef
Sicilian Meat Loaf

2 eggs, beaten
½ cup tomato sauce
¾ cup soft bread crumbs
2 tbsp. snipped parsley
½ tsp. dried oregano, crushed
¼ tsp. salt
¼ tsp. pepper
1 clove garlic, minced
2 lbs. ground beef
4 to 6 oz. thinly sliced ham
1 - 6 oz. pkg. sliced mozzarella cheese

In a bowl combine the eggs and tomato sauce. Stir in the bread crumbs, parsley, oregano, salt, pepper and garlic. Add ground beef. On waxed paper or foil pat meat into 8x10 inch rectangle. Arrange ham slices atop meat, leaving a small margin around edges. Reserve one slice of cheese. Tear up remaining cheese and sprinkle over ham. Starting from short end, carefully roll up meat, using paper to lift. Seal edges and ends. Place roll, seam side down in 13x9x2 inch baking pan. Bake at 350°F until done, about 1¼ hours (center of roll will be pink due to ham). Cut reserved cheese slices in 4 triangles, overlap on top of meat. Return to oven until cheese melts, about 2 minutes.
Serves 8.

Foam Lake United Church
Foam Lake, Sask.

Mystery Mini Meat Loaves

1½ cups soft bread crumbs
½ cup beef stock, milk or water
3 eggs, beaten
1 pkg. onion soup mix
3 lbs. ground beef

Soak bread crumbs in liquid. Mix meat with bread, soup mix and eggs. Add salt and pepper to taste. Shape into individual loaves. Recipe makes 18-20 loaves. Place in greased 9x13'' baking dish.

Sauce for Meat Loaves:
1 - 12 oz. bottle chili sauce
1⅓ cups water
½ cup brown sugar
1 - 16 oz. tin sauerkraut, drained
1 - 16 oz. tin cranberry sauce

Combine ingredients, simmer 5 minutes. Pour over meat loaves and bake at 350°F oven for approximately 1-1¼ hours. This dish freezes very well.

Trinity United Church
Shelburne, N.S.

Mary's Meat Pies

2 lbs. ground beef
2½-3 cups water
1 tbsp. onion soup mix or
  1 onion, finely chopped
1 tbsp. liquid Oxo
½ tsp. salt
⅔ cup frozen peas and carrots
1 tsp. oregano
4 tbsp. flour, mixed with water to thicken
  pastry for pies

Mix beef, water, onion, Oxo, salt and spices together in a large pot. Bring to a boil over medium heat using a fork to separate the beef. Thicken with the flour. Add peas and carrots. Let simmer 1 minute. Let cool. Line pie plates with pastry and meat filling and cover with pastry. They freeze well baked or unbaked then cooked. Bake 1 hour at 350°F.
Makes 24 - 9'inch pies

Fairfield United Church
Hamilton, Ont.

My Fair Lady

1 lb. ground beef
2 cups chopped celery
2 cups chopped onion
1 can cream of mushroom soup
1 can cream of chicken soup
8 oz. fine noodles, cooked

Brown ground beef well in butter. Remove from pan and sauté celery and onion. Stir in with beef in a casserole. Add mushroom and chicken soups and noodles. Bake at 350°F for 1 hour. About 10 minutes before serving, put 1 can button mushrooms on top. This recipe is a result of unexpected company after returning from a performance of My Fair Lady. Serves 8.

Blackwell United Church
Sarnia, Ont.

Oriental Casserole

1 lb. ground beef
2 onions
1 cup celery, chopped
½ cup Minute rice
1 can mushroom soup
½ can water
1 can Chinese vegetables
¼ cup soya sauce
1 tsp. salt
¼ tsp. pepper
1 can water chestnuts, drained and sliced
3 tbsp. butter

Brown beef in butter. Add other ingredients, put into a greased casserole. Sprinkle a few Chinese noodles on top. Bake uncovered in 350°F oven for 30 minutes (or longer).

Knox United Church
Shellbrook, Sask.

Poultry

Broccoli Stuffed Turkey Loaf

2½ cups chopped broccoli
Salt and pepper
1½ cups ground turkey
1 cup fresh bread crumbs
1 tsp. salt
½ tsp. marjoram
¼ tsp. pepper
Pinch of thyme

Tomato Sauce:
¼ cup water
1 onion, chopped
1 clove garlic, minced
1 - 19 oz. can tomatoes, undrained
2 tsp. chopped parsley

In saucepan heat water, add onion and garlic. Simmer 5-7 minutes. Set aside 1 tablespoon onion garlic mixture. Add tomatoes and simmer 20 minutes. Stir in parsley and season with salt and pepper. Cook broccoli until tender crisp, drain and refresh under cold water. Set aside to cool. Combine turkey, onion, garlic. Mix bread crumbs, salt and herbs. Mix thoroughly - place on waxed paper, pat into rectangle about 15x8 inches. Sprinkle broccoli over turkey, leave ½ inch border. Roll up from short end jelly roll style, lifting with paper. Place seam side down on greased baking sheet. Bake at 350°F 1 hour or until brown. To serve spoon sauce over roll. Pass remaining sauce.

St. James and St. John United Church
Newcastle, N.B.

Turkey Pie

1 cup thinly sliced onions
1 tbsp. chopped green pepper
1 - 10 oz. can condensed cream of mushroom
  soup
½ cup milk
2 cups cooked, chopped turkey
¾ cup frozen green peas or peas and carrots
Few grains pepper
Pastry for double crust pie

Line deep 9'' pie plate with pastry. Mix re-maining ingredients together. Pour into pie shell. Cover with pastry being sure to seal edges and leaving slits in top for steam to escape. Bake 20-25 minutes at 450°F. May be frozen and baked when desired.

Powassan United Church
Powassan, Ont.

Chicken & Cheddar Strata

5 cups bread, cubed
1½ cups cooked chicken or turkey
  coarsely chopped
1 - 10 oz. pkg. frozen, chopped broccoli,
  thawed and drained
2 cups (8 oz.) shredded cheddar cheese
6 eggs
3 cups milk
1 small onion, finely chopped
½ tsp. salt
1 tsp. dry mustard

Butter a six cup, deep, straight-sided baking dish. Layer ⅓ each of the bread, chicken, broccoli and cheese in the baking dish. Repeat to make 2 more layers. Beat eggs with milk, onion, salt and mustard until blended. Pour egg mixture over strata. Cover and refrigerate at least 3 hours or overnight. Bake uncovered 350°F for 1¼ hours, or until puffy and golden. Serves 6-8.

Variation: Instead of chicken and broccoli, you may substitute other cooked meats or vegetables. Try any combination of ham, turkey, tuna, salmon, crab, bacon, mushrooms, asparagus or cauliflower.

Mount Forest United Church
Mt. Forest, Ont.

Chicken and Rice Dinner

Rice:
½ cup butter or margarine
1 can chicken and rice soup
1 tsp. oregano
1 cup uncooked rice
1 small can mushrooms
1 chicken bouillon cube
5 green onions, chopped
Water, as needed

Combine ingredients in a baking dish. Cover tightly with foil and place a lid on top. Cook for 2 hours at 350°F. It may be necessary to add some more water during cooking.

Sauce:
3 tbsp. brown sugar
2 tbsp. cornstarch
½ tsp. salt
1 tbsp. soya sauce
¼ cup vinegar
½ cup ketchup
1 small tin crushed pineapple

Cook brown sugar, cornstarch, salt, soya sauce, vinegar and ketchup until thick. Add pineapple. Place cut up chicken in a pan. Cover with sauce. Cover tightly with foil. Cook 2 hours at 350°F. Serve with rice.

Foothills United Church
Calgary, Alta.

Fish

Microwave Kraft Dinner Casserole

1 pkg. Kraft dinner
1½ cups water
1 can cream of mushroom soup
1 can tuna, drained
2 tbsp. margarine or butter

Cover and microwave macaroni, sauce mix (grated cheese) and water in 1½ quart casserole 4 minutes (6 if doubling recipe). Stir. Cover and microwave 3 minutes more (5 minutes if dou-bling) HIGH setting. Stir in soup, tuna and mar-garine. Cover and microwave until macaroni is tender, 5 to 6 minutes (8 to 10 for doubling) HIGH setting.
Makes 6 servings, from a single recipe

Buchanan-Eastwood United Church
Edmonton, Alta.

Tuna Popover

¾ cup flour
¾ cup milk
2 eggs, beaten
2 hard-cooked eggs
1½ cups shredded cheese, divided
7 oz. can tuna, drained
¾ cup canned or frozen peas
⅓ cup chopped onion
¼ cup chopped celery
3 tbsp. mayonnaise
3 tbsp. plain yogurt
½ tsp. salt
¼ tsp. pepper

Mix flour, milk and eggs in a smooth batter and pour into 9" pie plate. Combine all other ingredients and spoon into the center of batter. Bake 30 minutes at 400°F. Sprinkle with ¼ cup cheese and bake 5 minutes longer.

Shubencadie United Church
Shubencadie, N.S.

Tuna Roll

2 cups flour
½ tsp. salt
4 tsp. baking powder
¼ cup shortening
1 egg, beaten
½ cup milk
1 cup flaked tuna
¼ cup milk
2 tsp. chopped onion
1½ tbsp. chopped parsley
¼ cup sweet pickle
½ tsp. salt

Sift dry ingredients. Cut in shortening until mixture resembles coarse crumbs. Add egg and milk. Mix only until dough follows fork around bowl. Roll out ¼" thick. Combine remaining ingredients, spread over dough. Roll it up and bake on ungreased sheet in 425°F oven for 30 minutes.

St. Mark's United Church
St. Thomas, Ont.

Mushroom Luncheon Dish

Make a fairly thick cream sauce - see below.

1 tin mushrooms, whole or pieces
1 tin mushroom soup
1 tin tuna fish (or salmon or chicken pieces)
1 pkg. cooked frozen green peas
Green pepper, cut in pieces
Sliced almonds

Combine mushrooms, mushroom soup, fish, peas and green pepper and heat until bubbly. Sliced almonds may be sprinkled on top. Serve over patty shells or tea biscuits. This can be served at a buffet in your prettiest casserole (over a candle). Serve along with a favorite salad.

Cream Sauce
2 tbsp. butter, melted
2 tbsp. flour, stirred into butter and heated
1 cup milk or milk and chicken stock added

Cook at medium heat for 2 minutes, stirring at intervals until thick and smooth. Season with salt, pepper, even a bit of Worcestershire sauce or celery salt.

St. Paul's United Church
Orillia, Ont.

Scallop Bake

1 lb. scallops
1 tsp. salt
½ cup chopped onion
¾ cup finely chopped celery
1 cup fresh mushrooms or 1 small can, drained
1 cup chopped green pepper
2 tbsp. butter or margarine
4 tbsp. butter
¼ cup flour
2 cups milk
1 cup bread crumbs
1 tbsp. butter, melted
¼ cup grated cheese
1 tsp. salt

Separate scallops and sprinkle with salt. Cook onion, celery, mushrooms and green pepper in 2 tablespoons butter until tender. Make cream sauce with butter, flour and milk. Combine scallops, vegetables and sauce in greased 1½ quart casserole dish. Combine crumbs, melted butter, cheese, salt and sprinkle over top. Bake in 375°F oven for 20 minutes or until bubbly.

Aylesford United Church
Aylesford, N.S.

Tuna Stroganoff on Rice

2 cups cooked rice
1 cup boiling water
1 chicken Oxo cube
2 - 7 oz. cans tuna
8 oz. fresh mushrooms
¼ cup butter
2 tbsp. flour
½ cup sour cream
½ tsp. Worcestershire sauce
2 tbsp. ketchup
Dash pepper

Dissolve Oxo cube in boiling water. Cook mushrooms in butter. Blend in flour and brown. Add bouillon gradually. Cook until thick stirring constantly. Add tuna (broken up), sour cream, Worcestershire sauce, ketchup and pepper. Stir until heated through. Serve over rice.

Shubenacadie United Church
Shubenacadie, N.S.

Salmon Wiggle

2 cups flaked, cooked salmon
2 cups cooked peas
2 cups white sauce
2 doz. crisp crackers
Paprika

Heat salmon and peas in white sauce. Serve on crackers and sprinkle with paprika.
Serves 6.

White Sauce:
2 tbsp. butter or other fat
2 tbsp. flour
1 cup milk
¼ tsp. salt
⅛ tsp. pepper

Blend butter and flour together in pan. Add milk, stirring constantly until mixture thickens. Cook for 3 minutes longer. Add ingredients.
Note: 1 - 7 ounce can of salmon works well in this amount of sauce.

Oriole Titus Westfield United Church
Westfield, N.B.

Salmon Ball Casserole

2 - 7¾ oz. cans salmon
½ cup uncooked rice
½ cup grated carrot
¼ cup chopped onion
1 egg
Salt and pepper to taste
1 - 10 oz. tin cream of mushroom soup
1 cup water

In medium size bowl mix salmon, rice, carrot, onion, egg, salt and pepper. Shape into balls and place in casserole dish, leaving room for expansion. Mix soup and water. Pour over top. Bake covered for 1 hour at 350°F.

York United Church
York, Ont.

Pork

Brunch Burritos

1 lb. ground pork
½ cup finely chopped green pepper
⅓ cup finely chopped onion
2 small cloves garlic, minced
¼ cup picante sauce
¼ tsp. salt
8 - 8" flour tortillas
3 cups (12 oz.) sharp cheddar cheese, shredded
Additional picante sauce (optional)
Dairy sour cream (optional)

Forty-five minutes or 24 hours before serving crumble ground pork into medium skillet. Over medium heat cook until lightly browned. Add green pepper, onion and garlic and sauté until vegetables are soft and pork is cooked through. Drain off fat. Stir in 1 cup picante sauce and salt. Place about ½ cup meat mixture down center of each tortilla then top with ¼ cup cheese. Fold up bottom side ½" then fold sides of tortilla, to make an envelope and roll up. Fold up remaining tortillas. Place seam side down in two ungreased 8x8x2" baking dishes. Sprinkle 2 tablespoons cheese on top of each burrito. Cover dishes with foil. If making ahead refrigerate up to 24 hours.

About 35 minutes before serving preheat oven to 350°F about 10 minutes. Bake burritos covered for 20-25 minutes or until cheese melts and center is heated through. Serve with warm picante sauce and sour cream if desired.

Fenwick United Church
Fenwick, Ont.

Ham Stacks

3 cups finely chopped ham
2 tbsp. red pimento, minced
2 tbsp. green pepper, minced
1 tbsp. onion, minced
1 - 10 oz. can mushroom soup

Make a regular pie pastry, cut circle out with large glass. Place 1 teaspoon filling and fold over and make a half moon. Wet edges first so they seal. Beat egg and add a little cold water and brush half moons. Make 2 small slits in top. Sprinkle with sesame seeds and bake at 400°F for 10-15 minutes.

Bruce Mines United Church
Bruce Mines, Ont.

Cauliflower and Ham Gratin

1 cauliflower, divided into florets, cooked
    tender crisp
3 cups diced cooked ham
1 red pepper, coarsely chopped
1 small onion, chopped
½ cup chopped fresh dill or
    fresh parsley and 2 tsp. dried dill
3 cups cheese sauce, recipe below
⅔ cup fresh bread crumbs

Arrange florets in greased shallow baking dish (4 L). Place ham and red pepper over top. Stir dill into cheese sauce and spread evenly over cauliflower. Sprinkle with bread crumbs. Bake at 375°F for 30 minutes or until bubbly. (Before baking, recipe can be covered and refrigerated for up to one day).
Serves 6-8.

Cheese Sauce
⅓ cup butter
⅓ cup flour
2½ cups milk
½ tsp. dried mustard
2 cups shredded cheddar cheese
Salt and pepper

Melt butter over medium heat, stir in flour and cook for 1 minute. Gradually add milk; cook for about 5 minutes or until mixture boils and has thickened, stirring constantly. Add cheese and mustard. Season with salt and pepper to taste.
Makes about 3 cups.

Central United Church
Port Colborne, Ont.

Ham Rolls with Sauce

Biscuit Dough:
2 cups flour
4 tsp. baking powder
½ tsp. salt
4 tbsp. shortening
¾ cup milk

Filling:
1 cup ground ham
2 tbsp. soft butter
1½ tbsp. prepared mustard
¼ cup minced onion (optional)
¼ cup diced green pepper (optional)

Roll biscuit dough ¼" thick and spread with ham mixture. Roll like jelly roll and cut into 1" slices. Bake in hot oven. May be served with cheese sauce or horseradish cream sauce. Makes 10.

Cheese Sauce:
2 tbsp. butter
½ tsp. salt
2 tbsp. flour
2 cups milk
¾ cup grated cheese

To make Horseradish Cream Sauce, substitute grated cheese with 2 tbsp. horseradish.
These ham rolls are delicious served with green peas or broccoli.

Aylesford United Church, Aylesford, Kings Co., N.S.
Fishburn-Marr United Church, Pincher Creek, Alta.
Zion Calvin United Church, Darlingford, Man.

Stuffed Onions

8 large onions, unpeeled
½ lb. sausage meat
1 cup fresh bread crumbs
1 - 8 oz. can tomato sauce
2 tbsp. chopped parsley
1 clove garlic, crushed
1 tsp. salt (or to taste)
¼ tsp. pepper
2 tbsp. butter or margarine

Boil onions, unpeeled in lightly salted water for 10 minutes. Drain and reserve 1 cup water. Cool drained onions. Peel and scoop out centers leaving a shell of 2 layers. Chop onion centers to measure 1 cup (reserve remaining onion for use in soups or stews). Sauté sausage meat until all pink colour has gone. Drain. Combine cooked sausage meat with 1 cup chopped onion, bread crumbs, tomato sauce, parsley, garlic, salt and pepper. Toss togehter lightly to mix well. Spoon into onion shells. Place stuffed onions in shallow baking dish. Dot each with a little butter or margarine. Pour in reserved 1 cup onion liquid. Bake 30 minutes at 400°F. Serves 6-8.

Ashton United Church
Ashton, Ont.

German Sausage Ring Loaf with Sauerkraut

2 cups (1 lb.) sauerkraut, drained and
finely chopped
½ cup finely chopped green pepper
½ cup grated carrots
1 cup loosely packed parsley sprigs, washed
and dried
2 lbs. bulk pork sausage
1 cup dry bread crumbs
1 egg, beaten
½ cup finely chopped onions
⅓ cup tomato juice
¾ tsp. thyme, crumbled
¼ tsp. pepper

Combine sauerkraut, pepper and carrots in medium size bowl. Combine sausage, bread crumbs, egg, onion, tomato juice, thyme, pepper in large bowl. With hands or large spoon, mix thoroughly. Press half of sausage mixture into lightly greased 6-cup ring mold (angel food pan),

Top with sauerkraut mixture, spreading evenly. Cover with remaining sausage mixture, packing firmly. Bake in a moderate oven (350°F) for 1¼ hours until loaf shrinks from edge of mold. Spoon off drippings twice during cooking. Remove from oven and spoon off all remaining drippings. Let stand 10 minutes. Invert serving plate on top of mold. Holding plate and mold together, turn right side up. Gently remove mold. Place parsley in center. Cut into slices to serve. Garnish with additional parsley, carrot curls, peas and julienne carrots if you wish.

St. Andrew's United Church
Chalk River, Ont.

Seven Layer Dinner

Raw potatoes, thinly sliced
Raw onions, thinly sliced
Raw carrots, thinly sliced
¼ cup uncooked rice
Salt and pepper
1 tin peas, undrained
1 lb. pork sausage
1 tin tomato soup, diluted with 1 tin water

Into a greased casserole place a 1 to 2 inch layer of potatoes, onions and carrots. Sprinkle uncooked rice over the three layers. Add salt and pepper to taste. Add peas and liquid. Arrange pork sausage on top. Pour diluted tomato soup over all. Cover and bake for 1 hour at 375°F. Uncover, turn sausage and bake 1 hour more. Garnish with pickled crab apples or apple wedges.

For variety replace sausage with 1 pound lean beef, cooked and drained and 1 can mushroom soup instead of tin of tomato soup.

Iondale Heights United Church, Scarborough, Ont.
Varna United Church, Varna, Ont.

Chicken Dinner for 500

Menu:
Baked Chicken Leg
Baked Potato   Green Peas
Coleslaw   Bun   Cake

500 whole chicken legs
500 potatoes, baking size
35 - 1 kg. bag frozen peas
500 rolls
25 heads cabbage
25 carrots
28 - 250 mL bottles of coleslaw dressing
300 serving size containers sour cream
600 pats butter
500 individual salt and peppers
14 Sara Lee cakes (to serve 36 each)

Have 20 people bake 25 chicken legs each. Cook with salt and pepper and bake for approximately 1-1½ hours at 350-400°F. Bake on a grill in the oven and drain the fat. Deliver warm in a foil pan covered with foil. Have another 10 people bake 50 potatoes for approximately one hour. Deliver warm. Have 8 people take 3 cabbages each (one person takes 4) and 3 carrots each and shred in food processor. Add a bit of shredded onion. Cook the frozen vegetables starting at least an hour or more before serving time using 8 large pots. Before serving, mix coleslaw with coleslaw dressing and top each serving dish with parsley.

Serve as follows: (at each of the 2 stations)
1 person - dish out 1 chicken leg on a plate
1 person - dish out 1 potato
1 person - dish out a serving spoonful of peas
1 person - dish out a small spoonful of coleslaw
1 person - put out the full plates for pickup

One person to look after the table with the condiments, rolls in the roll basket, butter pats in baskets, salt and peppers in baskets, and sour cream containers in basket. Two people (at two other stations) to cut up the cake and dish out onto paper plates.

If you follow this recipe, it is possible to serve all 500 people their main course in 17 minutes.

Dunbarton - Fairport United Church
Pickering, Ont.

Chicken Pot Pie

(Serves 20 people)

1 large (8 lb.) chicken
Cold water to almost cover
1 medium onion
4 whole cloves
Celery leaves
Carrot
1 tsp. salt
5 black peppercorns
Parsley
1 tsp. dried summer savory

Bring the above ingredients to boil and skim off any scum. Reduce heat and simmer for two hours or until chicken is cooked. Let chicken cool in stock for an hour. Remove chicken from stock, discard skin and bones, cut meat into bite-size pieces. Refrigerate. Strain stock and chill. Remove fat and return to stock pot (you should have 12 cups). Bring to boil and reduce stock to 8-10 cups.

Thicken stock - melt 1 cup butter, add 1 cup flour, cook for 1 minute. Whisk in the chicken stock and 1 can cream of chicken soup, cook until thick and smooth. Taste and correct seasoning by adding salt, pepper or a chicken bouillon cube. Arrange chicken in large pan and pour sauce evenly over chicken. Bake in 400°F oven until bubbly. Remove from oven and add tea biscuits. Return to hot oven and bake 20 minutes or until biscuits are brown and cooked through.

Tea Biscuits:
4 cups flour
2 tbsp. sugar
8 tsp. baking powder
1 tsp. salt
1 cup butter or margarine
1½ cups milk

Cut butter into dry ingredients. Add milk and blend with fork. Knead until smooth. Roll out dough ½ inch thick, cut in rounds. Cook at 400°F for 15-20 minutes.

Harwick United Church
Harwick, Que.

Suppers on the Go

Poultry

Chicken Breasts

Chicken Breasts with Curried Honey Sauce

1 tbsp. liquid honey
3 tbsp. ketchup
1 tbsp. vegetable oil
¼-½ tsp. curry powder
4 chicken breasts, boned and skinned

Preheat broiler. Combine honey, ketchup, oil and curry powder. Place chicken on broiler pan and brush with half of sauce. Broil 5 minutes; turn chicken over; brush with remaining sauce. Continue to broil until chicken is cooked, approximately 5-8 minutes (depends on size of chicken breast).

Vaughan's United Church
Windsor, N.S.

Chicken Maryland

4 deboned chicken breasts
1 envelope onion soup mix
1 - 12 oz. jar apricot jam
1 - 12 oz. bottle Russian salad dressing

Lay chicken in a 9" square casserole. Mix the other ingredients together and pour over chicken. Cover with foil or lid and bake at 375°F for 45-60 minutes. Remove lid for the last 10 minutes of cooking time. Chicken may be marinated in the sauce overnight before cooking.

Trinity United Church, Nanaimo, B.C.
Zion Evangelical United Church, Pembroke, Ont.
St. Lukes United Church, Fort St. John, B.C.

St. Luke's Chicken Breasts

6 chicken breasts
Salt and freshly ground pepper
¼ cup Dijon mustard
⅓ cup plain yogurt (2% small container)
½ cup fine fresh bread crumbs
1 tsp. thyme

Remove skin from chicken. Sprinkle chicken lightly with salt and pepper. Mix mustard into yogurt. In another bowl, mix bread crumbs, thyme, ½ teaspoon salt and ½ teaspoon pepper. Spread each piece of chicken with mustard mixture, then roll in bread crumb mixture. Place in single layer on lightly greased baking sheet. Bake in 350°F oven for 45-50 minutes for bone-in or 30-35 minutes for boneless chicken or until golden brown and meat is no longer pink. Serves 6.

St. Luke's United Church
Islington, Ont.

Eastern Kabob Chicken

8 - 8" bamboo skewers (or metal)
2 tbsp. soy sauce
1 tbsp. oil
1 tsp. granulated sugar
2" piece ginger, grated
2 cloves garlic, crushed
Dash Tabasco
4 chicken breasts, boned and skinned

Soak skewers in water 20 minutes. Stir all ingredients (except chicken). Cut chicken into ½" wide strips. Marinate at room temperature for 20 minutes. Stir often. Thread onto skewers. Broil 4" from broiler for 5 minutes, turning once. Easy and delicious. Serve with rice, mixed vegetables and slices of fresh fruit sprinkled with coconut.
Serves 4.

Brechin United Church
Nanaimo, B.C.

Chicken in Spicy Orange Sauce

2 chicken breasts
1 tbsp. cooking oil
¼ cup flour
¼ tsp. paprika
¼ tsp. salt
1 clove garlic
⅛ tsp. pepper
¼ tsp. crushed red pepper
½ tsp. ground cumin
½ tsp. oregano
1 med. onion, chopped
¾ cup orange juice
1 cup chicken stock
Grated rind of 1 orange
1 tbsp. lemon juice
2 tbsp. parsley flakes
1 small green pepper, cut in strips
4 thin slices of orange

Combine flour, salt, pepper and paprika. Roll chicken pieces in this. Brown them in oil and put in baking dish. Add onion and garlic to oil in pan; cook slowly until soft. Sprinkle in the leftover flour and stir. Remove from heat. Add stock and orange juice. Return to heat and add green pepper, orange rind, lemon juice, spices and parsley. Stir until boiilng, slightly thickened and smooth. Pour over chicken. Cover with foil and bake at 375°F about 40 minutes. Garnish with orange slices and parsley. Serves 2.

Merigomish United Church
Merigomish, N.S.

Lemon Rosemary Chicken

6 half chicken breasts
2 lemons
1 tsp. dried rosemary
2 cloves garlic
Pepper to taste

Finely grate all peel from lemons. Squeeze juice. Combine juice, peel, rosemary and pepper. Place in baking pan. Arrange chicken breasts in a single layer, flesh side down. Cut garlic in half and submerge in lemon mixture. Cover and cook at 375°F for 20 minutes. Uncover and continue cooking about 35 minutes till golden brown. Baste often.

Knox United Church
Nepean, Ont.

Oriental Casserole

2 cups Minute rice
3 whole chicken breasts, cooked and diced
2 tbsp. oil or fat
3 tbsp. cornstarch
1 tbsp. soya sauce
3 tbsp. prepared mustard
2 tbsp. vinegar
¼ cup molasses
1 or 2 green peppers
1 - 15 oz. can pineapple chunks
½ tsp. ginger
11 oz. can mandarin oranges
3 cups syrup drained from fruit plus water
Salt and pepper
2 chicken cubes
Chow mein noodles, fried

Cook rice in water with chicken cubes added. Sauté green pepper in fat. Add 3 cups syrup, salt, pepper and cornstarch. Cook until smooth. Add soya sauce, mustard, vinegar, molasses and ginger. Simmer until slightly thickened and clear. Add fruits and chicken. Put mixture on top of rice in a shallow casserole. Bake 30 minutes at 350°F. Sprinkle with noodles. Bake 5 minutes.

St. Pauls United Church
Ormstown, Que.

Chicken a la Gatineau

3 cups broccoli spears
3 cups cauliflowerets
2 cups sliced carrots
2 cups chicken pieces (leftover or uncooked breast meat)
1 - 10 oz. can cream of chicken soup
½ cup mayonnaise
1 tsp. lemon juice
Salt and pepper to taste

Layer vegetables and chicken in casserole. Mix together soup, mayonnaise, lemon juice, salt and pepper. Pour over vegetable mixture. Sprinkle with toasted croutons and shredded mozzarella cheese. Bake uncovered for 1 hour at 350°F.

Foote-Copeland United Church
Dafoe, Sask.

20 Minute Chicken a l'Orange

4 skinless, boneless chicken breasts
2 tbsp. flour
2 tbsp. butter

Pound chicken breasts to ¼" thick. Dust with flour and brown in butter about 2 minutes per side. Remove from pan.

⅓ cup minced onion
¼ cup raisins
¼ tsp. paprika
Dash each of pepper, rosemary and
   marjoram
½ cup orange juice
½ tsp. grated orange rind
¼ tsp. salt

Place these ingredients in the pan that the chicken was browned in and simmer 2 or 3 minutes. Return chicken to pan. Heat through, turning to coat with sauce, about 2 minutes. Garnish with **2 tablespoons sliced, blanched, toasted almonds** if desired.

Grace United Church
Trenton, Ont.

Annie's Sweet & Sour Chicken

3 or 4 chicken breasts, skinned, steamed,
   cooked and cut into small pieces (or use
   1 whole small chicken)

Sauce:
   ½ cup sugar
   ½ cup vinegar
   ⅓ cup juice from 1 - 14 oz. can pineapple
      chunks
   ¼ cup ketchup
   1 tsp. soya sauce
   2 tbsp. cornstarch
   1 tbsp. cold water

Prepare sauce in double boiler or heavy saucepan. Stir well until thick and clear. Add ½ green pepper, diced, and cooked chicken and the can of pineapple chunks. Pour in casserole dish and heat for 20-30 minutes in 350°F oven.

Salisbury United Church
Salisbury, N.B.

Chicken and Pineapple

6 chicken breasts
Flour, salt and pepper
1 cup grated old cheddar cheese
1 - 14 oz. can pineapple tidbits

Shake the chicken in a bag with flour, salt and pepper. Brown. Put into casserole and add the cheese and pineapple. Bake, covered in 350°F oven for 45 minutes. Take lid off for last 10 minutes.

Note: 1 large can of pineapple will do 24 breasts to serve 12 people.

Harrow United Church
Harrow, Ont.

Joyce's Chicken

8 chicken breasts (½'s)
1 - 19 oz. can cream of mushroom soup
2 tbsp. dry onion soup mix
½ pt. sour cream
1 tbsp. lemon juice
1 tbsp. dill seed (optional)
Butter
Pepper

Put chicken in buttered baking dish after removing skin. Place meat side up. Dot with butter and sprinkle with pepper and paprika. Combine remaining ingredients. Pour over chicken. Bake 1 hour at 350°F.

Powassan United Church
Powassan, Ont.

Company Lemon Chicken

6-8 skinless, boneless chicken breasts
Lemon juice
½ tsp. garlic powder
¼ tsp. lemon pepper
½ cup flour

Flatten chicken with the bottom of soup bowl. Soak for at least ½ hour in lemon juice. Put flour, garlic powder and lemon pepper in a paper bag. Coat chicken 1 piece at a time. Fry in 1 tablespoon butter and 1 tablespoon shortening for 10-15 minutes. Fabulous!

Note: Baked potatoes or squash go perfectly and are done in an hour at 350°F.

Bolton United Church
Bolton, Ont.

Chicken Vegetable Casserole

6 chicken breasts, deboned
⅓ cup flour
1 tsp. salt
1 tsp. paprika
Dash pepper and garlic powder
2 cups diagonally sliced carrots
1 can sliced mushrooms
½ cup sliced celery
¼ cup chopped onion
1 can mushroom soup
½ cup orange juice
½ cup white wine
¼ tsp. nutmeg
2 tsp. brown sugar

Combine flour, salt, paprika, pepper and garlic powder. Put in bag and shake with chicken to cover. Put oil in pan and brown chicken. Place in shallow casserole. Combine vegetables and put on top of chicken. Mix together remaining ingredients and pour over chicken. Bake at 350°F for 45 minutes. May be made ahead and refrigerated.

United Church in Meadowood
Winnipeg, Man.

Rush-Hour Chicken and Rice

(Microwave)

4 boneless chicken breasts, slivered
2 cups water
1 envelope golden onion soup mix
1 tbsp. chopped parsley
½ tsp. thyme
¼ tsp. pepper
1½ cups fresh or frozen vegetables
1½ cups Minute rice

In a non-metal dish combine chicken, water, soup mix, spices and vegetables. Cover and microcook on HIGH power for 5 minutes. Stir in rice; cover and microcook 5 minutes more. Let stand 3 minutes.
Makes 4 servings, about 350 calories each.

Innerkip United Church
Innerkip, Ont.

Swiss Party Chicken

1 - 10 oz. can cream of celery soup
½ cup white wine (cooking wine will do)
 or chicken broth
6 chicken breasts
6 slices Swiss cheese
½ cup fresh mushrooms, optional
1 tbsp. butter
½ cup bread crumbs
2-3 tbsp. Parmesan cheese
1 tsp. garlic powder
2 tbsp. melted butter

Combine soup, wine and seasonings in a bowl. Place chicken in lightly greased casserole and cover with cheese slices. Pour sauce over chicken and dot with butter. Top with mixture of bread crumbs, Parmesan cheese, garlic powder and melted butter. Bake at 350°F for 60 minutes.
   Note: ¼ cup sour cream may be added to sauce, but you may want to reduce wine to ¼ cup.
Serves 6.

Division Street United, Owen Sound, Ont.
Valois United Church, Point Claire, Que.

Easy Chicken Tetrazzini

2 tbsp. butter or margarine
1 med. onion, chopped
1 clove garlic, minced or garlic salt
4 chicken breasts or legs
1 - 10 oz. can condensed cream of mushroom
 soup
½ cup milk
1 tbsp. chopped parsley
½ lb. spaghetti, spaghettini or linguine
½ cup grated Parmesan cheese

Saute onion and garlic in butter until tender. Add chicken and brown on both sides. Stir in cream of mushroom soup, milk and parsley. Meanwhile, cook pasta while above simmers, covered for 30 minutes. Put cooked, drained spaghetti into baking dish. Arrange chicken pieces on top, cover with sauce and sprinkle with Parmesan. Bake at 400°F for 20 minutes.
Serves 4.

South Cayuga Pastoral Charge
Dunnville, Ont.

Chicken Charisma

½ lb. fresh mushrooms, sliced
¼ cup butter
3 whole chicken breasts, split
½ tsp. salt
¼ tsp. tarragon
1 tsp. Beau Monde
1 cup dry white wine
½ cup sour cream
3-4 green onions, sliced

Sauté mushrooms in 2 tablespoons butter. Remove mushrooms. Add remaining butter and brown chicken. Sprinkle chicken with salt, tarragon, Beau Monde while cooking. Pour wine over chicken. Cover and simmer 45 minutes. Keep heat low, so that wine will not cook away. If it does, add a little more water or wine. When chicken is tender, remove to serving dish. Add sour cream and mushrooms to pan juices. Stir with wooden spoon to loosen brown bits. Pour over chicken and sprinkle with green onions. Serve immediately with Savory Rice Casserole.

Savory Rice Casserole:
1 cup rice
1 cup beef broth
1 cup water
¼ tsp. Beau Monde
2 tbsp. butter or margarine

Combine ingredients. Cover and bake 1 hour at 350°F. Stir once. May add sautéed mushrooms during last 15 minutes or add chopped parsley.   United Church in Meadowood
Winnipeg, Man.

Cheddar Broccoli Chicken Supreme

6 boneless chicken breasts
Vegetable oil
1 can cream of broccoli soup
½ cup milk
1 cup cheddar cheese, shredded

Brown chicken on both sides in a small amount of oil. Drain off excess fat. Combine soup and milk. Pour over chicken. Bring to a boil; cover and cook over low heat until chicken is cooked. Remove chicken and keep warm. Add cheese to sauce, stir until melted. Pour over chicken. Sprinkle with additional cheese over all. Serve with hot cooked pasta or rice.
Bethesda of Forest Glen United Church, Mississauga, Ont.
Knox United Church, Fort Frances, Ont.

Skillet Chicken with Artichokes and Peaches

4 chicken breasts (halves), skinned, boned, cut into strips
2 tbsp. butter
1 cup long grain rice
1 cup chopped onion
½ red bell pepper, chopped
2 tbsp. capers
½ tsp. salt
¼ tsp. tarragon
1 clove garlic
1 - 16 oz. can peach slices in juice or light syrup
1 - 6 oz. jar marinated artichoke hearts

Sauté chicken strips in butter until browned. Stir in rice and onions - cook 2 minutes. Stir in red peppers, caper, salt, tarragon and garlic. Drain peaches and artichokes, reserving all liquid. Pour liquid into skillet and bring to boil. Reduce heat, cover and simmer 25 minutes until rice is tender. Fold in peaches and artichokes and heat through.
United Church in Meadowood
Winnipeg, Man.

Savory Chicken

4 whole deboned chicken breasts, skin removed
1 med. onion, diced
2 cups broccoli
1 - 28 oz. can diced tomatoes, drained
3 tbsp. chicken soup base (no MSG)
1 cup water
¼ tsp. pepper
¼ tsp. thyme
¼ tsp. tarragon

Lay chicken flat in the bottom of a large casserole dish. Layer onion, broccoli and tomatoes on top of the chicken. Mix soup base, water and spices and pour over top of the chicken and vegetables. Cover with lid or tinfoil and bake in the oven at 350°F for 1 hour. Serve with plain noodles or over rice for a fast, easy, low fat, low calorie meal. For thicker sauce 1 tablespoon of cornstarch may be added to the water mixture.
United Church in Meadowood
Winnipeg, Man.

Chicken and Almonds

⅔ cup flour
2 tsp. salt
½ tsp. pepper
1 tsp. paprika
½ tsp. garlic salt
8 chicken legs or breasts
⅓ cup shortening or oil
2-4 sliced onions
⅔ cup slivered almonds
2 cups orange juice
4 tsp. soya sauce
½ cup brown sugar
1 tbsp. vinegar
1 green pepper, sliced

Mix flour, salt, pepper and paprika together in a paper bag. Shake chicken pieces in bag until coated with the flour mixture. Brown in shortening (or oil) in a hot skillet. Remove chicken. Drain fat. Put chicken on paper towel. Saute onion rings and almonds until golden brown. Stir in 1½ tablespoons of flour mixture (in paper bag) into onion and almond mixture. Add remaining ingredients except green pepper. Stir until blended. Place chicken in roaster pan. Pour sauce over chicken, cover and cook in 350°F oven for 1 hour. Add green peppers 15 minutes before serving.
Serves 8.

Downsview United Church
Downsview, Ont.

Chicken Caccatori

3-4 chicken breasts, skinned
1 green pepper, sliced
1 onion, sliced
1 - 28 oz. can tomatoes, mashed with potato masher
1-2 cloves garlic
Salt and pepper to taste
2 tbsp. oil

Place oil in roaster and fry chicken until browned. Remove chicken and set aside. Add garlic, onion and green pepper to roaster and heat till tender. Add mashed tomatoes and simmer a few minutes. Place browned chicken into mixture and bake in covered roaster for 30 minutes, then uncover and bake for another 15-20 minutes. Serve over a bed of rice.

Alexander Grant United Church
Ainslui, N.S.

Chicken Stir Fry

Chicken Oriental Stir-Fry

1 tbsp. (15 mL) vegetable oil
4 boneless chicken breasts, skinned and cut into thin strips
5 cups (1.25 L) chopped vegetables of your choice: onion, celery, green and red pepper, broccoli, snow peas, mushrooms and bean sprouts
3 tbsp. toasted almonds, chopped
1 cup hot water
1 packet chicken instant bouillon or 2 tsp. chicken bouillon concentrate
2 tbsp. (30 mL) cornstarch
¼ cup (50 mL) soya sauce

In wok or large skillet, heat oil over high heat; add chicken and stir-fry just until barely cooked, 1-2 minutes. Add vegetables; stir-fry for 1 minute. Stir in stock (bouillon and water); cover and cook another minute or until chicken is tender. Blend cornstarch with soya sauce. Pour into wok and cook, stirring until liquid has thickened. Serve over white rice.

Eden United Church, Mississauga, Ont.
Varna United Church, Varna, Ont.

Zippy Chicken Stir-Fry

½ cup Miracle Whip salad dressing
1 tbsp. soy sauce
½ tsp. ground ginger
2 tbsp. oil
3 chicken breasts halved, skinned, deboned, cut into thin strips
1 cup each broccoli florets, red pepper strips and carrot slices
¼ cup green onion slices
1 garlic clove, minced
4 cups hot cooked rice

Stir together salad dressing, soy sauce and ginger. Set aside. Heat oil in wok or large heavy skillet over medium-high heat. Add chicken. Stir-fry 4 minutes. Add vegetables and garlic. Stir-fry 3 to 4 minutes, or until tender-crisp. Stir in salad dressing mixture; simmer 30 seconds. Serve over rice.
Serves 3-4.

Grace United Church
Brampton, Ont.

Chicken Stir-Fry

4 chicken breasts, deboned
Cooking oil (preferably peanut oil)
1 cup celery, chopped
2 med. carrots, sliced diagonally
1 cup red and green pepper each, sliced
1 cup snow peas
1 small zucchini, skin on, sliced
½ lb. fresh mushrooms, sliced
1 whole tomato, cut into eighths
¼ cup dry sherry, optional, or extra
   chicken broth
½ cup chicken broth
4 tbsp. soy sauce
Cornstarch and water (enough to make a
   paste)

In a wok or deep skillet, saute the chicken in oil. Remove chicken and set aside. Add the vegetables except the tomato and stir-fry; adding more oil as needed. Cook gently until all are al-denté. Add broth, sherry, soy sauce and simmer gently for 10 minutes on low heat. Return chicken to wok and thicken with cornstarch mixture. Add tomato wedges and cover and simmer for another 5 minutes. Serve on a bed of hot fluffy rice.

Northminster United Church
Peterborough, Ont.

Tangy Chicken Stir-Fry

½ cup (125 mL) orange juice
1 tsp. (5 mL) cornstarch
2 tbsp. (25 mL) vegetable oil
1 lb. (500 g) boneless chicken, cut in strips
1 medium onion, thinly sliced
1 cup (250 mL) thinly sliced carrots
1 cup (250 mL) thinly sliced celery
2 cups (500 mL) broccoli florets
1 tbsp. (15 mL) grated fresh gingerroot or
   ½ tsp. (2 mL) ground ginger
¼ cup (50 mL) chicken stock
1 tbsp. (15 mL) grated orange rind
½ tsp. (2 mL) salt
¼ tsp. (1 mL) pepper
2 tbsp. (25 mL) toasted almonds

Mix orange juice and cornstarch. Set aside in a wok or large skillet. Stir-fry chicken in oil for 5 minutes. Remove and set aside. Add onion, carrots and celery to wok and stir-fry 2 minutes. Add broccoli, gingerroot and chicken stock. Cover and cook 3-4 minutes or until vegetables are tender-crisp. Return chicken to wok. Add orange juice mixture, orange rind, salt and pepper. Cook until sauce is thickened, about 1 minute. Sprinkle with toasted almonds. Serve immediately.
Serves 4.

North Bedeque United Church
P.E.I.

Chicken and Pineapple Stir-Fry

2 chicken breasts, deboned and cut in 1"
   cubes
1 tsp. gingerroot, chopped fine
1 small egg white
2 tsp. cornstarch
Salt

Marinate chicken and these 4 ingredients 10 minutes.

1 green pepper, cut in 1" cubes on diagonal
2 med. carrots, sliced very thin on diagonal
1 or 2 cloves garlic, chopped very fine
1 cup pineapple chunks

Heat pan. Add 4 tablespoons peanut oil or your favorite. Add chicken mixture. Stir-fry 3 minutes. Remove. Add 1 tablespoon oil, garlic and stir-fry 1 minute. Add carrots and stir-fry 2 minutes. Add green pepper, stir-fry 1 more minute. Put chicken back in pan. Add pineapple. Add sauce and serve on bed of rice.

Sauce:
  2 tsp. sherry
  2 tsp. Chinese soya sauce
  ½ cup pineapple juice
  3 tsp. vinegar
  1 tsp. sugar
  1 tbsp. cornstarch
  1 tsp. salt

Cook together until clear in microwave or on stove, stirring regularly.
Serves 4.

St. Paul's United Church
Orillia, Ont.

Skillet Chicken Salad

4 boneless, skinless chicken breasts (1 lb.)
1 sweet red pepper
Half bunch broccoli
¼ cup vegetable oil
¼ cup chicken stock
3 tbsp. vinegar
1 tbsp. Dijon mustard
1 tsp. dried tarragon
Salt and pepper
1 cup tiny whole mushrooms
2 green onions, chopped

Cut chicken crosswise into ½" strips. Cut red pepper in strips. Cut broccoli into small florets. In skillet heat 2 tablespoons of the oil over medium heat. Saute chicken for 4 minutes. Using slotted spoon, transfer chicken to warm bowl to keep warm. In same skillet, heat remaining oil, cook red pepper and broccoli for 2 minutes. Stir in stock and reduce heat to low steam, covered for 2 minutes. Using slotted spoon, add vegetables to chicken. In same skillet pour in vinegar. Bring to boil. Stir in mustard, tarragon, salt and pepper. Stir in mushrooms and onions. Return chicken-vegetable mixture and any juices that have accumulated to skillet. Heat through for a few minutes. Serve over lettuce leaves or over hot cooked rice.

Mount Forest United Church
Mount Forest, Ont.

Miscellaneous Poultry

Apricot Glazed Chicken

2 fryers, quartered
Salt and pepper to taste

Combine and pour over chicken:
1 tsp. onion powder
1 tsp. garlic powder
1 cup apricot preserves
½ cup chili sauce
¼ cup dry white wine
2 tbsp. soya sauce
2 tbsp. liquid honey
1 tbsp. gingerroot

Bake at 350°F for 1 hour.

Bethany United Church
Ramsayville, Ont.

Chicken Jardin

3-5 lbs. chicken wings
1 cup soya sauce
⅛ cup lemon juice
Garlic powder

Cut tips off wings and cut in half. Mix in a large bowl soya sauce, lemon juice and lots of garlic powder. Soak wings overnight, mixing often. Deep-fry on high (375°F) for 3-4 minutes. Done when they float on top. Stir after putting in so they won't stick and they will float. Good hot or cold. Keep grease for use again with this recipe.

Franklin Centre United Church
Franklin Centre, Que.

Candied Chicken Wings

2-3 lbs. chicken wings
Salt, pepper and paprika

Clean and dry chicken wings. Season with salt, pepper and paprika. Place in a shallow baking dish.

Sauce:
½ cup honey
¼ cup soya sauce
4 tbsp. brown sugar
1 garlic clove, crushed
¼ cup ketchup

Mix sauce ingredients and pour over wings. Bake uncovered at 325°F, basting every 15 minutes for 1-1½ hours until tender.

Kintore Chalmers United Church
Kintore, Ont.

Oven Fried Chicken

½ cup margarine
Dry bread crumbs
Chicken pieces
Salt, pepper and paprika

Wash and dry chicken pieces. Melt margarine. Dip each piece of chicken in margarine, then coat in bread crumbs. Sprinkle with salt, pepper and paprika. Cover cookie sheet with foil. Place chicken on sheet. Bake 45 minutes at 350°F. No need to turn.

Robinson Memorial United Church
London, Ont.

Sweet & Sour Chicken Drumettes

3 lbs. chicken drumettes
1 egg, beaten
1 cup flour
1 cup butter

Dip drumettes in egg, then flour. Fry in butter till crisp and brown.

Sauce:
½ tsp. salt
½ cup vinegar
3 tbsp. soya sauce
3 tbsp. water
1 cup white sugar

Bake at 350°F for 30 minutes. Spoon sauce over drumettes (or wings) occasionally. Always a hit.

St. James United
Antigonish, N.S.
Crescent Fort Rouge United
Winnipeg, Man.

Today I may not be doing very well but I am doing better than yesterday.

Curry Chicken Wings

1 cup white sugar
1 tsp. dry mustard
1 tsp. paprika
1 tsp. salt
½ tsp. pepper
1 tsp. garlic powder
3 tbsp. Worcestershire sauce
½ tbsp. curry powder
1 cup vinegar
¾ cup ketchup

Cut the tips of the chicken wings and cut the remainder in two at the joint. Wash and dry (pat with paper towel) and place in baking dish, side by side. Heat to boiling in saucepan and pour over chicken wings that have been prepared and placed in baking dish. Bake 1 hour at 325°-350°F.

Hillsborough United
Hillsborough, N.B.

Chicken Burger Melts

1 egg white
½ cup minced green onions
¼ cup minced fresh parsley
2 tbsp. dry bread crumbs
2 tbsp. water
1 tsp. Dijon mustard
¼ tsp. each salt, dried basil or thyme
1 clove garlic, minced
1 lb. ground chicken
6 slices cheese

In a bowl, whisk egg white. Whisk in onions, parsley, bread crumbs, water, mustard, salt, basil and garlic. Mix in chicken and shape into patties about ½" thick. In lightly greased non-stick skillet over medium heat cook patties for about 5 minutes per side or until golden brown and no longer pink inside. Top with cheese slices. Cover pan and cook for about 1 minute longer until cheese melts. Nice grilled on the barbecue.
Serves 6.

Warren United Church
Warren, Man.

Chicken Tahiti

6 pcs. chicken - thighs
¼ cup flour
1 tsp. salt
¼ cup butter
¾ cup orange juice
½ cup orange marmalade
3 tbsp. cornstarch
½ cup cold water
¼ cup slivered almonds
1 tsp. paprika
⅛ tsp. pepper

Combine flour, paprika, salt and pepper. Coat chicken well. Melt butter in frying pan. Brown chicken pieces. Combine orange juice and marmalade in saucepan and heat until marmalade is completely melted. Combine cornstarch and water and add to orange mixture. Heat and stir until mixture is clear. Place chicken in 8x8" glass pan and pour orange sauce over chicken. Sprinkle with almonds. Bake uncovered in 325-350°F oven for approximately 50 minutes.
Serves 6.

Grace United Church
Port Dover, Ont.

Chicken Ragout

½ cup chopped celery
½ cup chopped onion
3 tbsp. margarine
3-4 lbs. chicken, cut up
1 can carrots, undrained
1 - 28 oz. can tomatoes
1 bay leaf
1 tsp. salt

In Dutch oven, saute celery and onions in margarine. Remove from pan. Add chicken, brown well on all sides. Add remaining ingredients. Simmer 1 hour. Thicken with 3 tablespoons cornstarch mixed in ⅓ cup cold water. Remove bay leaf and serve.
Serves 6.

St. Luke's United Church
Islington, Ont.

Citrus-Baked Cornish Hens

4 cornish game hens

Sauce:
¼ cup apricot preserves
2 tbsp. grated onion
1 tbsp. butter or margarine
1 tbsp. Dijon mustard
1 garlic clove, minced
Juice and grated peel of 1 lemon
Juice and grated peel of 1 orange

Remove giblets and necks from hens. Tie the legs of the hens together and turn the wing tips under the backs. If you cut the hens in half (lengthwise) before baking supper could be ready in just 45 minutes instead of 1¼ hours. In a saucepan combine all sauce ingredients. Simmer for 5 minutes. Brush the hens with the sauce and arrange, breast side up on a rack in a large roasting pan. Bake at 350°F for 1¼ hours or until tender (45 minutes if cut in half). Brush hens occasionally with sauce. Cut in half to serve or use whole. The mustard in this dish surprises people. Combined with the citrus it provides a real double "zing". Very tasty! You can also vary the ingredients, for example omit the garlic, or use orange marmalade instead of apricot.
Serves 4 or 8 (if cut in half).

St. Andrew's United Church
Admiral, Sask.

Tennessee Chili

(Excellent for those watching their cholesterol.)

1 lb. ground turkey
1 lge. onion, chopped
2 cans red kidney beans with liquid
1 - 28 oz. can tomatoes, chopped
1 - 6 oz. can tomato paste
3 tbsp. chili powder
1 tbsp. garlic powder
1 tbsp. vinegar
1 tbsp. sugar
Salt and pepper to taste

Brown meat and onions in small amount of olive oil. Blend all together and simmer on low heat. Freezes well.

Marshfield-Dunstaffnage United Church
Charlottetown, P.E.I.

Special Chicken

1 cup corn flake crumbs
½ pkg. onion soup mix
1 tsp. garlic powder
4 tbsp. dried parsley leaves

Mix all ingredients and store in a jar. When you cook chicken for dinner (legs or breasts) dip in a little melted butter and coat with some of the mix. Bake for 1 hour at 350°F.

Salem United Church
Colborne, Ont.

Maple Sweet & Sour Sauce for Chicken

¾ cup maple syrup (dark)
¾ cup ketchup
½ cup cold water
½ tsp. onion salt
¼ tsp. celery seed
A little salt and pepper to taste

Make right in the ketchup bottle using what ketchup is left after table use. Shake all together and pour over chicken. Bake in oven at your own regular time and temperature (approx. 350°F for 1 hour.) This is also good on pork chops.

Franklin Centre United Church
Franklin Centre, Que.

Chicken Skinny Shake

4 cups bread crumbs
½ cup vegetable oil
1 tbsp. salt
1 tbsp. paprika
1 tbsp. celery seed
1 tsp. pepper

Stir vegetable oil over bread crumbs in deep bowl with a fork until evenly distributed. Add salt, paprika, celery seed and pepper. Add other seasonings to your own taste such as onion or garlic powder, sesame or poppy seeds, dried herbs, lemon pepper. Store in refrigerator. Coat chicken parts in shake and bake 45 minutes to 1 hour in 350°F oven.

Harrow United Church
Harrow, Ont.

Casseroles

Creamy Turkey Casserole

6 slices bacon
¾ cup chopped onion
1 cup chopped green pepper
1 - 10 oz. can cream of celery soup or
    cream of chicken soup
1 cup sour cream
3 cups cooked turkey (cut into small pieces)
    or chicken
¼ tsp. salt
⅛ tsp. pepper

Topping:
2 cups Bisquick
½ cup milk
2 eggs
½ cup shredded cheddar cheese

Fry bacon until crisp. Crumble. Cook onions, celery, green pepper in bacon grease until tender. Stir in soup, sour cream, turkey, salt and pepper and bacon and heat until mixture bubbles. Spread mixture in casserole. Mix remaining ingredients (topping) until moistened. Spread over turkey mixture. Bake uncovered until golden brown in 350°F oven for 30-35 minutes. Serves 6-8.

Welland Avenue United Church
St. Catharines, Ont.

Turkey Creole

½ cup chopped green pepper
½ cup chopped celery
½ cup chopped onion
1 tbsp. margarine or butter
1 tbsp. flour
1 - 19 oz. can tomatoes, diced
1 - 8 oz. can tomato sauce
1 tsp. sugar
½ tsp. salt
½ tsp. crushed thyme
¼ tsp. garlic powder
Dash pepper
2 cups cooked turkey

Cook vegetables in butter or margarine until soft. Stir in flour. Add tomatoes and tomato sauce. Add spices. Cook and stir until thickened. Add turkey or chicken. Simmer for 5-10 minutes. Serve over hot cooked rice. Makes 4-5 servings.

Wesley United Church
Regina, Sask.

Chicken Chow Mein

2 cups cooked chicken, cut in good size
    pieces
1 cup celery, finely chopped
1 med. onion, finely chopped
1 cup chow mein noodles
¼ cup almonds or cashews, browned lightly
Pepper and salt to taste
1 can mushroom or cream of celery soup
1 cup chicken broth
1 tbsp. soy sauce

Mix all ingredients, reserving ¼ of the noodles for the top. After putting the combined ingredients in a buttered casserole sprinkle the top with ¼ cup noodles and cook for 30 minutes at 350°F. Serve hot and bubbly. May be served with rice or tossed salad and thick slices of homemade bread.

For variety replace the 1 cup chicken broth with one 14 ounce can crushed pineapple.

Middle River United Church
Gaddeck, N.S.
Wesley United Church
Port Elgin N.B.

Chicken, Broccoli & Cauliflower Casserole

2 cups cooked cubed chicken
1 cup grated cheese (old cheese)
2 tbsp. margarine or butter
1 cup sour cream
¼ tsp. pepper
½ tsp. salt
½ tsp. sugar
2 tbsp. flour
1 tbsp. grated onion
3 cups combined broccoli and cauliflower

Precook vegetables. Melt margarine or butter and saute onion. Blend in flour, salt, sugar and pepper. Stir in sour cream. Cook till thick. Add ¼ of grated cheese. Add vegetables and sauce alternately to casserole dish. Spread remaining grated cheese over top. Bake in 350°F oven for 20-25 minutes. This can be made ahead and reheated in oven.

Gilford United Church, Gilford, Ont.

Crusty Turkey Pie

2½ cups diced turkey or chicken
½ cup chopped celery
2 cups frozen peas or a combination of peas, cooked carrots or cooked cut green beans
1 cup fresh mushrooms or 1 - 10 oz. can drained (optional)
1 cup chopped onion
1 - 10 oz. can cream of mushroom or cream of chicken soup
½ cup water or ¾ cup milk
1 tbsp. margarine
¼ tsp. thyme or garlic powder or 1 tsp. lemon juice
Pepper to taste
1 tin Pillsbury buttermilk biscuits
¼ cup Parmesan cheese
1 tbsp. sesame seeds

Heat oven to 350°F. Rinse peas and thaw. Saute celery and onions in margarine. Add soup, milk or water, seasonings, turkey and vegetables. Pour mixture into 4-quart casserole. Separate biscuit dough. Cut each biscuit into 4. Toss the dough in a bag with Parmesan cheese and sesame seeds until coated. Arrange on top of casserole. Sprinkle with remaining cheese and seeds. Bake in oven 18-20 minutes.

Variation: Make a white sauce to replace the soup and liquid.

White Sauce:
¼ cup margarine
¼ cup flour
1 cup milk
1 cup hot water
1 chicken bouillon cube

Melt margarine, blend in flour. Stir in milk, hot water and bouillon cube. Cook until thick.
Variation: Make your own cheese biscuits.
1 cup flour
1½ tsp. baking powder
¼ tsp. salt
3 tbsp. butter
⅓ cup milk

Sift flour, baking powder and salt into a bowl. Cut in the butter. Add the milk all at once. Stir quickly with a fork. Press dough together and knead lightly. Roll dough into a rectangle ¼″ thick. Sprinkle with 1 cup grated cheese. Roll as for jelly roll. Cut into ½″ slices and place on hot filling. Bake at 425°F for 20-30 minutes.

Centre St. United Church, Shaunavon, Sask.
Landsdowne United Church, Landsdowne, Ont.
Pioneer Memorial United Church, Hamilton, Ont.
St. Paul's United Church, Estevan, Sask.
Harrow United Church, Harrow, Ont.

Sweet & Sour Turkey

2 cups grated carrots
2 cups sliced celery
2 cups chopped onion
2 tbsp. oil
14 oz. can pineapple tidbits, drained
Juice from pineapple with water to make 2 cups
5 tbsp. cornstarch
⅔ cup brown sugar
⅓ cup vinegar
¼ cup soy sauce
4 cups chopped cooked turkey or chicken

Saute vegetables in oil until tender-crisp. Combine juice and water, cornstarch, brown sugar, vinegar and soy sauce in saucepan. Cook, stirring constantly until sauce thickens. Add pineapple, vegetables and turkey. Heat and serve with rice.
Serves 8-10.

Mirror United Church, Mirror, Alta.

Chicken Casserole

6 oz. pkg. long grain and wild rice (e.g. Uncle
 Ben's)
2 cups cooked, cubed chicken or turkey
½ lb. mushrooms, sliced
1 - 10¾ oz. can cream of mushroom soup
 and ½ cup milk
1 - 4½ oz. can chopped black olives, optional
2 cups grated cheddar cheese
½ cup sliced almonds

Butter a 3-quart baking dish. Spread rice
evenly in bottom, then a layer of chicken,
mushrooms, soup, olives, cheese and almonds.
Bake at 350°F for 45 minutes.

For variation replace the olives, cheese and
almonds with 1 cup chopped celery, 1 small can
water chestnuts and 3 tablespoons soya sauce
and top with buttered crumbs.
Serves 6.

Cameron United Church
Cameron, Ont.
St. Giles United Church
Vancouver, B.C.

Chicken Jambalya

4 tbsp. margarine
¾ cup uncooked rice
1 chopped stalk celery
½ green pepper, chopped
1 small onion, chopped
2 cups cubed, cooked chicken
3 med. tomatoes, peeled and chopped or
 1 can tomatoes chopped with juice
1¼ cups chicken broth
Dash salt, pepper and cayenne pepper
¼ tsp. thyme or sage

Melt margarine in a large skillet, medium
heat. Add onion, green pepper, rice and celery.
Cook uncovered until the vegetables are tender,
about 10 minutes. Stir occasionally. Stir in
chicken, tomatoes, broth and spices. Cover and
simmer 30-35 minutes, stirring occasionally.
Leftover turkey is easily substituted.

Poplar Point United Church,
Poplar Point, Man.
Memorial United Church
Garden Cove, Nfld.

Chicken/Turkey Divan

1½ lbs. cooked chicken or turkey, sliced
1 cup chicken stock
1 lb. washed broccoli florets
1 tbsp. water
Pinch salt
1 tbsp. melted butter
2 oz. grated cheese
Pkg. of Hollandaise sauce mix
2 oz. grated Parmesan cheese

Place turkey and broth in casserole. Cover.
Cook on HIGH 3 minutes. Set aside. Place
broccoli, water and salt in casserole. Cover.
Cook on HIGH 6 minutes. Drain. Sprinkle with
melted butter and cheese. Arrange turkey over
broccoli. Pour prepared Hollandaise over top.
Sprinkle with grated cheese. Cook on MEDIUM
6-9 minutes until heated through.
Serves 6-8.

Grace United Church
Brampton, Ont.

Hot Chicken Salad Casserole

2½ cups diced cooked chicken
1 cup diced celery
1 cup sliced fresh mushrooms
1 tbsp. minced onion
1 tsp. lemon juice
½ tsp. crushed rosemary
¼ tsp. pepper
1 - 8 oz. can sliced water chestnuts, drained
2 cups cooked rice
¾ cup mayonnaise
1 - 10¾ oz. can cream of chicken soup,
 undiluted

Topping:
 3 tbsp. butter
 ½ cup corn flake crumbs
 ½ cup slivered almonds

In a large bowl, combine first nine ingredients. Blend mayonnaise and soup; toss with
chicken mixture. Spoon into a 2-quart greased
casserole. In a skillet, melt butter and combine
with the cornflakes and almonds. Top casserole
with crumb mixture. Bake at 350°F for 30
minutes.
Yield: 6 servings.

Salem United Church, Locksley
Pembroke, Ont.
St. Andrew's United Church
Millbrook, Ont.

Chicken Balls

Leftover pork, chicken or turkey

Batter:
1 cup flour
1 tsp. baking powder
1 tsp. salt
1 egg
Water

Dip small pieces of cooked meat into batter. Deep-fry in oil.

Sauce:
¾ cup white sugar
¼ cup ketchup
¼ cup vinegar
½-¾ cup water
1 tbsp. cornstarch

Pour sauce over meatballs and serve.

Ruthilda United Church
Ruthilda, Sask.

Tangy Chicken Bowl Salad

1 - 8 oz. can kidney beans, drained
1 cup cooked chicken or turkey, cut in strips
2 oz. American or cheddar cheese, cut in strips
½ of small cucumber, sliced
½ cup sliced celery
¼ cup vinegar
3 tbsp. sugar
1 tsp. grated onion
¼ tsp. salt
¼ tsp. celery seed
¼ tsp. dry mustard
⅛ tsp. paprika
½ cup salad oil
4 cups torn salad greens
1 lge. tomato, cut into wedges

Combine beans, chicken, cheese, cucumber and celery; chill. In mixer bowl or blender combine next 7 ingredients. Gradually add oil, beating constantly. Chill. Toss greens with bean mixture. Shake dressing. Pour some over salad; toss and pass remaining. Garnish with tomato. Serves 6.

United Church in Meadowood
Winnipeg, Man.

Chicken Salad Burritos

2 cups chopped chicken or turkey
½ cup finely chopped onion
¾ cup finely chopped celery
¼-½ cup sliced black or green olives
1 cup shredded cheddar cheese
½ cup salad dressing or mayonnaise
¼ cup picante sauce or chutney
½ tsp. salt
6 soft tortillas - or ½ pita breads or crepes (or use Tea Bisk and mix, refrigerating batter for a couple of hours)

Saute onion and celery briefly in microwave. Add remaining ingredients and heat through. Pack in tortillas, pita breads or crepes and hold warm. Serve with Minute rice to which you add frozen peas during the standing time.

Arundel United Church
Arundel, Que.

Some thrifty housewives who would say
That waste could cause them sorrow.
Will save leftovers today
But throw them out tomorrow.

Chicken Deluxe Casserole

8 slices bread
½ cup chopped onion
½ cup chopped green pepper
½ cup celery
½ cup mayonnaise
2 cups cooked, diced chicken or turkey
Salt and pepper
2 eggs, slightly beaten
1½ cups milk
1 can cream of mushroom soup
½ cup grated cheese

Place six slices of bread in the bottom of greased baking dish. Butter two slices of bread. Cut into cubes. Set aside. Combine onion, green pepper, celery, mayonnaise and chicken. Season with pepper and salt. Put this mixture over the bread. Combine eggs, milk and soup. Pour this mixture over the chicken mixture. Sprinkle cubed bread over the top, also grated cheese. Bake 1 hour at 325°F.

Central Avenue United Church
Fort Erie, Ont.

Beef

Helpful Hints

If you cook meat loaves in individual muffin tins, they will cook faster.

To make meatballs - form the ground beef into a log and slice into even slices. Then roll each slice to form a meatball.

Celery and green pepper can be diced in quantity and frozen for later use in casseroles.

Cheese can be grated in quantity and frozen for later use.

When making rice make in large quantities and freeze the leftovers. You will then have cooked rice on hand for those "Suppers on the Go."

Cook ground beef in large quantities and freeze in one-pound packages for use in recipes later.

Meat Pies

Cheeseburger Pie

1 lb. lean ground beef
1 medium onion
Salt and pepper to taste
Garlic powder (optional)
1 cup grated cheddar cheese
¾ cup Bisquick or Tea-Bisk
3 eggs
1¼ cups milk

Slightly cook beef and onion. Add spices. Put into 10-inch pie plate. Spread grated cheese on top. Mix the biscuit-mix, eggs and milk. Pour over cheese and meat. Do not stir! Bake at 400°F for ½ hour (or more) until set.

Mindemoya United Church, Mindemoya, Ont.
Highgate United Church, Highgate, Ont.
Kincardine United Church, Kincardine, Ont.
Warren United Church, Warren, Man.
St. Thomas United Church, Doaktown, N.B.
Guilford United Church, Guilford, Ont.
Brechen United Church, Nanaimo, B.C.

Hamburger Pie

1 pie shell
1 lb. lean ground beef
1 pkg. onion soup mix
3 tbsp. flour
⅓ cup powdered milk
1⅔ cups water
1 cup grated mozzarella cheese

Place pie shell in pie plate. Brown ground beef. Mix together onion soup mix, flour, and powdered milk and add to ground beef. Stir well. Add water and cook until thickened. Put into pie shell. Sprinkle cheese on top. Bake 30 minutes at 350°F.

High River United Church
High River, Alta.

Cheesy Meat Pie

1 unbaked 9" pie shell, chilled
1 medium onion, chopped
1 tbsp. butter or margarine
½ lb. ground beef
3 tbsp. white flour
½ tsp. salt
¼ tsp. pepper
8 oz. cheddar cheese, shredded
¾ cup milk
1 egg
1 tsp. Worcestershire sauce

Preheat oven to 400°F. In frying pan melt butter, add beef and onion and brown beef well. Remove from heat, drain fat and let cool. Stir into beef mixture, flour, salt and pepper and spread over pie shell. Cover with shredded cheese.

Beat well, milk, egg and Worcestershire sauce, pour over top of cheese.

Bake 35 minutes or until knife inserted in center comes out clean. Cool 10 minutes before serving.

Trinity United Church
London, Ont.

Country Pie

1 lb. ground meat
1 cup bread crumbs
½ - 7½ can tomato sauce
¼ cup chopped onion
¼ cup chopped green pepper
½ tsp. salt
⅛ tsp. oregano
⅛ tsp. pepper

Combine well, pat above mixture in 9-inch pie plate.

Filling:
1⅓ cups Minute rice
1 cup water
½ - 7½ oz. can tomato sauce
1 cup grated cheddar cheese
1 tsp. salt

Combine rice, water, tomato sauce, salt and ¼ cup cheese. Spread filling over meat mixture in pie plate. Cover with foil and bake at 350°F for 25 minutes. Uncover and sprinkle top with remaining cheese. Bake uncovered for an additional 15 minutes.

Trinity United Church
Vankleek Hill, Ont.

Hamburger Pie

1 lb. ground beef
½ cup chopped onion
½ tsp. salt
½ tsp. pepper
1 can mixed vegetables, drained
1 can mushroom pieces, drained
1 can tomato soup

Topping:
5 medium potatoes, cooked & mashed
½ cup warm milk
1 egg, beaten
½ cup shredded cheese

In skillet, fry meat and onions until browned. Add salt and pepper, mixed vegetables, mushrooms and soup. Pour into greased casserole. Mash potatoes, add milk and egg, season with salt and pepper. Spoon in mounds over meat and sprinkle with cheese. Bake at 350°F for 25-30 minutes.

Cambridge United Church
Lindsay, Ont.

Quick Hamburger Pie

9" unbaked pie shell
½ lb. lean ground beef
1 tin mushroom soup
2 eggs
2 tbsp. chives or onions
¼ tsp. each salt, pepper and dry mustard
1 tin mushroom pieces
4 Swiss cheese slices, broken

Brown meat, add onions. Mix together soup, beaten eggs, spices, mushrooms and cheese. Fill pie shell and bake at 425°F for 10 minutes. Reduce heat to 350°F for 45 minutes.

Grace United Church
Niagara-on-the-Lake, Ont.

Shepherd's Pie

1 lb. ground beef
1 large onion, finely chopped
3 tbsp. flour
1½ cups water
1 beef stock cube (OXO)
1 tbsp. Worcestershire sauce
½ tsp. salt
Pepper to taste
1 bay leaf
¼ cup frozen peas
¼ tsp. dried thyme

Topping:
6-8 medium potatoes
2 tbsp. butter
½ cup milk
Salt and pepper to taste
Grated cheddar cheese

Brown meat, breaking meat up, drain off excess fat, add finely chopped onion, fry meat until well browned. Sprinkle mixture with flour and stir to coat meat. Gradually add the water, then beef stock cube, sauce, salt, pepper, bay leaf and thyme. Add the frozen peas. Bring to boil, then simmer for 20 minutes. Put into a 13x9-inch dish.

Cook potatoes, mash and cream, with milk and butter. Put this on top of meat mixture. Sprinkle grated cheese on top. Bake at 325°F for another 20-30 minutes.

Exeter United Church
Exeter, Ont.

Quick Shepherd's Pie

1 can condensed vegetable soup
2 cups diced roast beef
1 cup chopped celery
3 cups mashed potatoes or instant potatoes

Mix first three ingredients in casserole dish. Cover with mashed potatoes. Heat in microwave 5-7 minutes then brown top under broiler. Serves 3.

Current River United Church
Thunder Bay, Ont.

Lasagna Pie
(no pastry to roll!)

1 lb. lean ground beef
1 tsp. dried oregano leaves
½ tsp. dried basil leaves
1 - 6 oz. can tomato paste
1 cup shredded mozzarella cheese
½ cup curd creamed cottage cheese
¼ cup grated Parmesan cheese
1 cup milk
⅔ cup Bisquick baking mix
2 eggs
1 tsp. salt
¼ tsp. pepper

Heat oven to 400°F. Grease 10x1½-inch pie plate.

Cook and stir beef over medium heat until brown, drain. Stir in oregano, basil, tomato paste and ½ cup mozzarella cheese. Layer cottage cheese and Parmesan cheese in plate. Spoon beef mixture over top. Beat milk, baking mix, eggs, salt and pepper until smooth, about 1 minute with hand beater. Pour into plate over beef mixture. Bake 30-35 minutes until knife inserted between center and edge comes out clean. Sprinkle with remaining ½ cup mozzarella cheese. Cool 5 minutes.

A tossed salad and fresh fruit completes the meal.

Serves 6 to 8.

Palermo United Church, Oakville, Ont.
Old Windham United Church, Simcoe, Ont.

Taco Pie

1 lb. lean ground beef
½ cup chopped onion
1 pkg. taco seasoning mix
Jalapeno peppers to taste
¾ cup Bisquick mix
3 eggs
2 tomatoes, sliced
1 cup shredded cheddar cheese

Fry ground beef and onion until brown. Stir in seasoning mix. Spread in pie plate. Top with peppers.

Beat milk, Bisquick, eggs until smooth, 15 seconds in blender or 1 minute by hand. Pourover beef mixture and bake at 375°F for 25 minutes.

Top with tomato slices, cheese and return to oven for an additional few minutes. Cool 5 minutes. Top with sour cream. Serve with a salad.

Vermillion Bay United Church
Vermillion Bay, Ont.

Crusty Beef and Vegetable Pie

4 thick slices crusty stale bread, cubed (whole wheat)
1 cup milk
2 egg yolks
1 medium onion, chopped
1 clove of garlic, minced
500 g ground beef
250 g zuchinni, sliced
Leftover vegetables (corn, pork and beans, etc.)
¼ cup raisins
¾ cup grated cheese

Soak bread in mixture of milk and egg yolks. Sauté chopped onion and minced garlic. Brown ground beef. Add zuchinni and cook for 5 minutes. Add any leftover vegetables and raisins. Simmer for 15 minutes. Pour mixture into 9-inch pie plate. Cover with bread cubes. Sprinkle with grated cheese. Bake at 375°F for approximately 15 minutes or until cheese melts.

St. Mark's United Church
Cannifton, Ont.

Beef and Onion Pie

2 medium onions, sliced
2 tbsp. bacon drippings
1 - 9" pie shell, unbaked
1 lb. minced beef
1 tsp. salt
2 tbsp. dry bread crumbs
½ cup canned tomatoes
1 egg, beaten
⅓ cup grated raw carrot
¼ tsp. garlic salt
¼ tsp. poultry seasoning
3 cups seasoned mashed potatoes

Sauté onions in drippings until limp and lightly browned and spread in bottom of pastry shell. Combine remaining ingredients except potato and spread evenly over onions. Bake at 400°F for 20 minutes. Cover the pie with the mashed potatoes and return to oven. Bake at 350°F for 30 minutes. Cut in wedges. May be served with creamed cauliflower or mashed squash.

College Hill United Church
Belleville, Ont.

Meat Loaf

Meat Loaf

1 lb. ground beef
½ cup bread crumbs
1 - 8 oz. tin of stewed tomatoes
1 egg
1 envelope dried onion soup mix
½ tsp. fresh ground pepper
½ tsp. parsley flakes
6 slices of processed cheese
4 slices of bacon

Mix all the above together except cheese and bacon. Form ½ of mixture into loaf. Overlap cheese slices on top. Cover cheese with remaining meat mixture, making sure cheese is completely sealed in at sides. Top meat mixture with bacon strips. If you like you can also top this with a tin of tomato soup. Bake 350°F for 1 hour.
Serves 6-10.

Charleswood United Church
Winnipeg, Man.

Yorkshire Steak Casserole

1 lb. ground beef
½ cup chopped onion
½ tsp. salt
½ tsp. sage
1 egg
1 cup milk
1 cup flour
½ tsp. salt
1 tsp. baking powder

Grease casserole, add ground beef. Mix, onion, salt, sage and sprinkle over meat. Beat egg, add milk, flour, salt and baking powder. Beat well then pour over meat. Bake in a moderate oven for 35 minutes.

St. Mark's United Church
St. Thomas, Ont.

Ground Chuck Meat Loaf

Sauce:
½ cup margarine
½ cup chopped onion
½ cup ketchup
¼ cup brown sugar
1½ tsp. chili powder
1 tsp. salt
⅛ tsp. pepper
3 tbsp. Worcestershire sauce
⅛ tsp. Tabasco sauce

Melt margarine and sauté onion. Add remaining ingredients and simmer for 5 minutes, stirring occasionally.

Loaf:
2 lbs. ground chuck
2 eggs
½ cup cracker crumbs
⅓ cup chopped green pepper
¼ cup milk
¼ cup ketchup
1½ tsp. salt
¼ tsp. pepper
Onion rings (optional)

Mix above loaf ingredients and firmly pack into 9x5 " pan or casserole. Arrange onion rings on top.

Pour the sauce over it and tightly cover with foil. Bake at 350°F for 1 hour.

Victoria St. United Church
Goderich, Ont.

Herbed Meat Loaf

1 egg, beaten
2/3 cup milk
2 cups soft bread crumbs
1 tbsp. prepared mustard
1 tsp. seasoned salt
Pepper to taste
1/2 tsp. dried basil leaves
1/4 tsp. dried thyme leaf
1 medium onion, chopped
1/2 cup diced celery and leaves
1 tbsp. dried parsley or 1/4 cup freshly
   chopped parsley
2 lbs. lean ground beef

In a bowl combine beaten egg, milk and crumbs. Let stand until bread absorbs milk.

Stir to break bread into smaller particles. Add next 5 seasonings and mustard. Stir in onions, celery, parsley and ground meat.

Bake in a loaf or flat square pan at 350°F until lightly browned, approximately 55 minutes, a little less for a flat pan. The loaf pan makes a moister, soft loaf. The flat, a crisper finish.
Serves 6.

St. Paul's United Church
Souris, Manitoba

Barbecued Hamburgers

1 cup soft bread crumbs
1/2 cup milk
1 lb. ground beef
1 tsp. salt
Pepper
1 1/2 tsp. Worcestershire sauce
1/4 cup vinegar
3 tbsp. granulated sugar
1/2 cup ketchup
1/2 cup water
1/2 cup chopped onion
1/2 cup chopped green pepper

Moisten bread crumbs with milk. Combine with beef, salt and pepper. Shape into 4 patties. Place in baking dish. Combine Worcestershire sauce, vinegar, sugar, ketchup, water, onion and pepper. Pour over patties. Bake for 50 minutes at 350°F.

Note: This recipe can be used in microwave. Cover baking dish with plastic wrap. Cook on high for 17 mintues, rotating at 8 minutes.

St. Paul's United Church
Sarnia, Ont.

Savory Supper Patties

2 cups ground beef cooked or other
   leftover roast
2 tbsp. minced onion
1 tsp. sage
1 tsp. salt
Pepper to taste
2 eggs
2-4 cups mashed potatoes

Combine all ingredients. Form into patties and roll in flour. Brown in hot fat in skillet.

Ste. Rose United Church
Ste. Rose du Lac, Man.

Meat Loaf

1 lb. lean ground beef
1 can vegetable soup
1 can mushrooms, drained
1 egg
1 medium onion, chopped
3/4-1 cup fine bread crumbs
Salt and pepper to taste
Dry mustard

Combine all ingredients and shape into 1 loaf. Bake at 350°F for 45 minutes or until done. May be served hot or cold.

Two Hills United Church
Two Hills, Alta.

Meatballs

Swedish Meatballs

1 lb. lean ground beef
1/4 cup chopped onion
1 tsp. salt
1/4 tsp. pepper
1/4 tsp. (or more) ground allspice
1/4 cup milk
1 or 2 slices bread, no crust
1 egg

Pour milk over bread, then put moistened bread over meat, add egg then mix together and roll into balls about plum size. Sauté in fat. Gravy can be made out of drippings.

Bruce Mines United Church
Bruce Mines, Ont.

Sweet & Sour Meatballs

1 lb. ground steak
Cracker crumbs
1 egg
Salt and pepper to taste

Make into small balls, brown in oven.

Sauce:
1 cup ketchup
1 cup water
½ bottle chili sauce
½ cup white sugar
1 green pepper
1 onion, chopped
1 tsp. prepared mustard
½ tsp. dry mustard
3 bay leaves

Make sauce, add meatballs, bake ½ hour at 350°F. Serve with rice or pasta.

Portland United Church
Saint John, N.B.

Hawaiian Meatballs

2 lbs. ground beef
2 eggs
¼ cup diced onion
1 tsp. salt
Sprinkle of flour

Sauce:
6 tbsp. brown sugar
¼ tsp. ginger
½ tsp. dry mustard
2 tbsp. cornstarch
¼ cup vinegar
1 - 10 oz. can crushed pineapple and juice

Mix together ingredients for meatballs, form into 1-inch balls. Brown well on all sides. Remove from pan. Add sauce ingredients to pan and stir until thick and boiling. Place meatballs in casserole, pour sauce over. Bake at 300°F for 30 minutes.
Serve with either rice or baked potato.

St. Andrew's United Church, Yorkton, Sask.
Stockholm United Church, Stockholm, Sask.
McKay United Church, Ottawa, Ont.

Sweet and Sour Meatballs

1 lb. (500 g) lean groud beef
1 egg, slightly beaten
½ cup (125 ml) oatmeal
2 tbsp. (25 ml) milk
Salt and pepper to taste
Dash of allspice
2 tbsp. (25 ml) chopped onion

Mix all ingredients gently and form into small meatballs. Arrange meatballs, ½ inch apart, in a microwave dish or pie plate. Microwave on HIGH 3-5 minutes. Transfer to another dish and pour off grease.

Sauce:
1 cup (250 ml) ketchup
½ cup (125 ml) water
¼ cup (50 ml) molasses
½ cup (125 ml) vinegar
1 tsp. (5 ml) dry mustard
3 tbsp. (45 ml) brown sugar (optional)
1 tsp. (5 ml) Worcestershire sauce
Dash cayenne pepper

Combine all ingredients in a large microwave dish. Add the meatballs and microwave on HIGH for 10 to 15 minutes - the longer the better. Stir occasionally and keep the meatballs immersed in the sauce.

Annesley United Church
Markdale, Ont.

Tangy Meatballs

24-36 medium meatballs

Prepare meatballs using your favorite recipe. Bake meatballs and drain. Place in bottom of 9x12'' baking dish.

Sauce:
2 - 12 oz. bottles chili sauce
1½ cups grape jelly
3 tbsp. lemon juice
1¼ tsp. dry mustard

Cook ingredients over low heat, stirring occasionally until the jelly is melted. Pour this mixture over the cooked meatballs. Bake 25 minutes at 350°F or until hot and bubbly. Transfer to serving dish.

Linden Park Community United Church
Hamilton, Ont.

Barbecued Meatballs

Meatballs:
  3 lbs. ground beef
  2 eggs, slightly beaten
  1 cup bread crumbs or cracker crumbs
  ½ tsp. salt and pepper
  1 small onion, chopped
  Milk

Mix above ingredients adding enough milk to moisten and hold meatballs together. Shape in walnut-size balls. Cook partially and drain.

Sauce:
  2 cups ketchup
  1 cup brown sugar
  1 tsp. liquid smoke (optional)
  ¼ cup chopped onion

Mix and pour over meatballs which have been placed in a baking dish. Bake 1 hour at 350°F.

Harriston United Church
Harriston, Ont.

Casseroles

Barbecued Beef

2 lbs. ground beef
1 can chicken gumbo soup
1 cup chopped onion
3 tbsp. ketchup
3 tbsp. mustard

Brown meat and onions. Add soup, mustard and ketchup and cook.

Bethel United Church
Forestburg, Alta.

Tasty Supper

1 lb. lean ground beef
1 cup chopped onion
1 medium can tomatoes
1 medium can pork and beans
1 small can creamed corn
Dash of pepper

Brown ground beef well. Add all other ingredients and allow to simmer for ½ hour.

Emmanuel United Church
Englehart, Ont.

Barbecued Beef, Pork, Chicken or Turkey

1 lb. leftover meat
½ cup ketchup
¼ cup barbecue sauce
1 tbsp. mustard
3 tbsp. brown sugar

Cook over medium heat, stirring often for about 30 minutes.

Oil Springs United Church
Oil Springs, Ont.

15-Minute Beef Stroganoff

1 lb. (¼ inch thick) round steak
13 oz. can or ⅔ cup broiled mushrooms, liquid too
1 pkg. dried onion soup
1 cup dairy sour cream
2 tbsp. flour

Trim fat from meat and reserve. Cut meat diagonally across grain in very thin strips. Heat fat in pan until you have about 3 tablespoons melted fat (or you can use 3 tablespoons corn oil). Brown meat. Add ⅔ cup liquid (water added) and mushrooms. Stir in soup mix. Heat to boiling. Add flour and sour cream. Cook and stir until mixture thickens. Sauce will be thin. Serve over noodles.
Serves 5-6

Arundel United Church, Arundel, Que.
Balzac United Church, Balzac, Alta.

Ontario Hash

1 lb. ground beef
1 large tin vegetable beef soup
1 pkg. macaroni and cheese mix
¾ tbsp. ketchup
⅓ cup chopped onion

Brown the beef and onion. Add ketchup and soup and simmer while preparing macaroni. Spoon servings on plates and pour meat sauce over. Serve with salad as desired.

Maple Grove United Church
Bowmanville, Ont.

Chop Suey

1 lb. ground beef
1 cup chopped onion
2 cups chopped celery
1 can mushrooms, reserve juice

Cook the above ingredients in frying pan.

4 cups chopped cabbage
1 can bean sprouts, reserve juice

In a large pan with a little butter, partially cook cabbage and bean sprouts and add:

1 can mushroom soup
4 tbsp. sugar
4 tbsp. soya sauce
Salt and pepper to taste

Let simmer for ½ hour to 1 hour. Add juice of mushrooms and bean sprouts if desired.

North Kildonan United Church
Winnipeg, Man.

Saucy Sloppy Joes

1 tbsp. salad oil
1 lb. lean ground beef
1 large onion, chopped
1 cup ketchup
1 cup water
3 tbsp. flour
½ cup cold water
½ tsp. dry mustard
½ tsp. chili powder
1 tsp. salt

Heat skillet and add salad oil. Over medium heat, lightly brown ground beef with onion, stirring with a fork to break up meat. Add ketchup with 1 cup water. Cook over medium heat until thoroughly heated. Combine ½ cup cold water with flour, stir until blended. Add dry mustard, chili powder and salt. Mix until smooth. Gradually add to meat mixture, while stirring constantly until thickened. Spoon over heated hamburger rolls.
Makes 4-6 servings.

Transcona Memorial Church
Winnipeg, Man.

Goulash

Brown:
    2½ lbs. ground beef
    1 large onion, chopped
    1 green pepper, chopped
    1 can mushrooms, drained

Sauce:
    1 - 23 oz. can tomatoes, chopped
    1 can tomato soup
    1 small can tomato paste
    2 tbsp. Worchestershire sauce
    Few drops Tabasco sauce
    Garlic salt

Mix in greased casserole meat and vegetables. Simmer 20 minutes.
Boil ½ - ¾ package of egg noodles and mix with meat and vegetables. Pour half of mixture into casserole and layer either 1 pound sliced or grated mozzarella cheese. Repeat layering. Bake ¾ hour at 350°F.

St. Paul's United Church
Aylmer, Ont.

Beefaroni Family Style

(Economical, quick and tasty)

1-1½ lbs. lean ground beef
1 can sliced mushrooms (optional)
2 small or 1 large onion, chopped
1 - 750 ml jar spaghetti sauce OR
    1 can tomatoes
1½ cups elbow or shell pasta
Grated parmesan cheese (optional)

Boil pasta until tender. In a large skillet or Dutch oven, brown beef, making sure it is broken into fine size pieces, add onion, continue cooking until onion is just browned. Add drained mushrooms and spaghetti sauce. Simmer 15 minutes. Drain pasta well, blanche. Add to simmered beef. Mix well, continue to simmer about 20 mintues. Top with grated Parmesan cheese before serving.

St. Giles United Church, Hamilton, Ont.
Balzac United Church, Balzac, Alta.

Country Hash

3 tbsp. oil
½ cup chopped onion
1-1½ cups chopped green pepper
1 lb. ground beef
½ cup rice
2 cups canned tomatoes
1 tsp. chili powder
1 tsp. salt
¼ tsp. pepper

Heat oil in skillet, add onion, greenpepper and ground beef. Brown well. Add remaining ingredients. Cover tightly. Cook over high heat until steaming freely, then turn heat down and simmer for about 30 minutes.
Serves 6.

Mount Bruno United Church
St. Bruno, Qué.

More Casserole

Cook:
1 lb. ground beef
1 cup chopped onion

Add:
1 - 8 oz. pkg. egg noodles, cooked
1 - 10 oz. pkg. frozen peas, thawed
1 - 12 oz. can kernel corn, drained
1 - 8 oz. can mushroom pieces, drained
1 - 8¼ oz. can water chestnuts, drained and diced

Toss well. Heat until bubbly:
1 - 10¾ oz. can celery soup, undiluted
1¼ cup milk
1 tbsp. chili powder
1 tbsp. Worcestershire sauce
2 tsp. salt
¼ tsp. pepper
¼ tsp. garlic powder

Add:
3 cups grated sharp cheddar cheese

Stir until melted. Pour hot cheese mixture over noodle mixture and mix well. Cover with foil and bake 40 minutes at 350°F. Sprinkle a bit of grated cheese on top.
Note: Can be doubled easily. Can be frozen and heated for later.
Serves 8

Adolphustown U.E.L. Centennial United Church
Napanee, Ont.

Macaroni Casserole

1 lb. ground beef
1 can mushrooms and liquid
1 onion
Green pepper
6 tbsp. fat
20 ozs. tomatoes
1 cup pasta, uncooked
Garlic salt
Bay leaf
Parsley flakes
Salt and pepper
Parmesan cheese
1 cup boiling water
1 can mushroom soup

Brown meat, remove from pan and keep warm. Drain fat and save 6 tablespoonfuls. Add mushrooms and liquid and let boil down. Add onion and green pepper and brown. Stir in macaroni and brown. Add tomatoes, soup, bay leaf, water, salt and pepper. Simmer 20 minutes, stirring often to keep from sticking to pan. Add more boiling water if needed. Pour into casserole. Add meat and stir. Sprinkle with parsley flakes and Parmesan cheese.
Serves 4-6.

Gilford United Church
Gilford, Ont.

German Skillet Dinner

1 tsp. butter
1 - 14 oz. can sauerkraut with liquid
⅔ cup uncooked regular white rice
1 medium onion, chopped
1 lb. ground beef
1¼ tsp. salt
¼ tsp. pepper
1 - 8 oz. can tomato sauce OR tomato soup plus 1 can water

Heat butter in large skillet (an electric frying pan is excellent). Brown ground beef and onion. Remove from pan. Spread sauerkraut over butter in skillet, sprinkle on rice. Top with ground beef and onion mixture, salt, pepper, tomato soup and water. Heat for 15 minutes, then serve right from skillet.
Serves 4-5.

St. Paul's United Church
Estevan, Sask.

Beef and Macaroni Combo

1 lb. lean ground beef
¾ cup chopped onion
½ cup chopped celery
1 large can stewed tomatoes
1 tsp. salt
1 cup uncooked macaroni
8 oz. shredded cheddar cheese
Snipped parsley (optional)

Sauté beef, onion and celery in a 3-quart saucepan until meat is browned. Add tomatoes and salt, bring to a boil. Stir in macaroni. Cover and cook over low heat stirring occasionally 10 minutes or until macaroni is done. Stir in cheese and melt on low heat (do not boil). Garnish with parsley if desired.

Grenfell United Church
Grenfell, Sask.

Quit worrying about hating your job so much. Someone else will have it soon.

Beef Fiesta

1 lb. ground beef
1 tbsp. salad oil
¼ cup diced onion
1½ tsp. salt
1 tsp. chili powder
¼ tsp. pepper
1 - 19 oz. can tomatoes, drained
1 - 12 oz. can whole kernel corn, drained
1 - 10 oz. can bouillon
½ cup thin strips green pepper
1½ cups Minute rice

Brown beef in oil over high heat in frying pan, leaving meat in coarse chunks, drain fat. Add onion; reduce heat to medium and cook until onion is tender but not browned. Add seasonings, tomatoes, corn and bouillon; bring to a boil, stir in green pepper. Boil again. Stir in rice; remove from heat. Cover. Let stand for 5 minutes. Fluff with fork.
Note: You may use 1 bouillon cube dissolved in 1¼ cups boiling water.
Serves 5.

St. Andrew's United Church
Tide Head, New Brunswick

Dinner in a Skillet

½ lb. ground beef
1 egg, slightly beaten
½ cup milk
¼ cup fine dry bread crumbs
1½ tbsp. finely chopped onion
½ tsp. salt
¼ tsp. dry mustard
2 tbsp. flour
¼ cup salad oil
1 - 10 oz. tin tomato OR cream of
   mushroom soup
10 oz. milk
1½ cups vegetables, cooked
½ tsp. salt

Combine first 7 ingredients, shape into 12 small meatballs, roll in flour, brown in oil. Arrange meatballs around outer edge of pan. Pour soup and milk mixture into center of pan. Place vegetables over soup, salt, cover and simmer 10 minutes. Serve hot.
Note: If vegetables are frozen allow extra 15 minutes cooking time.

St. Paul United Church
Kelliher, Sask.

Quick Hamburger and Vegetable Chili

1 medium can baked beans in sauce
1 medium can chili beans
1 stalk of celery, chopped
1 medium onion, chopped
1 large mushroom, chopped
1 medium carrot, chopped
Small piece green pepper, chopped
1 tsp. chili powder (optional)
1 cup ground beef

Fry ground beef in pan, drain fat. Mix in chopped vegetables and stir well. Add beans and mix all ingredients well. Simmer over medium heat for 30-45 minutes. If so desired, serve on a bed of white rice. This chili is quite mild and very filling.

Waterville United Church
Waterville, Quebec

Spaghetti Sauce

4 tbsp. oil
6 onions, chopped
5-6 cloves of garlic
1 lb. ground beef
1 lb. ground pork

Fry above ingredients until meat loses its color.

Add:
1 - 6 oz. tin tomato paste
1 small can red pimentoes
1 large tin tomato juice
1 large can tomato soup
¼ tsp. cinnamon
¼ tsp. chili powder
¼ tsp. cloves
4-5 bay leaves
Salt and pepper to taste
1 tsp. sweet basil
1 tsp. oregano
2 tbsp. tarragon vinegar
2 tbsp. white vinegar
2 tbsp. red wine vinegar
2 tbsp. Worcestershire sauce
2 tbsp. (or to taste) brown sugar
½ cup ketchup
½ cup water
1 cup chopped mushrooms

Simmer until well blended, approximately 1 hour or more. Serve on any type of pasta.
Kirkfield Park United Church
Winnipeg, Man.

Spanish Rice

½ cup rice
1½ lb. cooked ground beef or chopped
    leftover beef
    ½ cup grated cheese
1 can tomato soup
1 small onion, chopped
Salt and pepper

Cook rice in boiling salted water 10 minutes. Drain in sieve under cold water. Add meat, cheese, soup, onion and seasonings. Bake in 325°F 'till golden brown (20-30 minutes). Serve with tossed salad.
Maple Grove United Church
Bowmanville, Ont.

Potato-Pepperoni Supper

4 tbsp. margarine
5 large potatoes, unpeeled, cut into ⅛
    inch thick slices
1 small onion, diced
½ tsp. salt
⅛ tsp. pepper
1 - 8 oz. pkg. shredded mozzarella cheese
1 - 8 oz. can tomato sauce
1 - 3½ oz. pkg. sliced pepperoni
2 large tomatoes, cut into wedges

About 20 minutes before serving, over a medium heat, melt margarine in skillet. Remove from heat. Arrange potatoes and onion on bottom and slightly up sides of skillet. Sprinkle with salt and pepper. Cover skillet. Over medium-low heat, cook potatoes until tender, about 20 minutes. Sprinkle potatoes with cheese; top with ½ of the tomato sauce; arrange pepperoni and tomatoes over sauce; top with remaining sauce. Cover skillet; cook until cheese is melted and tomatoes are heated through.
St. Paul's United Church
Kenmore, Ont.

Chinese Casserole

1½ lbs. ground beef
1 large onion
1 can cream of chicken soup
1 can cream of mushroom soup
1 can sliced mushrooms including juice
    and add water to make 1 cup
1 cup water
1 cup diced celery
½ cup minute rice
2 tbsp. soya sauce
1 tin bean sprouts
1 tin Chinese noodles

Brown ground beef with onions. Add remaining ingredients, reserving ¼ cup of noodles to sprinkle top. Bake ¾ hour at 375°F.
St. Mark's United Church, St. Thomas, Ont.
Moorefield United Church, Moorefield, Ont.
Walton United Church, Walton, Ont.
Trinity United Church, Listowel, Ont.

Cheesy Casserole

12 oz. bow tie pasta
1 lb. ground beef
1 large onion, diced
1 green pepper
1 cup celery
1 - 28 oz. can spaghetti sauce
1 small can tomato soup
2 small cans mushrooms or mushroom
  pieces, drained
1 small pkg. Velveeta cheese, sliced
½ lb. shredded cheddar cheese
Parmesan cheese

Cook pasta in salted water until tender.
In a large frying pan cook ground beef, onion, green pepper and celery until vegetables are tender. Add spaghetti sauce, tomato soup and mushrooms.
In 2 casserole dishes, layer meat mixture with 3 cheeses. Sprinkle top with Parmesan cheese. Bake in oven at 350°F for 40-50 minutes until heated through and cheese is melted.
Note: Macaroni or other pasta may be used.

South Cayuga United Church
Dunnville, Ont.

Italian Delight

1 lb. lean ground beef, brown and drain
½ green pepper
1 medium onion, chopped
½ stalk celery, chopped
1 carrot, sliced
1 - 28 oz. can tomatoes, drained and
  chopped
1 can tomato soup
Soya sauce to taste
Tabasco sauce to taste
3 cups cooked noodles
1 can cheese soup

Mix first 5 ingredients and simmer until done. Add remaining ingredients except for cheese soup, and pour into buttered square baking pan. Pour cheese soup over top. Cover and bake for 20 minutes at 325°F. Uncover and brown last 5 minutes. Serve with a salad and rolls.

Bath United Church
Bath, Ont.

Quick Lasagna

1½ lbs. of ground beef
1 pkg. (1¾ oz.) onion soup mix
3 - 8 oz. cans tomato sauce
1 cup water
1 - 8 oz. pkg. lasagna noodles
½ lb. mozzarella cheese, sliced

Brown ground beef and stir in onion soup mix, tomato sauce and water. Bring to a boil. Cover, reduce heat and simmer 15 minutes.
Cook noodles according to directions on package. Drain well and let stand in cool water for easier separating.
Heat oven to 400°F.
In a 2-quart oblong baking dish, alternate layers of noodles, meat sauce and cheese, ending with cheese. Bake 15 minutes or until hot and bubbling.
Serves 6-8

Shubenacadie United Church
Shubenacadie, N.S.

Beef Noodle Casserole

1 lb. ground beef
1 cup minced onion
1 clove of garlic, minced
2 - 8 oz. cans tomato sauce
1 tsp. salt
¼ tsp. pepper
1 cup dairy sour cream
1 cup creamed cottage cheese
1 cup sliced carrots, cooked
¼ cup chopped fresh parsley
8 oz. medium noodles, cooked and drained
1 cup shredded cheddar cheese

Cook ground beef, onion and garlic in 10-inch skillet over medium heat 10 minutes or until meat is browned. Stir into tomato sauce, salt and pepper. Cook over high heat until mixture comes to a boil, about 2 minutes. Reduce heat to low and simmer, uncovered, 5 minutes. Remove from heat. Stir sour cream, cottage cheese, carrots and parsley into meat mixture. Add noodles and toss to coat. Turn mixture into greased 3-quart casserole and sprinkle with cheese. Bake in 350°F oven 30 minutes or until hot.
Note: Freezes well.

St. Paul's United Church
Boissevain, Man.

Italian Macaroni & Cheese

½ lb. ground beef
1 - 16 oz. can tomatoes
⅓ cup tomato paste
1 tbsp. instant minced onion
1 tsp. sugar
½ tsp. garlic salt
½ tsp. ground oregano
Dash pepper
2 cups cooked (1⅔ uncooked) shell
    pasta
1 cup creamed cottage cheese
1 cup shredded cheddar cheese
2 tbsp. grated Parmesan cheese

Cook meat in heavy saucepan until it loses its red color but is not brown, drain. Add tomatoes, tomato paste, onion and seasonings. Simmer slowly for 30 minutes. Stir as needed. Preheat oven to 325°F.

Combine cooked pasta and cottage cheese. Pour a small amount of sauce in bottom of a 2½-quart casserole. Top with ½ pasta mixture, ½ shredded cheese and ½ remaining sauce. Repeat. Sprinkle Parmasen cheese on top. Bake 40 minutes or until heated through. Serves 6.

Lamont United Church
Lamont, Alta.

Carmen's Caper

(one-dish meal)

1½ lbs. of ground beef
½ cup chopped onion
1½ tsp. salt
¼ tsp. pepper
½ lb. of spaghetti
1 - 19 oz. can tomatoes
1 - 10 oz. can cream of mushroom soup
1 cup grated cheddar cheese

Brown beef and onion in frying pan. Sprinkle with salt and pepper, stir. Transfer to bottom of 2-quart (2L) casserole. Break up spaghetti for easier serving. Cook according to package directions, drain. Layer over meat. Break up large tomato chunks. Pour over top. Spoon soup over tomatoes. Cover with cheese. Bake uncovered in 350°F (180°C) oven for 30 minutes or until hot and cheese is melted. Cover halfway through cooking time if cheese starts getting dry.
Serves 6

Invermay United Church
Invermay, Sask.

Mexican Dish

Layer:
  1 can refried beans
  1 lb. ground beef, cooked and drained
  1 pkg. taco seasoning
  1 - 16 oz. jar salsa sauce

Bake at 350°F for approximately 30 minutes. Add 8 oz. grated cheese and cook just to melt. Serve with taco chips and more salsa sauce.

Fleetwood United Church
Surrey, B.C.

Preacher's Casserole

1 lb. ground beef
4 medium onions
2 cups chopped celery
1 - 10 oz. can mushroom soup
1 - 10 oz. tomato soup
1¼ cups water
1 tsp. chili powder
2 cups chow mein noodles
Salt and pepper to taste

Brown beef, add onion and celery and cook till tender. Add remaining ingredients except a few noodles. Place in casserole and top with remaining noodles. Bake at 350°F for 45 minutes.

St. James United Church
Stroud, Ont.

Meat Muffins

½ lb. mushrooms, sliced
1 medium carrot, shredded
1 large onion, finely chopped
1½ lb. lean ground beef
1 cup bread rumbs
1 tsp. salt
¼ tsp. savory
½ cup ketchup
1 egg
Dash of pepper

Mix all together and form into 12 large balls and lightly pat into 3-inch muffin tins, leaving tops rounded. Bake 30 minutes at 400°F for moist tender muffins — a little longer for well-done muffins.
Note: Freezes well.

First United Church
Cambridge, Ont.

Pizza Casserole

3 cups small macaroni
1 lb. ground beef
1 onion, chopped
1 tsp. salt
½ tsp. pepper
1 large can tomato sauce
1 large green pepper
1 can mushrooms, drained
1 can pizza sauce
Pepperoni, sliced
1 lb. mozzarella cheese

Brown ground beef and onion. Combine with other ingredients. Save some mushrooms, pepperoni and cheese to sprinkle on top. Place in casserole. Bake at 350°F till bubbly.

Echo Bay United Church, Echo Bay, Ont.
Trinity United Church, Bowmanville, Ont.
Straffordville United Church, Straffordville, Ont.
Zion Evangelical United Church, Pembroke, Ont.
Kings Kirk United Church, Belleisle Creek, N.B.

Pizza Rice Casserole

Cook:
⅔ cup rice or 2 cups leftover rice

Brown in large skillet:
¾ lb. ground beef
1 onion, chopped

Add:
2 cups tomato sauce
¼ tsp. garlic salt
1 tsp. sugar
1 tsp. salt
Dash pepper
¼ tsp. oregano
1 tsp. parsley flakes

Cover and simmer 15 minutes.

Combine with cooked rice:
1½ cups cottage cheese

Put ⅓ of rice mixture into buttered casserole. Top with ⅓ of meat-tomato sauce. Continue to alternate layers ending with tomato sauce. Sprinkle with ½ cup shredded cheese. Bake at 325°F for 30 minutes.

Bissell Memorial United Church
Andrew, Alta.

Upside-down Pizza

1½ lbs. ground beef
1 medium onion, chopped
1 - 15½ oz. can pizza sauce
½ tsp. garlic salt
¼ tsp. oregano
8 oz. mozzarella cheese, grated
2 eggs
1 cup milk
1 tbsp. oil
1 cup flour
½ tsp. salt
½ cup grated Parmesan cheese

Preheat oven to 350°F. Brown ground beef and onion, drain off fat. Blend in pizza sauce, garlic salt and oregano. Put mixture in greased 9x13" pan. Sprinkle with mozzarella. In a small bowl mix eggs, milk, oil, salt and flour. Pour over meat mixture and sprinkle with Parmesan. Bake 30 minutes.
Variation: Mushrooms, bell pepper strips, Italian sausage and/or Canadian bacon may be added if desired.

Emmanuel United Church
Waterloo, Ont.

Hunter's Dinner

1 large bunch (1 lb.) celery, thinly sliced
2½ lbs. ground beef
1 can lima beans
2 tsp. salt
3 large onions, chopped
1 tin mushrooms
1 can tomatoes
1 - 7 oz. pkg. spaghetti

Cook spaghetti according to package directions. Brown ground beef in a heavy skillet. Add onions and celery. Cook until vegetables are transparent.

Combine cooked, drained spaghetti, tomatoes, lima beans, mushrooms, browned meat, celery and salt in casserole. Bake at 325°F for 30 minutes.

Knox United Church
Winnipeg, Man.

Killbear Hash

1 onion, chopped
1 - 19 oz. can spaghetti
1 can kernel corn
1 lb. ground beef
1 can mushrooms
Parmesan cheese

Brown and drain ground beef, add onion. Cook until done, add spaghetti, corn, mushrooms. Turn into casserole, sprinkle with cheese. Bake at 350°F for 20-30 minutes.
Note: Recipe can be doubled and freezes well.
Beverley Hills United Church
Downsween, Ont.

Lazy Day Lasagna

1 lb. ground beef
1 - 14 oz. can tomatoes, undrained
1 - 5 oz. tomato paste
1½ tsp. salt
1½ tsp. basil leaves
½ tsp. oregano
⅛ tsp. garlic powder
½ cup water
2 cups cottage cheese
¼ cup Parmesan cheese
1 egg
1 tbsp. parsley flakes
8 uncooked lasagna noodles
2 cups (8 oz.) shredded mozzarella cheese

Crumble ground beef into 1½-quart casserole. Microwave on HIGH 7 or 8 minutes until no longer pink, stirring once. Stir to break meat into pieces. Drain. Stir in tomatoes, tomato paste, salt, basil, oregano, garlic powder and water. Cover with casserole lid. Microwave on HIGH 7 or 8 minutes or until mixture boils. Combine cottage cheese, Parmesan cheese, egg and parsley. Mix well. Pour 1½ cups tomato sauce mixture into 9x13" baking dish and spread evenly. Place 4 uncooked noodles evenly over sauce. (They may overlap slightly). Top with ½ the cottage cheese mixture, spreading evenly. Sprinkle with ½ the mozzarella cheese. Spoon 1 cup sauce evenly over cheese. Place 4 more noodles on sauce. Top with layers of remaining cottage cheese mixture, mozzarella

cheese and tomato sauce. Cover tightly with plastic wrap. Microwave on HIGH 15 minutes. Rotate dish. Microwave on MEDIUM (50% power) 15-20 minutes or until noodles are tender. Let stand about 5 minutes before cutting. This appears to be a long procedure but really isn't and is ready to eat in less than 1 hour.
Bolton United Church
Bolton, Ont.

Olé

1 lb. ground beef
1 - 28 oz. can stewed tomatoes
1 - 12 oz. can of whole kernel corn
1 pkg. chopped broccoli, thawed
½-¾ cup mild salsa sauce or hotter
Garlic powder to taste
Salt to taste
½ cup grated cheese

Cook ground beef, add garlic and salt. While the meat is cooking, drain tomatoes and chop. Drain corn. Thaw broccoli in microwave and drain. Grate cheese. Put drained vegetables in shallow casserole. Add salsa sauce to meat and stir, add to vegetables. Add meat and top with grated cheese.
Wesley United Church
St. Andrew's, N.B.

Favorite Meat Loaf

1 - 8 oz. can tomato sauce, divided
  equally into 2 parts
¼ cup brown sugar
1 tsp. mustard
2 eggs, slightly beaten
⅓ cup cracker crumbs
2 lbs. lean ground beef
1½ tsp. salt
¼ tsp. pepper
1 medium onion, minced

In small bowl combine tomato sauce, brown sugar and mustard. Set aside.
In large bowl combine eggs, onions, cracker crumbs, ground beef and seasonings. Add ½ cup tomato sauce into mixture and mix well. Place meat mixture in glass-ring bowl. Pour remaining tomato sauce over the top of the meat, cook uncovered on microwave HIGH for 12-14 minutes or until done. Let stand 5-10 minutes before serving.
Zion Evangelical United Church
St. Pembroke, Ont.

All At Once Spaghetti

1 tbsp. margarine
1 cup chopped onion
1 lb. lean ground beef
1 tsp. salt
½ tsp. basil
¼ tsp. pepper
2 - 8 oz. tins tomato sauce
1½ cups water
½ tsp. oregano
¼ lb. uncooked spaghetti
Grated Parmesan cheese

Place margarine and onion in 2-quart casserole in microwave - HIGH 3-4 minutes or till onion is tender.

Add beef and cook 3-4 minutes on HIGH until beef loses its pinkness. Stir ½ way into cooking time, drain fat.

Add salt, pepper, tomato sauce, oregano and basil. Cook covered on HIGH for 4 minutes.

Break spaghetti in ½, stir into sauce, cook covered on HIGH 18-20 minutes or until spaghetti is tender. Stir twice during cooking time. Sprinkle with Parmesan cheese.

Sundre United Church
Sundre, Alta.

Quick-Cook Beef & Mushroom Stew

2 tbsp. vegetable oil
1 lb. beef sirloin, cut into ½" cubes
2 tbsp. flour
1 tbsp. paprika
¾ cup beef broth
¼ cup dry red wine
1½ cup quartered mushrooms
¾ tsp. thyme
Salt and pepper to taste
1 - 8 oz. pkg. wide egg noodles

Preheat oven to 350°F.

Heat oil in 3-quart casserole, add beef; cook about 5 minutes, stirring frequently, until all sides browned. Sprinkle with flour and paprika, stirring to coat well, gradually stir in broth and wine. Cook, stirring constantly until mixture boils and thickens. Stir in mushrooms, thyme, salt and pepper. Bake, covered about 20 minutes. Meanwhile prepare noodles according to package directions. Drain and toss with butter. Arrange noodles around beef mixture of rimmed serving platter.

Ste. Rose United Church
Ste. Rose du Lac, Man.

Wild Rice Casserole

1 lb. ground beef
1 cup wild rice, soaked overnight
1 cup barley, pearl or pot
1 can mushrooms
1 large onion
3 stalks celery, chopped
1 tsp. chopped garlic
2 cans consomme
2 cans water
3 tbsp. soya sauce
1 tsp. olive oil
Ground pepper

Sauté beef, barley, onion and garlic in oil. Put all ingredients in a large casserole. Cover and microwave on HIGH for 40-60 minutes, stirring occassionally.

Soaking wild rice the night before serves to "open up" the rice kernels. This can also be accomplished by cooking the rice in water in the microwave on HIGH for 8 minutes.

After 40 minutes check the casserole, add more water if too dry. Check the barley to see if it is tender. If not, continue to cook until barley is tender.

Winnipeg Presbytery
Winnipeg, Man.

Japanese Steak

1 lb. round steak
2 tbsp. brown sugar
½ tsp. garlic powder
½ tsp. salt
½ tsp. pepper
½ tsp. M.S.G.
¼ cup soya sauce
2 large onions, chopped
1½ cups chopped celery
1 - 20 oz. can tomatoes
1 can water chestnuts, sliced
1 can mushrooms, drained
3 tbsp. cooking oil

Cut steak in thin strips. Brown in oil. Add sugar, garlic, salt, pepper, MSG and soya sauce. Cover and simmer for 10 minutes. Add onions and celery, simmer another 10 minutes. Add remaining ingredients and simmer 5-10 minutes. Serve over rice.

First United Church
Corner Brook, Nfd.

Beef on a Bun

Mix together:
2 tbsp. sugar
2 tbsp. vinegar
2 tsp. prepared mustard
2 tsp. lemon juice
1 tsp. salt
1 tsp. paprika
¼ tsp. pepper
¾ cup water
4 tbsp. butter
1 medium onion, thinly sliced
¼ green pepper, cut in strips

Simmer uncovered for 20 minutes and add:
¼ cup ketchup
1 tsp. monosodium glutamate (optional)
1½-2 cups cooked roast beef OR roast pork, cut in strips

Refrigerate. About 30 minutes before serving, simmer slow to heat. To serve, sprinkle with chopped parsley and celery leaves. May be served on a bun, over rice, buttered noodles or mashed potatoes.
Note: Make it up the day before and refrigerate overnight.

Mount Forest United Church
Mount Forest, Ont.

Chinese Casserole

1 lb. minced steak, cut in pieces
1 large Spanish onion
3 stalks celery, cut in chunks
1 green pepper, cut in slices
1 can mushroom soup
1 can sliced mushrooms
½ can water, may use juice of mushrooms instead)
Salt and pepper to taste
Soya sauce

Brown steak in oil. Then add soya sauce to taste. Add other ingredients. Simmer in oven ½ hour or until done. Sprinkle 1 can of Chinese noodles on top and heat for another 10 minutes.

Lafleche United Church
Lafleche, Sask.

Marinated Teriyaki Flank Steak

1 flank steak
2 tbsp. brown sugar
¾ tsp. ground ginger
1 tbsp. vinegar
2 tbsp. Worcestershire sauce
½ cup soya sauce
1 clove of garlic, finely minced

Combine all of the ingredients, except the steak. Marinate the steak in the mixture at least 6 hours. Barbecue to your taste, but medium is the best for this type of steak. Remove from grill and thinly slice across the grain.

Robinson Memorial United Church
London, Ont.

Pepper Steak

1½ lbs. steak, cut in bite-size pieces
3 tbsp. soy sauce
1 tbsp. cooking oil
Dash of pepper
½ tsp. grated gingerroot or ground ginger
1-2 cloves of garlic, minced
1 tbsp. cooking oil
1 medium green pepper, sliced
2 cups sliced fresh mushrooms
6 green onions with tops, cut in ½ inch pieces or regular onion
½ cup beef broth
1 tbsp. cornstarch
2 medium tomatoes, cut in wedges
Rice

In large bowl combine soy sauce, 1 tablespoon oil and pepper. Add beef, toss to coat well. Let stand several hours in refrigerator. Drain beef, reserving marinade. In wok or skillet heat ginger, garlic and 1 tablespoon oil. Add beef, stir fry till it is browned. Remove beef with slotted spoon. Add green pepper, mushrooms and onions to wok. Cook and stir fry till vegetables are done, approximately 2 minutes. Return beef to wok, combine reserved marinade, beef broth and cornstarch and pour over beef mixture. Cook and stir till thick and bubbly. Add tomatoes, cover and cook till heated. Serve with rice and or egg rolls.

Makes 6 servings.

Note: Partially frozen meat is easier to slice.

Alexander Grant United Church
East Lake Ainslie, N.S.

Steak Oriental

1 lb. ½ inch thick round steak
2 tbsp. salad oil
1 cup green pepper strips
2 stalks celery, cut on bias
1 cup thinly sliced onion
1 can bean sprouts, (optional)
2 tbsp. soy sauce
1½ cups water
2 tbsp. cornstarch
1 tsp. sugar
1 tsp. salt
2 medium tomatoes, peeled and quartered
2 cups hot cooked rice
½ tsp. ginger

Steak should be partly frozen for easy slicing. Cut meat into thin strips across grain. Stir fry peppers, celery and onion in oil until tender. Remove vegetables from pan and brown meat quickly. Add 1 cup water to meat. Simmer until tender. Add bean sprouts (optional). Mix cornstarch with ½ cup water and stir in. Add other seasonings to taste and cook until thick and bubbly. Return vegetables to pan. Add tomatoes, heat through. Serve over hot fluffy rice sprinkled with ginger.

St. Andrew's United Church
Maryfield, Sask.

Oriental Beef with Broccoli and Carrots

1 lb. round steak
2 tbsp. cornstarch
2 tbsp. sherry OR water
2 tbsp. soya sauce
3 green onions
1 bunch (approx. 6 cups) broccoli
6 (approx. 4 cups) carrots
1 tbsp. vegetable oil

Seasoning sauce:
1 cup water
2 tbsp. cornstarch
2 tbsp. soya sauce

Slice beef into thin 1-inch long strips and place in a bowl. Sprinkle with cornstarch. Toss with water or sherry and soya sauce. Let stand for 15 minutes. Blanch broccoli and carrots for 2 or 3 minutes or until tender crisp. Heat oil over high heat, add beef and stir fry for 1 or 2 minutes or until browned. Add broccoli,carrots and onion. Stir in seasoning sauce. Bring to a boil and boil for one minute or until sauce thickens.

Brechin United Church
Brechin, Ont.

Mom's Main Dish

2 lbs. round steak
1 cup ketchup
1 cup water
1 medium onion

Cut meat into large bite-sized pieces. Lay in bottom of 2-quart casserole. Slice onion on top. Mix ketchup and water in measuring cup and pour over meat. Bake at 350°F for 1 hour.

Clavet United Church
Clavet, Sask.

Beef and Peppers Paprikash

(A complete and colorful meal in one skillet!)

3 cups fine egg noodles
1 lb. round steak, cut into thin strips
1 tbsp. all-purpose flour
2 tbsp. vegetable oil
1 - 28 oz. or 1 - 19 oz. can stewed tomatoes
1 medium red pepper, cut into thin strips
1 medium green pepper, cut into thin strips
1 tsp. paprika
1 tsp. Worcestershire sauce
½ tsp. salt
½ cup sour cream

Cook noodles according to package directions for 6 minutes, drain. Coat beef strips with flour. Heat oil in large frying pan, sauté beef in frying pan, over high heat, until browned on all sides. Stir in stewed tomatoes, peppers, paprika, Worcestershire and salt. Bring to a boil, then simmer for 3-5 minutes, stirring occasionally, until peppers are tender. Stir in sour cream, then gently stir in drained noodles. Or serve beef and peppers over the noodles for a tasty variation.

Zion Evangelical United Church
Pembroke, Ont.

Steak and Onion Stir-Fry

½ lb. round steak, thinly sliced into
   bite-sized strips
2 small unpeeled potatoes, cut in ½ inch
   wedges
2 small onions, sliced and separated into
   rings
1 clove of garlic, peeled and minced fine
¼ lb. fresh mushrooms, thickly sliced
1 cup frozen peas
1 cup frozen or fresh beans
2 tbsp. vegetable oil
2 tbsp. butter
¼ tsp. thyme
Pinch salt
Black pepper

Heat oil in wok or electric frying pan. Add
meat, stir fry over high heat until meat loses red
color, add more oil if needed. Add butter, when
melted, add the potatoes, continue to stir fry
until they start to brown. Then add onions,
garlic, mushrooms, peas, beans, and seasonings
and stir fry over high heat until vegetables are
heated through and the meat is done as you like,
about 4 minutes. Serve hot with a salad.
Serves 4.

Fordwich United Church
Fordwich, Ont.

Rueben Casserole

1 - 28 oz. jar sauerkraut
2 tbsp. butter or margarine
½ cup chopped onion
12 oz. corned beef, cut up
¾ cup Russian dressing
4 slices Swiss cheese

Drain sauerkraut, rinse well and drain again.
Put in 2½-quart casserole. Heat butter in medium saucepan. Sauté onions until soft. Add
corned beef and dressing to onions. Stir
together. Spoon over sauerkraut. Layer cheese
over top. Bake uncovered at 350°F for 30
minutes. Serve with rye bread.

Heartz Memorial United Church
Weymouth, N.S.

Cheaters' Shepherd Pie

1 can corned beef
1 cup grated carrot
1 tbsp. chopped onion
2 tbsp. ketchup

Mix together well. Place in loaf tin and cover
generously with fairly moist mashed potatoes.
Bake at 375°F until potatoes are lightly
browned.

Gibsons United Church
Gibsons, B.C.

Corned Beef Pie

2 eggs
1 - 12 oz. can corned beef, flaked
⅓ cup chopped onion
½ tsp. prepared mustard
½ tsp. horseradish
1 - 8 oz. can tomato sauce
2 cups cooked macaroni (1 cup uncooked)
¾ cup shredded cheese
½ tsp. basil
2 tbsp. parsley
Pepper to taste
¾ cup soft bread crumbs
1 tbsp. butter, melted

Beat 1 egg in medium size bowl. Stir in corned
beef, onion, mustard, horseradish and ¼ cup
tomato sauce. Press into a lightly greased 9-inch
pie plate and set aside.

Beat remaining eggs, add macaroni, basil,
pepper, parsley and remaining tomato sauce.
Spoon into meat shell. Toss bread crumbs with
butter and sprinkle over macaroni mixture.
Bake 350°F for 25-30 minutes.
Serves 4-6

Brooklin United Church
Brooklin, Ont.

Veal Oscar

4 boneless veal steaks
All-purpose flour
3 tbsp. margarine
12 fresh asparagus spears
½ lb. crab meat
1 pkg. Hollandaise Bernaise sauce mix

Pound meat between sheets of waxed paper until thin. Dip in flour. In frying pan, brown both sides in margarine until cooked. Keep hot. Cook asparagus in salted water until tender. Drain. Heat crab meat. Prepare Bernaise sauce according to package directions. To serve: place 3 asparagus spears in each steak, along with crab. Spoon Bernaise sauce over top.

United Church in Meadowood
Winnipeg, Man.

Veal Casserole
(Ideal for buffet)

1½-2 lbs. veal, cubed
½ cup butter
1 medium onion, chopped
2 tbsp. lemon
Bay leaf
1 tsp. salt
Freshly ground black pepper
1¼ cups red wine
½ cup white flour
1 cup chicken stock
1 cup sliced mushrooms
2 cloves of garlic, crushed
2 tbsp. butter
⅔ cup white wine
1 cup sour cream or yogurt

Cube the veal. Melt the butter in a large pan and gently fry the onions for 5 minutes. Add the veal, lemon juice, bay leaf, salt, pepper and ½ the red wine, cover and cook gently for 15 minutes. Lift the veal out. Add the flour to the pan and cook over a medium heat, stirring continuously, for 2 minutes. Add the chicken stock and remaining red wine and bring to a boil, stirring continuously. Sauté the mushrooms and crushed garlic in a saucepan in melted butter for 2 to 3 minutes. Add the white wine, cover and simmer gently for 10 minutes. Return the veal to the red wine mixture, add the mushroom mixture and simmer for 10 minutes. Add the sour cream and reheat without boiling.

Lakeshore Drive United Church
Morrisburg, Ont.

Sausage and Veal

½ lb. pork sausage
2 lbs. boneless veal, cut in 2-inch cubes
1 cup flour
¾ cup dry white wine
1 tsp. paprika
½ tsp. basil
½ tsp. thyme
1 onion, finely chopped

Brown sausage. Remove from pan. Dredge veal with flour and brown in fat, drain excess fat. Add other ingredients. Bake covered at 350°F for 1½ hours. Serve over hot noodles, using the juice from casserole as gravy.
Note: Freezes well.
Serves 5.

St. David's United Church
Truro, N.S.

Thought For The Week

Give us Lord a bit o sun
A bit o work and a bit o fun;
Give us all in this struggle and sputter;
Our daily bread and a bit o butter.
Give us Lord a chance to be
Our goodly best, brave, wise and free;
Our goodly best for ourselves and others
Till all men learn to live as brothers.

(From an old English prayer)
Trinity United Church
Coronation, Alta.

Even The Kids Will Like it Liver

6 slices bacon, chopped
¼ cup flour
1½ cups milk
¼ cup fine, dry bread crumbs
1 cup chopped onion
1 lb. beef liver, cut in serving pieces
1 tbsp. butter melted

Combine bacon and onion in frying pan. Cook until bacon is crisp and onion tender. Remove, reserving drippings in pan. Combine flour, 1 teaspoon salt and dash of pepper. Coat liver with flour, reserve rest of flour. Brown liver in bacon drippings, remove liver to 10x6x1½" baking dish. Blend reserved flour with drippings in pan till smooth. Add milk. Cook and stir till thickened. Pour sauce over liver. Sprinkle bacon and onion over all. Combine crumbs and melted butter. Sprinkle on top of liver. Bake uncovered 350° for 25-30 minutes. Serves 4

Knox United Church
Russell, Man.

Liver in a Skillet

4 bacon slices
1 medium onion, chopped
2 tbsp. all-purpose flour
1 tbsp. chili powder
1 lb. beef liver, thinly sliced
2 cups canned tomatoes, with liquid
1 - 12 oz. can kernel corn, drained
1 tsp. salt or to taste

In large skillet, fry bacon until crisp. Drain and crumble into pieces. In 2 tablespoons of bacon fat sauté onions. Combine flour and chili powder. Roll liver slices in it. Push onions to side of skillet and brown liver on both sides. Add bacon to tomatoes and corn. Simmer 5 minutes or until fork-tender. Serve with parsley boiled potatoes or rice.

Trinity United Church
Grimsby, Ont.

Liver & Vegetable Casserole

4 slices baon
1½ cups sliced onions
1 cup peas OR beans
2 cups cooked rice (½ cup uncooked)
1 can mushroom soup
1 cup grated cheese
1 lb. liver, thinly sliced
¾ cup celery
1 cup milk
½ cup buttered crumbs

Cut bacon in small pieces, fry to delicate brown and remove bacon, dredge liver in seasoned flour, brown in bacon fat and remove. Cook onions and celery in fat until brown then add bacon, liver, rice, peas, soup and milk. Mix well and heat to boiling. Stir in ⅔ cup of cheese and little salt. Put in casserole, top with buttered crumbs, sprinkle with remaining cheese. Bake for 30 minutes at 350°F.

Crescent Fort Rouge United Church
Winnipeg, Man.

Throw It Together Lasagna

(will feed 200 for a luncheon meal)

27 pans (9x13)
5 cartons (2 kg each) cottage cheese
45 lbs. hamburger
20 lbs. mozzarella cheese, shredded
11 boxes lasagna noodles
9 tins spaghetti sauce
Tomatoes, (donated)
1 large bag cooking onions
Garlic to taste
Salt and pepper
Oregano

Cook 2½ to 3 pounds hamburger per pan. Add as many tomatoes, garlic, onions and sauce as you prefer. Cook until quite a bit of the juice is gone. Put all together in a large pot. Put a little sauce on the bottom of the pans, then add noodles, meat, cottage cheese, mozzarella cheese. Repeat until 3 layers have been completed. Cover with foil. Put in oven at 350°F for 20 minutes or until cheese is melted and warmed through.

We have this every year, as a money maker. Served with a salad and dessert.

Smithville United Church
Smithville, Ont.

Pork

Miscellaneous Pork

French Canadian Tourtiere

1 lb. minced pork
1 envelope onion soup mix
1 tsp. garlic powder or 1 clove fresh, crushed
   garlic
1 tsp. cinnamon
1 tsp. nutmeg or ground cloves
1 cup water
Pastry for double crust 9'' pie
1 tbsp. brown sugar

Mix all ingredients in a saucepan except the pastry, brown sugar and bread crumbs. Bring to a boil and simmer for ½ hour then stir in the bread crumbs and cool. Make pastry with 1 tablespoon brown sugar added to dry ingredients. Line a 9'' pie pan. Fill with meat filling. Cover with pastry. Cut slit in top of pastry to allow steam to escape and flute edges. Bake at 425°F for 30 minutes.

Grace United Church
Hanover, Ont.

Pork Meat Loaf

1½ lbs. minced fresh pork
1½ lbs. minced cured pork
1 cup cracker crumbs
⅔ cup brown sugar
1 tsp. mustard
1 cup grapefruit juice
½ cup water

Combine first 5 ingredients, form into a loaf and place in a loaf pan. Pour grapefruit juice and water over the top. Bake at 350°F for up to 1 hour, basting often. Good hot or cold.

Grace United Church
Hanover, Ont.

Mock Veal Cutlets

4 breaded pork cutlets
Mozzarella cheese slices
Spaghetti sauce
Sliced fresh mushrooms

Cut cutlets in half. Brown briefly in oil. Pepper and salt them. Place in micro-safe pan and cover with plastic wrap leaving one corner free. Microwave 4 minutes on HIGH. Drain and cover with cheese slices, sauce and mushrooms. Recover and microwave 1 minute until bubbly. Serve with noodles on side plus a salad. Serves 4.

St. John United Church
Hamilton, Ont.

Pork-Rice Oriental

1 small clove garlic, minced
2 tbsp. oil
1½ cups diced or slivered cooked pork,
   ham, beef or chicken
½ medium red or green pepper, cut into
   strips
⅛ tsp. pepper
2 cups water
1½ cups Minute rice
1½ cups shredded raw spinach or lettuce
1 tbsp. soy sauce

Sauté garlic in oil in skillet until lightly browned. Add pork, red pepper, pepper and water. Bring quickly to a boil over high heat. Stir in rice. Cover. Remove from heat and let stand 5 minutes. Just before serving add spinach and soy sauce, tossing lightly. Serve with additional soy sauce if desired. Makes 4 servings.

Kirk McCall United Church
St. Stephen, N.B.

Quick Pork Chow Mein

2 cups cooked pork, cut into thin strips
1 cup diced celery
½ cup chopped onion
½ cup coarsely chopped red or green
  peppers
1 tsp. chicken flavoured instant bouillon
1 tsp. sugar
⅛ tsp. pepper
1½ cups water
2 tbsp. soya sauce
1 - 16 oz. can bean sprouts, drained, rinsed
2 tbsp. cornstarch
¼ cup cold water
Chow mein noodles or hot rice

In large skillet, combine pork, celery, onion, red pepper, bouillon, sugar, pepper, 1½ cups water, and soya sauce. Cover. Bring to boil; simmer 10 minutes or until vegetables are tender. Stir in bean sprouts. In a small bowl, combine cornstarch and ¼ cup water until smooth. Over medium-high heat, carefully add to skillet mixture, stirring constantly until thickened. Serve over noodles or rice.
Makes 4 servings.

Essex United Church
Essex, Ont.

Pineapple Pork and Cauliflower

1 - 8 oz. can pineapple chunks
1 tbsp. oil
1 garlic clove, minced
1 lb. boneless pork, cut into 1 inch cubes
2 cups cauliflower florets
1 medium green pepper, cut into 1-inch pieces
1 tbsp. brown sugar
½ tsp. ginger
1 tbsp. vinegar
1 tbsp. cornstarch
2 tbsp. soy sauce
12 cherry tomatoes, halved
Hot cooked rice

Drain pineapple, reserving liquid in cup, adding water to measure ½ cup. In large skillet heat oil. Add garlic and pork. Stir-fry until pork is no longer pink. Add cauliflower, green pepper, brown sugar, ginger, vinegar and ½ cup pineapple liquid. Blend well. Cover. Cook over medium heat for 4 to 5 minutes or until vege-tables are tender crisp. Stir in pineapple. In small bowl combine cornstarch and soy sauce. Add to skillet, stirring constantly until thick-ened. Arrange tomatoes around edge of skillet. Cover and cook for 1 minute. Serve over hot cooked rice.
Serves 4.

Grace United Church
Brampton, Ont.

While at a church supper - eat lots - food for the soul has no calories.

Pork Kabobs

(Marinate in the morning, cook at night)

2 lbs. lean boneless pork (leg or shoulder),
  cut into 1'' cubes

Marinade:
½ cup dry white wine
¼ cup ketchup
2 tbsp. vinegar
1 tsp. Worcestershire sauce
⅓ cup brown sugar
1 tsp. dry mustard
½ tsp. ground pepper

Place pork cubes in a plastic bag and set in a bowl. Combine marinade in a saucepan and bring to a boil (can be done in the microwave). Cool and pour over pork cubes. Close bag tight-ly with a twist tie. Marinate 2 hours at room temperature or overnight in the fridge. Thread pork cubes onto skewers with any four of the following:

1 large onion, cut into 1½'' pieces
1 red pepper, cut into 1½'' pieces
1 green pepper, cut into 1½'' pieces
½ lb. large mushrooms
6 pineapple slices, cut into 1½'' pieces
6 cherry tomatoes

Barbecue kabobs over low to medium heat turning often and baste with marinade through-out cooking time - about 30 minutes or until meat just loses its pinkness. Meat will lose its full flavorful juices if over cooked.

Moorefield United Church
Moorefield, Ont.

Pork Tenderloin a la Asparagus

8 pieces pork tenderloin (approx. 2 lbs.)
2 tbsp. butter or margarine
1 tin condensed cream of asparagus soup
¼ cup milk
½ cup chopped onion
1 - 3 oz. can sliced mushrooms, drained
½ tsp. curry powder

Pound pork slices to flatten. In skillet brown tenderloin in butter. Set aside. In same skillet blend together soup and milk. Stir in remaining ingredients. Return meat to skillet. Cover and simmer 40 minutes or until tender. Serve over rice.
Serves 4.

Iondale Heights United Church
Scarborough, Ont.

Apple Pork Chops

4 pork chops
2 red apples
2 celery stalks, including leaves
¼ tsp. each garlic powder and basil
Pinch of salt and pepper

Trim excess fat from chops. Heat oil in large frying pan. Add chops and cook over medium heat for 4-5 minutes until browned. Meanwhile, coarsely chop apples and thinly slice celery. Sprinkle garlic powder and basil over chops. Scatter apples and celery on top. Add salt and pepper. Cover. Reduce heat to low and cook, turning once, about 30 minutes.

Bethany United Church
Ramsayville, Ont.

Pork Chops

Breaded Pork Chops with Mozzarella and Ham

4 pork chops, deboned
Salt, pepper and flour
1 egg, lightly beaten
1 cup finely crushed cracker crumbs
2 tbsp. vegetable oil
1 tbsp. butter or margarine
½ tbsp. lemon juice
1 tbsp. grated Parmesan cheese
4 slices cooked ham
4 slices mozzarella cheese

Season chops lightly with salt and pepper, then dust with flour. Dip each chop into beaten egg, then into crumbs to coat both sides. In skillet, heat oil and butter; cook chops on both sides until golden brown and cooked through. Sprinkle with lemon juice, then Parmesan cheese. Place a slice of ham and then a slice of cheese on each chop. Place under broiler until the cheese melts. Ready to serve.

Consul United Church
Consul, Sask.

Pork Chop Supreme

4 pork chops
1 tbsp. vegetable oil
1 can beef consommé
1 cup water
3-4 carrots, sliced
1 can mushrooms (optional)
2 medium onions, slivered lengthwise
Salt and pepper
Poultry seasoning (optional)
2 broken bay leaves
1 tbsp. prepared mustard
1-1⅓ cup long grain rice

Preheat oven to 350°F.
Brown the pork chops in the vegetable oil in a frying pan. Sprinkle salt, pepper and seasonings on top. Place in 8x11'' baking dish. Spread mustard evenly on chops. Sprinkle bay leaves, carrots and onions over chops. Heat the consommé and water in saucepan. Brown rice in hot frying pan until lightly brown. Then add to the hot consommé and water (liquid from the mushrooms may also be used). Spread rice and liquid evenly over chops and vegetables. Cover tightly and bake for 30 minutes. Stir carefully and/or move rice into liquid and continue baking for approximately 30 minutes covered.
Variation: Replace the consomme with 1 envelope onion soup mix and increase the liquid by 1 cup.

Sutton Knox United Church, Sutton West, Ont.
Emmanuel United Church, Saskatoon, SK

Easy Pork Chops

4-6 pork chops
1 medium onion, sliced
1 can mushrooms or 1 cup fresh mushrooms
1 envelope gravy mix

Preheat oven to 350°F. Brown chops in electric frying pan for 4-5 minutes. Remove to casserole dish. Sauté onions and mushrooms for 2-3 minutes. While chops are browning make up gravy mix. Pour this while still hot over the chops, onions and mushrooms. Pop in the oven for 50 minutes. Serve with rice and a tossed salad, plus rye or pumpernickle bread (if so desired).

Ardrossan United Church
Ardrossan, Alta.

Stuffed Pork Chops

1 can mixed or 1 cup frozen mixed
  vegetables
4 to 6 pork chops
1 box Stove Top dressing
Salt and pepper
1 can mushroom soup or brown gravy

Heat oven to 350°F. Empty mixed vegetables into small roasting pan. Place browned chops on top of vegetables. Prepare Stove Top dressing (or make your own) and spread over meat. Spoon soup or gravy over all. Bake 30 minutes, or 1 hour if chops have not been browned.

Embro Knox United Church
Embro, Ont.

Dijon Pork Chops

3 tbsp. dried bread crumbs
1 tbsp. grated Parmesan cheese
1 tbsp. chopped fresh parsley
1 tbsp. vegetable oil
1/8 tsp. pepper
2 pork chops
2 tsp. Dijon style mustard

In shallow mixing bowl, combine bread crumbs, cheese, parsley, oil, pepper. Mix and set aside. Spread both sides of each pork chop with mustard, then press each into bread crumbs. Spray cookie sheet with Pam. Bake at 400°F for 40-45 minutes.

Warren United Church
Warren, Man.

Braised Pork Chops with Wine

6 pork chops, cut 1 inch thick
1 tbsp. vegetable oil
2 cups sliced onion
1 - 10 oz. can consommé
1/2 cup red dinner wine
1 tsp. rosemary leaves, crushed
Salt and pepper, to taste
2 tbsp. flour

Brown chops in oil in a large frying pan over high heat for 3-4 minutes on each side. Remove from pan. Add onions and cook over medium heat until transparent; return chops to pan; add consomme, wine, rosemary, salt and pepper. Cover pan and simmer over low heat until chops are tender, for about 30 minutes, turning once. Remove chops to platter to keep warm. Mix flour with 1 cup of juices from pan. Cook over medium heat, stirring, until smooth and thick; pour over chops to serve.

St. Andrew's United Church
Tide Head, N.B.

Microwave Stuffed Pork Chops

1 cup chopped, unpeeled apple
2 tsp. grated orange peel
1 tbsp. butter
2 tsp. brown sugar
1/4 cup raisins
1/8 tsp. cinnamon
1/2 cup dry bread crumbs, seasoned
8 pork chops, 1/4" thick

Combine apple, raisins, orange peel, cinnamon and butter in 2 cup measure. Cook on HIGH for 2-4 minutes or until apples are tender. Stir in 1/4 cup bread crumbs and brown sugar. Place 1/2 cup dressing on four pork chops. Top each with another pork chop. Secure with wooden toothpicks. Coat chops with 1/4 cup crumbs. Arrange chops on outer edges of rack. Cook 5 minutes on MEDIUM, turn and cook 12-18 minutes on MEDIUM until no pink shows. Serves 4.

Welland Ave. United Church
St. Catharines, Ont.

High in the Sky Pork Chops

(Air Canada)

6 pork chops
Sage
Salt and pepper

Cook pork chops which have been seasoned with sage and salt and pepper.

Sauce:
2 tbsp. brown sugar
1 tbsp. cornstarch
1 cup apple juice
½ cup cranberry sauce
1 apple, sliced

Mix brown sugar, cornstarch and apple juice. Add cranberry sauce, bring to a boil. Add to chops in pan. Then slice apple into 12 slices. Arrange around chops. Cover and cook 5 to 7 minutes or until apple is cooked. Serve at once.

Streetsville United Church
Streetsville, Ont.

One Pot Pork Chop Supper

4 pork chops (1 lb.)
1 - 10¾ oz. can tomato soup or
   1 envelope onion soup mix with
   1 cup water
½ cup water
1 tsp. Worcestershire sauce
½ tsp. salt
½ tsp. oregano
Desired potatoes, carrots, peeled and sliced
   for 2 or 4 people

Brown chops. Pour off fat. Add remaining ingredients. Cover and simmer for 45 minutes.

Banner United Church, Thamesford, Ont.
St. Andrews United Church, Scotstown, Que.

Yummy Pork Chops

6-8 pork chops
Shake and Bake or your favorite bread crumb
   mix
2 tbsp. brown sugar
⅔ cup ketchup
⅔ cup water

Coat chops with crumb mixture and bake at 350°F for ½ hour. Mix together sugar, ketchup and water and pour over chops and bake an additional ½ hour. Baste frequently.

North Bedeque United Church
Summerside, P.E.I.

Sausage

Sausage Peach Balls

1 lb. ground pork sausage
2 tbsp. minced onion
2 cups soft bread crumbs
¼ tsp. salt
⅛ tsp. pepper
1 egg, beaten
8 peach halves, canned
24 cloves
Peach syrup

Combine sausage, onion, bread crumbs, seasoning and egg. Form into eight balls. Stick 3 cloves around edge of each peach half on cut side in baking dish. Place sausage ball in center of each peach. Bake for 45 minutes in moderate oven (350°F). Drain off fat and add heated peach syrup. Serve with rice. Serves 4.

Ardrossan United Church
Ardrossan, Alta.

Sausage Loaf

1 lb. sausage meat
2 tbsp. parsley flakes
1 cup instant potato flakes
1 medium onion, chopped
1 egg

Combine above ingredients. Roll in dry bread crumbs. Place in loaf pan. Bake 1 hour at 350°F.

Knox St. Paul's United Church
Cornwall, Ont.

Country Sausage Casserole

1 lb. country sausage meat
3 cups cooked rice
1 onion, finely chopped
1 can condensed cream of tomato soup
2 tbsp. shredded cheddar cheese

Brown sausage and drain off fat. Arrange rice and meat in alternate layers in greased casserole. Sprinkle each layer with onion. Pour on undiluted soup. Top with shredded cheese. Cover and bake in moderate oven (350°F) for 30 minutes. Makes 4-6 servings.

Grace United Church
Hanover, Ont.

Sweet and Sour Sausage

1 lb. sausage, fried, drained and cut in half

Sauce:
 ¾ cup water
 ¾ cup brown sugar
 ¼ cup vinegar
 ¼ tsp. ginger
 ½ tsp. garlic salt or powder
 ½ tsp. curry powder
 ½ tsp. cloves
 2 tbsp. cornstarch
 1 tbsp. Worcestershire sauce
 2 tbsp. soya sauce
 1 onion, finely chopped

Cook sauce until thickened. Pour over sausage.

North Bedeque United Church
Summerisde, P.E.I.

Baked Sausages & Apples

1 pkg. (500 g) pork sausages
6 medium apples, peeled, cored and cut
 into ¼ inch slices
⅓ cup maple syrup

Sauté sausages in frying pan until lightly browned on all sides. Place apples in 9 inch square casserole dish. Arrange sausages in single layer on top of apples. Pour syrup evenly over all. Bake at 400°F for 10 minutes. Then reduce heat to 325°F and continue baking for 15 minutes longer.
Makes 6 servings.

College Hill United Church
Belleville, Ont.

Limas! Loisiana

½ lb. little pork sausages
2 cups cooked, dried lima beans
2 tbsp. chopped onion
1 tsp. sugar
¼ tsp. mace
1 tsp. salt
¼ tsp. poultry seasoning
1 cup milk
½ cup finely chopped green pepper
1 tbsp. butter or margarine

Parboil sausages for 5 minutes. Combine lima beans, sausages, onion, sugar, mace, salt and poultry seasoning and place in oiled baking dish. Pour milk over the top and scatter bits of butter or margarine and green pepper over the top. Bake at 350°F for 25 minutes. This is a one dish meal.

Linden Park Community United Church
Hamilton, Ont.

Vegetable-Meat Medley

1 lb. bulk pork sausage (or substitute
 ground beef and increase salt in meat
 mixture to ¾ tsp.)
¼ cup chopped onion
3 tbsp. all-purpose flour
1 - 16 oz. can tomatoes, cut up
1 - 8¾ oz. can whole kernel corn
1 - 8 oz. can cut green beans
1 cup sifted all-purpose flour
1½ tsp. baking powder
½ tsp. dry mustard
2 tbsp. shortening
⅔ cup milk
3 oz. (¾ cup) sharp cheese, shredded

Cook meat with onion until meat is brown and onion is tender, breaking up meat as it cooks. Drain off excess fat. Blend in 3 tablespoons flour, ¼ teaspoon salt and dash pepper. Stir in tomatoes and cook until slightly thickened. Drain corn and beans, add to meat mixture. Heat to boiling; spoon into 4 individual casseroles.

Meanwhile, sift together 1 cup flour, baking powder, ½ teaspoon salt and mustard. Cut in shortening, blend in milk and add ½ cup of the cheese to form soft dough. Drop biscuit dough onto boiling hot mixture. Sprinkle with remaining ¼ cup cheese. Bake uncovered at 350°F for 30 minutes until brown.
Serves 4.

Maple Grove United Church
Bowmanville, Ont.

Sausage, Broccoli, Sweet Potato Stir-Fry

1 lb. link sausage, cut into chunks
2-3 sweet potatoes
1 bunch broccoli
½ cup orange juice
Pinch cinnamon and nutmeg

Brown sausages in large frying pan. Cut potatoes French fry style and broccoli into bite-size pieces. Add to sausages, along with juice and seasonings. Cover and reduce heat and simmer about 20 minutes, stirring often.

United Church in Meadowood
Winnipeg, Man.

Stove Top Casserole

1 lb. pork sausages
1 large can tomatoes
1 small onion, chopped
2 tbsp. cornstarch, dissolved in cold water

Prick sausages with fork then sauté until well browned. Drain off all fat. Cut into bite-size pieces and place in frying pan. Cover with tomatoes, stir in onion and dissolved cornstarch. Bring to boil then simmer 10 minutes. Children love this casserole when weiners are used instead of sausages, but do not fry first.

Gibsons United Church
Gibsons, B.C.

Sausage Supper

1 lb. sausage links
5 medium potatoes, sliced
2 large onions, sliced
3 tbsp. chopped green pepper
1½ tsp. salt
⅛ tsp. pepper
1 tin tomato soup

Brown sausages and set aside. Add potatoes and brown. Place onions over potatoes, then sprinkle green onion on top. Season with salt and pepper. Lay sausages over vegetables and pour soup over all. Cook at 425°F for 25 minutes, until potatoes are done.

St. Giles United Church
Hamilton, Ont.

Sausage Casserole

1 lb. sausage, cut into 1 inch pieces
1 - 8 oz. can tomato sauce
½ cup brown sugar
Dash chili powder
½ tsp. onion salt
¼ tsp. salt and pepper
1 medium onion, sliced
1 medium apple, cut in thin wedges
1 - 19 oz. can kidney beans

Place sausage in casserole dish. Bake 15 minutes at 400°F. Drain off fat. To baked sausage add onion and apple. Place over meat in layers. Cover with kidney beans and tomato sauce. Combine brown sugar with seasoning and sprinkle over top. Bake at 350°F for 30-40 minutes. Remove cover for last 10 minutes. Use 2 L (quart) casserole.

St. James United Church
Upper Musquodoboit, N.S.

Favorite Supper Dish

2 cups cream style corn
1 egg, beaten
Salt to taste
Pepper to taste
2 cups cooked rice
1 tbsp. minced onion
1 tbsp. green pepper, finely chopped
Skinless sausage or bacon

Combine first 7 ingredients. Turn all mixture into greased casserole dish. Cover with sausages or bacon and bake at 400°F until sausages or bacon are brown. Very delicious for a Sunday supper.

Kirkfield Park United Church
Winnipeg, Man.

Ham and Weiners

Ham and Noodle Casserole

4 oz. broad egg noodles
½ cup milk
2 tsp. prepared mustard
2 cups chopped, cooked ham
1½ tbsp. melted butter
1 can cream of mushroom soup
1 tsp. minced onion
1 cup sour cream
½ cup bread crumbs
1 tbsp. grated Parmesan cheese

Grease a 1½ quart casserole. Add noodles to boiling water and boil for 3 minutes. Drain well and rinse with cold water and drain again. Combine soup and milk and stir until smooth. Add onions, mustard and sour cream and mix well. Place ½ noodles, ½ ham and ½ sauce in a 9x13 pan. Repeat and then combine crumbs and butter and spread on top. Add cheese. Bake at 350°F for approximately 20-25 minutes.

Linden Park Community United Church
Hamilton, Ont.

Spanish Skillet Dinner

½ cup raw rice
2 tbsp. shortening
1½ cup cubed cooked ham
½ cup chopped onion
½ cup chopped green pepper
¾ cup ketchup
1 can undrained green beans
¾ cup water
⅛ tsp. thyme
1 tsp. apple cider or salad vinegar

Lightly brown rice in shortening. Add ham, onion and green pepper and sauté until tender. Stir in remaining ingredients, cover and simmer, stirring occasionally until rice is tender. Serve as main dish.

Maple Grove United Church
Bowmanville, Ont.

Ham-Potato Bake Casserole

3-4 cooked potatoes, sliced
2 medium shredded carrots (1 cup)
1-2 cups fully cooked cubed ham
1 can cream of mushroom soup
1 cup shredded cheddar cheese
¼ cup milk
1 tablespoon chopped onion
1 cup soft bread crumbs
1 tablespoon melted margarine
⅛ tsp. pepper

Preheat oven to 350°F. Place half of the potatoes, half of the carrots in a 2-quart casserole dish. Combine ham, soup, half of the cheese, milk, onion and pepper. Pour half of this mixture over the potatoes. Repeat layers. Combine crumbs, remaining cheese and melted margarine. Sprinkle over the casserole. Bake until heated through (approximately 45 minutes). Can be prepared ahead and popped into oven.

Cameron United Church, Cameron, Ont
Trinity United Church, Hazlet, Sask.

Casserole Supper Dish From Leftover Meat

2 cups cubed ham, chicken or cold meat
½ cup chopped celery
¼ cup pimento (optional)
1 tbsp. onion
1 - 12 oz. can kernel corn or off the cob
1 cup bread crumbs
½ cup grated cheese

Sauce:
¼ cup butter or margarine, melted
3 tbsp. flour
1 cup broth or milk
2 eggs, well beaten

Melt butter and blend in flour. Gradually add milk. Cook and stir constantly. Add beaten eggs to cooked sauce. Mix meat, celery, pimento, onion and corn. Put into greased casserole, cover with sauce. Sprinkle crumbs and grated cheese over all. Bake 30 minutes or more in 350°F oven.

St. Andrew's United Church
Scotstown, Que.

Ham and Rice Casserole

1 cup rice, uncooked
3 cups diced ham
1 onion
1 can chinese vegetables
1 can mushroom soup
1 can pineapple chunks, drained and reserve juice
½ cup vinegar
3 tsp. dry mustard
3 tbsp. cornstarch
½ tsp. salt
1½ tbsp. soya sauce

Heat pineapple juice and vinegar. Add onion, vegetables, soup and pineapple. Combine dry ingredients and add to hot liquid. Stir until thickened and add soya sauce. Pour over rice and ham. Bake 45 minutes at 325°F.

St. David's United Church
Truro, N.S.

Bologna Cups

6 slices bologna
1 tin tomato soup
2 medium onions, diced
Salt, pepper, garlic salt and onion salt, to taste
½ soup can of water

Put bologna in deep pan. Put in oven on 350°F and cook for 15 minutes or until bologna curls. Turn bologna over. Mix remaining ingredients and pour over bologna. Put back in oven and cook for 15 minutes.

St Andrew's United Church
Norton, N.B.

Barbecued Weiners

2 tbsp. butter
1 onion, chopped
1 tsp. mustard
¼ cup vinegar
⅓ cup water
2 tbsp. sugar
⅔ cup sweet pickle
8 weiners

Mix all together, then add weiners and simmer.

Echo Bay United Church
Echo Bay, Ont.

Jiffy Delight

½ cup chopped onion
½ cup chopped green pepper
¼ cup chopped pimento
½ cup chopped, pitted ripe olives
¾ lb. slivered pressed ham*
1 cup Minute rice
1 cup water
1 - 12 oz. pkg. frozen peas
1½ cups grated cheddar cheese

Sauté onion, green pepper, and ham on medium-high. Add pimento, olives, rice, water and peas. Turn to high heat; when boiling turn to low heat. Cook 10 minutes. Add grated cheese and mix.
*Chicken may be used instead of ham.

St. Paul's United Church
Bancroft, Ont.

Zippy Franks

10 frankfurters
½ cup ketchup
½ cup corn flake crumbs

Place frankfurters in a greased baking pan. Pour enough ketchup to cover frankfurters. Spread enough corn flake crumbs to cover ketchup and frankfurters.
Gently turn over frankfurters and again cover with ketchup and corn flake crumbs. Bake in 200°C (400°F) oven about 12 minutes or until crisp and thoroughly heated. Serve withe additional ketchup if desired.
Yield: 5 servings.

Eastend United Church
Eastend, Sask.

Fancy Franks

4 or 6 slices bacon, cut in small pieces
¼ cup chopped onion
½ cup chopped green pepper
1 cup ketchup
1½ cups unsweetened pineapple juice
½ tsp. chili powder
Weiners, cut in bite-size pieces

Fry bacon, add onion, green pepper. Fry and add ketchup, pineapple juice and chili powder. Add weiners. Serve in hot dog buns.

St. Andrew's United Church
Wakefield, Que.

Ham and Green Bean Bake

(Good for using leftover ham)

1⅓ cups Minute rice
1 cup diced leftover ham
1 cup green beans
⅓ cup mayonnaise
2 tbsp. chopped onion
2 tbsp. diced olives
½ tsp. savory
Dash nutmeg
1⅓ cups hot chicken bouillon or chicken
  in a mug

Combine all ingredients in a 1½ quart casserole. Dot with butter. Bake at 400°F for 20 minutes. (You may use any leftover vegetables from table). Serve with green salad and buns or biscuits.

Battleford United Church
Battleford, Sask.

Skillet Franks

1 lb. weiners
1 cup diced onions
3 tbsp. butter
1 big can kernel corn
1 - 19 oz. can tomatoes
1 cup mashed potatoes (instant if you prefer)
Salt and pepper

Slice weiners into 1-inch pieces. Brown the weiners and onion in butter. Add the corn and tomatoes, salt and pepper. Place in casserole and top with mashed potatoes. Bake at 350°F for 45-60 minutes. Can be made the night before.

Zion United Church
Thessalon, Ont.

Pigs in Blankets

6 weiners, partially slit through lengthwise
Cheddar cheese
6 slices side bacon

Insert slivers of cheddar cheese in the lengthwise slits of weiners. Wrap each weiner with a slice of cheese and a piece of bacon. Fasten each end of bacon with a toothpick. Place on an oven-proof plate under oven broiler with cheese side down for 5 minutes. Turn and broil other side for 5 minutes. This recipe may also be used in a microwave - 1½ minutes each side.

Mt. Elgin United Church
Mt. Elgin, Ont.

Ham and Broccoli Noodle Casserole

1½ cups cooked noodles
1½ cups cooked ham
1 small onion, minced
1½ cups broccoli (partially cooked and drained)
1 - 10 oz. can cream of mushroom soup
1½ cups shredded sharp cheese
¼ cup milk
½ cup buttered crumbs

Grease casserole. Layer noodles, ham, onions and broccoli. Mix together soup, cheese and milk and spread over the broccoli. Bake at 375°F for 20 minutes.

Grace St. Andrew's United Church
Arnprior, Ont.

Saucy Dogs

1 lb. frankfurters, finely chopped
1 tbsp. onion, finely chopped
1 tsp. mild mustard
1 tsp. Worcestershire sauce
1 cup grated cheddar cheese
½ cup undiluted condensed tomato soup
¼ cup sweet relish
12 frankfurter buns

Preheat oven to 400°F. Combine all ingredients except the buns. Spoon ⅓ cup of the mixture between bun halves. Wrap each bun in aluminum foil. Heat 10-15 minutes. Serve hot.

Grenfell United Church
Grenfell, Sask.

Bacon and Potato Bake

½ lb. bacon
¾ lb. onions
1½ cups potatoes (sliced)
Salt and pepper
1 cup water or beef stock
1 tbsp. melted butter

Fry bacon slightly. Remove bacon and fry onions until soft. Arrange layers of potatoes, bacon and onions in a casserole - salting onion layers. End with layer of potatoes. Pour over liquid. Brush with melted butter and bake at 375°F for 45 minutes.

Carstairs United Church
Carstairs, Alta.

Fish & Seafood

Tuna Casseroles

Tuna Vegetable Pie

1½ cups sliced carrots
1½ cups cubed, pared potatoes
Milk
¼ cup butter or margarine
¼ cup chopped onion
2 tbsp. all-purpose flour
½ tsp. salt
Dash of pepper
¼ tsp. diced rosemary, crushed
1 stick pie crust mix
1 - 8 oz. can of peas, drained or frozen peas
2 - 6½ oz. cans tuna, drained and flaked

Cook carrots and potatoes in a small amount of water. Drain, reserving liquid. Add enough milk to make 2 cups. Melt butter in a saucepan. Add chopped onion. Cook until tender, but not brown. Blend in flour, salt, pepper, rosemary. Add milk mixture all at once. Cook stirring constantly, until mixture thickens and bubbles. Add carrots, potatoes, peas and tuna. Turn into a 13x9x1½ inch baking dish. Prepare 1 stick of pie crust mix according to directions. Cut into triangles or shapes and place on tuna mixture. Bake at 425°F for 30-35 minutes or until lightly browned.
Serves 6.
Variations: Sauce may be creamed soups. Vegetables - celery, green beans, broccoli instead of peas. Topping - tea biscuits or buttered crumbs or buttered slices of bread.
Columbus United Church, Columbus, Ont.
St. James United Church, Antigonish, N.S.
South Cayuga Pastoral Charge, Dunnville, Ont.

Tuna Noodle Casserole

1 tbsp. chopped onion
1 can mushroom soup, cream of chicken or cream of celery
1 - 7¾ oz. can tuna
⅓ cup milk
2 cups cooked noodles
1 tbsp. butter or margarine

Cook onions in butter, add soup, milk, then noodles and tuna. Place in casserole. Sprinkle top with corn flakes or crushed potato chips. Bake at 350°F for 30 minutes. 1 cup grated cheddar cheese and 1 cup cooked green peas may be added to mixture.
Knox United Church, Redvers, Sask.
Trinity United Church, Grimsby, Ont.
Happy Valley-Goose Bay United Church
Happy Valley-Goose Bay, Labrador
Maple Grove United Church, Bowmannville, Ont.
Almonte United Church, Almonte, Ont.

Quick Economy Casserole

1 - 15 oz. can cut green beans, drained
2 - 7 oz. cans solid pack tuna, drained and broken
1 cup shredded medium cheddar cheese
1 small onion, chopped
¼ cup butter
¼ cup flour
½ cup milk
½ cup bean juice or water
1 - 10 oz. can cream of celery soup
Dried or chopped parsley
Salt and pepper
Cereal or cracker crumbs

Mix beans, tuna and cheese in a greased 1½ quart casserole. In a skillet, sauté onion in butter until transparent. Stir in flour, then add milk and bean juice. Cook until thickened and add undiluted soup, parsley and season to taste. Pour over tuna mixture. Stir with a fork. Sprinkle with a few crumbs. Bake at 450°F, 15 to 20 minutes. Make ahead of time, then just put in oven. Can substitute different meat, vegetables and soup.
St. Paul's United Church
Ajax, Ont.
Serves 4 or 5.

Company Tuna Bake

1 - 3 oz. pkg. cream cheese
1 can condensed cream of mushroom soup
1 - 185 gr. can tuna, drained and flaked
1½ tbsp. chopped pimento (optional)
1 tbsp. chopped onion
1 tbsp. prepared mustard
¼ cup milk
1 cup 7 minute macaroni, cooked and
  drained
½ cup dry (medium) bread crumbs or
  crackers
2 tbsp. butter or margarine, melted

Cook macaroni and drain. Soften cream cheese, blend in soup (using electric or rotary beater). Stir in tuna, pimento, onion, mustard, milk and macaroni. Spoon into 1½ quart casserole. Mix crumbs and butter and sprinkle over top. Bake in moderate oven 375°F for 20-25 minutes. Garnish with pimento flowers and parsley.
Serves 4 or 5.

Moorefield United Church
Moorefield, Ont.

Captain's Casserole

1 - 10¼ oz. can condensed cream of
  mushroom soup
¼ to ⅓ cup finely chopped onion
1⅓ cups water
1 tsp. lemon juice
¼ tsp. salt
Dash of pepper
1⅓ cups (4⅝ g box) Minute rice
1½ cups cooked peas
1 - 7 oz. can tuna, drained and flaked
½ cup grated cheddar cheese
Paprika

Combine soup, onion, water, lemon juice, salt and pepper in a saucepan. Bring to a boil over medium heat, stirring occasionally. Pour half the soup mixture into a greased 1½ quart casserole. Then, in layers add Minute rice (right from the box), peas and tuna fish. Add remaining soup. Sprinkle with cheese and paprika. Cover and bake in moderate oven (375°F) for 15-20 minutes. Cut through mixture with knife or fork after 10 minutes of baking to help distribute soup mixture.
Makes 4 servings.
For 8 servings double all ingredients.

St. Andrew's United Church
Scotstown, Que.

Mardi Gras Dinner

3 tbsp. flour
Pepper
¼ tsp. salt
¼ cup melted butter
1 large tin evaporated milk
1 cup shredded cheddar cheese
1⅓ cups Minute rice
Parsley
Dash of cayenne
½ tsp. oregano
1⅓ cups water (use juice from canned
  tomatoes)
1 - 28 oz. can tomatoes, drained
½ onion, thinly sliced
1 or 2 cans tuna fish, drained and flaked
Paprika

Mix together flour, pepper, salt, butter, evaporated milk and cheese. Cook and stir until thick. Place rice, parsley, oregano, cayenne, juice from tomatoes and water to make 1⅓ cups and ½ teaspoon salt in an 8x1'' baking dish and stir well. Place on top ⅔ of the canned tomatoes (that have been strained), onion and tuna fish. Spread cheese sauce on top. Add remaining tomatoes. Sprinkle with paprika. Bake at 350°F for ½ hour. If regular rice is used add only half the juice from the tomatoes.
Serves 6.

Trinity United Church
Iroquois Falls, Ont.

Tuna Casserole

1 - 12½-13 oz. can tuna, packed in water
2 large celery stalks
1 green onion
1½ cups shredded cheddar cheese
¾ cup mayonnaise
1 tbsp. lemon juice
2 cups croutons
Celery leaves for garnish

About 1 hour before serving: drain tuna, separate into large chunks. Chop celery and onion. Preheat oven to 350°F. In large bowl mix celery, onion, cheddar cheese, mayonnaise, lemon juice and 1 cup croutons. Stir in tuna gently. Spoon mixture into 2-quart casserole. Top with remaining croutons. Bake uncovered 35 to 40 minutes until hot and bubbly. Garnish with celery leaves.
Serves 6.

St. Paul's United Church
Ormstown, Que.

Quick Holiday Casserole

1 pkg. Stove Top stuffing mix
1 small can flaked tuna
1 can cream or mushroom or celery soup
½ cup grated medium cheese
1 cup bread crumbs or soda biscuits

Prepare Stove Top stuffing mix as directed on package. Put stuffing in bottom of casserole. Mix tuna with creamed soup and put on top of stuffing. Top with grated cheese and bread crumbs. Bake at 375°F for ½ hour.

St. John United Church
Hamilton, Ont.

Salmon

Tuna & Salmon Puff

6 slices stale bread, buttered and cubed
2 eggs
½ tsp. Worcestershire sauce
½ pint (1¼ cups) milk
½ cup finely grated cheee
1 cup flaked, cooked or canned fish
Salt and pepper to taste
Dash of cayenne pepper

In a greased baking dish, place layers of bread cubes, cheese, fish alternately ending with bread cubes. Beat eggs, add milk, sauce and seasonings. Pour over contents of dish. Bake at 325°F for approximately 1 hour. Serves 6.

Greenwood United Church
Greenwood, Ont.

Salmon-Potato Bake

2 cups cold, mashed potatoes
1 half tin salmon
2 tbsp. shortening, melted
2 eggs, lightly beaten
1 cup milk or cream
Salt to taste

Blend mashed potates with salmon and shortening. Add eggs, milk and salt. Beat all together. Pour into deep dish. Bake in quick oven until lightly browned. Serve hot.

Grace United Church
Hanover, Ont.

Salmon Scallop

1 small can salmon
½ can peas
4 medium potatoes, sliced
2 tbsp. flour
2 tbsp. butter
1½ cups milk
½ onion
Salt and pepper to taste

Prepare milk sauce - melt butter and flour, gradually stir in milk. Line casserole with sliced potatoes. Add a little sauce, onion, salt and pepper, layer of salmon, layer of peas. Pour remaining sauce over all. More milk may be added. Bake at 350°F for 1 hour.

Embro Knox United Church
Embro, Ont.

Salmon Newburg

1 can condensed cream of shrimp soup
1½ cups milk
1 tbsp. Worcestershire sauce
1 - 7 oz. can salmon, drained and flaked
3 cups cooked rice
1 - 10 oz. pkg. frozen peas, cooked and drained

Combine soup, milk and Worcestershire sauce in large saucepan. Heat slowly, stirring often until bubbly. Fold in salmon and rice. Spoon into 6 cup shallow casserole. Bake at 350°F for 20 minutes or until bubbly hot. Spoon cooked peas around edge of dish.

Camlachie United Church
Camlachie, Ont.

Salmon & Corn Casserole

2 eggs
1 - 12 oz. can whole kernel corn
½ cup half and half cream
1 - 7½ oz. can salmon
⅛ tsp. pepper
¾ cup shredded cheese
1 tsp. instant minced onion

Beat eggs in medium bowl. Add remaining ingredients, except cheese. Mix well. Pour into a greased 1½ quart casserole. Sprinkle with cheese. Bake in preheated 350°F oven for 45-50 minutes.

High Bluff United Church
High Bluff, Man.

Salmon or Chicken Delight

⅓ cup butter or margarine
½ cup finely chopped onion
⅓ cup flour
½ tsp. salt
Dash of pepper
1½ cups milk
¼ cup cheese
1 - 7½ oz. can salmon or
   1 cup cut up chicken
½ cup tomato ketchup
½ tsp. Worcestershire sauce

Melt butter in saucepan. Add onion and cook until tender. Blend in flour, salt and pepper. Slowly stir in milk. Cook until thickened and stir in cheese, salmon, ketchup and Worcestershire sauce. Pour into buttered 2-quart casserole dish.

Topping:
1¾ cups flour
4 tsp. baking powder
1 tsp. salt
⅓ cup butter
1¼ to 1½ cups milk

Combine flour, baking powder, salt and butter. Add milk. Stir to make a drop batter. Drop by large spoonsful around the edge of the casserole. Bake in preheated oven at 450°F for 35-45 minutes with lid on dish. Uncover and bake for 10-15 minutes more. Casserole dish may be lined with pastry. Trinity United Church
Grand Centre, Alta.

Salmon Supper Casserole

1½ cups elbow macaroni
1 can condensed cream of celery soup
½ cup milk
1½ cups grated old cheddar cheese
1 lb. canned salmon (pink or combination pink and red)

Cook macaroni until tender in plenty of boiling salted water. Drain. Carefully blend in milk into cream of celery soup. Stir 1 cup of grated cheese into the soup mixture. Drain and mash canned salmon. Stir salmon and drained macaroni into celery sauce. Turn into oven dish, arrange remaining cheese as a border on top. Bake in 350°F oven for 30 minutes. Very tasty. Serves 5. Rexdale United Church
Rexdale, Ont.

Celery Salmon Souffle

1 small onion, chopped
1 - 10 oz. can cream of celery soup
1 lb. tin pink salmon, drained and broken into pieces
1 tbsp. butter or margarine
4 eggs, separated
1 tbsp. lemon juice

Cook onion in butter over low heat for 5 minutes. Stir in soup and remove from heat. Lemon juice may be added to the salmon. Add salmon to mixture. Beat egg yolks slightly and add to mixture. Beat egg whites until stiff, but not dry. Fold into mixture gently. Pour into a greased 1½-quart casserole. Bake at 350°F for 1 hour or until souffle is golden brown. Serve immediately.
Serves 6.
Trinity United Church, Ottawa, Ont.
St. Paul's United Church, Souris, Man.

Salmon Loaf

1 can (1 lb.) salmon
1 egg, slightly beaten
¾ cup soft bread crumbs
¼ cup undiluted evaporated milk
½ cup chopped celery
½ cup chopped onion
¼ tsp. salt
2 tsp. lemon juice
Parsley and lemon wedges

Flake salmon in a large bowl. Add remaining ingredients (except parsley and lemon wedges). Mix thoroughly. Put into loaf pan and bake in 325°F oven 20 to 25 minutes. Before serving garnish loaf with parsley sprigs and lemon wedges.
Variation: Use 3 eggs instead of 1 and 1 cup of milk instead of ¼ cup evaporated milk. Omit lemon juice and onion and add ½ cup grated cheese.
St. Andrew's United Church, Beaverton, Ont.
Grace United Church, Gananoque, Ont.
Pinedale United Church, Sunderland, Ont.
Beverley Hills United Church, Downsview, Ont.

Shellfish and Fish Fillets

Seafood Casserole

2 lbs. one or several of the following:
  scallops, lobster, haddock, crab, shrimp
  and cod
2 chicken bouillon cubes
6 tbsp. butter
6 tbsp. flour
1 cup cereal cream
2 egg yolks
1 cup or ¼ lb. cheddar cheese, grated
1 cup or 4 oz. mushrooms, sliced
1 tbsp. butter
⅛ tsp. Worcestershire sauce
Pinch cayenne pepper
3 cups bread cubes (½x½-inch)
2 tbsp. butter, melted

Cut all fish into bite-size pieces. Bring 2 cups of water to boil. Add raw fish and simmer 3 or 4 minutes. Reserve fish and dissolve chicken bouillon cubes in cooking liquid. Pour into a 2 cup measure, including any liquid from canned shellfish. Heat butter in top half of a double boiler. Stir in flour and cook several minutes. Gradually beat in the 2 cups of hot liquid. Continue to stir and cook until sauce thickens. Add cheddar cheese, cook and stir until well blended. Remove from heat, combine egg yolks and cream. Beat with a fork and add slowly to the sauce while stirring. Wash and slice mushrooms and cook in 1 tablespoon butter. Add mushrooms, Worcestershire sauce cayenne pepper and shellfish to the sauce. Taste sauce and salt if necessary. Pour mixture into 1½-quart slightly greased casserole. Toss bread cubes in melted butter and sprinkle over top. Bake until bread cubes are brown. Bake at 450°F for 35 minutes.
Serves 8.

St. John's United Church
Wallace, N.S.

Seafood Supreme

1 cup crushed rice cereal
2 tbsp. margarine
⅓ cup flour
½ pint light cereal cream
1¾ cups milk
2 - 4½ oz. tins shrimp
1 - 2½ oz. can lobster
1 - 4½ oz. can crab meat
⅓ cup butter
2 cups sliced mushrooms
¼ cup chopped onion

Melt rice cereal and 2 tablespoons margarine for topping. Melt ⅓ cup butter and sauté onions and mushrooms. Add flour and remove from stove. Add milk and cream gradually and return to stove stirring until thickened. Add seafood and mix well. Pour into greased casserole, cover with cereal topping and bake at 375°F for 30 minutes.

Birtle United Church
Birtle, Man.

Blessed is she who opens the door to welcome both stranger and well-loved friend. For gracious hospitality is a test of brothery love.

Seafood Creole

2 tbsp. margarine
1 onion, diced
½ green pepper, diced
½ stalk celery, diced
1½ tbsp. flour
1 - 19 oz. can tomatoes
Garlic salt to taste
Bay leaves
½ tsp. thyme
Worcestershire sauce to taste
1 can chunk style tuna
1 can crab meat
1 can shrimp

Melt margarine in saucepan. Cook onion, celery and pepper until tender. Add flour, tomatoes, garlic salt, bay leaves, thyme and Worcestershire sauce. Simmer 15 minutes. Add tuna, crab meat and shrimp. Simmer another 15 minutes. Serves 6.

St. James United Church
Upper Musquodoboit, N.S.

V8 Seafood Casserole

1 cup V8 juice
1 cup mayonnaise
1 can crab meat
1 can shrimp
2 cups cooked rice
1/3 cup chopped green pepper
Salt and pepper

Combine all ingredients in a casserole. Sprinkle top with buttered crumbs and toasted almonds. Bake 1/2 hour at 350°F.
Serves 4 generously.

Crescent Fort Rouge United Church
Winnipeg, Man.

Scallops and Linguine in Spicy Tomato Sauce

1 tbsp. vegetable oil
1 small red onion, coarsely chopped
1 small yellow squash or
     zucchini, cut in 1/2-inch cubes
1/8 to 1/4 tsp. red pepper flakes
12 oz. linguine or spaghetti
1 lb. scallops or medium sized shrimp,
     shelled and deveined
1 can whole tomatoes in tomato purée
2 tsp. red wine vinegar or cider vinegar
1 tbsp. brown sugar
2 tsp. grated orange rind

Heat oil in a deep 12 inch skillet over moderate heat for 1 minute. Add onion, squash and pepper flakes. Cover and cook, stirring occasionally for 5 minutes or until almost soft. Meanwhile cook linguine according to package directions. Add scallops to skillet and cook, uncovered, until opaque 1 to 2 minutes. Mix in tomatoes with their purée, breaking them up with a spoon. Add sugar, vinegar and orange rind. Heat just until the sauce simmers - 2 minutes - turn off heat.
Drain linguine, transfer it to a serving dish. Bring sauce to serving temperature over low heat, then ladle over the linguine.
Serves 6.
For a poultry recipe, use 1 pound chicken or turkey cutlets, cut into thin strips.

St. James United Church
Upper Musquodoboit, N.S.

Curried Scallops
(Microwave)

1 tbsp. butter or margarine
1 lb. scallops, rinsed and drained
1/4 cup sliced green onions
1 1/2 tsp. cornstarch
1/2 tsp. curry powder
1/4 tsp. salt

Place butter in 9-inch glass pie plate, heat in microwave on HIGH for 20 seconds or until melted. Add scallops and onions. Cover with plastic wrap. Cook covered on HIGH for 2 1/2 to 3 1/2 minutes or until scallops are almost opaque. Stir halfway through cooking time. Reserve 2 tablespoons of liquid.
Combine cornstarch, curry powder and salt with the 2 tablespoons of reserved liquid. Stir into scallops. Cover wth plastic wrap. Cook covered on HIGH for 2 minutes or until sauce is thickened and smooth. Scallops should be opaque. Serve with rice and salad.
Yield: 4 servings.

St. Paul's United Church
Fairview, Alta.

Seafood Salad Casserole

1 cup celery
1/4 cup onion
1/4 cup green pepper
1 can mushrooms
1 can tuna
1 can shrimp
1 can crab
1 cup mayonnaise
3 tbsp. flour
3 tbsp. butter
1/4 tsp. salt
1 tsp. Worcestershire sauce or lemon juice
1 1/2 cups milk
Dash of cayenne pepper
1 cup buttered crumbs

Cook vegetables slowly for approximately 20 minutes in 1/8 pound butter. Make a white sauce of the flour, butter, salt, milk and lemon juice. Add the fish, vegetables and mayonnaise. Cover with buttered crumbs and bake at 350°F for 30-35 minutes. Serve over rice.
Note: A tin of cream of mushroom or chicken soup can be used to replace the white sauce. If this is done reduce the mayonnaise to 1/2 cup.

Knox United Church, Redvers, Sask.
St. Vital United Church, Winnipeg, Man.

Linguine with Clam Sauce

¾ lb. linguine
4 tbsp. butter
1 small onion, chopped
2 cloves garlic, minced
Salt and pepper
⅓ cup dry white wine
⅓ cup clam nectar or chicken broth
1 cup whipping cream
1 - 10 oz. tin baby clams
3 tbsp. fresh parsley, chopped

Cook linguine in boiling water. Melt butter and add onion and garlic. Cook until softened but not brown. Add wine, nectar and cream. Simmer 10 minutes or until thickened. Rinse clams and add along with parsley. Heat through. Serve over linguine.

Eastend United Church
Eastend, Sask.

Curried Shrimp au Gratin

1 lb. cooked shrimp
3 tbsp. butter or margarine
⅓ cup minced celery
⅓ cup chopped onion
3 tbsp. flour
1 tsp. salt
2 tsp. curry powder
¼ tsp. ginger
2 cups milk
2 tbsp. lemon juice
3 cups cooked rice
1 cup grated cheese

Melt butter, sauté onion and celery, stirring occasionally until tender. Stir in flour and seasonings. Stir in milk gradually and continually, stir while heating to boiling. Stir in shrimp, lemon juice and half the cheese. Butter one large or six individual casserole dishes. Cover bottom with cooked rice, pour in shrimp mixture, sprinkle with remaining cheese over top. Bake on top shelf of oven at 375°F for 20 minutes or until mixture is heated and cheese is melted. Serves 6.

Carol United Church
Labrador City, Nfld.

Crab Fettucine

6-8 oz. frozen crab meat
2 cloves garlic, minced
½ cup chopped green onion
¼ cup olive oil
½ cup chopped ripe olives
2 tbsp. chopped sweet red pepper
¼ cup minced parsley
½ cup chopped walnuts
2 tsp. lemon juice
½ tsp. salt
⅛ tsp. freshly ground pepper
½ tsp. each basil and oregano
8 oz. fettucine, cooked and drained
Grated Parmesan cheese

Thaw, drain and slice crab. Sauté garlic and onion in oil. Add crab, olives, pimento, parsley, walnuts, lemon juice and seasonings; heat thoroughly. Toss crab sauce with hot fettucine. Serve with Parmesan cheese.

Ashton United Church
Ashton, Ont.

Cod au Gratin

Boil cod and flake it. (Make sure bones are all out, and use only fresh or frozen cod, not salted). Quantity needed is 2 to 2½ cups cooked.

White Sauce:
4 tbsp. butter
3 tbsp. flour
1 tsp. salt
½ tsp. pepper
2 cups milk
1 cup grated old cheese

Melt butter, add flour, salt and pepper. Make a paste, add milk gradually and stir constantly until thickened. Grease casserole dish. Pour a little of the sauce on the bottom. Layer cooked flaked cod, sauce, and cheese as many times as desired, ending with the cheese on top. Bake at 350°F for half an hour without cover, until brown.

Salisbury United Church, Salisbury, N.B.
Port de Grave United Church, Port de Grave, Nfld.

Baked Fish au Gratin

1 lb. fish fillets
1 can cream of celery or cream of mushroom
** soup**
½ cup shredded mild cheese
Dash black pepper

Place fillets in lightly greased shallow baking dish. Combine soup and cheese with pepper and pour over fish. Bake at 375°F for about 45 minutes.   Westminster United Church,Whitby, Ont.
St. Paul's United Church, Ormstown, Que.
Ontario St. United Church, Clinton, Ont.

Cod Fish with Grapefruit

1 lb. cod fillets
1 large grapefruit
3 tbsp. butter
½ tsp. salt
⅛ tsp. pepper
¼ tsp. paprika

Preheat oven to 375°F. Arrange cod fillets in shallow baking dish. Pare and section grapefruit, reserving 4 tablespoons juice. Set sections aside. Combine juice and melted butter. Pour over fish. Sprinkle with salt, pepper and ⅛ teaspoon paprika. Bake 30 minutes. Place grapefruit sections on top of fillets and bake an additional 15 minutes. Garnish with parsley.

Hant's Harbour United Church
Trinity Bay, Nfld.

Lobster Casserole

White Sauce:
** ½ cup flour**
** 2½ cups milk**
** ½ cup butter, melted**

Cook white sauce in a double boiler until thick.

Add:
** 1 can lobster cold pack**
** 1 can mushrooms**
** 3 hard boiled eggs, sliced**
** Chopped green pepper to taste**

Top with buttered bread crumbs. Bake at 350°F for 20-30 minutes.

North Bedeque United Church
Summerside, P.E.I.

Shrimp Linguine

½ lb. linguine
1 cup (more or less) shrimp, fresh or canned
½ cup butter or margarine
4 cloves garlic, minced
½ cup mushrooms
¼ cup Romano cheese
Salt and pepper to taste

Cook linguine until al dente. Drain, rinse in cold water and set aside. Dice or cut shrimp in half, depending on preference. Melt butter or margarine in large skillet and add shrimp and garlic. Slice or dice mushrooms, add to pan and cook slowly, about 5 minutes. (If using precooked shrimp, add to mushrooms and garlic for last minute of cooking time.) Add linguine to skillet; sprinkle with cheese, salt and pepper. Toss until linguine is heated through. Turn on to a warm serving platter and garnish with extra cheese, if desired. Serves 4.

Trinity United Church
Nanaimo, B.C.

Fish Casserole

1 lb. fish fillets, one or several varieties
1 chicken bouillon cube
3 tbsp. butter
3 tbsp. flour
½ cup cereal cream
1 egg yolk
½ cup grated cheese
½ cup sliced mushrooms, cooked in
** 1 tbsp. butter**
Dash of Worcestershire sauce
Pinch of pepper

Bring 1½ cups of water to boil. Add fish, simmer 3-4 minutes. Remove fish, dissolve bouillon cube in liquid. Heat butter, add flour and cook. Gradually beat in 1 cup of hot liquid. Continue to stir, cook until it thickens. Add grated cheese. Remove from heat, combine egg yolk and cream. Add slowly to sauce. Add cooked mushrooms, salt and pepper. Mix with fish. Toss 1½ cups bread cubes in 1 tablespoon butter. Sprinkle over top. Bake about 15 minutes.

Portland United Church
Saint John, N.B.

Cod Fish Cakes

1 lb. salt cod fish (freshened) - yield about
  2 cups
3 cups mashed potatoes (may be leftover
  from previous day)
1 medium onion, finely grated
⅛ tsp. pepper
1 egg, beaten

Blend well and form into balls and flatten like
a hamburger. Fry over moderate heat in about
3 tablespoons oil until browned on both sides.
Serve with chutney or chili sauce and salad.
Yield: 12 fish cakes.
  Note: To freshen boneless salt cod, soak overnight in cold water to cover. Drain. Add fresh
water and slowly bring to simmer. Drain and
repeat if fish is still too salty. To cook, simmer
until fish flakes easily. If fish and potatoes are
cooked, it only takes 15-20 minutes to have these
on the table.

Trinity United Church
Hopewell Hill, N.B.

Sweet and Sour Fish

4 cod fillets, about 150 g (5 oz.) each
1 tbsp. soy sauce
2 tbsp. lemon juice
2 tsp. white wine vinegar
1 tbsp. clear honey
2 level tsp. tomato ketchup
1 clove garlic, crushed
¼ level tsp. paprika
Oil
1 red pepper, cut in strips
4 oz. (125 g) mushrooms, sliced
4 oz. (125 g) spring onions, sliced
4 oz. (125 g) frozen green beans
Black pepper

Divide each piece of fish in half. Roll up with
skinned side inside. Mix together next seven ingredients. Place in large skillet. Add fish and
baste with sauce. Bring to gentle simmer. Cover
and cook for 10-12 minutes. Meanwhile heat a
little oil in another skillet and stir-fry vegetables
for 3-4 minutes until just tender. Season well
with black pepper. Spoon sauce over fish and
accompany with vegetables. (Not suitable for
freezing). Cooking Time - 15 minutes.
Serves 4.

St. Andrew's United Church
Halifax, N.S.

Baked Fish Fillets

2 lbs. sole, salmon steaks, whitefish or
  any favourite
Salt and pepper
1 cup sour cream or plain yogurt
½ cup mayonnaise
4 tbsp. lemon juice
4 tbsp. flour
½ tsp. dried dill weed (1 tsp. if fresh)
Paprika

Cut fish into serving-sized pieces and arrange
in single layer in 9x13'' baking dish. Sprinkle
lightly with salt and pepper. In a bowl, combine the next 5 ingredients. Stir until smooth and
well blended. Spread over fish. Cover and bake
at 400°F for 20-25 minutes or until flesh is
opaque and flakes. Sprinkle with paprika. Serve
with rice, spinach salad and bread sticks.
Serves 6.

Bruce Mines United Church
Bruce Mines, Ont.

Baked Stuffed Salmon

1 salmon (5-8 lbs.)
2 tsp. salt
3 tbsp. lemon juice
⅓ cup margarine
1 medium onion, chopped
½ cup chopped celery
½ cup grated carrot
2 cups bread crumbs
1 tsp. savory
½ tsp. salt
¼ tsp. pepper
1 egg
Vegetable oil for basting

Wash fish and remove scales and fins. Combine salt and lemon juice. Rub the clean salmon
inside and out with mixture. Stuffing - melt butter, add onion and celery, cook until soft. Combine with bread crumbs, carrot, savory, salt and
pepper. Add beaten egg and mix well. Stuff
salmon with this mixture and skewer closed.
Brush salmon with oil and place on greased baking sheet. Bake at 425°F, allow 10 minutes per
inch of fish thickness (1-1 ½ hours). Baste with
oil during baking.
  (You may use arctic char or trout instead of
salmon). Instead of oven cooking, you could
wrap your fish in greased foil and put on your
barbecue.
Approximately 8 servings.

Clarke's Beach United Church Women
Clarke's Beach, Nfld.

Healthy Low-Cal Supper in 45 Minutes

1 lb. fish fillets or scallops
1 envelope Shake & Bake, barbecue flavor

Wash fish or scallops. Dry on paper towels. Oil cookie sheet. Cut fish in 1-inch pieces. Coat with shake and bake and place on cookie sheet. Bake at 350°F for 30 minutes. Serve with baked potatoes (scrubbed and microwaved). Add tossed salad of choice and fresh fruit dessert.

Kirk Memorial United Church
Aspen, N.S.

Fish Lasagna

1½ lbs. fish fillets
Dot of butter
¼ cup onion
⅓ cup green pepper
1 - 5½ oz. can tomato paste
1 - 19 oz. can tomato sauce or soup
½ tsp. each basil, pepper
Salt to taste

Preheat oven to 350°F. Place fish in casserole dish. Top with mixture of other ingredients. Bake at 350°F for 30 minutes until fish is flaky and top brown.

Heartz Memorial United Church
Weymouth, N.S.

Salmon Supper

2 lbs. salmon fillets, thawed
1 large onion, in rings
1 large green pepper, sliced
2 fresh tomatoes, sliced
1 lemon, sliced
3 strips side bacon

Place salmon on a sheet of foil on a cookie sheet. Put on the top a layer of onions, green pepper, tomato and lemon. Place the strips of side bacon over top. Fold up foil at top. Leave a small opening to let the steam out. Bake at 375°F (190°C) oven for 1 hour. Serve with rice and a green salad.
Serves 4-6.

Trinity United Church
Cobourg, Sask.

New Brunswick Lobster à la Mornay

2 cups hot mashed potatoes
2 tbsp. butter
2 tbsp. flour
1 cup milk
Salt and pepper
½ cup grated cheddar cheese
1 egg yolk
1 cup lobster meat
½ cup buttered crumbs

Place mashed potatoes in a greased casserole. Make sauce with butter, flour, milk and pepper. Remove from heat and add grated cheese and beaten egg yolk. Pour half the sauce over potatoes. Add flaked lobster. Pour remaining sauce over and top with crumbs. Bake in 350°F oven for 20-25 minutes until thoroughly heated and nicely browned.

Wilmot United Church
Fredericton, N.B.

Oriental Fish (Salmon Steaks)

¼ cup margarine or butter
2 tbsp. grated ginger root
2 clvoes garlic, minced
¼ cup lime juice
1 tbsp. soy sauce
1 tsp. Dijon mustard
1 tsp. sesame oil (optional)
1 tsp. brown sugar
Dash cayenne
4 salmon steaks or fish fillets of your choice

Heat skillet, add margarine. Saute ginger and garlic until golden. Stir in remaining ingredients. Place fish fillets/salmon steaks in baking dish. Pour sauce over fillets. Cover with foil. Bake 425°F oven for 10-12 minutes per inch. Serves 4.

Alternate: Microwave oven - cover dish with waxed paper or plastic wrap. Bake 6-8 minutes on HIGH or until flakes easily.

Brechin United Church
Nanaimo, B.C.

Pasta, Rice & Vegetables

Microwave Macaroni and Cheese

½ lb. macaroni
2 cups hot water
3 tbsp. margarine or butter
¼ cup finely chopped onion
¼ tsp. salt
¼ tsp. pepper
2¼ cups milk
12 oz. cheese, cubed (3 cups)
⅓ cup flour

Combine macaroni, water, butter, onion, salt and pepper in 2-quart casserole. Cover. Cook at full power in microwave 6 minutes, then half power (level 5) for 5 minutes. Stir twice during cooking. Drain. Stir in remaining ingredients. Cover. Microwave on HIGH for 12-15 minutes until sauce is thickened and bubbly, stirring every 3 minutes.
Serves 4.

Trinity United Church
Grimsby, Ont.

Macaroni & Cheese

1 cup broken macaroni
2 qts. boiling water
1 tbsp. salt
3 tbsp. margarine or fat
3 tbsp. flour
¼ tsp. dry mustard
¾ tsp. salt
Dash pepper
2 cups hot milk
1 tbsp. chopped onion
2 cups grated cheddar
½ cup bread crumbs

Cook macaroni in boiling, salted water until tender. Drain and rinse. Blend margarine or fat and flour in saucepan. Let bubble 3 minutes. Add seasonings, hot milk and onion. Add grated cheese. Stir until melted. Mix sauce and macaroni, turn into well oiled 1½-quart casserole. Top with crumbs. Bake at 400°F till brown, approximately 20 minutes.
Serves 4.

McClure United Church
Winnipeg, Man.

Macaroni-Cheese Custard

½ lb. elbow macaroni, cooked and drained
2 cups milk
2 eggs, slightly beaten
2 cups shredded medium or old cheddar cheese
Salt and pepper to taste
½ tsp. dry mustard
⅔ cup buttered bread crumbs

Mix together all ingredients except crumbs and spread in a well greased 1½-quart baking dish. Sprinkle with crumbs and set in a pan of hot water. Bake at 350°F for 35-50 minutes or until set. Length of baking time depends on depth of mixture. Serve with your favorite chili sauce and a tossed salad.
Serves 8.

Camlachie United Church
Camlachie, Ont.

Spaghetti Cheese Casserole

1-1½ lbs. spaghetti - 2" pieces
Sliced onion
⅓ lb. butter
2 tbsp. flour
2 cups milk or more
Salt and pepper
1 tsp. dry mustard
1 or 2 12" wedges med. cheese

Cook spaghetti with sliced onion. Meanwhile, make sauce of butter, flour, milk, salt, pepper, mustard and cheese. Stir until melted. Add more cheese if desired. Layer spaghetti and sauce. Top with seasoned bread crumbs and bits of butter. Bake at 350°F for ½ hour. Top with cooked bacon bits just before serving.

Grace United Church
Niagara-on-the-Lake, Ont.

Pat's Macaroni & Tomato Supper Dish

1 tbsp. butter or margarine
½ cup chopped onions
1½ cups uncooked macaroni
1 cup finely cubed cheese (or grated)
1 - 19 oz. can tomatoes
1 cup water
1 tsp. salt

In microwave, cook onions in margarine in 2-quart casserole for approximately 1 minute. Stir all ingredients together. Bake in 350°F oven for 1 hour covered.

Foote Copeland United Church
Dafoe, Sask.

Rotini alla Sialiana

2 zucchini, sliced ¼" thick
1 green pepper, chopped
1 lge. onion, chopped
1½ cups canned tomatoes, drained or fresh tomatoes
¼ cup tomato juice
3 cups uncooked Rotini pasta (spiral shaped)
½ lb. mozzarella cheese, in small dices

Heat some oil in a large pot. Add zucchini, peppers, onions and garlic to taste. Saute a few minutes. Add tomatoes (drained and cut in pieces), juice, salt, pepper and basil to taste. Meanwhile, cook Rotini according to package instructions. Drain. Add to vegetables. Add mozzarella cheese and mix gently. Serve at once.

United Church in Meadowood
Winnipeg, Man.

Ken's Pesto

Pesto:
1 cup fresh basil, tightly packed
½ cup olive oil
⅓ cup pine nuts
¼ cup parsley, fresh
2 cloves garlic
1 tsp. salt
½ cup Parmesan cheese

Place all ingredients in blender. Cook pasta of choosing as directed on package. Mix pesto and pasta together. Serve with a salad.

United Church in Meadowood
Winnipeg, Man.

Vegetable Noodle Casserole

3 cups medium egg noodles
2 tbsp. butter or margarine
2 med. carrots, chopped
1 med. onion, chopped
½ cup chopped celery
½ tsp. dried basil leaves
1 can cut green beans, drained
½ cup milk
1½ cups shredded cheddar cheese
¼ tsp. salt
¼ tsp. pepper
2 tbsp. fine dried bread crumbs
2 tbsp. grated Parmesan cheese

Cook noodles according to package directions. Drain. Meanwhile, in frying pan, melt 1 tablespoon butter over medium heat. Saute carrots, onions and celery with basil until tender, about 3 minutes. Stir in noodles, green beans, milk, cheddar, salt and pepper. Pour into a greased 1½-quart casserole. Combine bread crumbs, Parmesan cheese and 1 tablespoon butter, melted. Sprinkle over casserole. Bake at 350°F for 20 to 30 minutes until golden.

Zion Evangelical United Church
Pembroke, Ont.

Tasty Rice and Egg Casserole

1 cup white rice
1 tsp. salt
2 cups boiling water
1 can vegetable soup
1½ cups milk
Dash pepper
Sliced hard-boiled eggs
Grated cheese

Cook rice and salt in boiling water over low heat for approximately 14 minutes. Add 1 can vegetable soup, milk and dash of pepper. Layer this mixture with sliced hard-boiled eggs in a greased baking dish. Top with grated cheese. Bake in moderate oven for ½ hour or until cheese is melted.

Heartz Memorial United Church
Weymouth, N.S.

Presbytery Office Pasta

Pasta for 4 (spaghetti, linguini, etc.)
1 can cream of mushroom soup
½ soup can of milk
⅓ cup grated Parmesan cheese
½ tsp. Italian seasoning
½ tsp. Mrs. Dash
1 cup chopped fresh tomatoes and green
  onions

Cook the pasta al dente. Combine soup, milk, cheese and seasoning. Microwave 5 minutes - MEDIUM power. Transfer pasta to serving platter. Pour sauce over pasta. Garnish with tomato/onion mixture.

Winnipeg Presbytery
Winnipeg, Man.

Baked Bean Casserole

2 lbs. tin pork and beans
½ cup maple syrup
¾ tsp. dry mustard
2 tbsp. ketchup

Mix above in casserole. Bake at 400°F for 40-50 minutes.
Serves 8.

Charleswood United Church
Winnipeg, Man.

Scalloped Corn Crisp

1¾ cups (15 oz.) cream style corn
2 tbsp. finely chopped onion
2 tbsp. finely chopped green pepper
1 cup coarsely broken cracker crumbs
⅓ cup (small can) undiluted evaporated milk
¼ tsp. salt
⅛ tsp. pepper
2 tbsp. butter

Mix corn, onion and green pepper in bowl. Place half mixture in bottom of buttered casserole. Sprinkle half the cracker crumbs over corn. Add remaining corn mixture. Top with cracker crumbs. Mix milk and seasonings. Pour over top. Place pieces of butter on top and bake in moderate oven (350°F) for about 30 minutes. Serve at once with ham slices or crisp bacon slices.

Westmount Park United Church
Westmount, Que.

Cheese and Broccoli Casserole

1 head broccoli or 1 pkg. frozen
1½ cups grated Velveeta cheese
1 can cream of mushroom soup
1 can water chestnuts, sliced and drained
2 cups croutons

Cook broccoli until barely tender. Drain and add cheese, soup and water chestnuts. Mix well. Place in greased casserole and cover with croutons. Cook at 350°F until mixture starts to bubble.

St. Mark's United Church
Douglastown, N.B.

Baked Vegetable Frittata

2 tbsp. (25 mL) unsalted butter
1 onion, finely chopped
1 clove garlic, minced
1 green pepper, diced
¼ cup (50 mL) chopped fresh or frozen
  parsley
1 - 19 oz. can (540 mL) tomatoes or equivalent
  fresh, chopped and drained
5 eggs
½ cup (125 mL) fresh bread crumbs
1 tsp. (1 mL) salt
¼ tsp. (1 mL) freshly ground pepper
1 tsp. (5 mL) Worcestershire sauce
2 cups (500 mL) shredded Swiss cheese

In skillet, melt butter. Over medium heat, cook onion and garlic until tender. Add diced green pepper and parsley and cook for 1 minute longer. Remove from heat - add tomatoes. In large mixing bowl, beat eggs until well mixed. Stir in bread crumbs, salt, pepper, Worcestershire sauce and cheese; gently stir in vegetables. Pour mixture into 9'' (2-litre) round dish, buttered. Bake in 350°F (180°C) oven for 30-35 minutes or until top is golden and mixture firm in the centre. Let stand 5 minutes before serving. This frittata is delicious served hot for brunch or cold as an appetizer or addition to a salad plate.
Serves 6.

Minto United Church
Moose Jaw, Sask.

Broccoli Bake

3 eggs
2 cups cottage cheese
Broccoli (cooked, drained and chopped)
1 onion
1 cup shredded cheddar cheese
¼ cup flour
1 can mushrooms (optional)

Mix together and bake at 350°F for 45 minutes.

Wolfe Island United Church
Wolfe Island, Ont.

Zesty Potato Quarters

(Microwave)

4 med. potatoes
3 tbsp. butter
½ tsp. garlic powder
½ tsp. paprika
2 tbsp. Parmesan cheese grated and/or
　mozzarella grated

Melt butter in microwave in an 8'' round cake dish or pie plate at HIGH for 1 minute or until melted. Blend in garlic powder, paprika and cheese. Leave skins on potatoes and quarter potatoes lengthwise. Dip cut edges in butter mixture and arrange cut side down in dish. Cover with paper towelling to prevent splattering. Micro-cook at HIGH for 10-13 minutes or until potatoes are tender. Stir twice.

First United Church
St. Thomas, Ont.

Cabbage Dish

2 tbsp. butter or margarine (oil)
1 lge. onion
1 small cabbage
1 tbsp. dill weed or seeds
Salt and pepper to taste

In skillet melt butter. Add chopped onion. Cook till clear, then add shredded cabbage. Cover and cook for 8 minutes on low heat till soft. Add dill, salt and pepper. Let set for a couple of minutes. Stir well. Meat may also be added to this to make a main dish. To serve for a dish on table add croutons. This dish very adaptable to anyone's changes. Very inexpensive.

Kirk McCall United Church
St. Stephen, N.B.

Sweet Potato with Pecan Topping

(A Texas Favourite Dish)

3 cups cooked and mashed sweet potato
¼ cup milk
⅓ cup melted butter
1 tsp. vanilla
2 beaten eggs
½ tsp. salt

Mix sweet potato, milk, butter, vanilla, eggs and salt. Spoon into 1½-quart oiled casserole.

Combine:
1 cup chopped pecans
1 cup brown sugar
3 tbsp. flour
⅓ cup melted butter
1 cup coconut (optional)

Sprinkle over sweet potato mixture. Bake at 375°F for 25 minutes. This is also good with squash in place of potatoes.

Grace United Church
Port Dover, Ont.

Cheesy Broccoli and Potato Casserole

6 med. potatoes
1 tsp. butter
⅓ tsp. pepper
⅓ tsp. dried parsley
2 cups broccoli florets
1 small onion, sliced
1 cup shredded old cheddar cheese

Cook potatoes until tender. Drain and mash with milk, butter and seasonings. Meanwhile, steam broccoli and onion until barely tender (in microwave on HIGH for 5-8 minutes). In lightly greased cup casserole spread potato mixture. Top with broccoli, onion and cheese. Microwave covered on HIGH for about 8 minutes. Serves 6.

Grace United Church
Port Dover, Ont.

Stuffed Zucchini

1 zucchini, cut in half
Mashed potatoes
Cheese
Butter

Fill zucchini with mashed potatoes. Sprinkle with cheese and butter. Bake in 300°F oven till warmed through.

Knox United Church
Sutton West, Ont.

Crispy Fried Mushrooms

8 oz. whole fresh mushrooms
½ cup flour
½ tsp. salt
¼ tsp. mustard
¼ tsp. paprika
Dash pepper
½ cup buttermilk
Crisco oil for frying

Mix flour, salt, mustard and paprika and pepper in plastic storage bag. Dip a few mushrooms at a time in buttermilk. Place in bags of flour mixture and shake to coat. Heat 2-3 inches of oil and fry a few mushrooms at a time until golden brown, turning over several times. Drain on paper towels. Serve hot.

Zion United Church
Thessalon, Ont.

Tomatoed Potatoes

1 - 5.5 oz. pkg. scalloped potatoes
2 cups water
1 - 1 lb. can tomatoes
¼ tsp. basil (optional)

Heat oven to 400°F. Place potatoes and seasoned sauce mix in ungreased 2-quart casserole. Heat water, tomatoes and basil to boiling. Stir into potatoes. Cover and bake 35-40 minutes. Serve with fried hamburger pals or sausages and coleslaw.

Maple Grove United Church
Bowmanville, Ont.

Party Scalloped Potatoes

2 tbsp. margarine
¼ cup chopped onion
¼ cup chopped green peppers
2 tbsp. flour
½ tsp. salt
1 cup milk
1 tin mushroom soup
½ cup grated cheese
4 cups cubed, cooked potatoes

In frying pan melt margarine. Add and cook until tender the onion and green peppers. Blend in flour and salt. Stir in milk, soup and cheese. Put potatoes in a 1½-quart baking dish. Pour all liquid over them. May put a few bread crumbs over top. Bake 30-35 minutes in 350°F oven.
Serves 8.

Ste. Rose United Church
Ste. Rose du Lac, Man.

Souper Cheese Potatoes

(Microwave)

4 lge. potatoes, peeled and cubed (about 4 cups)
¼ cup water
½ - 10 oz. can cheddar cheese soup
1 tbsp. snipped chives or onion
½ tsp. garlic salt
½ cup sour cream
½ cup cereal cream
½ cup shredded cheddar cheese
Paprika

Combine potatoes and water in 1½-quart microwave safe casserole. Cover with casserole lid. Microwave on HIGH 12-14 minutes until potatoes are about tender, stirring once. Stir in soup, sour cream, cereal cream, chives, and garlic salt. Microwave on HIGH uncovered, 4-5 minutes until heated through, stirring once. Sprinkle with cheese and paprika. Let stand covered about 5 minutes or until cheese is melted.
Yield: 6 servings.

St. Andrew's United Church
Atwater, Sask.

Butter Baked Taters

¼ cup butter
3 tbsp. minced green onion
3 lge. baking potatoes, peeled
Salt and pepper
2 tbsp. Parmesan cheese or grated
  mozzarella cheese

Preheat oven to 500°F. Melt butter in small saucepan. Add onion, saute until tender, about 3 minutes. Halve potatoes lengthwise, then slice crosswise into ⅛'' thick slices. (Do not put potatoes in water after slicing. Immediately line up in buttered 18x9'' baking pan with slices overlapping. Pour butter mixture over potatoes. Season with salt and pepper. Bake 20 minutes. Remove from oven. Sprinkle with Parmesan cheese. Bake an additional 5-7 minutes, or until cheese is melted and slightly browned.
Serves 4.

Wilkie United Church
Wilkie, Sask.
Ste. Rose United Church
Ste. Rose, Man.

Scalloped Turnip & Apples

1 large turnip
1 tbsp. butter
1½ cups apples, peeled
¼ cup brown sugar, lightly packed
Pinch of cinnamon

Topping:
⅓ cup all-purpose flour
⅓ cup brown sugar, lightly packed
2 tbsp. butter

Peel, dice and cook turnip. Drain and mash adding butter. Slice apples and toss with sugar and cinnamon. Arrange alternate layers of mashed turnip and sliced apples in greased casserole beginning and ending with turnip. Mix together until crumbly the three ingredients for topping. Sprinkle over top of casserole. Bake at 350°F for 1 hour. Serve hot.
Makes 6-8 servings.

St. Paul's United Church
Perth, Ont.
Vankleek Hill United Trinity Church
Vankleek Hill, Ont.

Potato Puff

3 cups mashed potatoes
¾ cup milk
1 egg
2 tbsp. melted butter
1 tsp. baking powder
Salt and pepper to taste

Mix together mashed potatoes, milk, egg, melted butter, baking powder, salt and pepper. Place in loaf pan. Bake in 375°F oven 35-40 minutes till well heated through and golden brown on top.
Serves 4-6.

Knox United Church
Nepean, Ont.

Orange Glazed Vegetables

Glaze:
½ cup orange juice
¼ cup cider vinegar
¼ cup orange marmalade
2 tbsp. brown sugar
1 tbsp. cornstarch
2 tbsp. chicken soup mix
¼ tsp. curry powder
¼ tsp. nutmeg
2 tbsp. parsley

1 medium onion, chopped
3 large carrots, diagonally sliced
1 cup cubed turnip
1 cup brussels sprout, fresh or frozen,
  cut in halves, or equivalent of other green
  vegetables
3 celery stalks, cut diagonally
½ cup sliced fresh mushrooms
2 tbsp. vegetable oil
2 tsp. salt

In a covered jar, shake glaze ingredients together thoroughly. Set aside. Prepare veggies. Heat oil and salt in wok and stir-fry onions, carrots and turnips for 3-4 minutes at high heat. Push veggies up the side. Add sprouts, celery and mushrooms and stir-fry at medium heat for 2-3 minutes. Blend in glaze; stir and simmer covered about 2 more minutes. Serve at once. Delicious, nutritious and ready in minutes.
Yield: 5 servings (1 cup each).

St. Paul's United Church
Ormstown, Que.

Glazed Carrots

2 bunches small carrots
1 tbsp. lemon juice
⅓ cup sugar
½ cup water
1 tsp. salt
2 tbsp. butter or margarine

Scrape carrots; cut in fourths, lengthwise; place in heavy skillet. Add remaining ingredients; cover; cook over low heat, turning often until tender and glazed.
Makes 6 servings.

Emmanuel United Church
Saskatoon, Sask.

Savory Carrots

1½ cups sliced carrots
⅛ tsp. salt
2 tsp. butter or margarine
2 tsp. chopped onion
2 tbsp. chopped green pepper
Salt and pepper to taste

Cook carrots with salt and a little water for 5 minutes. Drain and push carrots to one side of saucepan. Add butter to other side of pan, add onion and green pepper. Stir over low heat 1 min. Stir all together. Add seasoning and continue cooking over low heat, stirring occasionally, until everything is tender - about 5 minutes.
Serves 2.

Merigomish United Church
Merigomish, N.S.

Turnip Carrot Casserole

1 med. turnip, diced
6 med. carrots, diced
3 med. parsnips, diced
Salt and pepper
¼ cup butter
1 egg, slightly beaten

Steam vegetables until cooked and mash thoroughly (or put through food processor). Add salt and pepper, and butter. Cool slightly and blend in the egg. Pour into a well buttered casserole. Dot with butter or crumb topping. Bake in 375°F oven for 35 minutes.

Wesley United Church
Vandorf, Ont.

Baked Cauliflower Casserole

1 lge. head cauliflower, broken apart
½ tsp. salt
1 - 10 oz. can cream of chicken soup
1 - 4 oz. pkg. shredded cheese (1 cup)
⅓ cup mayonnaise
½ tsp. curry powder
¼ cup dried bread crumbs
2 tbsp. melted butter

In covered saucepan in 1" boiling water cook cauliflower in salt for 10 minutes. Drain. In casserole stir undiluted soup, cheese, mayonnaise and curry powder. Add cauliflower and mix well. Toss bread crumbs in melted butter and sprinkle on top. Bake 30 minutes or until casserole is hot and bubbly in 350°F oven. To freeze do not cook first. Thaw and bake 45 minutes at 350°F.

Elimville United church
Exeter, Ont.

Company Vegetable Casserole

1 lge. pkg. frozen mixed vegetables
1 cup chopped onion
1 cup chopped celery
1 cup grated cheese
1 cup mayonnaise
1 cup margarine
1-2 pkgs. soda crackers, crushed

Cook vegetables until just tender. Put in greased casserole or 9x13" pan. Mix onions, celery, cheese and mayonnaise. Spread over drained vegetables. Melt margarine and combine with cracker crumbs. Put on top. Bake 30 minutes at 350°F.

Acme United Church
Acme, Alta.

Parsley Rice Ring

3 cups cooked rice
¼ cup snipped parsley

Combine hot cooked rice with parsley. Pack into an ungreased 5 ½ cup ring mold. Turn out at once on a warm platter.
Serves 6.

Columbus United Church
Columbus, Ont.

Broccoli Squares

3 tbsp. butter
3 eggs
1 cup milk
1 tsp. baking powder
2 tbsp. chopped onion
1 cup flour
1 tsp. salt
1 bunch broccoli
½ cup grated cheddar cheese

Melt butter in 9x13" pan. Steam broccoli (no stems). Chop fine. Beat eggs with beater. Add flour, milk, baking powder and salt. Mix together. Add cheese, broccoli and onion. Pour into pan. Bake at 350°F for 35 minutes or until done in middle.   Zion United Church
                               Thessalon, Ont.

Squash and Apple Bake

2 lbs. butternut or buttercup squash
½ cup brown sugar
¼ cup butter or margarine, melted
1 tbsp. flour
1 tsp. salt
½ tsp. mace
2 baking apples, cored and cut into ½" slices

Heat oven to 350°F. Cut each squash into ½" slices. Stir together remaining ingredients except apple slices. Arrange squash in ungreased baking dish - 12x8x1½" and top with apples. Sprinkle sugar mixture over top. Cover with foil. Bake 50 to 60 minutes or until squash is tender.   Orono United Church
                                 Orono, Ont.

Rice Casserole

1 cup cooked rice, salt added
1 cup milk
½ cup chopped onion
½ cup grated cheese
1 egg, beaten
4 tbsp. butter
¼ cup parsley

Mix all ingredients and pour into dish. Place in pan of water. Bake at 300°F for 30 minutes. A delicious casserole. May be served with cold sliced chicken and a salad.
        Waterville United Church
                      Waterville, Que.

Chinese Fried Rice

2 cups water
2 cups Minute rice
½ tsp. salt
2 celery stalks
1 lge. or 2 small onions
½ green pepper
¾ cup sliced mushrooms
2 med. fresh tomatoes (optional)
Oil or margarine
Soya sauce
Leftover chicken or ham, diced or some crumbled bacon (optional)

Bring water and salt to a boil. Stir in rice. Cover and remove from heat. Let stand 5 minutes. Add oil or margarine to a frying pan (preferably electric). When hot, add cut-up celery and onions. Cook until onions are golden. Add cut-up pepper and sliced mushrooms. Leave this only till mushrooms and peppers are half cooked. Add rice and soya sauce as desired. Cook only until everything is well mixed or until rice gets hot. Add tomatoes (optional) and serve hot. If using chicken, ham or bacon add just before rice. Great with a tossed salad!
        Shanly United church
                    Spencerville, Ont.

Baked Squash

3 cups squash
2 tbsp. butter
Salt and pepper
½ cup celery
¼ cup green pepper
½ cup grated cheese
Crushed crackers
¼ cup grated cheese

Cook squash until just undercooked. Drain squash and mash. In a 1-quart baking dish, place mashed squash. Mix butter, salt and pepper, celery, green pepper and ½ cup grated cheese. Mix all together with the mashed squash. Sprinkle finely crushed crackers and grated cheese on top of squash. Place in 350°F oven for 10 minutes.
       St. Andrew's United Church
                       Tide Head, N.B.

Quick Rice Dish

2 cups raw rice (white)
1 pkg. dry onion soup (Liptons)
¼ cup vegetable oil
3 tbsp. soy sauce
1 tin mushrooms (optional)
4 cups boiling water (3½ cups if you use
   the liquid from the mushrooms)

Place all ingredients in 9x13'' pan or large casserole. Cover with foil wrap. Bake in 350°F oven for 1 hour.

Note: 2 cans undiluted beef consomme can replace the onion soup and 2 cups of water, then add 6 chopped green onions. Leftover cooked vegetables or meats can be added to the rice dish to make a one dish supper or luncheon meal.

Kirkfield Park United Church, Winnipeg, Man.
St. Andrew's United Church, Yorkton, Sask.
Nipawin United Church, Nipawin, Sask.
Onanole United Church, Onanole, Man.
Orono United Church, Orono, Ont.
Knox United Church, Redvers, Sask.
St. Giles United Church, Hamilton, Ont.

Spanish Rice

¾ cup uncooked rice
1½ cups sliced onions
3 tbsp. cooking oil
1 tsp. white sugar
1 can tomatoes (large or medium size)
1½ tsp. salt
Dash pepper
4 tbsp. diced green pepper
4 whole cloves
1 bay leaf

Cook rice till tender. Meanwhile cook onions in oil. Add remaining ingredients and simmer 15 minutes. Remove bay leaf and cloves. Add the rice. Turn into greased casserole. Bake at 350°F for 30 minutes. Leftovers may be reheated in double boiler or steamed.

St. Mark's United Church
Scarborough, Ont.

Spanish Rice with Cheese

4 slices bacon, diced
1 cup chopped onion
¼ cup chopped green pepper
½ cup celery
1 can mushrooms or ½ lb. fresh
1 cup rice
1 tsp. salt
1 cup water
1 - 28 oz. can tomatoes
2 cups grated cheese

Cook bacon until crisp. Cook onions, green pepper, celery and mushrooms in bacon fat until brown. Add rice, salt, water and tomatoes. Stir to blend. Layer rice mixture and 1¾ cups grated cheese into large buttered casserole. Cover and bake at 350°F until rice has absorbed liquid about ¾-1 hour. Uncover and top with ¼ cup grated cheese. Return to oven uncovered for 10 minutes.

Greenbank United Church
Uxbridge, Ont.

Baked Corn Casserole

1 egg
2 - 12 oz. cans kernel corn, drained
1 - 5½ oz. can evaporated milk
¼ cup shredded Swiss cheese
2 tbsp. chopped onion
2 tbsp. green pepper
Pepper

Beat egg. Stir in rest of ingredients. Pour into greased baking dish and sprinkle with topping.

Topping:
½ cup grated soft bread crumbs
2 tbsp. melted butter
¼ cup shredded cheese

Bake at 350°F for 35 minutes.

Donminister United Church
Don Mills, Ont.

Spanish Rice

1 tbsp. shortening or oil
1 med. onion, chopped
1 green pepper, chopped
1 - 28 oz. can tomatoes put through blender
1 cup water
1¼ tsp. salt
⅛ tsp. pepper
1 tsp. sugar
1 tbsp. prepared mustard
1 tsp. Worcestershire sauce
¾ cup rice

Saute onion and pepper in oil. Add all other ingredients and cook over low heat for 45 minutes to 1 hour. Serve with pork chops, steak or fish.

Emmanuel United Church
Englehart, Ont.

Infallible Rice

1 med. onion, minced
1 cup long grain, raw white rice
2 tbsp. butter
2 cups chicken broth (hot)

Saute onions in butter until transparent. Combine onions, rice and hot broth. Bring to a boil on top of range. Cover and place in 325°F oven for 20 minutes. Serve and listen to the compliments. Serves 4 hungry people or 6 polite people.

Fleetwood United Memorial Church
Surrey, B.C.

Scalloped Corn with Mushroom Soup

1 tsp. salt
¼ tsp. pepper
¾ cup mushroom soup
1 tin whole kernel corn
2 tbsp. flour
2 eggs, beaten
½ cup bread crumbs

Drain liquid from corn and add to soup. Melt butter, add flour and seasoning. Mix until blended, add soup mixture stirring until smooth and thick. Combine corn and eggs, add to the above. Pour into a greased baking dish and top with bread crumbs. Place dish in pan of hot water and cook at 350°F for about 40 minutes or until mixture is set.

Battle River United Church
Manning, Alta.

Cheesy Veggie Casserole

Cheese slices
Broccoli
Cauliflower
Croutons
Onions
Carrots
Mushrooms
1 can mushroom soup

Line 9x13'' pan with cheese slices on the bottom and sides. Microwave or panbroil vegetables for 1-2 minutes before putting in pan. Cover vegetables with mushroom soup. Put cheese slices on top and cover with croutons or bread crumbs seasoned with **basil, thyme** and **margarine.** Bake at 350°F till bubbly, about 30 minutes.

Beachville United Church
Beachville, Ont.

Cottage Cheese and Broccoli Bake

1½ cups partly cooked broccoli
½ cup cubed cheddar cheese

Spread in baking dish.

Combine:
2 eggs, beaten
⅔ cup cottage cheese
1 tbsp. flour
1 tbsp. butter
Salt
Pepper

Pour mixture over broccoli and cheese. Top with **buttered bread crumbs.** Bake at 350°F for 20 to 30 minutes.
Serves 2.

Eastend United Church
Eastend, Sask.

Desserts

Cookies

Minnie's Cookies

2 cups white chocolate wafers
Peanut butter
Ritz crackers

Melt white chocolate wafers. Spread peanut butter between 2 Ritz crackers. Dip in white chocolate. Let cool on wax paper.

Westworth United Church
Winnipeg, Man.

Peanut Butter Cookies

1 cup white sugar
1 cup brown sugar
1 cup butter or margarine
1 cup peanut butter
1 tsp. vanilla
2 eggs, beaten
3 cups flour
2 tsp. baking powder

Make balls. Bake at 300°F for 10 minutes, then place a chocolate rosebud (or colored wafer) in the middle of each. Return to oven for 5 minutes.

St. Andrew's United Church
Millbrook, Ont.

Julia's Brown Sugar Cookies

½ cup shortening or margarine
2 cups brown sugar
1 cup hot water with 1 tsp. soda dissolved
   in it
1 egg, beaten
1 tsp. vanilla or 1 tsp. lemon extract
1 tsp. salt
3¼ cups flour
Nuts, raisins, coconut or chocolate chips
   (optional)

Bake at 350°F.

Trinity United Church
Hopewell Hill, N.B.

Chocolate Fingers

1¾ cups sugar
½ cup butter
½ cup milk
3 cups oatmeal
1 cup shredded coconut
½ tsp. vanilla
Dash salt
2 squares unsweetened chocolate
2 squares semi-sweet chocolate
¼ bar parafin wax

Bring sugar, butter and milk to boil until it bubbles. Add oatmeal, coconut, vanilla and salt. Pack in 8x12" glass pan. Cool, cut into squares and shape into fingers. Lay on cookie sheet and freeze. Melt chocolate and wax. Drop in the fingers and lay on wax paper.

Wilkie United Church
Wilkie, Sask.

Coconut Crisps Cookies

1 cup margarine
1 cup white sugar
1 cup brown sugar
1 egg
1½ cups flour
1¼ cups rolled oats
½ tsp. soda
1 tsp. baking powder
½ tsp. salt
¾ cup coconut

Cream margarine, sugars and egg. Combine and add flour, oats, soda, baking powder, salt and coconut. Grease cookie sheets. Make small balls of batter (1") and put on cookie sheet. Press down with fork dipped in milk. Bake at 375°F for 6-8 minutes.

Variation: Add chocolate chips or sprinkles. Makes 10-12 dozen.

Wyoming United Church, Wyoming, Ont.
North Street United Church, Goderich, Ont.

Poppy Seed Cookies

1 cup butter
1 cup sugar
2 eggs, beaten
2 tbsp. sour cream
2¾ cups flour
Pinch salt
½ cup poppy seeds
1 tsp. baking soda

In large bowl cream butter, beat in sugar until light and fluffy. Gradually blend in eggs and sour cream. In separate bowl, sift together flour, baking soda and salt. Stir in poppy seeds. Add flour mixture to butter mixture. Mix thoroughly. Form into ball; wrap and refrigerate for 1 hour. On floured surface roll out ⅓ dough to ⅛" thickness or so. Cut with 2" cutter and arrange on greased baking sheet. Bake at 375°F for 6-8 minutes or until light brown around edges. (This recipe is excellent all year round, especially for your child's special occasions, especially angel and heart shaped cookies.) Great tasting.

Meadowood United Church
Winnipeg, Man.

Chocolate Scotcheroos

1 cup sugar
1 cup corn syrup
1 cup peanut butter
6 cups rice krispies or Special K
1 cup semi-sweet chocolate morsels
1 cup butterscotch morsels

Combine sugar and syrup in a 3-quart saucepan. Cook over moderate heat until mixture bubbles. Remove from heat. Stir in peanut butter mix. Add cereal. Press into 9x13" pan. Melt morsels together over low heat and stir until blended. Spread over mixture. Cut into squares.
Variations: Add 1 cup raisins or peanuts. Omit the butterscotch chips and stir the chocolate chips into the mixture instead of using as a topping. ⅓ cup of peanut butter can replace the butterscotch morsels in the topping.

Kincardine United Church, Kincardine, Ont.
St. Giles United Church, Hamilton, Ont.
Wyoming United Church, Wyoming, Ont.
St. James United Church, Antigonish, N.S.
Waterville United Church, Waterville, Que.
Westminster United Church, Whitby, Ont.
St. John's United Church, Elmvale, Ont.

Sunflower Seed Cookies

2 cups white sugar
3 cups flour
1 cup sunflower seeds, raw, shelled
1 cup desicated coconut
1 tsp. baking soda
1 tsp. baking powder
1 cup butter or margarine
1 cup shortening
2 eggs
1 tsp. vanilla

Mix all dry ingredients together. Cream butter and add shortening, eggs, vanilla and dry ingredients. Drop cookies. Bake at 325°F for about 8 minutes or until brown.

McClure United Church
Winnipeg, Man.

Chinese Almond Cookies

1 cup butter or margarine
1 cup sugar
2 egg yolks, slightly beaten
1 tsp. almond extract
2 cups sifted flour
1 cup chopped almonds

Work butter with a wooden spoon until soft. Gradually add sugar while beating. Beat until light and add eggs and extract. Beat until light and fluffy. Gradually add flour. Mix after each addition and beat until smooth. Add almonds. Mix until blended. Shape into balls the size of a walnut. Place on ungreased cookie sheets. Flatten with a glass tumbler which has been dipped in flour. Bake at 350°F for 15 minutes or until done. Cool and frost with tea frosting. Top each cookie with whole or slivered almond.

Tea Frosting:
½ cup butter or margarine
2½ cups sifted icing sugar
4 tbsp. instant tea
2 tbsp. milk

Work butter with wooden spoon until soft. Gradually add icing sugar. Beat until blended. Combine tea and milk and mix well. Add to sugar and butter mixture. Mix until light and fluffy. Add a few drops of milk if too thick.

St. Paul's United Church
Souris, Man.

Chocolate Cookies with Butterscotch Chipits

1 cup butter, soft
1½ cups white sugar
2 eggs
2 tsp. vanilla
2 cups all-purpose flour
⅔ cup Fry's cocoa (sift out lumps first, before using)
¾ tsp. baking soda
½ tsp. salt
2 cups butterscotch chipits

Cream together butter, sugar, eggs and vanilla in bowl. In another large bowl, mix together flour, cocoa, baking soda, salt and chipits. Add the creamed butter mixture to the above mixture and mix. Chill until firm enough to handle (you may omit this) and shape into 1'' balls and flatten (or drop by teaspoon onto ungreased baking sheet). Bake at 350°F for 12 minutes. Cool 2 minutes before removing from cookie sheet, to cool on cookie rack. Secret to having nice soft cookies is to bake only a while, so they still appear undercooked when you take them out of oven. But by the time they cool, they'll be just right. (Most delicious cookies ever.)

Imperial United Church
Imperial, Sask.

Belgian Cookies

½ cup butter
1½ cups flour
½ cup brown sugar

Mix together to a crumbly mass like pie crust. Put into a flat buttered 9x9'' pan and bake in 350°F oven until lightly browned. Spread **raspberry jam** over above and pour over all.

1 cup brown sugar
2 eggs
1 tsp. vanilla
2 tbsp. flour
½ tsp. baking powder
¼ tsp. salt
1-1½ cups coconut
½-1 cup nuts

Bake again at 350°F until browned (20-25 minutes). When cool, cut in bars.

Bowman United Church
Ancaster, Ont.

Oatmeal Sunflower Seed Cookies

1 cup margarine
½ cup white sugar
½ cup brown sugar
1 egg
1½ cups flour
¼ tsp. salt
1 tsp. soda
1 tsp. baking powder
1½ cups oatmeal
¾ cup coconut
⅓ cup shelled sunflower seeds

Beat margarine, sugars and egg together. Add remaining ingredients. Mix well. Drop into a greased cookie sheet. Press lightly with a floured fork. Bake at 350°F until slightly browned.

Trinity United Church
Portage la Prairie, Man.

Fruit Drop Cookies

2 eggs
1 cup brown sugar
¾ cup margarine
1 tsp. vanilla
1 tsp. soda, dissolved in 2 tbsp. hot water
Pinch of salt
2 cups flour
1 cup chopped dates
1 cup mixed fruit
1 cup raisins
1 cup coconut

Mix well. Drop on cookie sheet with teaspoon and bake at 350°F for 12-15 minutes.

Glenboro United Church
Glenboro, Man.

Corn Flake Drop Cookies

20 large marshmallows
3 tbsp. butter
2 tbsp. cocoa
2 cups corn flakes

Mix first three ingredients in a double boiler. Remove from heat and stir in corn flakes. Drop on waxed paper and cool.

Ste. Rose United Church
Ste. Rose Du Lac, Man.

Almond Puffs

1 cup butter
⅓ cup icing sugar
¾ cup cornstarch
1¼ cups all-purpose flour
Almonds

Cream butter. Add icing sugar gradually and cream well, using mixer. Sift together cornstarch and flour and add gradually to creamed mixture. Roll in balls, flatten with hand to approximately ½'' thick. Place ½ almond on each cookie, pushing in well. Bake at 350°F and watch closely. Bake until delicately browned - about 15 minutes. Roll in granulated sugar while hot. Handle carefully.
Makes about 4 dozen.

Stanley United Church
Stanley, N.B.

Biscuits de Noël

(MiPans)

1⅔ cups flour
1 tsp. baking powder
½ tsp. baking soda
½ cup sugar
1 lemon rind or 1 tbsp. lemon juice
Pinch salt
½ cup butter or margarine
2 eggs

Mix together with hands adding eggs and mix rapidly. Form into ball. Let stand covered for ½ hour to 24 hours. Roll with rolling pin ½ centimetre thick. Cut out into shapes. Lay on greased pan (cookie sheet). Bake at 325°F for 10-15 minutes until golden.

Westlock United Church
Westlock, Alta.

Lemon Cookies

½ cup white sugar
1 cup butter
1 egg
2 cups flour
1 tsp. cream of tartar
½ tsp. soda
½ tsp. salt

Mix all ingredients thoroughly and roll very thin. Bake in 350°F oven until golden brown (don't overbake).

Filling:
1 cup sugar
½ cup coconut
1 egg, well beaten
1 tbsp. cornstarch
Juice and rind of 1 lemon

Cook in double boiler till it thickens. When cookies are cool, spread between two cookies.

Trinity United Church, Capreol, Ont.
St. Andrews United Church, Rexton, N.B.

Six Week Butter Cookies

2 cups soft butter
⅔ cup white sugar
2 cups chopped pecans or walnuts
1 tbsp. vanilla
4 cups sifted white flour
2 cups icing sugar for dredging (optional)

Preheat oven to 375°F. Cream butter and sugar in a large bowl with electric mixer until light and fluffy. Beat in nuts and vanilla by hand. Sift, then measure flour and beat into butter mixture. Wrap and chill dough in fridge until stiff enough to shape with hands. Place one teaspoon at a time in hand. Shape into balls and flatten to make cookies 1-1½''. Place on ungreased cookie sheet and bake 8-10 minutes until light brown. Sift icing sugar on platter and dredge both sides of warm cookies in it. Store in cookie tin with layers of foil between. Will keep for 6 weeks.
Yield: 7 dozen.

Crescent Fort Rouge United Church
Winnipeg, Man.

Applesauce Cookies

½ cup shortening
1 cup brown sugar
1 egg
½ cup chopped raisins
2 cups sifted cake flour
1½ tsp. baking powder
¼ tsp. soda
½ tsp. cinnamon
¼ tsp. cloves
1 tsp. salt
1 cup thickened, unsweetened applesauce

Cream together shortening and brown sugar. Beat in egg. Add raisins. Add sifted dry ingredients alternately with applesauce. Drop by spoonsful on oiled cookie sheet. Bake at 350°F for 10-12 minutes.

St. Paul's United Church
Ormstown, Que.

Honey Cookies

4 cups flour
1 cup honey
1 cup sugar
3 eggs
1 tsp. cinnamon
1 tsp. cloves
1 tsp. baking soda

Make evening or day before. Warm honey till clear. Make a deep hole in flour and spice mixture and add eggs (slightly beaten) and honey. Work dough very well and cover. Leave overnight. Roll out next day to thickness of thumb and leave for 3 or 4 hours. Cut with small cutter as cookies (bake to triple in size). Place on greased sheet and bake at 375°F, if risen in 6 minutes - leave for 8 minutes only. If slower, leave for 10 minutes.

Icing: Sugar boiled with a little water till syrupy, but not to stringy stage. Dunk cookies in and let dry (individually). Coat with icing sugar. You can also ice with 7-minute frosting covering completely, or a chocolate syrup. Great for Christmas.

Emmanuel United Church
Saskatoon, Sask.

Shirley's M&M Cookies

1 cup shortening
1 cup brown sugar
½ cup white sugar
2 tsp. vanilla
2 eggs
1 tsp. baking soda
1 tsp. salt
½ cup M&M candy
2¼ cups flour

Blend shortening and sugars. Add eggs and vanilla and beat. Blend baking soda and salt and add to mixture. Mix M&M candy with flour and add to mixture. Drop from teaspoon onto ungreased cookie sheet. Decorate tops with more M&M candies. Bake at 375°F for 10 minutes or till brown. You may substitute chocolate chips for M&Ms.

United Church in Meadowood
Winnipeg, Man.

Giant Cookies

⅓ cup shortening
⅓ cup butter or margarine
½ cup white sugar
½ cup brown sugar
1 large egg
1 tsp. vanilla
1½ cups all-purpose flour
½ tsp. salt
½ tsp. soda
6 oz. pkg. chocolate chips
½ cup broken walnuts

Cream fat mixture and sugars. Add egg and vanilla and dry ingredients. Using two sideless baking sheets form dough into two large cookies ½'' deep. Bake in 375°F oven for 12-15 minutes.

Innerkip United Church
Innerkip, Ont.

Pumpkin Cookies

1 cup brown sugar, firmly packed
½ cup margarine
2 eggs
1 cup cooked pumpkin
2 cups flour
2 tsp. baking powder
½ tsp. salt
½ tsp. cinnamon
½ tsp. nutmeg
¼ tsp. ginger
½ cup chopped nuts
½ cup raisins (optional)

Preheat oven to 400°F. Mix everything together, except the nuts and raisins, in a large bowl. Add nuts and raisins and mix until blended. Bake for 8-10 minutes.

Hearts Memorial United Church
Weymouth, Digby Co., N.S.

Easy Peanut Butter Cookies

1 cup white sugar
1 cup peanut butter
1 egg, well beaten

Blend together sugar and peanut butter. Add egg and mix well. Roll into teaspoon size balls. Place on ungreased cookie sheet. Press with fork. Sprinkle with a pinch of sugar. Bake 10-12 minutes at 350°F. Taste best when completely cooled. A-1 for kids to make!

Moorefield United Church
Moorefield, Ont.

Squares

Cream Cheese Almond Squares

½ cup butter or margarine, softened
2 tsp. sugar
2 tbsp. milk
½ tsp. grated lemon rind
1⅓ cups all-purpose flour
2 - 8 oz. pkgs. cream cheese, softened
1 cup sugar
1 egg, beaten
1 tsp. grated lemon rind
1 cup chopped almonds, toasted
1 cup sifted icing sugar
1 tbsp. water
1 tsp. ground cinnamon
Toasted sliced almonds (optional)

Combine first 5 ingredients. Mix well. Press mixture into the bottom of a 9" pan. Set aside. Combine next 4 ingredients and beat until smooth. Stir in chopped almonds. Pour mixture over layer in pan. Bake at 300°F for 1 hour and 10 minutes or until set. Combine icing sugar, water and cinnamon; mix well. Spread over hot mixture and let cool. Chill 3-4 hours. Cut into squares. Garnish with toasted, sliced almonds if desired. These are rich and delicious
United Church of Canada, Caledonia, N.S.
Caledonia United Church, Queens County, N.S.

Life is a measure to be filled; not a cup to empty.

One who thinks by the inch and talks by the yard needs to be moved by the foot.

Cheesecake Squares

⅓ cup margarine
⅓ cup brown sugar
1 cup flour
½ cup chopped pecans
8 oz. cream cheese
¼ cup white sugar
1 tsp. vanilla
1 egg
¾ cup Smarties

Crumble together the margarine, brown sugar, flour and pecans. Save some crumbs for top. Pat the remaining crumbs into an 8" square pan and bake at 350°F for 10 minutes. Let cool. Beat until smooth the softened cream cheese and sugar. Add the egg and vanilla and continue to beat till smooth. Put mixture on top of baked crust, top with the Smarties and then the remaining crumbs. Bake at 350°F for 25 minutes.
North Bedegue United Church
Summerside, P.E.I.

Cream Cheese & Jelly Squares

1½ cups flour
½ cup butter
4 oz. cream cheese
3 tbsp. icing sugar
1 tsp. baking powder
¼ tsp. salt

Blend flour, butter, cream cheese, icing sugar, baking powder and salt. Save ¾ cup of crumbs for top. Spread remainder in 8" pan. Over this spread marmalade, jelly or jam. Top with crumbs. Bake just until brown at 350°F.
St. Andrew's United Church
Norton, N.B.

Fluffy Pink Icing Squares

20 single graham wafers, crushed or 1¼ cups graham cracker crumbs
½ cup butter, (measure, then melt)
½ cup brown sugar
1 heaping tbsp. flour

Mix well. Press into a 9x11" pan. Bake 15 minutes at 275°-300°F. Mix:
1 tin Eagle Brand milk
2 cups desicated coconut (don't use any other kind)

Place on top of base and bake 30 minutes at 275°-300°F. Let stand until very cold. Ice with:
½ cup soft butter
¾ cup icing sugar
2 tbsp. milk
2 tbsp. boiling water
Pink colouring
½ tsp. vanilla

Beat butter and icing sugar two minutes. Add milk. Beat two minutes more. Add water and beat two minutes more. Add pink colouring if desired and vanilla and spread over cooled cake.

Calvin United Church
Pembroke, Ont.

Dutch Treat

⅔ cup butter
1 cup sugar
1 tsp. almond extract
1 egg, beaten
1½ cups all-purpose flour
½ tsp. baking powder

Cream butter and sugar. Add beaten egg and almond extract. Sift flour and baking powder and add to first ingredients. Press in bottom of 8x8" square pan.

Topping:
1 egg
1 tbsp. milk
Sliced almonds

Beat egg and add milk. Put this on top of first mixture. Spread almonds evenly over egg mixture. Bake in 350°F oven for 30 minutes.

Shanly United Church
Spencerville, Ont.

Lemon Custard Squares

Bottom:
1 cup flour
1 cup graham wafer crumbs
1 cup coconut
1 cup brown sugar
½ tsp. baking soda
½ tsp. salt
½ cup butter

Rub together. Press half of mixture into 8x8" pan.

Filling:
1 tin condensed milk
2 egg yolks
½ cup lemon juice

Topping:
2 egg whites
2 tbsp. sugar

Beat milk, add egg yolks and lemon juice. Beat 1 minute. Put on bottom mixture. Beat egg whites and sugar. Spread on top of filling. Sprinkle with remaining crumbs. Bake in 350°F oven until brown.

Garnish United Church
Garnish, Nfld.

Easy Mix Cookie Bars

2 eggs
2 cups moist brown sugar
1 cup shortening
1 cup raisins
3 cups all-purpose flour
1 tsp. cinnamon
1 tsp. soda
1 tsp. baking powder
1 cup boiling water

Measure all ingredients into a large mixing bowl before stirring. Then beat thoroughly. Spread ¼" thick on a greased cookie sheet (17½x11½"). Bake at 375°F about 20 minutes until rich brown. Sprinkle with icing sugar while hot.

Varna United Church
Varna, Ont.

Caribbean Bars

Bottom Layer:
½ cup butter or margarine
¼ cup granulated sugar
1¼ cups all-purpose flour

Crumble first three ingredients together well. Pack into 9x9" pan, ungreased. Bake in 350°F oven for 15 minutes.

Top Layer:
2 eggs
1 cup brown sugar, packed
½ cup crushed pineapple, drained (save liquid for icing)
1 cup coconut
⅓ cup chopped candied cherries
1 tsp. rum flavouring
2 tbsp. flour
½ tsp. baking powder

Beat eggs slightly. Add remaining ingredients. Spread over bottom layer. Bake in 350°F oven for 25-30 minutes, until a medium brown colour and is set. Frost with icing below. Cut into 36 squares.

Icing:
1½ cups icing sugar
3 tbsp. butter or margarine
½ tsp. rum flavouring
1½ tbsp. pineapple juice

Combine all together in bowl. Beat, adding more juice if icing is too stiff. Spread over bars. Allow to set before cutting.

Lakeshore Drive United Church
Morrisburg, Ont.

Mincemeat Squares

1½ cups all-purpose flour
1⅓ cup brown sugar
½ tsp. soda
1 tsp. salt
2 beaten eggs
½ cup margarine
1⅓ cup mincemeat

Make batter, fold in mincemeat. Bake at 350°F for 30-35 minutes in 9x13" pan. Frost with butter icing.

Innerkip United Church
Innerkip, Ont.

Christmas Fruit Bars

1½ cups sifted all-purpose flour
¼ cup sugar
1 tsp. baking powder
1 tsp. salt
1 cup chopped nutmeats
2 cups chopped candied fruit
3 eggs, unbeaten
1 cup corn syrup
1 tsp. vanilla
½ cup corn oil

Sift together first four ingredients. Dredge nuts and fruits with ⅓ cup dry ingredients. Place eggs in mixing bowl; beat until light. Add syrup, vanilla and oil; beat until well mixed. Stir in nuts and chopped fruit; mix well. Fold in sifted dry ingredients. Bake in well-greased (10½x15½x¾") pan in 350°F oven for 30-35 minutes. Remove from oven; cool, then cut into bars. Dust with icing sugar, if desired.

For variety replace ½ cup of the fruit with ½ cup chopped dates.
Yield: 40 bars.

St. Paul's United Church, Kenmore, Ont.
Grace United Church, Port Dover, Ont.

Chocolate Chip Cookie Bars

¾ cup margarine
1 cup sugar (brown or combination)
1 egg
1 tsp. vanilla
1⅓ cups flour
1 cup oatmeal
¼ tsp. baking soda
½ tsp. salt
¾-1 cup chocolate chips

Cream margarine and sugar. Add egg and vanilla and beat until well mixed. Combine flour, oatmeal, soda and salt. Stir into batter. Stir in chocolate chips. Press dough onto cookie sheet (10½x16") with edges. Bake at 350°F for 15 minutes. Cut while warm.

Variation: Omit the oatmeal and decrease the margarine to ½ cup and increase the flour to 1½ cups and the baking soda to ½ teaspoon.

Streetsville United Church, Mississauga, Ont.
St. Andrew's United Church, Beaverton, Ont.

Applesauce Bars

½ cup butter
1 cup brown sugar
1 cup applesauce
1 egg
½ cup nuts
¼ tsp. salt
½ tsp. cloves
½ tsp. soda
1 cup raisins
2¼ cups sifted flour
1 tsp. cinnamon
1 tsp. nutmeg

Mix butter, sugar, applesauce and egg together. Sift together flour, soda, salt and spices. Add raisins and nuts. Mix with first mixture. Spread in 9x13" baking pan. Bake at 350°F for 35-40 minutes. Ice if you wish while warm.

Cloudslee United Church
Bruce Mines, Ont.

Rhubarb Bars for Microwave

Crust:
1 cup flour
1 tsp. baking powder
¼ tsp. salt
¼ cup margarine
1 egg
1 tbsp. milk
2 cups rhubarb
1 pkg. strawberry or raspberry jelly powder

Sift together dry ingredients. Cut in margarine. Add egg and milk, mix well to form soft dough. Pat into 9" square glass pan. Prick well with a fork all over crust. Let sit about 5 minutes. Microwave on full power for 5 minutes. Cool slightly. Chop rhubarb into ½" size pieces. Spread over crust. Sprinkle dry jelly powder evenly over rhubarb.

Topping:
¾ cup brown sugar
½ cup flour
¼ cup margarine

Cut in margarine until crumbly. Sprinkle topping evenly over mixture in pan. Microwave full power 5½ to 6 minutes or until rhubarb is tender. Let cool, then refrigerate. Cut into bars or squares.

Poplar Point United Church
Poplar Point, Man.

Carrot Bars

3 cups finely grated carrots
2 cups flour
2 cups white sugar
1 tsp. salt
2 tsp. cinnamon
2 tsp. soda
1½ cups oil
4 eggs, beaten

Sift dry ingredients and add the rest in order. Pour onto cookie sheet. Bake at 350°F for 30-35 minutes.

Frosting:
8 oz. Philadelphia cream cheese
¼ lb. butter
1 cup icing sugar
1 cup chopped nuts
2 tsp. vanilla

Emmanuel United Church
Saskatoon, Sask.

Butterscotch Brownies

¾ cup flour
1 tsp. baking powder
¼ cup butter
1 cup brown sugar
1 egg, slightly beaten
¼ tsp. salt
1 tsp. vanilla
½ cup nuts (optional)

Stir dry ingredients together. Melt butter and brown sugar over low heat. Stir in slightly beaten egg. Blend in dry ingredients. Add vanilla and nuts and bake in greased, floured 8" square pan in slow oven (300°F) for 25-35 minutes. Cut while warm.

Icing:
¼ cup butter
½ cup brown sugar
⅛ cup milk
1 cup icing sugar

Boil butter and brown sugar two minutes, slowly. Add milk and bring to boil, stirring constantly. Cool. Add icing sugar until desired consistency.

Hampstead United Church
Gadshill, Ont.

Almond Rocco Bars

1 pkg. graham crackers
1 cup slivered almonds
1 cup butter
¾ cup brown sugar
1 cup chocolate chips

Fill cookie sheet with crackers and sprinkle with nuts. Cook butter and sugar until well blended. Pour over squares and nuts. Bake 8 minutes at 350°F. Sprinkle with chocolate chips and swirl. Keep refrigerated.

Forest United Church
Forest, Ont.

Double Chocolate Crumble Bars

¾ cup all-purpose flour
2 tbsp. unsweetened cocoa powder
¼ tsp. baking powder
¼ tsp. salt
½ cup butter or margarine
¾ cup sugar
2 eggs
1 tsp. vanilla
2 cups mini marshmallows
½ cup chopped pecans or walnuts
1 - 6 oz. pkg. chocolate chips (1 cup)
1 cup peanut butter
1½ cups rice krispies cereal

Grease a 13x9x2'' baking pan. Stir together flour, cocoa and baking powder. In mixing bowl beat butter or margarine on medium speed of electric mixer about 30 seconds. Add sugar and beat till fluffy. Add eggs and vanilla. Beat till well blended. Add dry ingredients and blend well. Stir in nuts. Spread in prepared pan and bake at 350°F for 15-20 minutes or until done. Sprinkle with marshmallows and bake 3 minutes more. Cool. In a saucepan combine chocolate chips and peanut butter. Cook and stir over low heat till chocolate is melted. Stir in rice krispies cereal. Spread over marshmallow layer. Cover and chill. Cut into bars. Store in fridge. Makes about 48 squares.

St. Lukes United Church,
Fort St. John

Caramel Pecan Bars

Crust:
1 cup (250 mL) butter
½ cup (125 mL) lightly packed brown sugar
3 cups (750 mL) all-purpose flour
1 egg

Filling:
3 cups (750 mL) pecan halves
¾ cup (175 mL) butter
½ (125 mL) liquid honey
¾ cup (175 mL) lightly packed brown sugar
¼ cup (50 mL) whipping cream

Combine all crust ingredients and mix until blended. Press evenly in jelly roll pan. Bake at 350°F (180°C) for 15 minutes.

Filling: Spread pecans evenly over crust. (Take time to place pecans or walnuts right side up.) In large heavy saucepan, melt butter and honey. Add brown sugar. Boil 5-7 minutes, stirring constantly until a rich caramel colour. Remove from heat. Stir in cream. Mix well and pour over pecans. Bake 15 minutes longer. Cool - then cut in squares.

Hampstead United Church
Gadshill, Ont.

Chocolate Caramel Squares

14 oz. wrapped caramels
1 cup Carnation milk
2 cups flour
2 cups rolled oats
1½ cups lightly packed brown sugar
1 tsp. baking soda
½ tsp. salt
1½ cups butter or margarine, softened
1 - 300 g pkg. chipits
1 cup walnuts, chopped

Melt caramels and milk together on low heat, stirring until smooth. Combine flour, rolled oats, brown sugar, soda and salt in large bowl. Cut in butter until mixture is crumbly. Press ½ mixture in 15x10'' pan, or two 9'' pans. Bake at 350°F for about 5 minutes. Sprinkle chipits and walnuts evenly over crust. Pour caramel mixture over top. Sprinkle with remaining crumbs. Bake 15-20 minutes longer or until golden. Cut in squares when cool.

Westmount Park Church
Westmount, Que.

Butterscotch Squares

Whole graham wafer crackers
½ cup butter
1 cup brown sugar
⅓ cup milk
1 egg, beaten
1 cup coconut
½ cup walnuts
1 cup graham wafer crumbs
½ tsp. vanilla

Place whole graham wafers in 12x8'' pan. Melt butter and sugar; add milk and egg. Cook for 5 minutes. Stir in coconut, walnuts, graham crumbs and vanilla. Spread mixture on graham crackers. Cover with a layer of graham crackers. Cool. Cover with a thin icing.

Plevna United Church
Plevna, Ont.

Almond and Marshmallow Bars

30 lge. white marshmallows
⅓ cup butter or margarine
2½ cups Special K cereal or frosted flakes
1 cup flaked coconut
1 cup roasted, slivered almonds

Melt cut up marshmallows and butter over low heat or in top of double boiler until well blended. Remove from heat. Add other ingredients. Put in a buttered 9x9'' pan. Pat lightly. Do not press. Do not freeze.

Hillview United
Liskeard, Ont.
Riverview United Church
Winnipeg, Man.

Grace's Bars

1 can sweetened condensed milk
1½ cups coconut
23 crushed graham crackers
1 cup chocolate chips
1 tsp. vanilla

Mix all ingredients together. Pat into well-greased 9x13'' pan. Bake at 225°F for 15 minutes. Do not overbake.
Yield: 24 servings.

St. Andrews United Church
Bow Island, Alta.

Date Squares

1½ cups all-purpose flour
½ tsp. baking soda
1½ cups quick oats
1½ cups brown sugar
1 cup butter

Date filling:
1 lb. pitted dates, chopped
½ cup hot water
¼ cup sugar
Pinch of salt
¼ cup orange juice
Rind of ½ orange
2 tsp. lemon juice
1 tsp. vanilla

Combine dates, hot water, sugar, salt, orange juice, orange rind and lemon juice together in a saucepan. Cook over medium heat until dates are soft and water is absorbed. Add vanilla and let cool. Stir flour and baking soda together; add oats and brown sugar and mix well. Work in butter, with fork, until mixture is crumbly. Spread ½ mixture in bottom of greased 8'' square pan and pat down. Cover with cold date filling. Pat remaining mixture on top. Bake in a moderate oven, 350°F, for 30 minutes.
Note: For thinner date squares use larger pan (9x13'').
Yield: 22 squares (2''x2'')

Memorial United Church
St. Catharines, Ont.

Orange Coconut Bars

¼ cup butter
1 cup brown sugar
1 egg
½ tsp. vanilla
2 tsp. grated orange rind
½ cup flour
½ tsp. salt
1 tsp. baking powder
1 cup coconut
1 cup chopped dates

Melt butter in saucepan. Remove from heat and add sugar. Blend in egg, vanilla and orange rind. Stir in flour, salt and baking powder. Add coconut and dates. Spread in shallow pan, approximately 9x13''. Bake at 350°F for 30 minutes. While warm, cut into 24 bars.

Emmanuel United Church
Saskatoon, Sask.

Two-tone Brownies

½ cup margarine
1 cup white sugar
2 eggs
¾ cup flour
½ tsp. baking powder
¼ tsp. salt
¼ cup milk

Cream margarine and sugar. Add eggs and remaining ingredients. Divide mixture into two bowls. In first bowl add **3 teaspoons cocoa** and **1 teaspoon vanilla flavouring.** In second bowl add **½ cup coconut** and **½ teaspoon almond flavouring.** Place in 8x11'' pan, putting chocolate mixture on the bottom. Bake at 350°F approximately 30 minutes. Ice with chocolate frosting.

George St. United Church
St. John's, Nfld.

Kahlua Brownies

1¼ cups flour
¼ tsp. baking powder
½ tsp. salt
½ cup butter or margarine
¾ cup brown sugar
1 large egg
¼ cup and 1 tbsp. Kahlua or any coffee
liqueur or very strong coffee
1 cup chocolate chips
¼ cup chopped walnuts

Preheat oven to 350°F. Sift flour, baking powder and salt together and set aside. Cream butter, sugar and egg. Stir in ¼ cup liqueur. Add flour mixture and blend well. Fold in chocolate chips and walnuts. Spread mixture in 9'' square pan and bake for 30 minutes. Cool and brush with remaining coffee liqueur.

Kahlua Brown Butter Icing:
2 tbsp. butter
1 tbsp. coffee liqueur or very strong coffee
2 tbsp. cream
1¼ cups sifted confectioners sugar

Heat butter till lightly brown. Remove from heat and add coffee liqueur, cream and icing sugar. Beat until smooth. Put on top of brownies and cut into squares.

Streetsville United Church
Mississauga, Ont.

Grandma Graham's Brownies

1 cup white sugar
½ cup butter
½ cup flour
2 eggs
2 squares semi-sweet chocolate, melted
1 cup chopped pecans

Cream sugar and butter. Add flour, eggs, chocolate and pecans. Spread mixture in an 8x8'' pan. Bake at 350°F for 30 minutes. These are so good, there is no need to ice! This is an old recipe - so easy to make and delicious!

Aurora United Church
Aurora, Ont.

Ten Commandments of Human Relations

1. SPEAK TO PEOPLE — there is nothing so nice as a cheerful word of greeting.

2. SMILE AT PEOPLE — it takes 72 muscles to frown, only 14 to smile.

3. CALL PEOPLE — the sweetest music to anyone's ears is the sound of his own name.

4. BE FRIENDLY and helpful, if you would have friends, be a friend.

5. BE CORDIAL — speak and act as if everything you do is a genuine pleasure.

6. BE GENUINELY interested in people — you can like almost everybody if you try.

7. BE GENEROUS with praise — cautious with criticism.

8. BE CONSIDERATE with the feelings of others — there are usually three sides to a controversy: yours, the other fellow's, and the right side.

9. BE ALERT to give service — what counts most in life is what we do for others.

10. ADD TO THIS a good sense of humour, a big dose of patience and a dash of humility, and you will be rewarded many-fold.

United Church in Meadowood
Winnipeg, Man.

Puddings

Cheese Apple Crisp

5 cups apples, peeled and sliced
¼ tsp. cinnamon
¾ cup water (room temp.)
¾ tbsp. lemon juice
1½ cups white sugar
1 cup all-purpose flour
¼ tsp. salt
½ cup butter or margarine
½-¾ cup shredded cheese

Arrange apples in shallow baking pan. Sprinkle with cinnamon. Add water and lemon juice. Combine sugar, salt and flour. Work in butter to form a crumbly mixture. Lightly stir in shredded cheese. Spread this mixture over apples. Bake at 350°F until apples are tender and crust is golden brown (about 40 min.)

Berwick United Church
Berwick, N.S.

Rhubarb Shortbread

3 cups diced rhubarb
¾ cup white sugar
¼ cup shortening
½ cup granulated sugar
½ tsp. vanilla
1 egg
1 cup sifted flour
¼ tsp. salt
1½ tsp. baking powder

Mix together rhubarb and ¾ cup sugar. Let stand 10 minutes. Simmer gently until tender. Pour into baking dish (8x8"). Cream shortening, sugar and vanilla. Add egg, then sifted dry ingredients. Batter is stiff. Drop by spoonful on top of rhubarb. Bake at 350°f for 30 minutes. Serve warm with whipped cream for variety.

Lachute United Church
Lachute, Que.

Apple & Peanut Butter Crisp

6 cups apples, sliced (or canned)
1 tsp. cinnamon
¾ cup brown sugar
⅔ cup flour
¼ cup margarine
¼ cup chunky peanut butter

Place apples in greased 8" pan. Mix in cinnamon. Combine sugar and flour. Cut in margarine and peanut butter till coarse crumbs are formed. Add ½ cup to apple mixture. Sprinkle remaining over apples. Bake uncovered in 375°F oven for 40 minutes. Serve warm, as is or with ice cream or topping. This recipe can be successfully doubled or quadrupled for quantity serving.

Wesley United Church
Regina, Sask.

Blueberry Grunt

1 qt. blueberries (4 cups)
½ cup sugar (or to taste)
½ cup water

Put berries, sugar and water in a pot. Cover and boil gently until there is plenty of juice. In the meantime make dumplings.

Dumplings:
2 cups flour
4 tsp. baking powder
½ tsp. salt
1 tsp. sugar
2 tbsp. shortening
¼-½ cup milk

Sift together flour, baking powder, salt and sugar into a bowl. Cut in the shortening. Add enough milk to make a soft biscuit dough. Drop by spoonful onto the hot blueberries. Cover tightly and simmer. Do not peek for 15 minutes. Serve hot.

Zion United Church, Liverpool, N.S.

Rhubarb Cobbler

1 cup sugar
⅓ cup pancake mix
1 tsp. grated lemon peel
4 cups (about 1½ lbs.) fresh or frozen
rhubarb cut in 1'' pieces

Heat oven to moderate (375°F) temperature.
For base combine sugar, pancake mix and lemon peel. Add rhubarb and toss lightly. Place in a 9'' square baking pan.

Topping:
¾ cup pancake mix
⅔ cup sugar
1 egg, beaten
¼ cup melted butter or margarine

Combine mix and sugar. Stir in egg until mixture resembles coarse crumbs. Sprinkle evenly over rhubarb base. Drizzle with melted butter. Bake in preheated oven (375°F) 35-40 minutes. Serve with cream, ice cream or Cool Whip.

Central United Church
Sarnia, Ont.

Fruit Cobbler

4 cups sliced apples, plums, peaches, apricots
or berries or any frozen fruit
½-¾ cup sugar
⅛ tsp. nutmeg, cinnamon or 1 tsp. lemon
juice

Topping:
2 tbsp. shortening or margarine
⅓ cup sugar
1 egg, beaten
⅞ cup sifted flour
1½ tsp. baking powder
½ cup milk

Butter a 9'' deep pie plate or cake pan. Spread fruit and sprinkle with sugar and spice or lemon juice. If using frozen fruit, thaw in oven while preparing topping. Cream shortening and sugar; add beaten egg. Mix well. Add sifted flour and baking powder alternately with milk. Pour over fruit. Bake 35-40 minutes at 350°F. Delicious served plain, or with ice cream, cream or milk.

Wilkie United Church, Wilkie, Sask.
Franklin Centre United Church, Franklin Centre, Que.

Baked Partridgeberry Pudding

2 cups flour
1 cup sugar
3 tbsp. melted butter
⅔ cup milk
1 egg
2½ tsp. baking powder
½ tsp. salt
1 tsp. vanilla
2 cups partridgeberries

Sift dry ingredients into mixing bowl. Add butter, milk, vanilla and egg. Beat 2 minutes. Stir in berries. Bake in greased 9x9'' pan at 350°F for 40 minutes.
Note: Blueberries or saskatoons can be used instead of partridgeberries.

St. Andrews United Church,
Whiteway, Nfld.

Baked Pumpkin Pudding

6 tbsp. butter
¾ cup brown sugar
¼ cup white sugar
2 eggs
1½ cups flour
½ tsp. salt
½ tsp. baking soda
½ tsp. cinnamon
½ tsp. ginger
¼ tsp. nutmeg
¾ cup mashed cooked pumpkin
½ cup buttermilk

Cream butter and sugars until light. Beat in eggs. Stir together flour, salt, soda, cinnamon, ginger and nutmeg. Combine pumpkin and buttermilk. Add to creamed mixture alternately with dry ingredients, mixing well after each addition. Also add ½ cup chopped walnuts if desired. Spoon mixture into a greased and floured 6½ cup ring mold, cover tightly with foil. Bake at 350°F for 1 hour. Let stand 10 minutes. Unmold. Serve with whipped cream if desired.
Serves 8-10.

Trinity United Church, Hazlet, Sask.

Cranberry Pudding

1 cup flour
½ cup white sugar
2 tsp. baking powder
¼ tsp. salt
1 tsp. vanilla
½ cup milk
1 cup raw cranberries

Mix together and pour into a small casserole dish. Make a sauce of:
1 cup brown sugar
2 cups boiling water
Butter size of a walnut

Pour over pudding and bake 20-30 minutes in a 350°F oven.
Serves 6.

Trinity United Church, Shelburne, N.S.
Port Mouton United Church, Port Mouton, N.S.

Quick Fruit Pudding

½ cup butter or margarine
1 cup flour
1 cup white sugar
2 tsp. baking powder
¾ cup milk
Dash salt
16 oz. cherries, raspberries or other fruit

Place butter in 8x10'' pan and put in 350°F oven till melted. Mix flour, ¾ cup sugar, baking powder and salt. Add milk and beat until smooth. Pour batter in hot butter, do not stir. Scatter fruit on top of batter and sprinkle with remaining ¼ cup sugar. Bake 30 minutes until top is brown. This is a quick and easy dessert when unexpected company drops in.

Westcott United Church
Conn, Ont.

Batter Pie

(Pudding)

Slice several apples into a saucepan and add a little water. Gently cook on stove while mixing batter.

Batter:
1 tbsp. butter
1 tbsp. sugar
1 egg, beaten
½ cup milk
1 cup flour
1½ tsp. baking powder
1 tsp. cinnamon

Mix batter and pour over apples in an 8x8'' pan. Bake at 350°F for 30 minutes. Serve with caramel sauce.

Caramel Sauce:
1 tbsp. butter
2 tbsp. flour
1 cup brown sugar
¼ cup water

Mix in order given in pan on stove until thickened.

Lansdowne United Church
Lansdowne, Ont.

Snow Pudding

1 tbsp. gelatin soaked in ¼ cup cold water
1 cup boiling water
1 cup sugar
¼ cup lemon juice
3 egg whites

Dissolve gelatin in boiling water. Add sugar and lemon juice. Set aside in cool place. Occasionally stir mixture and when it is thick enough to hold mark of spoon, beat until frothy. Add egg whites, beaten stiff and continue beating until stiff enough to hold its shape. Mold. Serve with custard sauce.

Custard Sauce:
3 egg yolks
¼ cup sugar
⅛ tsp. salt
2 cups scalded milk
½ tsp. vanilla

Beat egg yolks. Add sugar and salt. Add milk gradually, stirring constantly. Cook and stir in double boiler over hot, not boiling water until mixture coats a spoon, or about 7 minutes. Chill and flavour.
Serves 6.

Aylesford United Church
Aylesford, N.S.

Magic Carmel Pudding

1 or more unopened cans Eagle Brand sweetened condensed milk

Place condensed milk (unopened tins) in pot of boiling water. Keep at boiling point for 3 hours. Be sure to keep can covered with water. You can serve right away or it may be left till later. If left, place can in hot water for 1 minute before serving.

To serve, punch hole in bottom of can to let the air in. Remove top with opener. Loosen carmel from sides of can with a knife dipped in hot water. Turn on plate and cut in slices, with knife dipped in hot water. Garnish with whipped cream, fruit or nuts, or place a slice of carmel on a slice of pineapple or cake before garnishing. May also be used in sherbet glasses. Blend magic carmel pudding with hot water, fruit juices or coffee. Beat till smooth, then put in glasses. Garnish however desired. If pressure cooker is used, use 15 pounds pressure for 1 hour.

Cape North United Church
Cape Breton, N.S.

Economy Pudding

¼ cup shortening, melted
1 cup white sugar
2 tbsp. molasses
1 cup dried bread crumbs
1 cup milk
½ cup sifted all-purpose flour
1 tsp. cinnamon
½ tsp. cloves
½ tsp. allspice
1 tsp. soda
½ cup walnuts

Soak dried bread crumbs in milk. Mix in melted shortening, sugar and molasses. Add dry ingredients and walnuts. Bake in casserole dish - uncovered at 350°F until toothpick comes out dry, about 1 hour. Can be served hot with caramel sauce. Can be reheated another time by adding a bit of hot water and covering with casserole lid. Nice with vanilla ice cream.

Grace United Church
Gananoque, Ont.

Kingston Pudding

1 cup sugar
2 cups flour
3 tbsp. margarine or butter
Pinch of salt
1 tsp. baking powder
1 tsp. vanilla
Milk to make a soft batter (about 1½ cups)

Bake in muffin tins at 375°F for about 35 minutes or until done. Serve with brown sugar sauce.

Brown Sugar Sauce:
2 cups brown sugar
1 cup water
2 tbsp. cornstarch
1 tsp. vanilla

Mix together sugar, water and cornstarch and cook until thick. Add vanilla and stir.

Renfrew United Church
Calgary, Alta.

Pineapple Custard

3 eggs, beaten
½ cup sugar
½ pt. (8 oz.) sour cream
1 tsp. flour, heaped
1 tsp. vanilla
1 small can crushed pineapple

Drain pineapple and save juice. Combine eggs, flour, sugar and juice in a double boiler. Stir until thick. (Can be made without a double boiler but heat must be on low.) Cool; add vanilla and refrigerate until cold. Stir in pineapple. Fold in sour cream.

St. James United Church
Stroud, Ont.

Pistachio Dessert

1 small pkg. instant pistachio pudding mix
1 - 28 oz. can fruit cocktail, including juice
1 cup mini marshmallows
1 cup cooked rice
1 large container Cool Whip (1 litre)

Blend together. Serves 10-12.

Wesley Memorial United Church
Moncton, N.B.

Maple-Walnut Cream Pudding

2 cups milk
1 cup maple syrup
2 tbsp. cornstarch
Salt
2 eggs, well beaten
½ cup chopped walnuts
Whipped cream

Scald 1¾ cups milk with maple syrup in top of double boiler. Combine remaining milk with cornstarch, gradually stirring cornstarch mixture into scalded milk and syrup. Cook 25 minutes. Add beaten eggs; cook 5 minutes. Pour into serving dishes, sprinkle with walnuts. Chill and serve with a swirl of whipped cream.

Danville-Asbestos Trinity United Church
Danville, Que.

Cherry Parfaits

1 cup milk
1 cup sour cream (commercial)
¼ tsp. almond extract
3¾ oz. pkg. instant vanilla pudding
1 can cherry pie filling
Toasted slivered almonds

Combine milk, sour cream, almond extract. Add pudding mix and beat 2 minutes. Fill parfait glasses with alternate layers of pudding, cherry filling and almonds. Chill. Garnish with almonds.

Wesley United Church
Vandorf, Ont.

Apple Amber

4 cups peeled, sliced apples
⅔ cup sugar
¼ cup soft butter or margarine
Grated rind and juice of 1 lemon
3 eggs separated
1 tsp. water
3 tbsp. sugar

Put first four ingredients in a pot, cover and cook 4 minutes on high. Remove and stir apples with a fork, crushing large pieces here and there. Beat egg yolks lightly and add 1 teaspoon water, then add to hot apples and mix thorough-ly. Cook 3 minutes at medium heat. Stir well - mixture should be creamy at this point. Beat egg whites with 3 tablespoons sugar and fold into apple mixture. Cook 2 minutes on high heat. Let stand until ready to serve, hot or cold. Serves 4.

St. Mark's United Church
St. Thomas, Ont.

Orange Pudding

3 oranges, peeled and sectioned
3 tbsp. white sugar
2 cups milk
2 tbsp. cornstarch
1 tsp. salt
¾ cup white sugar
2 eggs, separated
1 tsp. vanilla
2 tbsp. white sugar

Shake 3 tablespoons sugar over oranges and arrange in casserole dish. Heat milk in double boiler. Slowly add cornstarch, salt and ¾ cup white sugar. Stir until thickened. Beat egg yolks and vanilla. Add to milk mixture. Pour over oranges. Beat egg whites and 2 tablespoons sugar until stiff. Spread on top and brown in oven at 350°-375°F for 5-10 minutes. Serves 6-8.

St. James United Church
Antigonish, N.S.

Easy Christmas Pudding

2 cups finely ground suet
1½ cups brown sugar
1 tsp. salt
2½ cups flour
1 tsp. baking soda
1 tsp. cinnamon
1½ cups boiling weak coffee
Speck of ginger and allspice
2 cups raisins
1 cup dates
1 cup currants
Chopped blanched almonds (optional)
1 cup mixed fruit

Mix all the ingredients, then pour hot coffee over them and put in a greased pan and steam for three hours without lifting the cover. I use all raisins instead of any currants.

Highgate United Church
Highgate, Ont.

Cakes

Lazy Daisy Cake

2 eggs
1 cup sugar
1 tsp. vanilla
1 cup flour
½ tsp. salt
1 tsp. baking powder
½ cup milk
2 tbsp. butter

Beat eggs until thick. Add sugar and vanilla. Add the sifted dry ingredients and mix. Add butter to milk and heat until butter melts. Add this to the batter and mix. Pour into greased 8x8" pan. Bake 30 minutes in moderate oven (350°F).

4 tbsp. butter
10 tbsp. brown sugar
1 cup coconut
3 tbsp. light cream

Melt butter. Add sugar, coconut and cream. Spread on top of hot cake and brown in oven. Mixture is thick, but will run later. Using the broiler to brown is good.

Rosemont United Church
Regina, Sask.

No-Icing Sugar Icing

¾ cup shortening
¾ cup white sugar
½ tsp. vanilla
¾ cup milk
3 tbsp. flour or cornstarch
Pinch of salt

Combine flour (cornstarch) and milk in saucepan over low heat, stirring constantly until mixture thickens. Put in fridge to cool. Combine remaining ingredients in bowl. Beat on high speed. Add thickened milk mixture gradually till all is thick and smooth. Frosts a 13x9" cake.

St. Paul's United Church
Sarnia, Ont.

Microwave Yummy Cake

1 - 16 oz. pkg. cake mix
1 - 22 oz. can pie filling
2 eggs
½ cup sour cream (optional)

In large mixing bowl blend ingredients. Rest 10 minutes. Spoon into 12 cup plastic bundt pan. Microwave on HIGH for 9-12 minutes, rotating ¼ turn every 4 minutes. Rest 10 minutes before you loosen sides and middle. Invert on serving dish. May use spice cake with apple filling, chocolate cake with cherry filling or whole cranberry sauce, or gingerbread with brandied mincemeat. May use round casserole in place of bundt pan.

Bruce Mines United Church
Bruce Mines, Ont.

Fluffy Shadow Frosting

1 cup sifted icing sugar
⅓ cup water
¼ tsp. salt
¼ tsp. cream of tartar
Scant tbsp. corn syrup
1 egg white
3 drops green food coloring
½ oz. melted unsweetened chocolate
1 tsp. melted butter

Combine sugar, water, salt and cream of tartar in saucepan. Bring to boil, simmer 1 minute. Gradually pour hot syrup in thin steady stream over unbeaten egg white, beating constantly until straight peaks are formed when beater is raised. Stir in vanilla and food coloring; frost cooled cake; allow to stand a few minutes. Combine melted chocolate and butter. Cool slightly, spoon around top edge of cake, allowing to drip down sides.

Wesley United Church
Regina, Sask.

Fruit Cocktail Crunch

2 - 28 oz. cans fruit cocktail
1 - 500 g white cake mix
1 cup butter

Drain fruit cocktail and put in a 9x13'' pan. Melt butter. Put the cake mix in a bowl and pour melted butter over. Mix well by hand. Batter will be gooey! Drop spoonsful of batter to completely cover the fruit cocktail. Bake in a 350°F oven for 50 minutes till nicely browned. A swirl of topping dresses it up. Yummy, quick and easy.

Wellington Square United Church
Burlington, Ont.

Watergate Cake

1 - 500 g box white cake mix
1 - 106 g box pistachio pudding
1 cup oil
3 eggs
1 cup ginger ale
½ cup chopped nuts

Bake 30-40 minutes at 350°F in 9x13'' pan.

Topping:
2 envelopes Dream Whip
1 - 106 g box pistachio pudding
1¼ cups cold milk
Beat all ingredients together. Add nuts at the end. Bake 30-40 minutes at 350°F in 9x13'' pan.

Forest Home United Church
Orillia, Ont.

Poppy Seed Cake

1 pkg. golden layer cake mix
1 cup sour cream
½ cup oil
¼ cup sugar
¼ cup water
4 eggs
½ cup poppy seeds

Preheat oven to 375°F. Beat all ingredients together. Add poppy seeds at the end. Bake in tube pan or bundt pan for 45-55 minutes. Cool right side up for at least 25 minutes. Sprinkle with powdered icing sugar when cake is cool. This cake is also good after its been frozen. Stays moist for days.

Harrow United Church
Harrow, Ont.

Apple Spice Crumb Cake

1 pkg. spice layer cake mix
3-4 apples, peeled and cored (Macs are good)
½ cup white or brown sugar
½ cup all-purpose flour
½ tsp. cinnamon
¼ cup butter
½ cup chopped nuts or coconut

Combine sugar, flour, cinnamon and butter until crumbly, then add nuts. Preheat oven and prepare cake batter according to directions on package. Pour into greased 13x9x2'' pan. Slice apples very thin and overlap in rows down the cake batter. Sprinkle crumb mixture over apples and bake according to package directions. Serve warm or cold. Top with whipped cream if desired.

Embro Knox United Church
Embro, Ont.

Apricot Cake

4 tbsp. (60 mL) brown sugar
2 tbsp. (30 mL) butter or margarine
1 pt. (254 g) apricot preserves (or fresh stewed in 50% sugar)

Melt the butter or margarine in a round 8'' (20 cm) pan. Add sugar and stir until well blended. Drain fruit, reserving juice for cake. Cut fruit in slices and press into syrup in pan. Cover with the following batter:

¼ cup (57 g) butter or margarine
⅓ cup (80 mL) white sugar
¼ tsp. (1 mL) almond extract
1 egg, well-beaten
1 cup (250 mL) all-purpose flour
2 tsp. (10 mL) baking powder
¼ tsp. (1 mL) salt
2 tbsp. (30 mL) wheat germ
½ cup (125 mL) apricot juice

Cream together first three ingredients. Add well beaten egg. Sift together all dry ingredients and add to first mixture alternately with the fruit juice. Spread batter over fruit slices. Bake at 350°F (180°C) for 25-30 minutes, or until done. Serve warm with cream or vanilla ice cream. Serves 6-8.

Kirkfield Park United Church
Winnipeg, Man.

Mandarin Orange Cake

2 cups flour
2 tsp. baking soda
1 can mandarin oranges and juice
1½ tsp. vanilla
2 cups white sugar
2 eggs
1½ tsp. salt

Put all ingredients together and mix for 3-4 minutes. Bake at 350°F for 30-40 minutes in 9x13" pan.

Topping:
¾ cup brown sugar
½ cup margarine or butter
1 cup nuts (pecans best) or coconut
¼ cup milk

Mix together. Pour over cooled cake. Place under broiler for 1 minute.

Camlachie United Church
Camlachie, Ont.
St. Pauls United Church
Kenmore, Ont.

Easy Special Rhubarb Cake

2 cups flour
1 tsp. baking powder
1 cup butter or margarine
¼ tsp. salt
1 egg, beaten

Mix first four ingredients until crumbly. Save one cup for top. Add beaten egg and press in a 9x13" pan.

Filling:
1 cup white sugar
1 box (85 g) strawberry Jell-O
½ cup flour
½ cup melted butter or margarine
2 eggs, beaten
4 cups fresh or frozen rhubarb

Mix first three ingredients. Add melted butter and beaten eggs. Stir in rhubarb. Spread filling on crust. Sprinkle with saved crumbs. Cinnamon can be added. Bake one hour at 350°F.
Note: This cake freezes well, made up in individual servings.

Wilkie United Church
Wilkie, Sask.

Macaroon Cake

Bottom:
½ cup butter or margarine
4 egg yolks
1 tsp. baking powder
½ cup white sugar
1 cup flour
3 tbsp. milk or more

Topping:
4 egg whites, beat stiff
1 tsp. vanilla
½ cup white sugar
1 cup dessicated coconut

Spread bottom layer in 8" pan, cover with topping. Bake at 350°F for 30 minutes. Needs no icing and stays fresh a long time.

Foam Lake United Church
Foam Lake, Sask.

Prize Applesauce Cake

½ cup shortening
2 eggs, beaten
2 tsp. baking powder
1½ tsp. cinnamon
Salt
1⅓ cup sugar
2¾ cups flour
¼ tsp. baking soda
½ tsp. cloves
2 cups applesauce
1½ cups raisins and chopped nuts (combined)

Cream shortening and sugar. Add eggs, dry ingredients and applesauce. Add nuts and raisins last. Bake in 9x13" pan at 350°F for 35 minutes. Spread cake with praline topping.

Praline topping:
½ cup butter
¾ cup brown sugar
¼ cup sour cream
⅔ cup coconut
¾ cup chopped nuts

Combine above. Spread on warm cake. Place under broiler for 5 minutes. Serve warm.

Knox - St. Pauls United Church
Cornwall, Ont.

Pineapple Tart Cake

½ cup butter
1 cup flour

Blend butter and flour. Press into a 9x9'' pan and bake at 325°F for 20 minutes.

Cook till thick:
1 - 20 oz. can crushed pineapple
3 egg yolks
1 tbsp. butter
1 tbsp. cornstarch

When cooked, spread on base. Beat **3 egg whites** till peaked. Beat in ⅓ **cup sugar** and ½ **teaspoon vanilla, salt.** Spread on pineapple mixture and bake at 325°F for 20 minutes. Cool.

St. Pauls United Church
Estevan, Sask.

Busy Day Cake

2 cups sifted cake flour
2½ tsp. baking powder
1¼ cups white sugar
1 tsp. salt
⅓ cup soft shortening
⅔ cup milk
1 egg
⅓ cup milk
1 tsp. vanilla

Grease and flour two 9'' cake pans or one 9x13'' pan. Sift flour, sugar, baking powder and salt into a large mixing bowl. Make a well in ingredients and add shortening, ⅔ cup milk and vanilla. Beat until well blended. Add ⅓ cup milk and egg. Beat thoroughly. Pour into prepared pans. Bake 30 minutes in 350°F oven until top springs back when lightly touched with finger. Remove and cool 10 minutes. Finish with caramel boiled frosting.

Easy Caramel Frosting:
½ cup butter
1 cup firmly packed brown sugar
¼ cup milk
Sifted icing sugar
Melt butter in saucepan. Add brown sugar and cook over low heat for two minutes, stirring constantly. Add milk, continue cooking until mixture comes to a boil. Remove from heat, cool and add enough sifted icing sugar to make an icing of spreading consistency.
Yield: about 2 cups.

Wilkie United Church
Wilkie, Sask.

Kay's Chocolate Cake

Step 1:
2 cups white sugar
⅔ cup vegetable oil
2 eggs
2 tsp. vanilla

Beat the above for 4 minutes with electric beater.

2⅔ cups flour
⅔ cup cocoa
2 tsp. baking powder
1 tsp. salt
2 tsp. baking soda

Sift all dry ingredients together in a bowl. Add alternately with 2 cups boiling water to Step 1 ingredients. Beat well after each addition. Pour batter in 8x12'' pan. Bake at 325°F for 50 minutes. Ice with chocolate or your favorite icing. This is a very moist chocolate cake.

Emmanuel United Church
Saskatoon, Sask.
Wolfe Island United Church
Wolfe Island, Ont.

Mothers Fudge Cake

½ cup margarine
½ cup flour
½ cup nuts
1 tsp. vanilla
1 cup brown sugar
3 tbsp. cocoa
1 egg

Cream sugar, margarine and add egg. Sift flour and cocoa together. Add to creamed mixture. Add vanilla and nuts. Pour into greased 8x8'' pan. Bake in 400°F oven for 17 minutes or 350°F oven for 25 minutes. Sugar can be reduced to ½ cup.

Icing:
2 tbsp. warmed milk
2 tbsp. cocoa
1 tbsp. margarine
1 cup icing sugar

Frost as soon as removed from oven.

Transcona Memorial
Winnipeg, Man.
Trinity United Church
Riverview, N.B.

Best Chocolate Cake
(Eggless)

3 cups flour
2 cups white sugar
2 tsp. baking soda
½ cup cocoa
2 tsp. vinegar
1 cup salad oil
1 tsp. salt
2 tsp. vanilla
2 cups cold water

Put all ingredients in one bowl. Mix well. Put in greased and floured 9x13" pan. Bake at 350°F for 35-40 minutes. Ice as you wish. Will also make 2 dozen cupcakes.

Harrington United Church
Calumet, Que.
Trinity United Church
Hopewell Hill, N.B.

"Healthy" Chocolate Cake

½ cup cocoa powder (for darker chocolate cake increase to ¾ cup cocoa)
1¼ cups white sugar
2 cups flour
1 cup skim milk powder
2 tsp. baking soda
1 tsp. baking powder
½ tsp. salt
½ cup unsweetened applesauce
2 cups plain low-fat yogurt (less than 2% M.F.)
⅓ cup oil
2 eggs (may use 4 egg whites instead of 2 whole eggs)
2 tsp. vanilla

Mix dry ingredients. Beat liquid ingredients together. Add liquid ingredients to dry ingredients all at once - beat until smooth. Pour into greased 9x13" pan (sprayed with Pam). Bake at 325°F for approximately 45 minutes. Place doily over cake and sift with icing sugar. Remove doily and serve at once. For a richer dessert, top with this icing:

1 cup white sugar
1 tbsp. margarine
½ cup milk

Bring to boil and boil one minute. Remove from heat and add 6 ounces semi-sweet chocolate. Pour over top of warm cake.

Golden Valley Church
Val d'Or, Que.

Pineapple Cake

1 lb. raisins
½ lb. red cherries
½ lb. green cherries
½ lb. mixed peel
1 - 16 oz. can crushed pineapple

Put this fruit in a bowl and let stand overnight. 1 hour before mixing, sprinkle with ½ cup flour.

2 tsp. baking powder
3 eggs
¾ cup butter
1 cup white sugar
2¼ cups flour
½ tsp. salt

Mix all together. Put into foil lined pan (1 very deep 8x8" or 2 loaf pans). Bake at 325°F for approximately 1-2 hours, depending on size of cake pan, or till skewer comes out clean.

Franklin United Church
Franklin Centre, Que.

Grumdrop Cake

1 lb. seeded raisins
2 cups sweetened applesauce
1 lb. gumdrops (no black ones)
1 cup white sugar
1 cup butter
1 tsp. salt
2 eggs
2 cups flour
2 tsp. baking powder

Boil raisins in small amount of water for 5 minutes. Drain and cool. Cream butter and sugar. Add eggs. Sift flour with salt and baking powder. Add 1 cup flour to batter. Add applesauce and raisins. Slice gumdrops and sprinkle with flour. Add remaining flour and gumdrops. Put in a tube pan that has been greased and floured. Bake in slow 325°F oven for approximately 1 hour or until toothpick inserted near centre comes out clean.

St. John's United Church
Kemptville, Ont.

If you have a narrow mind education will broaden it. But there is no cure for a big head.

Lemon Sponge

4 egg yolks
¾ cup sugar
2 tbsp. lemon juice
1 tsp. lemon extract
½ cup potato flour
1 tsp. baking powder
¼ tsp. salt
4 egg whites
½ tsp. cream of tartar

Beat together first four ingredients. Mix next three ingredients and add. Beat egg whites, cream of tartar and fold in. Bake in a tube pan at 325°F for 40 minutes.

Salem United Church
Colborne, Ont.

Sherry's Christmas Cake

2 tsp. brandy
3 lbs. seedless raisins
1 lb. mixed fruit
1 lb. glazed pineapple
1 lb. glazed cherries
1 lb. walnuts
1 jar maraschino cherries and juice
¼ cup fruit juice
1 lge. pkg. gum drops
½ lb. almonds

Mix together and let stand 2-3 days, mixing once a day. (You may pour some brandy, rum or rye over when mixing.)

12 eggs
1 lb. butter
2 cups white sugar
2 cups brown sugar
4 cups flour
½ tsp. salt
1 tsp. soda
2 tsp. cinnamon
1 tsp. each allspice, nutmeg, cloves and mace

Cream butter, sugars and eggs. Dredge fruit with some of the flour mixture before adding to creamed mixture. Put into lined cake pans and bake at 250°-275°F for 2-4 hours, depending on the size of cake pans. This also makes a very nice wedding cake.

Ochre River United Church
Ochre River, Man.

Winnipeg Birthday Cake

Base:
⅓ cup shortening
¼ cup icing sugar
1 tsp. vanilla
1 cup flour
½ tsp. baking powder

Cut shortening into dry ingredients. Mix well. Pat firmly and evenly into an 8" square wax paper lined pan. Bake at 350°F for 10-12 minutes. Cool.

Cake:
½ cup shortening
¾ cup sugar
2 eggs
1 tsp. vanilla
1½ cups flour
2 tsp. baking powder
½ tsp. salt
½ cup milk

Cream shortening and sugar. Add eggs and vanilla, beating well until fluffy. Sift flour, baking powder and salt together. Add to creamed mixture alternately with milk. Pour batter into a greased and floured 8" square pan. Bake at 350°F for 35-40 minutes. Cool.

Frosting:
½ cup milk
2 tbsp. flour
½ cup butter
¼ cup shortening
½ tsp. vanilla
1 cup icing sugar
Dash of salt

In a small saucepan stir together the milk and flour. Cook, stirring constantly until mixture is thickened and smooth; cool. On highest speed of mixer beat cooled flour mixture with butter, shortening and vanilla until smooth and fluffy. Blend in icing sugar and salt. Continue beating until frosting is fluffy (about 15 minutes). To assemble cake place shortbread base on serving plate, spread with small amount of frosting. Place cake on base. Cover top and sides of cake with remaining frosting. If desired, garnish with chocolate sprinkles.

Silver Heights United Church
Winnipeg, Man.

Pies & Tarts

Mince-Pumpkin Pie

Pastry:
1¼ cups stirred, but not sifted, pastry flour
½ tsp. salt
⅓ cup shortening
3 tbsp. butter
1 tbsp. cold water

Cut shortening and butter into flour and salt until size of peas. Drizzle in water, tossing with fork. Shape into ball between palms and roll out on a well-floured board with well-floured rolling pin to fit deep nine inch pie plate.

Filling:
1 cup mincemeat
1 cup canned pumpkin
2 eggs
½ cup granulated sugar
1 cup milk
⅜ tsp. each of cinnamon, nutmeg, ginger and salt

Spread mincemeat evenly over bottom. Mix together pumpkin filling and other ingredients in the order given and pour over mincemeat. You may have too much so bake the pie adding surplus at centre when pie is half baked. Bake at 425°F at centre of oven for 10 minutes. Then reduce heat to 325°F until nearly set, about 50 minutes more.

Grace United Church
Port Dover, Ont.

Gram's Pie Crust

¼ cup butter (or ½ cup margarine)
½ lb. lard
1 tsp. salt
3 cups flour
½ cup cold water

Beat butter, lard and salt with mixer or spatula. Add flour and water. Knead until smooth. Roll out on floured surface.

Wilmot United Church
Fredericton, N.B.
River Hebert United Church
River Hebert, N.S.

Peanut Butter Pie

2 - 6" baked pie shells or 1 - 9" baked
  pie shell
92 g vanilla instant pudding
¼ tsp. nutmeg
¼ cup honey
¾ cup peanut butter
¼ tsp. cinnamon
250 mL whipping cream

Make pudding and add nutmeg. Set aside until firm. Blend honey, peanut butter, (smooth or crunchy) and cinnamon. Whip whipping cream. Carefully, fold prepared pudding mixture into honey and peanut butter mixture. Fold in whipped cream. (Leave a little for decorating.) When carefully folded, set mixture into pie shells or shell. Garnish with whipped cream and chocolate slivers. Set in fridge overnight.

St. John United Church
Hamilton, Ont.

Vanilla Fruit Tart

¾ cup butter or margarine, softened
½ cup confectioners' sugar
1½ cups all-purpose flour

Heat oven to 300°F. Beat butter and confectioners' sugar until light and fluffy; blend in flour. Press mixture onto bottom and up side of 12'' round pizza pan. Bake 20 to 25 minutes or until lightly browned. Cool completely. Prepare vanilla filling; spread on cooled crust. Cover; chill. Prepare fruit topping. Cover; chill.

Vanilla filling:
1 pkg. white chocolate, melted
¼ cup whipping cream
1 - 8 oz. pkg. cream cheese

In microwave-safe bowl microwave vanilla chips and whipping cream at HIGH 1-1½ minutes or until chips are melted and mixture is smooth when stirred. Beat in cream cheese. Now spread on cooled crust.

Fruit Topping:
¼ cup sugar
1 tbsp. cornstarch
½ cup pineapple juice
½ tsp. lemon juice
Assorted fresh fruit

In small saucepan combine sugar and cornstarch; stir in juices. Cook over medium heat, stirring constantly, until thickened; cool. Meanwhile, slice and arrange fruit on top of filling; pour juice mixture or glaze over fruit.

Franklin Centre United Church
Franklin Centre, Que.

Fresh Fruit Tarts

24 baked tart shells
1 - 250 g pkg. cream cheese
1 tin sweetened condensed milk
¼ cup lemon juice
1½ tsp. vanilla
Fresh fruit - strawberries, kiwi, etc.

In large bowl beat cream cheese until fluffy. Beat in sweetened milk, lemon juice, and vanilla until smooth. Spoon filling into baked tart shells. Decorate with fresh fruit. Chill 3 hours.

Carol United Church
Labrador City, Nfld.

Rhubarb Custard Pie

Unbaked 9'' pie shell
2½ cups cut rhubarb
2-3 egg yolks
1 cup sugar
2 tbsp. flour
1 tbsp. melted butter
2-3 egg whites

Beat egg yolks until thick. Gradually add sugar, flour and butter. Fold in rhubarb. Pour into unbaked shell. Bake at 450°F for 10 minutes, then at 325°F until filling is cooked. Make a meringue of egg whites and ¼ cup sugar. Put on hot pie. Return to oven to brown.

Moorefield United Church, Moorefield, Ont.
Frontier United Church, Frontier, Sask.
Wellington Sg. United Church, Burlington, Ont.

Nellie's Cake

2 cups currants
½ cup sugar
1 cup water or more

Cook above for 20 minutes. Thicken with **cornstarch** (approximately 1 tablespoon). Add ½ **teaspoon cinnamon** and **butter.** Cool. Line pie plate with **pie pastry** and cover with the currant mixture. Cover with pastry. Bake in 425°F oven for approximately 30 minutes. Ice with vanilla icing when cool.

St. Andrew's United Church
Ripley, Ont.

Strawberry Glazed Pie

1 - 4 oz. pkg. vanilla Jell-O pudding and
   pie filling
2 cups milk
1 - 9'' baked pie shell, cooled
1 - 3 oz. pkg. strawberry Jell-O powder
1 cup boiling water
1 cup sweetened, sliced, fresh strawberries
   (or frozen)
¾ cup cold water

Prepare Jell-O pie filling as directed. Cool 5 minutes, stirring twice. Pour into pie shell. Chill thoroughly. Dissolve Jell-O powder in boiling water. Stir in cold water and add strawberries. Chill until slightly thickened. Spoon over pie filling. Chill until firm.

St. Andrew's United Church
Hemmingford, Que.

Peanut Butter Fudge Pie

1 - 8 oz. (250 g) pkg. cream cheese, softened
1 cup creamy peanut butter
2 tbsp. butter
2 cups plus 2 tbsp. confectioner's sugar
  (icing sugar)
1 tbsp. vanilla
½ cup 35% cream
1 graham cracker pie shell

Topping:
½ cup 35% cream
1 - 6 oz. (170 g) pkg. semi-sweet chocolate
  chips

Beat cream cheese, peanut butter and butter in an electric mixer. When soft, add confectioner's sugar and vanilla. Reserve. Whip cream to stiff peaks. Fold into peanut butter mixture. Spoon into prepared pie shell and chill at least two hours. Make the topping by heating the cream and chocolate in a small saucepan over medium heat, stirring until chocolate is melted. Chill, then spoon over chilled pie.

Embro Knox United Church
Embro, Ont.

Self Crusting Apple Pie

1 - 9'' pie plate, buttered
5 apples, peeled and thinly sliced (more
  or less)
½ cup sugar
½ tsp. cinnamon
1 egg, beaten
½ cup sugar
6 tbsp. melted butter
¾ cup all-purpose flour
1 tsp. vanilla
½ cup chopped nuts (pecans or walnuts)

Fill pie plate even with brim with apples. Mix ½ cup sugar with the cinnamon and sprinkle over the apples. Combine egg, remaining sugar, flour, butter, vanilla and nuts. Spread mixture over apple slices. Bake in 350°F oven for 50 minutes or until lightly browned.

Grace United Church
Thornbury, Ont.

Ever feel like a doughnut? You're either in the dough or in the hole.

Chocolate Peanut Butter Pie

1 - 9'' baked pie shell
1 - 125 g pkg. cream cheese, softened
1 cup icing sugar
½ cup peanut butter
1 - 500 mL container Cool Whip
1½ cups milk
1 - 99 g pkg. instant chocolate pudding
Cool Whip
Chopped peanuts
1 sq. semi-sweet chocolate

Beat together cream cheese, icing sugar and peanut butter until well blended. Fold in Cool Whip. Spread above mixture in pie shell. Add pudding mix to milk and blend. When pudding mix is firm spread over peanut butter filling. Chill well. Before serving top with more Cool Whip, chopped peanuts and semi-sweet chocolate curls (warm chocolate before cutting).

Moorefield United Church
Moorefield, Ont.

Ummy, Nummy Lemon Pie

1 pkg. lemon pie filling (single pie)
2 egg yolks
¼ cup lemon juice
1¾ cups water

Mix above in microwavable dish on HIGH for 5-6 minutes or till thick.

Add:
1 - 250 g pkg. cream cheese
1 tsp. lemon rind
2 egg whites, beaten stiff
¼ cup white sugar

Mix well. Add mixture to either a ready made graham crumb pie shell, or a pre-made graham cracker crumb pie shell (already cooked and cooled.) Refrigerate till set. Pie may be decorated with lemon or lime slices. Keep refrigerated.

Zion Evangelical United Church
Pembroke, Ont.

Old English Mincemeat Pie Filling

3 or 4 lb. lean blade roast beef
1 lb. ground suet
"Spy" (or any hard apples)
1 cup broth from boiled meat
2 cups seeded raisins
2-3 cups seedless raisins
1½ tsp. salt
2 cups currants
1 tbsp. each of nutmeg, cloves and mace
1 - 20 oz. can crushed pineapple
1 cup white vinegar
2 cups light molasses
½ cup brandy
2½-3 cups white sugar

Boil meat till tender. Grind meat (there should be about 4-5 cups packed). Grind enough apples so there is twice as much apples as meat. Stir all ingredients together. Simmer for 1½ hours, stirring to keep from burning. This keeps in fridge indefinitely or it freezes well. Wonderful for Christmas pies or tarts.

Courtice United Church
Courtice, Ont.

Chocolate Sundae Pie

1 cup evaporated milk
Pinch nutmeg
½ cup hot water
1 cup sugar
3 egg yolks
1 tbsp. plain gelatin
3 tbsp. cold water
1 tsp. vanilla
3 egg whites
Pinch salt
3 tbsp. grated bitter chocolate

Add well beaten egg yolks to first four ingredients and let cook in double boiler until like thick cream. Soak gelatine in cold water for 3 minutes and add to custard mixture when removing from heat. Add vanilla and let cool. When it begins to thicken, fold in stiffly beaten egg whites and salt. Put this mixture into cooked pie shell. Top with whipped cream which has been sweetened and flavored. Grate bitter chocolate over the surface (about 3 tablespoons).

St. Paul's United Church
Ormstown, Que.

Fresh Fruit Pies

3 cups fresh fruit (strawberries, peaches, etc.)
2 cups white sugar
½ cup cornstarch
2 cups boiling water
1 lge. pkg. of Jell-O, same flavor as fruit
Dream Whip

Boil sugar, cornstarch and water until thickened and clear. Add Jell-O and mix together. Put fruit in baked pie shell, pour over thickened glaze. Refrigerate. Top with Dream Whip. Best to let set for 4-5 hours before serving. Makes 2 pies.

Beachville United Church
Beachville, Ont.

Pineapple Pie

1 cup white sugar
1 cup cold water
3 egg yolks
1 cup crushed pineapple and juice
2 tbsp. cornstarch
3 egg whites, beaten stiff

Bring first four ingredients to a boil. Add cornstarch and remove from heat. Add egg whites. Pour into baked pie shells. Top with whipped cream. Makes 2 pies.

Kincardine United Church
Kincardine, Ont.

Scotch Village Squash Pie

2 cups squash
2 egg yolks, beaten
½ cup milk
1 tsp. vanilla
1 cup sugar
½ tsp. cinnamon
½ tsp. nutmeg
⅛ tsp. cloves
2 egg whites, beaten stiff

Mix squash, egg yolks, milk and vanilla. Add sugar, blended with spices and a pinch of salt. Fold in stiffly beaten egg whites. Pour into uncooked pie shell and bake at 400°F for 10 minutes. Lower heat to 350°F and bake for 30 minutes. Delicious!

Scotch Village United Church
Hants County, N.S.

Cranberry Pie

2 cups cranberries (fresh or frozen)
½ cup sugar
½ cup chopped nuts
2 eggs
1 cup sugar
1 cup flour
½ cup butter or margarine, melted
¼ cup shortening, melted

Grease a 10'' pie plate. Spread cranberries over bottom of plate. Sprinkle with ½ cup sugar and nuts. Beat eggs well. Add 1 cup sugar gradually and beat until thoroughly mixed. Add flour, melted butter and shortening to egg mixture. Beat well. Pour batter over top of cranberries. Bake in slow oven (325°F) for 60 minutes or until crust is golden brown. Cut like a pie. Serve either warm or cold with a scoop of ice cream.

Trinity United Church
Iroquois Falls, Ont.

Upside-Down Peace Cake

Pastry for double crust 9'' pie
2 tbsp. soft butter
⅔ cup toasted, sliced almonds or pecans
⅓ cup brown sugar
5 cups sliced, fresh peaches (8)
¾ cup granulated sugar
¼ cup brown sugar
2 tbsp. quick cooking tapioca
½ tsp. grated nutmeg
½ tsp. cinnamon

Line 9'' pan with foil. Rub with butter. Press sugar into butter and place nuts in the butter and sugar. Line with pastry shell. Mix remaining ingredients and place in shell. Cover with top pastry. Bake in 450°F oven about 10 minutes. Lower heat to 375°F until done (35 minutes). Cool and turn onto serving dish.

Gilford United Church
Gilford, Ont.

Black Bottom Pie

Crust:
14 crisp ginger cookies (1½ cups)
5 tbsp. melted butter

Roll out the cookies fine. Mix with melted butter. Line a 9'' pie tin, sides and bottom, with the buttered crumbs, pressing flat and firm. Bake 10 minutes in a slow oven to set.

Basic Filling:
1 tbsp. cornstarch
4 tbsp. cold water
1 tbsp. gelatine
1¾ cups milk
½ cup sugar
4 egg yolks
Pinch salt

Chocolate Layer:
2 squares melted semi-sweet chocolate
1 tsp. vanilla

Rum-flavoured Layer:
4 egg whites
½ cup sugar
⅛ tsp. cream of tartar
1 tbsp. white rum (optional)

Topping:
2 tbsp. confectioner's sugar
1 cup whipping cream
Grated chocolate

Soak gelatine in cold water. Scald milk, add ½ cup sugar mixed with the cornstarch, salt and beaten egg yolks. Cook in double boiler, stirring constantly, until custard thickens and will coat the back of the spoon. Stir in the dissolved gelatine. Divide custard in half. To one half add the melted chocolate and vanilla. Turn while hot into the cooled crust, dipping out carefully so as not to disturb crust. Let the remaining half of the custard cool. Beat the egg whites and cream of tartar, adding ½ cup sugar slowly. Blend with the cooled custard. Add rum (if desired). Spread carefully over chocolate layer. Chill thoroughly (may leave overnight). When ready to serve, whip the heavy cream stiff, adding 2 tablespoons confectioner's sugar slowly. Pile over the top of the pie. Sprinkle with grated bitter or semi-sweet chocolate.

Lakeshore Drive United Church
Morrisburg, Ont.

Date Sesame Pie

Pastry:
- 2-4 tbsp. sesame seeds
- 1 cup all-purpose flour
- ½ tsp. salt
- ⅓ cup shortening
- 3-4 tbsp. cold water

Toast sesame seeds in a pie pan at 450°F 2 minutes until light brown, watching carefully; remove and cool. Sift flour and salt in mixing bowl. Add sesame seeds. Cut in Crisco until size of small peas. Sprinkle water a little at a time, tossing lightly with a fork. Form into ball, flatten to about ½''. Roll to fit 9'' pie pan. Prick generously and bake in 450°F oven 10-12 minutes. Cool.

Filling:
- 1 envelope plain gelatin
- ¼ cup cold water
- 1 cup milk
- 2 egg yolks
- ¼ cup sugar
- ¼ tsp. salt
- 1 tsp. vanilla
- 1 cup dates, cut in small pieces
- ¾ cup whipping cream, whipped
- 2 egg whites
- 2 tbsp. sugar
- Sprinkle of nutmeg

Soften gelatin in cold water. Beat milk, egg yolks, sugar and salt in top of double boiler; cook over hot water, stirring constantly until mixture coats metal spoon. Add gelatin; stir until dissolved. Chill, stirring occasionally until thickened and partially set. Stir in vanilla and dates. Fold in whipped cream. Beat egg whites until slight mounds form; add sugar gradually until glossy peaks form. Fold gently into date mixture. Spoon into cooled baked pie shell. Chill until firm, at leat one hour. Sprinkle lightly with nutmeg. For a stronger date flavour, the dates can be added to the hot custard after adding the gelatin.

Hampton United Church
Hampton, N.B.

Recipes for the best speeches should always include shortening.

No-Roll Cherry Pie

- ½ cup butter
- 1 tbsp. sugar
- 1 cup flour
- 1 can cherry pie filling

Melt butter with sugar. Add flour and stir until mixture forms a ball. Press onto bottom and sides of a 9'' pie pan. Pour in pie filling.

Topping:
- 1 egg
- ½ cup sugar
- ¼ cup flour
- ¼ cup milk

In small bowl, beat egg with sugar. Blend in flour and milk until smooth. Spoon the topping over the pie filling. Bake at 350°F for 50-60 minutes until crust is golden brown. Cool.

Note: Blueberry or apple pie filling may be used instead of cherry.

Grace United Church
Hanover, Ont.

Strawberry-Rhubarb Pie

- 1½ cups diced rhubarb
- 1½ cups strawberries, sliced
- 2 tbsp. flour
- ½ tsp. salt
- 1 cup sugar
- 2 tbsp. butter
- Pastry for 2 crust pie

Line a plate with your favorite pastry. Mix prepared fruit and fill plate. Combine flour, sugar, and salt and spoon over the fruit. Dot the filling with butter. Add top crust, either lattice or one piece, slashing the latter to allow for the escape of steam as the pie bakes. Bake at 425°F for 40 minutes, or until filling bubbles.

St. Stephen United Church
St. Stephen, N.B.

Fancy Desserts

Mystery Cream Cheese Pecan Pie

1 - 250 g pkg. cream cheese
⅓ cup white sugar
4 eggs
2 tsp. vanilla
½ tsp. salt
1¼ cups coarsely chopped pecans
1 cup golden corn syrup
¼ cup packed brown sugar

Prepare your favorite pie crust and place into 9'' pie plate. In small bowl beat cream cheese, white sugar, one of the eggs, one teaspoon vanilla and ½ teaspoon salt until smooth. Pour over prepared crust. Sprinkle pecans over cream cheese layer. In a small bowl, combine brown sugar, remaining 3 eggs and remaining one teaspoon vanilla. Blend well - gently pour mixture over layer in pie crust. Bake at 425°F for 10 minutes, reduce heat to 375°F and bake 20-25 minutes longer. Cool. Chill well before serving.

Forest United Church
Forest, Ont.

Blender Cheesecake

(Easy - Ready in about 50 minutes.)

1⅔ cups graham cracker crumbs
½ cup melted butter or margarine
½ cup boiling water
1 pkg. (3 oz. or 84 g) lemon Jell-O
2 tbsp. lemon juice
2 cups (500 mL) cottage cheese
1 container (9 oz. or 257 g) frozen Cool Whip

Combine cracker crumbs and butter; mix well. Press into bottom of 7x11'' pan. Set aside. Assemble blender. Pour boiling water into blender container, add Jell-O and process at BEAT until Jell-O is dissolved. Add lemon juice and 1 cup cottage cheese. Process at LIQUIFY until smooth. Add remaining cottage cheese and process until smooth. Pour into large mixer bowl. Add frozen whipped topping and mix until smooth. Pour over graham cracker crust. Chill until set (this takes only 30 minutes - a quick dessert!) Flavour of Jell-O may be varied. Top with pie filling or make your own. Delicious when topped with fresh blueberry sauce.
It's not enough to save
And a little too much to dump
And there's nothing to do but eat it
That makes the housewife plump.

Grace United Church
Port Dover, Ont.

Blueberry Deluxe

Whole vanilla or graham wafers
1 cup butter
2 - 250 g pkgs. cream cheese
2 cups icing sugar

Line a 9x12'' pan with wafers. Mix in bowl butter, cream cheese and icing sugar. Spread over wafers, being sure they are completely covered so Jell-O won't seep through to wafers. Sprinkle a few crushed walnuts over cream.

2 small or 1 large Jell-O (grape)
1¾ cups boiling water
2 pkgs. frozen blueberries
2 pkgs. Dream Whip

Dissolve Jell-O in boiling water and add frozen berries. Let stand to gel while you whip Dream Whip. Spread Jell-O over cream, then Dream Whip. Sprinkle a few wafer crumbs on top. Refrigerate several hours or overnight. Other fruits (frozen) may be used, being sure to use corresponding Jell-O flavor.

Trinity United Church
Portage la Prairie, Man.

Praline & Pumpkin Harvest Cheesecake

Crust:
¾ cup (175 mL) graham wafer crumbs
½ cup (125 mL) finely chopped pecans
¼ cup (50 mL) brown sugar
3 tbsp. (45 mL) butter or margarine, melted

Filling:
3 pkgs. (250 g each) cream cheese, softened
½ cup (125 mL) brown sugar
½ cup (125 mL) granulated sugar
3 eggs
1½ cups (375 mL) canned pumpkin
1½ tsp. (7 mL) cinnamon
½ tsp. (2 mL) nutmeg
½ tsp. (2 mL) ginger
2 tbsp. (30 mL) milk
1 tbsp. (15 mL) cornstarch
1 tbsp. (15 mL) rum (optional)

Topping:
2 cups (500 mL) sour cream
2 tbsp. (25 mL) sugar
1 tbsp. (15 mL) rum (optional)

Crust: Combine crust ingredients and press firmly onto bottom and ½'' up sides of a 9'' (23 cm) springform pan. Chill.

Filling: In a large bowl, using electric mixer, beat cream cheese and sugars until smooth. Beat in eggs until blended. Beat in pumpkin, spices, milk, cornstarch and rum, until thoroughly combined. Pour into pan. Bake at 350°F (180°C) for 50-55 minutes or until center is just set.

Topping: Blend sour cream, sugar and rum. Spread over hot cheesecake. Bake 5 minutes longer. Remove cake from oven and run knife around sides of pan. Cool at room temperature. Chill, covered overnight. To serve, remove sides, garnish as desired.

Elimville United Church
Exeter, Ont.

Success is doing something usual and doing it unusually well.

Hawaiian Cheesecake

(or Chinese Wedding Cake)

1 Celebration (or any pouch size) white cake mix
1 - 4 oz. (125 g) pkg. cream cheese
1 vanilla instant pudding (6 portion size)
1½ cups milk
1 - 19 oz. can crushed pineapple, drained well
1 tub Cool Whip or 2 envelopes Dream Whip or Lucky Whip (whipped) or equal amount of whipped cream
Angel flake coconut

Mix cake as directed on package. Pour into greased 9x12'' cake pan. Bake 15 minutes at 325°F. Cream the cheese. Mix pudding with 1½ cups milk. Fold in creamed cheese. Spread over cooled cake. Sprinkle drained pineapple over above. Spread whipped topping on top of pineapple. Add coconut over top. (May be toasted, if desired.) Set for 24 hours. Store in fridge. This freezes well.

Kirkfield Park United Church
Winnipeg, Man.

Apricot 'n Cream Cheesecake

2 cups water
¼ cup sugar
1½ cups chopped apricots
¼ cup golden sultana raisins
1 cup margarine
1 - 8 oz. pkg. cream cheese
1½ cups white sugar
1½ tsp. vanilla
4 eggs
2¼ cups flour
1½ tsp. baking powder

Bring to a boil the first four ingredients. Reduce heat and simmer for 15-20 minutes. Drain and cool, discarding juice. Cream together the next four ingredients. Add eggs, one at a time. Combine flour and baking powder. Add to creamed mixture. Fold in fruit. Bake in a greased and floured tube pan or bundt pan at 250°F for 15 minutes. Increase heat to 300°F and bake for another 40-50 minutes.

Central United Church
Bay Roberts, Nfld.

Peanut Butter Cheesecake

Crust:
 ⅓ cup butter
 1½ cups graham cracker crumbs
 ¼ cup granulated sugar
 ¼ cup cocoa

Filling:
 8 oz. cream cheese, softened
 1 cup powdered sugar
 ⅔ cup milk
 ½ cup peanut butter
 2 cups Cool Whip

Crust: Melt butter. Stir in crumbs, sugar and cocoa. Mix well. Press into bottom and up ¾ sides of ungreased 10" springform pan. Do not bake.

Filling: Beat cheese and sugar together. Add milk and peanut butter. Fold in Cool Whip. Pour over crumb crust. To serve remove from pan. Ice with Cool Whip. Sprinkle with crushed peanuts or grated chocolate.
Serves 10.

First United Church
Wawa, Ont.

Smooth Cheesecake

 ⅓ cup graham wafer crumbs
 3 - 8 oz. pkgs. cream cheese, softened
 4 egg whites
 1 cup sugar
 ½ tsp. vanilla
 2 cups sour cream
 2 tbsp. sugar
 ½ tsp. vanilla

Butter a 9" springform pan and dust with crumbs. Cream cheese. Beat egg whites until stiff and blend in 1 cup sugar. Combine egg whites with cheese and add vanilla. Pour into pan and bake at 350°F for 25 minutes. Combine sour cream, 2 tablespoons sugar and ½ teaspoon vanilla and spread on top of cake. Return to oven at 475°F for 5 minutes. Chill at least 2 hours and serve. Cherry pie filling or any other goes good on the top when served.

Cheltenham United Church
Cheltenham, Ont.

Raspberry Cheesecake

 2½ cups graham cracker crumbs
 ½ cup brown sugar
 ½ cup margarine

Mix and pat in bottom of 9x13" pan. Bake at 325°F for 10 minutes.

 2 cups raspberries
 1 cup water
 1 cup white sugar
 1 tbsp. lemon juice
 Pinch salt
 3 tbsp. (heaping) cornstarch

Cook until mixture thickens. Cool.

 1 - 8 oz. pkg. cream cheese
 1 cup icing sugar
 1 litre dessert topping

Cream cheese and sugar; add prepared dessert topping. Spread on top of crust. Cover with the cooked raspberry mixture.

Tobermory United Church
Tobermory, Ont.

Cherry Cheesecake

 1 cup Oreo cookie crumbs
 3 tsp. sugar
 3 tbsp. butter, melted

Combine crumbs, sugar and butter. Press into bottom of 9" springform pan. Bake at 325°F for 10 minutes.

 3 - 8 oz. pkgs. cream cheese, softened
 ½ cup sugar
 3 eggs
 1 tsp. vanilla
 1 - 20 oz. can cherry pie filling

Combine cream cheese and sugar, mixing at medium speed on electric mixer until well blended. Add eggs, one at a time, mixing well after each egg. Blend in vanilla. Pour over crust. Bake at 450°F for 10 minutes. Reduce heat to 250°F and bake for 45 minutes to 1 hour or until fork comes out clean. Remove from oven and leave on counter until cool. Chill and put on filling just before serving.

Knox United Church
Fort Frances, Ont.

Creamy Baked Cheesecake

Crust:
¼ cup margarine or butter, melted
1 cup graham cracker crumbs
¼ cup white sugar

Preheat oven to 300°F. Combine margarine or butter, crumbs and sugar. Pat firmly into bottom of greased 9'' springform pan.

Filling:
2 - 8 oz. pkgs. cream cheese
1 - 14 oz. can Eagle Brand sweetened
   condensed milk
3 eggs
¼ tsp. salt
¼ cup Realemon

In large bowl beat cheese until fluffy. Beat in Eagle Brand milk, eggs and salt until smooth. Stir in Realemon. Pour into prepared pan. Bake 50-55 minutes or until knife comes out clean. Cool to room temperature and chill.

Topping:
1 - 8 oz. sour cream
1 - can of pie filling or fresh fruit

Spread sour cream on top of cheesecake and garnish with canned pie filling or fresh fruit as desired.

St. Andrew's United Church
Fitzroy Harbour, Ont.

Berry Brownies

4 purchased frosted brownies
½ cup soft-style cream cheese with
   strawberries
Fresh strawberries

Split each brownie in half horizontally. Spread the bottom half with about 1 tablespoon of the cream cheese. Slice some of the strawberries; arrange sliced berries over cream cheese. Top with remaining brownie half.

Grace United Church
Brampton, Ont.

Raspberry Trifle

1 pound cake (or raspberry jelly roll)
1 - 15 oz. pkg. frozen raspberries, thawed
   and drained (use unsweetened berries)
⅓ cup raspberry juice
1 - 6 oz. pkg. vanilla instant pudding
   prepared with 4 cups of milk
½ cup whipping cream, whipped or 1 pkg.
   prepared Dream Whip
2 tbsp. toasted almonds or coconut

Cut cake in half-inch pieces. Put in layer of cake on bottom of bowl, 8'' or 9'' in diameter and 3½'' deep. Spoon raspberries over cake. Cover with half of the prepared pudding. Add another layer of cake. Drizzle raspberry juice over cake, then add remaining pudding. Chill for 2 hours or overnight. Top with whipped cream or Dream Whip and garnish with toasted almonds. Is better made the day before you serve it.
Serves 10-12.

Glen Morris United Church
Glen Morris, Ont.

Orange Sponge Cake Dessert

Sponge or angel cake, 6-7'' size
28 marshmallows
¾ cup orange juice
½ pint whipping cream, whipped stiff

Cut cake into four layers. Melt marshmallows and juice in double boiler. Cool. Gently fold whipped cream into marshmallow mixture. Place first layer of cake in large bowl, cover with ¼ of the marshmallow mixture. Repeat layers.

Grace United Church
Hanover, Ont.

Strawberry Fluff

2 - 85 g pkgs. strawberry Jell-O
3 cups boiling water
2 pkgs. frozen strawberries
1 pt. whipping cream (Dream Whip can be substituted)
1 pkg. vanilla wafers

Dissolve Jell-O in boiling water. Stir in frozen fruit. Partially set, then add whipped cream. Pour into bowl lined with vanilla wafers. Chill. Recipe can be doubled. Looks best in glass bowl. Ideal for diabetics if proper Jell-O is used.

Adolphustown U.E.L. Centennial United Church
Napanee, Ont.

Strawberries & Cream Dessert

1 can sweetened condensed milk
1½ cups (375 mL) cold water
1 pkg. (4 serving size) vanilla instant pudding mix
2 cups (500 mL) whipping cream, whipped
1 - 285 g pkg. frozen pound cake, thawed, cubed
4 cups (1 L) fresh strawberries, cleaned, hulled, sliced
½ cup (125 mL) strawberry jam
Additional fresh strawberries
Toasted, slivered or sliced almonds

In large mixing bowl combine condensed milk and water. Add pudding mix; beat well. Chill until thickened, about 20 minutes. Fold in whipping cream. Spoon 2 cups of the pudding mixture into 4-quart round glass serving bowl. Top with half the cake cubes, half the strawberries, half the jam and half the remaining pudding mixture. Repeat layering, ending with pudding mixture. Chill at least 4 hours. Garnish with additional strawberries and almonds. Cover leftovers. Refrigerate.
Makes 10-12 servings.

Westminster United Church
Mississauga, Ont.

Pumpkin Ice Cream

1 tbsp. boiling water
10 large marshmallows

Melt marshmallows in double boiler with water. Add:
1 cup pumpkin
⅓ cup brown sugar
2 egg yolks, beaten
2 tbsp. orange juice
½ tsp. ginger
½ tsp. nutmeg
1 tsp. cinnamon
½ tsp. salt

Cook 10 minutes. Let cool. Whip **1 small (250 mL) carton whipping cream.** Fold into mixture. Freeze.

Innerkip United Church
Innerkip, Ont.

Easy Homemade Ice Cream

7 cups milk (homo)
4 eggs
7 tsp. flour
2 cups sugar
Dash salt
2 tsp. vanilla extract
3 cups heavy cream (or 3½ cups thin cream)

Scald milk. Beat eggs. Add flour, sugar and salt. Mix together. Slowly add hot milk to egg mixture, while stirring constantly. Bring to a boil. Remove from heat and cool thoroughly. Add vanilla to cream, whip slightly, but not so much as to make it stiff. Mix cream with milk and egg mixture. Pour into containers and freeze. For smoother ice cream, strain milk and egg mixture after cooking and before adding to cream.

Robert McClure United Church
Calgary, Alta.

Almond Fruit Float

1 envelope unflavored gelatin
1 cup water
½ cup sugar
½ cup milk
1 tbsp. almond extract
13 oz. can of fruit with syrup or fresh fruit

Dissolve gelatin in water. Place over high heat and bring to boil. Reduce heat to low. Add sugar. Stir to thoroughly dissolve. Stir in milk and almond extract. Mix well. Pour into deep square pan and allow to set at room temperature. Put into fridge to cool. When cool, cut into cubes and serve topped with fruit and syrup.

Broadview United Church
Broadview, Sask.

Chocolate Charlotte

8 oz. (225 g) plain chocolate, broken into pieces
6 tbsp. (6x15 mL) brandy
8 oz. (225 g) ground almonds
4 oz. (100 g) unsalted butter, softened
½ pt. (300 mL) whipping cream
Oil for preparing mold
20 sponge fingers

Decoration:
4 oz. (120 mL) whipping cream
1 oz. (25 g) chocolate, grated

Put the chocolate and 2 tablespoons brandy in heat-proof bowl, standing it over pan of simmering water. Heat gently until chocolate has melted, stirring once or twice. Remove from heat and work in butter gradually until melted. Stir in almonds and leave to cool. Line base of a 1½ pint (900 mL) mold with spray or wax paper. Brush the paper and inside the rim of the mold lightly with oil. Dip the sponge fingers one at a time into remaining brandy. Use to line sides of mold. Trim to fit if necessary. Whip cream until firm, then fold into the chocolate mixture. Spoon into mold and level. Cover and chill overnight. Next day turn the Chocolate Charlotte out of mold onto serving plate. Whip cream for decoration and pipe or swirl around top. Sprinkle grated chocolate over the top. Chill until serving time.
Serves 8.

Hillsburgh United Church
Bear River, N.S.

Jell-O and Dream Whip Christmas Garland

Red Layer:
1 - 3 oz. pkg. strawberry Jell-O
1 cup hot water
¾ cup cold water
1 med. banana, sliced

Dissolve Jell-O in hot water. Add cold water. Chill until slightly thickened. Fold in banana. Pour into a 6-cup ring mold or a 9x5x3'' loaf pan. Chill until almost firm.

White Layer:
1 - 3 oz. pkg. lime Jell-O
1 cup hot water
¾ cup cold water
¾ cup pineapple juice
2 envelopes Dream Whip

Dissolve Jell-O in hot water. Add cold water. Add pineapple juice, then chill ½ cup of this liquid until slightly thick. (Chill remainder for green layer.) Prepare Dream Whip according to package directions. Fold 1 cup of prepared Dream Whip into ½ cup slightly thickened liquid. Pour over strawberry Jell-O in mold. Chill until almost firm. (Cover and refrigerate remaining Dream Whip.)
Green Layer:
1 - 20 oz. can pineapple tidbits, drained

Use slightly chilled lime-pineapple mixture from white layer. Fold in pineapple tidbits. Pour over Jell-O in mold. Chill until firm. Unmold just before serving. Put remaining Dream Whip into centre of mold or spread onto top if using loaf pan. Garnish with maraschino cherries and almonds.
Serves 10.

Memorial United Church
Garden Cove, Nfld.

Jelly Magic

1 lg. pkg. jelly powder
1 litre ice cream
2 cups boiling water

Dissolve jelly powder in boiling water. Add ice cream and stir till melted. Place in 10x10'' container. Refrigerate to set, approximately ½ hour. Cut in pieces and serve with dab of whipped cream.

Newtonville United Church
Newtonville, Ont.

Black Forest Trifle

1 pkg. pound cake or 2 chocolate jelly rolls
28 oz. sour red pitted cherries (available
  in most supermarkets in glass jar) or
  1 can cherry pie filling
2 pkgs. 4-serving chocolate instant pudding
  powder beaten with 4 cups milk (skim, 2%
  or whole)
2 pkgs. Dream Whip or equivalent in
  whipping cream or Nutri-Whip topping
2-3 tbsp. cornstarch

Thicken cherries with cornstarch and add
some sugar if desired. Let cool. Prepare the pudding powder with milk. Whip topping. In a large
decorative glass bowl layer the four ingredients
starting with a ¼ of the cake cubed, a ¼ of
the cherry mixture, a ¼ of the pudding and fi-
nally the whipped cream. Continue in this man-
ner ending with whipped cream. A few grated
chocolate curls sprinkled on top adds a festive
touch. Some cherry brandy may be sprinkled
over the cake cubes.

Note: to make your own chocolate pudding
use the following recipe.

Chocolate Pudding:
1¼ cups white sugar
¼ cup cornstarch
2⅓ cups milk
½ cup cocoa
½ cup butter or margarine
2 tsp. vanilla

Combine sugar, cornstarch and cocoa in
medium saucepan. Add milk gradually. Cook
over medium heat, stirring constantly until mixture thickens and it starts to boil. Reduce heat
and cook 2 minutes longer. Remove from heat.
Add margarine and stir until melted. Add vanilla. Cover and cool.

Wesley-Willis United Church, Clintin, Ont.
St. James United Church, Antigonish, N.S.

Chocolate Trifle

Lady fingers or pound cake
Orange juice
Raspberry jam
Vanilla pudding mix
6 oz. pkg. chocolate chips, melted
½ cup milk
8 oz. tub sour cream

Line bowl with lady fingers or cake. Sprinkle orange juice over cake. Spread jam over.
Mix together the next four ingredients. Pour
over cake. Cover with sliced bananas or other
desired fruit. Top with whipped cream. Garnish
as desired.

Central United Church
Bay Roberts, Nfld.

Pineapple Chocolate Dessert

2 envelopes Whip 'n Chill
2 - 14 oz. cans crushed pineapple
1 pkg. chocolate wafers
1 cup whipping cream

Carry out the first step on the Whip 'n Chill
package. Drain crushed pineapple and use the
juice instesad of water in the second step of
Whip 'n Chill directions. Add the crushed
pineapple. In a serving bowl, layer the pineapple mixture with the chocolate wafers. Top with
whipped whipping cream. Chill until served.

Central United Church
Bay Roberts, Nfld.

Cherries in the Snow

1 angel food cake
8 oz. cream cheese
1 cup white sugar
1 tsp. vanilla
1 cup milk
1 large tub Cool Whip (1 L)
1 can cherry pie filling

Mix cheese and sugar together. Add milk,
vanilla and Cool Whip. Mix all above well.
Break cake into small pieces, then put layer in
bottom of large glass bowl. Cover cake with a
layer of mixture. Alternate layers, ending with
mixture. Pour cherry pie filling over and chill.

St. Paul's United Church
Mildmay, Ont.

A Nice Dessert

1 - 3 oz. pkg. raspberry Jell-O
1 cup hot water
1 pkg. frozen raspberries
1 pkg. Dream Whip or ½ pt. whipping
  cream
About ½ a small angel cake (use more
  if desired)

Dissolve Jell-O in hot water. Add frozen berries. Stir till berries are mostly thawed and mixture begins to set or thicken (takes only a few
minutes). Have Dream Whip or cream whipped
and cake torn in small pieces. Put layer of mixture into mold, then a layer of cake. Continue
with mixture and cake in layers. (I use a loaf
pan and cut in slices.) Put in fridge till ready
to use. Unmold and serve very cold. May be
made day before. This will keep 2 or 3 days.
Strawberries and strawberry Jell-O may be used
instead.
Serves 6-8.

St. Paul's United Church
Orinstown, Que.

Luscious Orange Mold

1 small angel food cake
2 envelopes unflavoured gelatin
⅔ cup granulated sugar
⅛ tsp. salt
1 - 6 oz. can frozen orange juice concentrate,
  thawed
2 envelopes Dream Whip
1 - 11 oz. can mandarin oranges
Seedless green grapes

Remove brown crust from cake, then break
up in small to medium pieces. In saucepan,
sprinkle gelatin on ½ cup water, place over low
heat and stir until dissolved. Add sugar and salt;
stir well. Remove from heat and add orange
juice and let sit until slightly thickened. Beat
Dream Whip until stiff. Add to orange juice
mixture. Place in greased bowl, a layer of
orange mixture, the crumbled cake, then more
orange mixture until all is used. Refrigerate for
at least 1 hour or overnight. Unmold and
decorate with oranges and grapes.

Sharon St. John United Church
Stellarton, N.S.

Springtime Dessert

Baked angel cake (use half)
Small coloured marshmallows
Lemon pie filling
2 whole eggs
3 cups water
19 oz. can drained pineapple (optional)

Topping:
1 pkg. Dream Whip
1 pkg. lemon instant pudding
1½ cups cold milk

Break cake in small pieces to cover a Pyrex
11x7x2'' dish. Cover cake pieces with marshmallows. Make pie filling according to directions using eggs and water. Pour hot mixture
over marshmallows and cake (pineapple may be
added to lemon filling.) Whip Dream Whip, instant pudding and milk until thick and put on
top and chill overnight.
Variation: Add 1 - 14 ounce can fruit cocktail to filling. Topping may be Dream Whip
only.

Zion United Church, Crediton, Ont.
St. Andrews United Church, Scotstown, Que.

Quick Strawberry Shortcake

1 cup miniature marshmallows
2 cups fresh or 2 - 10 oz. pkgs. frozen
  strawberries in syrup, completely thawed
3 oz. pkg. strawberry Jell-O
2¼ cups all-purpose flour
1½ cups sugar
½ cup solid shortening
3 tsp. baking powder
1 cup milk
3 eggs
1 tsp. vanilla
½ tsp. salt

Generously grease bottom only of 13x9'' pan.
Sprinkle marshmallows over bottom of pan.
Thoroughly combine Jell-O and strawberries.
Set aside. Combine rest of ingredients and blend
at low speed until moistened. Pour batter evenly
over marshmallows. Spoon strawberry mix over
all. Bake at 350°F for 45-50 minutes. Delicious
with whipped cream.

Iondale Heights United Church
Scarborough, Ont.

Blueberry Squares

Graham wafers
½ cup margarine
4 oz. cream cheese
½ cup icing sugar
1 - 85 g pkg. grape or cherry Jell-O
1 cup boiling water
2 cups frozen blueberries
1 cup whipped cream (Nutri Sweet)

Line 9x9'' pan with graham wafers. Cream together margarine, cream cheese and icing sugar and spread over wafers. Dissolve Jell-O in boiling water, add bluberries and pour over mixture in pan. Top with whipped cream. Chill until serving time.

George St. United Church
St. John's, Nfld.

Blueberry Dessert

2 cups graham wafers
½ cup melted butter

Topping:
8 oz. cream cheese
1 cup white sugar
½ tsp. lemon juice
¼ tsp. salt
2 tsp. vanilla
500 mL Cool Whip
3 cups blueberries

Mix graham wafers and butter. Use most for base; save some for top. Press crust into an 8x8'' pan. Mix cream cheese, sugar, lemon juice, salt and vanilla very well. Fold in Cool Whip quickly. Fold in blueberries and spread on base. Sprinkle with rest of crumbs. May be frozen.

Saint Andrews United Church
Tabusintoe, N.B.

Chocolate Cake Desert

6 chocolate bars (with almonds)
1 angel food cake mix
1 pt. whipping cream

Mix cake mix. (Remove 2 tablespoons mix and replace with 2 tablespoons cocoa.) Bake as directed and cool. Cut cake across in two layers. Whip cream and fold in 6 melted chocolate bars. Frost bottom layer. Put top layer on bottom and frost. Let set at least four hours.

Forest Home United Church
Orillia, Ont.

Strawberry Squares

1 regular size strawberry Jell-O
⅔ cup boiling water
1 cup strawberries
2 cups vanilla ice cream
1 litre tub Cool Whip

Crust:
2 cups graham wafer crumbs
½ cup melted butter
3-4 tbsp. sugar

Mix ingredients for crust. Put in 9x13'' pan. Dissolve Jell-O in water and add ice cream. Stir until dissolved. Add Cool Whip and stir until thickened. Add strawberries. Put on top of crust. Sprinkle with extra graham wafer crumbs and chill.

Zion Calvin United Church
Darlingford, Man.

Brunch Dessert

⅓ cup (75 mL) butter, melted
1¼ cups (300 mL) graham wafer crumbs
¼ cup (50 mL) sugar
3 cups (750 mL) pared, fresh peach halves or
    1 - 28 oz. (796 mL) can peach halves, drained
2 pkgs. (250 g each) cream cheese, softened
1 can Eagle Brand sweetened condensed milk
2 tbsp. (30 mL) lemon juice
1-2 tsp. (5-10 mL) almond extract (optional)
1 container (500 mL) frozen whipped topping, thawed

Combine butter, crumbs and sugar. Press on bottom of 9'' (23 cm) springform pan. In blender container, blend peaches until smooth. In large mixer bowl beat cheese until fluffy. Gradually beat in condensed milk until smooth. Stir in lemon juice, almond extract and peach puree. Fold in whipped topping; pour into prepared pan. Freeze several hours or overnight. Remove from freezer to refrigerator 15 minutes before serving. Garnish. Freeze leftovers. Makes 10-12 servings.

Rossendale United Church
Rossendale, Man.

Praline Dessert

2 cups graham wafer crumbs
½ cup melted margarine

Make graham wafer crust in 9x13'' pan.

Pecan layer:
3 eggs
1 cup brown sugar
½ cup corn syrup
1 cup pecan halves
1 tsp. vanilla extract

Cook in double boiler. When cooked, spread on graham wafer crust.

Topping:
1 vanilla instant pudding
1½ cups milk
½ cup NutriWhip

Mix pudding with milk. Let stand to set. Whip NutriWhip until firm. Mix with instant pudding. Spread on top of pecan layer. Decorate with pecans.

St. James United Church
Stroud, Ont.

Chocolate Log Roll

5 eggs, separated
½ cup icing sugar, sifted
2 tbsp. cocoa
2 tbsp. flour
½ pt. (250 mL) whipping cream

Separate eggs and beat the yolks until thick. Add the sifted sugar and continue beating until well blended. Add the cocoa and flour sifted together. Beat the egg whites until stiff, but not dry. Add the yolk mixture and beat hard for 10 minutes. (Important because it incorporates air into cake.) Pour into jelly roll pan lined with wax paper and bake in 400°F oven for 10 minutes. Turn out on cloth that is sprinkled with icing sugar and peel wax paper off gently and immediately. Allow to cool. Whip the cream and sweeten to taste. Reserve 4 heaping tablespoons of this and spread the remainder over the cake. Roll up as for jelly roll. To the remaining cream add sufficient icing sugar (¾-1 cup) and cocoa (2½ teaspoons) to make icing. Spread over the whole cake using a hot, wet spreader.
Serves 6-8.

Riverview United Church
Winnipeg, Man.

Soda Crackers for Dessert

1 box unsalted soda crackers
1 - 500 mL whipping cream
2 boxes instant pudding (4 serving) vanilla, chocolate or pistachio
2 cups milk
1 - 19 oz. can pie filling - blueberry, cherry, or raspberry

In a mixing bowl place whipping cream, milk and puddings. Beat 2 minutes. On a flat pan or plate place soda crackers, 3 across and 5 down. Spread with whipped mixture. Repeat for 6 or 7 layers, until all whipped mixture is used up. Top with a layer of crackers and then pie filling. Let stand 24 hours and serve.

Zion United Church
Kitchener, Ont.

Chipits Polka-dot Dessert

2 - 6 oz. (or 1 - 12 oz. pkg.) Chipits
1½ cups fine graham crumbs
¼ cup firmly packed brown sugar
¼ cup melted butter or margarine
1 pt. whipping cream
1 cup miniature marshmallows
2 tsp. grated orange rind

Melt Chipits over hot water, cool. Mix graham wafer crumbs, brown sugar and butter. Press crumb mixture into 8'' pan. Reserve some of the crumbs. Beat cream until stiff (reserve ½ for topping). To remaining half, fold in melted Chipits until well mixed. Fold in marshmallows. Spread onto crumbs, lightly press remaining crumbs on top. Spread reserved whipped cream on top. Sprinkle with orange rind. Chill 2 hours until firm.
Serves 9.

Keswick United Church
Keswick, Ont.

Grapes en Creme

2 cups (or whatever) green, seedless grapes
⅓ cup commercial sour cream
¼ cup brown sugar
1 tbsp. grated lemon rind

Mix last three ingredients. Fold in grapes. Chill at least 1 hour.

St. Andrew's United Church
Millbrook, Ont.

Rhubarb Delight

6 cups rhubarb, cut up fine
1 cup white sugar
1 pkg. strawberry Jell-O (85 g)
2 cups miniature marshmallows
½ cup white sugar
¼ cup shortening
1 egg
½ cup milk
¾ cup flour
1½ tsp. baking powder
½ tsp. salt

Spread rhubarb in bottom of 9x13" pan. Sprinkle the sugar over it, and then sprinkle the Jell-O powder over the sugar. Cover with the marshmallows. Mix together the shortening, sugar, egg, flour, etc. in a bowl and spread over rhubarb mixture. Bake for 50 minutes at 300°F.

Wesley United Church
Port Elgin, N.B.

Lemon Fluff Pudding

Base:
1¾ cups graham cracker crumbs
1 tsp. sugar
½ cup melted butter or margarine

Combine ingredients together and press into a 9x9" pan, reserving some crumbs for the garnish.

Filling:
1 small box (85 g) Jell-O, raspberry or lemon
1 cup boiling water
1 - 8 oz. pkg. cream cheese
1 cup sugar
¾ cup evaporated milk, chilled

Melt Jell-O in boiling water. Cool. Cream the cream cheese with sugar. Whip chilled, evaporated milk. Add whipped milk to Jell-O mixture. Add creamed cheese and sugar mixture. Pour pudding mixture on top of base and sprinkle remaining crumbs on top.

Zion Evangelical United Church
Pembroke, Ont.

Lemon Dessert
(No Bake)

Crumb crust:
¼ cup butter
¼ cup brown sugar
1¼ cups crumbs

Topping:
1 small (85 g) pkg. lemon Jell-O (partially set - use juice of pineapple in place of water)
1 pkg. Dream Whip

Make Dream Whip as per instructions on box. Fold into Jell-O. Add:
1 cup miniature marshmallows
1 small can crushed pineapple, drained

Press crumb crust into bottom of 9x9" pan. Add topping and refrigerate until set. When set, cut into squares and serve. (Recipe may be doubled for 9x13" pan).

Gilford United Church
Gilford, Ont.

Cherry or Strawberry Cha Cha

Base:
2½ cups graham wafer crumbs
½ cup cooking oil
¼ cup icing sugar

Press ⅔ of this mixture into a 9x13" pan.

Filling:
½ pt. whipping cream or 1 pkg. Dream Whip
4 cups miniature marshmallows
1 can pie filling (either cherry or strawberry)

Whip the whipping cream. Fold in marshmallows. Put half of this mixture over base. Spread pie filling on top, then the remainder of the marshmallow mixture. Now put the rest of the crumbs on top. Press firmly. Chill at least 24 hours.
Makes 2 servings.

Ardrossan United Church, Ardrossan, Alta.
Zion Evangelical United Church, Pembroke, Ont.

Banana "Icebox" Cake

1½ cups scalded milk
2 eggs
2 tbsp. flour
½ cup sugar
1 tbsp. butter
3 bananas
16 graham wafers, crushed (1½-2 cups)
½ tsp. vanilla or lemon flavoring

Scald milk. Mix beaten eggs, flour and sugar and pour on milk and cook till thick and smooth. Add butter and flavouring; cool. Line oblong Pyrex pan with wax paper. Put layer of crumbs and layer of bananas, then layer of custard. Repeat till mixture is used up, ending with crumbs. Chill for 6 hours or more. Serve in squares topped with whipped cream.

Foam Lake United Church
Foam Lake, Sask.

Orange Dessert

1½ cups graham crumbs
½ cup butter or margarine, melted
½ cup brown sugar

Spread half of crumb mixture in Pyrex pan 11¾x7½".

Filling:
2 - 85 g pkgs. orange Jell-O
Juice and rind of 1 orange or 2 tbsp. orange Tang
1 tbsp. lemon juice or lemon crystals
1 cup boiling water

Stir together and let stand until it starts to set. Whip **1 package Dream Whip** and fold in.
Spread filling in pan and cover with rest of crumb mixture. Leave in fridge 3-4 hours or overnight.

Caledonia United Church
Caledonia, N.S.

Pudding Cake

1 box chocolate pudding and pie filling
1 box butterscotch pudding and pie filling
1 box vanilla pudding and pie filling (6½ cup serving size)
Graham crackers

Line a 9x13" pan with graham crackers. Cook vanilla pudding and pour over crackers. Put crackers over vanilla pudding and put cooked butterscotch pudding over this. Put more crackers on butterscotch pudding and top with cooked chocolate pudding. Chill for several hours.

Bowman United Church
Ancaster, Ont.

Mount Vernon Dessert

½ cup firmly packed brown sugar
1 - 19 oz. can cherries, drained
1¾ cups sifted flour
2 tsp. baking powder
½ tsp. salt
1 cup white sugar
⅓ cup shortening
¾ cup milk
1 tsp. vanilla
1 egg, beaten

Cherry sauce:
½ cup sugar
2 tbsp. cornstarch
1½ cups juice from cherries
Water
⅛ tsp. almond flavoring

Prepare 12x8x2" pan by greasing well with butter. Sprinkle brown sugar over bottom of pan. Add can of cherries. Keep juice for sauce. Sift together flour, baking powder, salt and white sugar. Add shortening, milk and vanilla. Beat until batter is well blended. Add egg. Beat well and pour over cherries in pan. Bake at 350°F for 35-45- minutes. Add enough water to the juice from the cherries to make 1½ cups. Combine sugar, cornstarch and juice. Cook until thickened, stirring constantly. Remove from heat and add almond flavoring. Serve warm over cake.

Vaughan's United
Hants Co., N.S.

Pineapple Delight

2 cups graham cracker crumbs
¼ cup brown sugar
Dash cinnamon
¼ lb. melted butter

Mix together and press into 9x13'' pan. Bake at 325°F for 10 minutes. Let cool.

1 lge. pkg. vanilla pudding
1 pkg. Dream Whip
1 - 19 oz. tin crushed pineapple

Cook vanilla pudding and let cool. Pour over crust. Drain the crushed pineapple and fold into prepared Dream Whip. Spread on pudding and sprinkle with graham cracker crumbs and top with maraschino cherries. Refrigerate. Can also be frozen. Remove from freezer 5 minutes before serving.
Serves 8 or more.

St. John's United Church, Hamilton, Ont.
Wesley United Church, Port aux Basques, Nfld.

Pineapple Delight

2½ cups graham wafer crumbs
¾ cup melted butter or margarine

Mix together and spread in 9x13'' pan. Bake at 350°F for 10 minutes. Cool.

1½ cups icing sugar
½ cup butter or margarine
2 eggs, well beaten
1 pt. whipping cream
1 tsp. vanilla
2 tbsp. sugar
1 - 19 oz. can crushed pineapple, drained

Cream together icing sugar and butter. Add eggs. Beat till nice and creamy and then spread over top of crumbs. Whip the cream until stiff. Add vanilla and sugar. Add pineapple. Spread over top of mixture. Sprinkle a few crumbs over top. Chill and serve.

Glenboro United Church
Glenboro, Man.

Poached Pears

4 pears, peeled, cored and halved

Sauce:
¼ cup maple syrup or substitute
½ cup cream
2 tsp. brown sugar
Mincemeat

Fill centre of pears with mincemeat. Blend remaining ingredients in saucepan. Pour over pears in a shallow pan. Heat for 15 minutes in 375°F oven.

St. Paul's United Church
Bancroft, Ont.

Pumpkin Pie Squares

1 cup sifted flour
½ cup rolled oats
½ cup brown sugar
½ cup melted butter

Combine above ingredients. Mix together until crumbly and press into an ungreased 13x9'' pan. Bake at 350°F for 15 minutes.

1 lb. can pumpkin
1 - 13½ oz. can of evaporated milk
2 eggs
¾ cup sugar
1 tsp. cinnamon
½ tsp. cloves
½ tsp. ginger
½ tsp. salt

Combine above ingredients and beat well. Pour into baked crust. Bake at 350°F for 20 minutes.

½ cup chopped nuts
½ cup brown sugar
2 tbsp. melted butter

Combine. Remove pan from oven. Sprinkle over the pumpkin filling and return to oven. Bake 15-20 minutes longer or until filling is set. If desired serve with whipped topping or ice cream.

Harrow United Church
Harrow, Ont.

Pumpkin Custard Squares

1 - 19 oz. pkg. yellow cake mix
½ cup butter or margarine, softened
3 eggs
1 - 28 oz. can pumpkin
¾ cup milk
½ tsp. each allspice, cloves and ginger
½ tsp. salt
1 tsp. cinnamon (½ and ½ in topping)
¼ tsp. nutmeg
½ cup brown sugar, packed (¼ & ¼)
¼ cup butter or margarine, softened
1 cup chopped pecans or walnuts
1 cup whipping cream
1 tsp. vanilla
1 tsp. grated orange peel
2 tsp. sugar
½ tsp. cinnamon

Empty cake mix into a bowl. Cut in ½ cup butter until mixture forms moist, even crumbs. Reserve 1 cup of mixture for topping. To remaining crumb mixture add one of the three eggs. Stir to blend. Spoon into greased 9x13" baking dish. Press lightly into even layer. Bake at 350°F for 10 minutes or until puffy - set aside. Meanwhile, beat remaining two eggs until foamy. Gradually beat in pumpkin and milk. Stir in allspice, cloves, ginger, salt, ½ teaspoon cinnamon, nutmeg and ¼ cup brown sugar. Pour over baked cake layer. Combine reserved 1 cup crumb mix with ½ teaspoon cinnamon and ¼ cup brown sugar. Add ¼ cup butter and stir to blend. Stir in nuts. Drop by spoonful to form an even layer of crumbs on top of pumpkin mixture. Bake at 350°F until custard sets in center - about 30 minutes. Let cool completely. Shortly before serving, cut into 3" squares and top each with a peak of spiced whipped cream. Top with chopped nuts.

Spiced Whipped Cream: Beat cream until soft peaks are formed. Add vanilla, cinnamon, grated orange peel and sugar.
Serves 12-15.

Arundel United Church
Arundel, Que.

Fruit and Cake Dessert

1 large cake mix
¼ cup oil
2 eggs
½ cup water
1 can fruit pie filling

In 9x13" pan, pour oil. Tip pan to cover. Add dry cake mix, eggs and water. Mix with fork for 2-3 minutes. Spread evenly in pan. Spoon fruit filling in about six places on batter, then draw fork through to marble through the batter. Bake 35-40 minutes at 350°F. Serve with whipped cream topping. Good, easy and quick.

Brechin United Church
Nanaimo, B.C.

Strawberry-Orange Ice

1 pt. fresh strawberries or frozen
Juice and finely grated peel or 1 large orange
2 tbsp. fresh lemon juice
⅔ cup granulated sugar
1 tbsp. Grand Marnier (optional)

Measure ingredients into blender. Blend until no lumps remain. Pour into an ice-cube tray, or shallow dish. Freeze just until a layer of frozen crystals forms on the top, about 45 minutes. Turn into a mixing bowl and beat until light, even texture. Pour back into freezing dish. Cover and freeze. To serve: Garnish with a little whipped cream and mint.
Serves 6-8.

Lakeshore Drive United Church
Morrisburg, Ont.

Pumpkin Ice Cream Pie

¼ cup honey or brown sugar
¾ cup pumpkin
½ tsp. cinnamon
¼ tsp. ginger
¼ tsp. salt
Dash nutmeg
1 quart vanilla ice cream
½ cup pecan pieces (optional)

Combine honey or brown sugar, pumpkin, spices and salt. Bring just to a boil, stirring constantly. Cool. Beat the mixture into the softened ice cream, adding nuts if desired. Spread into a baked pastry shell or graham cracker crust. Freeze until firm. Decorate with whipped cream graham cracker crumbs on top adds to the appearance of the dessert.

St. Mark's United Church
St. Thomas, Ont.

Lemon Tart

Crust:
> 3 cups (750 mL) vanilla wafer crumbs or digestive biscuit crumbs
> ½ cup (125 mL) melted butter

Filling:
> 6 large eggs, separated
> 2 - 14 oz. (398 mL) cans sweetened condensed milk
> 1 - 12½ oz. (355 mL) can frozen lemonade, thawed
> 1 pt. (500 mL) whipping cream, whipped
> ¾ cup (250 mL) sugar

Combine wafer crumbs and butter and press into a foil-lined 13x9" (22x23 cm) pan. Bake in 350°F (180°C) oven for about 7 minutes. Cool. Beat egg yolks, add condensed milk and lemonade (undiluted), and fold in the whipped cream. Pour into cooled crust. Beat egg whites until foamy. Beat in sugar 1 tablespoon (15 mL) at a time and continue beating until stiff. Spread over the filling. Put under the broiler, 4 inches (10 cm) from the heat, and brown lightly. This takes just seconds so don't turn your back. Cover pan without crushing meringue and seal well with foil. Wrap and store in freezer. Remove from freezer about 20-25 minutes before serving to soften slightly. Transfer from pan and decorate with lime and lemon slices and fresh strawberries. Cut into 2" (5 cm) squares to serve. It can be made days or weeks ahead. Half of this recipe will fill a 9" (22 cm) pie. For variety, substitute limeade for the lemonade, or use a combination of both.
Serves 16.

Trinity United Church
Shediac, N.B.

Lemon Cream Dessert

1 cup Miracle Whip
1 litre Cool Whip
1 cup (250 g) frozen lemonade, undiluted
½ box (250 g) graham crackers or vanilla wafers

Combine all but wafers. Arrange whole crackers or wafers in bottom of 8" square pan. Spoon above mixture over crackers and cover. Freeze at least 2 hours or until firm. Refrigerate 10 minutes before serving. A sprinkling of graham cracker crumbs on top adds to the appearance of the dessert.

Wellington Square United Church
Burlington, Ont.

Oreo Cookies and Cream

Crust:
> 1 - 16 oz. pkg. Oreo cookies, crushed (reserve 5 cookies for garnish)
> ½ cup melted butter

First layer:
> ½ gallon vanilla ice cream, softened

Second layer:
> 4 - 1 oz. squares unsweetened chocolate
> 2 tbsp. butter
> 1⅓ cups evaporated milk
> 1 cup sugar
> 1 tsp. vanilla
> 1 - 12 oz. Cool Whip

Reserve five Oreo cookies for garnish. Mix crushed Oreos and melted butter and press into 9x13" buttered pan. Spread softened ice cream over crust and place in freezer. Cook chocolate, butter, evaporated milk, sugar and vanilla until thickened. Stir continuously. Cool chocolate sauce and spread on top of ice cream. Spread Cool Whip over chocolate sauce. Sprinkle 5 crushed Oreos on top for garnish. Freeze. Remove 5-10 minutes before serving.
Makes 16 servings.

Union Church
Ste. Anne de Bellevue, Que.

Peanut Buster Parfait

1 pkg. chocolate wafers, crushed
½ cup melted butter

Mix and press into two 9" pans. Chill.

2 litres vanilla ice cream
1½ cups Spanish peanuts
1 cup chocolate chips
½ cup margarine
⅔ cup icing sugar
1½ cups evaporated milk

Spread ice cream over crumbs. Press peanuts in. Freeze well. Mix chocolate chips, margarine, icing sugar and evaporated milk. Bring to a boil on medium heat. Simmer for 8 minutes, stirring. Cool well. Spread on top of ice cream and nut mixture. Freeze.

Emmanuel United Church
Saskatoon, Sask.

Cherry-Choco Squares

1 small pkg. miniature marshmallows
1 chocolate cake mix
1 cup cherry pie filling
500 mL Cool Whip or 1 pkg. Dream Whip

Grease 9x13" pan. Sprinkle marshmallows on bottom of pan. Mix chocolate cake mix as per directions on box. Put in pan on top of marshmallows. Top with cherry pie filling. Bake at 350°F for 1 hour or until knife comes out clean. Cut into squares and top with whipped topping.

St. Andrews United Church
Peterborough, Ont.

Quick Torte

1 lge. pkg. Devils Food cake mix
250 g or 8 oz. frozen whipped topping, thawed
1 - 540 mL or 19 oz. can cherry pie filling

Heat oven to 350°F. Grease and flour a 10" tube pan. In large mixing bowl add cake mix, 3 eggs, 1¼ cups water or milk and ⅓ cup cooking oil. Blend at low speed. Pour batter into pan and bake 45-50 minutes. Cool in pan on rack for 20 minutes. Remove from pan. Split cake into 3 layers (using thread or dental floss). Spread ⅓ whipped topping, then ⅓ pie filling between each layer and on top. Chill until set.

Westminster United Church
Whitby, Ont.

Crème de Menthe Cake

1 baked angel food cake
3 pts. vanilla ice cream
1 pt. whipping cream (or chocolate sauce)
1 cup Crème de Menthe (real or imitation)

Rub brown from cake with your hand. Slice cake into three layers. Tear smallest layer into pieces and put into an angel food cake pan. Cover with 1 pint of softened ice cream. Pour ⅓ cup Crème de Menthe over ice cream. Repeat for other two layers. Return to freezer, covered. When ready to use, unmold on plate and cover with whipped cream or serve plain slices and pour hot chocolate sauce over each. Can be made 2-3 weeks ahead. Cuts into 12-14 pieces.

Lachute United Church
Lachute, Que.

Frozen Pumpkin Squares

1 litre vanilla ice cream, softened
1 cup cooked pumpkin
½ cup brown sugar
½ tsp. cinnamon
¼ tsp. ginger
¼ tsp. nutmeg
Crumb crust of your choice
½ cup chopped nuts (optional)
2 tbsp. reserved crumb topping (optional)

Graham Cracker Crust:
1¼ cups graham cracker crumbs
¼ cup butter, melted

Spice Graham Cracker Crust:
1¼ cups graham cracker crumbs
3 tbsp. sugar
½ tsp. cinnamon
¼ tsp. nutmeg
⅓ cup butter

Combine ice cream, pumpkin, sugar, cinnamon, ginger and nutmeg. Beat until well blended. Pour mixture into crumb crust. Sprinkle with nuts or reserved crumb topping if desired. Cover tightly with foil and freeze until firm - about four hours. Before serving, let stand at room temperature 10-15 minutes to make cutting easier.

Moorefield United Church
Moorefield, Ont.

Pistachio - Ice Cream Dessert

35 Ritz crackers, crumbled
¼ lb. margarine, melted
2 - 3 oz. pkgs. *pistachio instant pudding
1½ cups milk
1 qt. (4 cups) soft vanilla ice cream
9 oz. Cool Whip
2 Heath/Skorr bars

Combine crackers with margarine. Press in 9x13" pan and bake 10 minutes at 350°F. Cool. Blend pudding with milk. Add to ice cream and spread over base and freeze for 6 hours. Cover with Cool Whip. Crush and sprinkle bars over Cool Whip. Freeze again until you wish to use dessert. Remove from freezer 5-10 minutes before serving. *Butterscotch instant pudding may be used for a change.

St. Andrew's United Church
Chateauguay, Que.

Indexes

Brunches & Lunches

Suppers on the Go

Desserts

Many thanks to these churches whose wonderful recipes appear in this cookbook.

Adolphustown U.E.L., Centennial United Church - Napanee, Ontario
Advocate United Church - Advocate Harbour, - Nova Scotia
Alexander Grant United Church - East Lake Ainslie, Nova Scotia
Almonte United Church - Almonte, Ontario
Alsask United Church - Alsask, Saskatchewan
Androssan United Church - Androssan, Alberta
Annesley United Church - Markdale, Ontario
Arundel United Church - Arundel, Quebec
Asbury and West United Church - Toronto, Ontario
Ashton United Church - Ashton, Ontario
Athens United Church - Athens, Ontario
Aurora United Church - Aurora, Ontario
Aylesford United Church - Aylesford, Nova Scotia

Balzac United Church - Balzac, Alberta
Banner United Church - Thamesford, Ontario
Bath United Church - Bath, Ontario
Battleford United Church - Batterford, Saskatchewan
Battle River United Church - Manning, Alberta
Beachville United Church - Beachville, Ontario
Beaconsfield United Church - Beaconsfield, Quebec
Bells Corner United Church - Nepean, Ontario
Belmont United Church - Belmont, Ontario
Berwick United Church - Berwick, Nova Scotia
Bethany United Church - Ramsayville, Ontario
Bethel United Church - Forestburg, Alberta
Bethesda of Forest Glen United Church - Mississauga, Ontario
Bethesda United Church - Ancaster, Ontario
Beverley Hills United Church - Downsview, Ontario
Binbrook United Church - Binbrook, Ontario
Birch Hills United Church - Birch Hills, Saskatchewan
Birtle United Church - Birtle, Manitoba
Bissell Memorial United Church - Andrew, Alberta
Blackwell United Church - Sarnia, Ontario
Bloomingdale United Chuch - Bloomingdale, Ontario
Bolton United Church - Bolton, Ontario
Bowman United Church - Ancaster, Ontario
Brechin United Church - Brechin, Ontario
Brechin United Church - Nanaimo, Brithish Columbia
Britannia United Church - Ottawa, Ontario
Broadview United Church - Broadview, Saskatchewan
Brooklin United Church - Brooklin, Ontario
Bruce Mines United Church - Bruce Mines, Ontario
Brucefield United Church - Brucefield, Ontario
Buchanan - Eastwood United Church - Edmonton, Alberta
Buchin United Church - Buchin, Ontario
Burgessville United Church - Burgessville, Ontario

Caistorville United Church - Canfield, Ontario
Caledonia United Church - Caledonia, Nova Scotia
Calvin United Church - Pembroke, Ontario
Cambray Pastoral Charge - Cambray, Ontario
Cambridge Street United Church - Lindsay, Ontario
Cameron United Church - Cameron, Ontario
Camlachie United Church - Camlachie, Ontario
Camrose United Church - Camrose, Alberta
Cape North United Church - Cape North, Nova Scotia
Carberry United Church - Carberry, Manitoba
Carlisle United Church - Carlisle, Ontario
Carlyle United Church - Carlyle, Saskatchewan
Carol United Church - Labrador City, Newfoundland
Carstairs United Church - Carstairs, Ontario
Carville United Church - Richmond Hill, Ontario
Central United Church - Port Colborne, Ontario
Central United Church - Sarnia, Ontario
Central United Church - Lunenburg, Nova Scotia
Central United Church - Unionville, Ontario
Central United Church - Bay Roberts, Newfoundland
Central Avenue United Church - Fort Erie, Ontario
Centralia United Church - Centralia, Ontario
Centre Street United Church - Shaunavon, Saskatchewan
Charleswood United Church - Winnipeg, Manitoba
Cheltenham United Church - Cheltenham, Ontario
Chilliwack United Church - Chilliwack, British Columbia
Chinese United Church - Vancouver, British Columbia
Clarke's Beach United Church - Clarke's Beach, Newfoundland

Clavet United Church - Clavet, Saskatchewan
Cliffcrest United Church - Scarborough, Ontario
Cloudslee United Church - Bruce Mines, Ontario
Coaldale United Church - Coaldale, Alberta
Cole Harbour United Church - Dartmouth, Nova Scotia
College Hill United Church - Belleville, Ontario
Columbus United Church - Columbus, Ontario
Como Lake United Church - Coquitlam, British Columbia
Consul United Church - Consul, Saskatchewan
Cooksville United Church - Mississauga, Ontario
Courtice United Church - Courtice, Ontario
Cresent Fort Rouge United Church - Winnipeg, Manitoba
Crystal City United Church - Crystal City, Manitoba
Current River United Church - Thunder Bay, Ontario

Danville - Asbestos Trinity United Church - Danville, Quebec
Delta United Church - Hamilton, Ontario
Division Street United Church - Owen Sound, Ontario
Donminister United Church - Don Mills, Ontario
Downsview United Church - Downsview, Ontario
Dublin Street United Church - Guelph, Ontario
Dunbarton - Fairport United Church - Pickering, Ontario
Dundas Street United Church - Woodstock, Ontario

Eastend United Church - Eastend, Saskatchewan
Echo Bay U.C.W. - Echo Bay, Ontario
Eden United Church - Mississauga, Ontario
Elimville United Church - Exeter, Ontario
Embro Knox United Church - Embro, Ontario
Emmanuel United Church - Sebringville, Ontario
Emmanuel United Church - Saskatoon, Saskatchewan
Emmanuel United Church - Waterloo, Ontario
Emmanuel United Church - Englehart, Ontario
Ennismore United Church - Ennismore, Ontario
Erie Street United Church - Ridgetown, Ontario
Essex United Church - Essex, Ontario
Exeter United Church - Exeter, Ontario
Fairfield United Church - Hamilton, Ontario
Fallowfield United Church - Nepean, Ontario
Fenwick United Church - Fenwick, Ontario
First United Church - Wawa, Ontario
First United Church - Hopeall Trinity Bay, Newfoundland
First United Church - Corner Brook, Newfoundland
First United Church - St. Thomas, Ontario
First United Church - Truro, Nova Scotia
First United Church - Cambridge, Ontario
First United Church - Trenton, Nova Scotia
Fishburn Marr United Church - Pincher Creek, Alberta
Fleetwood United Church - Surrey, British Columbia
Foam Lake United Church - Foam Lake, Saskatchewan
Foote-Copeland United Church - Dafoe, Saskatchewan
Foothills United Church - Calgary, Alberta
Fordwich United Church - Fordwich, Ontario
Forest Hills United Church - Dartmouth, Nova Scotia
Forest United Church - Forest, Ontario
Forest Home United Church - Orillia, Ontario
Franklin Centre United Church - Franklin Centre, Quebec
Fraser Road United Church - Gander, Newfoundland
Frontier United Church - Frontier, Saskatchewan

Garden City United Church - Victoria, British Columbia
Garnish United Church - Garnish, Newfoundland
George Street United Church - St Johns, Newfoundland
Gibbons United Church - Gibbons, Alberta
Gibsons United Church - Gibsons, British Columbia
Gilford United Church - Gilford, Ontario
Glen Morris United Church - Glen Morris, Ontario
Glenboro United Church - Glenboro, Manitoba
Golden Valley United Church - Val D'or, Quebec
Gordon Providence United Church - Bridgetown, Nova Scotia
Goshen United Church - Varna, Ontario
Grace United Church - Niagara-on-the-Lake, Ontario
Grace United Church - Caledonia, Ontario
Grace United Church - Gananoque, Ontario
Grace United Church - Trenton, Ontario
Grace St. Andrew's United Church - Arnprior, Ontario
Grace United Church - Thornbury, Ontario
Grace United Church - Port Dover, Ontario
Grace United Church - Hanover, Ontario

Grace United Church - Brampton, Ontario
Grace United Church - Dunnville, Ontario
Grantham United Church - St. Catharines, Ontario
Greenbank United Church - Uxbridge, Ontario
Greenwood United Church - Greenwood, Ontario
Grenfell United Church - Grenfell, Saskatchewan

Hamiota United Church - Hamiota, Manitoba
Hammond United Church - Maple Ridge, British Columbia
Hampstead United Church - Gadshill, Ontario
Hampton United Church - Hampton, New Brunswick
Hant's Harbour United Church - Trinity Bay, Newfoundland
Happy Valley-Goose Bay United Church - Happy Valley- Goose Bay, Labrador
Harrington United Church - Columet, Quebec
Harriston United Church - Harriston, Ontario
Harrow United Church - Harrow, Ontario
Hawthorne United Church - Ottawa, Ontario
Heartz Memorial United Church - Weymouth, Nova Scotia
Hickson United Church - Hickson, Ontario
High River United Church - High River, Alberta
High Bluff United Church - High Bluff, Manitoba
Highgate United Church - Highgate, Ontario
Hillsborough United Church - Hillsborough, New Brunswick
Hillsburgh United Church - Bear River, Nova Scotia
Hillview United Church - New Liskeard, Ontario
Howick United Church - Howick, Quebec
Hudson Bay United Church - Hudson Bay, Saskatchewan
Humbervale United Church - Etobicoke, Ontario
Humphrey Memorial United Church - Moncton, New Brunswick

Imperial United Church - Imperial, Saskatchewan
Innerkip United Church - Innerkip, Ontario
Invermay United Church - Invermay, Saskatchewan
Iondale Heights United Church - Scarborough, Ontario

Keswick United Church - Keswick, Ontario
Kilbride United Church - Kilbride, Ontario
Killarney United Church - Killarney, Manitoba
Kincardine United Church - Kincardine, Ontario
Kings Kirk United Church - Belleisle Creek, New Brunswick
Kingston United Church - Kingston, Nova Scotia
Kingsview United Church - Oshawa, Ontario
Kintore Chalmers United Church - Kintore, Ontario
Kipling United Church - Kipling, Saskatchewan
Kirk Memorial United Church - Aspen, Nova Scotia
Kirk McCall United Church - St Stephen, New Brunswick
Kirkfield Park United Church - Winnipeg, Manitoba
Knox United Church - Gainsborough, Saskatchewan
Knox United Church - Winnipeg, Manitoba
Knox United Church - Redvers, Saskatchewan
Knox United Church - Sutton West, Ontario
Knox United Church - Manitowaning, Ontario
Knox United Church - Didsbury, Alberta
Knox-St Paul's United Church - Cornwall, Ontario
Knox United Church - Russell, Manitoba
Knox United Church - Shellbrook, Saskatchewan
Knox United Church - Fort Frances, Ontario
Knox United Church - Nepean, Ontario

La Riviere United Church - La Riviere, Manitoba
Lachute United Church - Lachute, Quebec
Lafleche United Church - Lafleche, Saskatchewan
Lake Cowichan United Church - Lake Cowichan, British Columbia
Lakeshore Drive United Church - Morrisburg, Ontario
Lamont United Church - Lamont, Alberta
Lansdowne United Church - Lansdowne, Ontario
Lavenham United Church - Lavenham, Manitoba
Linden Park Community Church - Hamilton, Ontario
Lucan United Church - Lucan, Ontario

Mackay United Church - Ottawa, Ontario
Macoun U.C.W. - Macoun, Saskatchewan
Maple Grove United Church - Bowmanville, Ontario
Marsden United Church - Marsden, Saskatchewan
Marshall Memorial Church - Ancaster, Ontario
Marshfield-Dunstaffnage United Church - Charlottetown, Prince Edward Island

Special acknowledgements go to these churches who also submitted recipes.